W9-DAT-975

Guerrilla Warrior

The Early Life of John J. Pershing

Guerrilla Warrior

The Early Life of
John J. Pershing

Donald Smythe

CHARLES SCRIBNER'S SONS · NEW YORK

To my father and mother

Acknowledgment

For permission to quote from books copyright by them, the author is obliged to the following publishers: Biblo and Tannen for Anita Brenner, *Idols Behind Altars;* Hawthorn Books, Inc. for Everett T. Tomlinson, *The Story of General Pershing* and for Hugh L. Scott, *Some Memories of a Soldier;* Houghton Mifflin Company for Charles G. Dawes, *A Journal of the Great War,* Vol. 1; Random House, Inc.-Alfred A. Knopf, Inc. for Herbert Molloy Mason, Jr., *The Great Pursuit* and for Glendon Swarthout, *They Came to Cordura;* The Macmillan Company for Clarence C. Clendenen, *Blood on the Border;* Stackpole Books for Avery D. Andrews, *My Friend and Classmate, John J. Pershing,* for Frederick Palmer, *John J. Pershing,* and for Frank Tompkins, *Chasing Villa;* The Viking Press Inc. for Alvin Johnson, *Pioneer's Progress.*

The following periodicals have permitted quotation from articles as here specified: *American Legion Monthly* for Frank Elser, "Pershing's Lost Cause," July, 1932, and for Robert Ginsburgh, "Pershing as His Orderlies Know Him," October, 1928; *The American West* for Karl Young "A Fight That Could Have Meant War," Spring, 1966; The U.S. Armor Association for Samual Dallam, "The Punitive Expedition of 1916", which appeared in the *Cavalry Journal,* July, 1927; *Mexican*

Acknowledgment

Border Veterans Bulletin for the poem, "Fifty Miles to Carrizal," March-April, 1957.

To say "Thank you" to those individuals who helped on this book is the most pleasant part of what has been, in general, a pleasant task over the last thirteen years. In particular I should like to mention the staffs of the Library of Congress, the National Archives, and the Office of the Chief of Military History, as well as those of the other archives and libraries which are listed in the Bibliography. My gratitude also to those who permitted me to use their private manuscript collections, wrote me their recollections, or granted interviews.

I am grateful to various historians who, over the years, aided with advice and counsel: Martin Blumenson, Haldeen Braddy, Clarence C. Clendenen, Edward M. Coffman, I. B. Holley, Jr., D. Clayton James, Tom Mahoney, Al and Marge Moe, Francis Munch, George Prpic, Harry Sievers, S. J., W. Richard Walsh, and George Walton.

At John Carroll University James A. Mackin, S.J., Florence Krueger, and Mary K. Sweeny were unfailingly kind. I am grateful to the Administration, which released me from teaching to research the book; to Donald Gavin, Dean of the Graduate School, who aided in obtaining three grants from the American Philosophical Society which helped finance it; to William Ulrich and the History Department for many kindnesses; to Marybeth Muehle, Michael Stary, Christine Ulrich and James Webber, who served as research assistants; and to Margie Wasdovich, Elizabeth Catalano, Mary Dempsey, Ann Glowe, Anne Hillyard, and Helen Lawson, who typed various drafts of the manuscript.

My gratitude to F. Warren Pershing for permission to consult his father's Papers, and to the following for various kinds of assistance: Carol Cutler, H. Bruce Fant, Arther S. Trace, Sr. Leona Eberhardt, Mary Beth Hayes, Joseph Osuch, S.J., Susan Navish, Roberta Mendel, Joyce Tianello, Cecilia Connare, Julian A. Maline, S.J., Paul V. Siegfried, S.J., Roger Billings, Gladys Williams, Vickie Cicek, Daniel J. Homick, James E. Price, Robert Carver, Sanford Slutzker, Richard and Lynne Horner, Dayton Haskin, S.J., and William F. Butler.

One or more chapters of the manuscript were read by William D.

Acknowledgment

Aeschbacher, Richard S. Brownlee, John W. Caughey, James L. Collins, James Dehn, Donald J. Delaney, Margaret Egeland, Robert H. Ferrell, Victor Gondos, Jr., James W. Goodrich, Vivian A. Paladin, Frank D. Reeve, Wendell Tripp, and Heath Twitchell. Of these, I wish to thank in particular Dr. Robert H. Ferrell of Indiana University, whose advice and encouragement came at a time when they were badly needed.

Approximately half of the book was read by Eugene H. Bacon, Jr., J. Joseph Huthmacher, Joseph T. Durkin, S.J., and Vada Hummel. I profited much by their comments.

The book was read in its entirety, in various drafts, by N. J. Anthony (who prepared the Index), Mark Boatner III, Harold C. Gardiner, S.J., Riley Hughes, Harold King, M.D., Dolores Kratzer, Gerald F. McCauley, Allan R. Millett, and Forrest C. Pogue. Dr. Riley Hughes, Professor of English at Georgetown University, was extraordinarily helpful. Dr. Allan R. Millett, Professor of History at Ohio State University and biographer of Lt. Gen. Robert L. Bullard, furnished valuable research leads and made a very perceptive critique of the manuscript. Dr. Forrest C. Pogue, Executive Director of the George C. Marshall Research Foundation and General Marshall's distinguished biographer, was friend, mentor, and editor, all rolled into one. His kindness and graciousness shall always be remembered. Thanks too to three good friends, Herman Duncan, Barbara Kraft, and Keith E. Eiler, for all sorts of kindnesses; to my brother Jesuits, for friendship and mutual support through the years; and to all those others, too numerous to mention, who in any way helped.

Finally, to my father and mother, my thanks for more than I can say. To them I dedicate this book.

Donald Smythe, S.J.

John Carroll University
Cleveland, Ohio

List of Illustrations

Pictures:

Pershing as a Cadet, U. S. Military Academy, Class of 1886–*page 9*

Officers' quarters, Fort Bayard, New Mexico–*page 10*

Fort Wingate, New Mexico, where Pershing was stationed in 1889 –*page 17*

Pershing as a 2nd Lieutenant of the 6th Cavalry–*page 18*

Pershing as Commandant of Cadets at the University of Nebraska, 1891–1895–*page 31*

Pershing (at center, seated) with members of the Cadet Battalion, University of Nebraska, 1895–*page 32*

A Moro leader with his retinue–*page 83*

Approach to the house on Zamboanga where Pershing lived while Governor of Moro Province–*page 177*

The Pershing family "at home" in Zamboanga–*page 177*

Scene at top of Bud Bagsak, Island of Jolo, Philippines, after the June, 1913, battle–*page 201*

Amil, Moro leader at Bud Bagsak, with his son–*page 201*

John J. Pershing, and his son, Warren–*page 215*

Pershing leading cavalry during Mexican campaign, 1916–*page 223*

Pershing (at center) inspecting a mountain battery at Laredo, Texas, February, 1917–*page 267*

Major General John J. Pershing–*page 281*

Maps:

Siege of Santiago–*page 49*

Department of Mindanao–*page 63*

The Lake Lanao Region–*page 72*

Bacalod Fort–*page 98*

Mount Bagsak–*page 191–192*

Mexican Punitive Expedition, 1916: Area of Operations–*page 219*

Table of Contents

1	Frontier Cavalryman	1
2	Commanding Cadets	27
3	"The Splendid Little War"	46
4	Iligan: Making Friends with the Moros	66
5	Camp Vicars	79
6	The March Around Lake Lanao	94
7	Love and Marriage	111
8	Promotion and Scandal	121
9	Fort William McKinley	133
10	Governor of the Moro Province	144
11	Disarming the Moros	161
12	"The Good Old Days at Zamboanga"	175
13	The Bud Bagsak Campaign	186
14	Tragedy at the Presidio	205
15	Chasing Villa	217
16	Parral and Carrizal	241
17	The Last Campaign	261
	APPENDIX	283
	NOTES	285
	BIBLIOGRAPHY	331
	INDEX	363

1

Frontier Cavalryman

At four o'clock on the afternoon of June 18, 1864, Henry Lomax, a clerk in the Pershing General Store at Laclede, Missouri, ran excitedly into the building, fright written all over his face. "Bushwhackers are riding into town," he cried. "They're headed right this way!"

It came as no surprise to John Fletcher Pershing, the proprietor, that they were heading for his store. The Civil War was in its fourth year and Missouri, a border state, frequently suffered from Southern sympathizers who terrorized Unionists and looted towns. Pershing was known as an outspoken Union man, his store was the largest in town, and his safe served as a vault for the townspeoples' valuables. No wonder bushwhackers were headed his way.

Soon the town square whereon Pershing's store fronted was a scene of confusion. The raiders fired shots to terrify the people, then went from house to house, herding the townsmen under gun point to the square. Inside the store Pershing discovered with disgust that his shotgun was empty. Usually kept loaded, it had been emptied that morning as a safety measure when John, his three-year-old son, was playing around the store. With no time to reload (bushwhackers were even then heading across the square), Pershing locked the safe with a quick turn of the key and hustled his son into the back alley as the raiders entered by the front door.

Five doors down the alley was the Pershing home. Two Confederate guerrillas had just left, after Mrs. Pershing had satisfied them that her husband was not at home. Pershing entered by the back, entrusted his son to his wife, reloaded his gun, and looked out from the front room window. While the townspeople stood corralled like helpless cattle, brigands were looting the stores. Two citizens already lay dead. Pershing raised his shotgun and took aim.

Before he could fire his wife's arms were around his neck. "Don't shoot," she pleaded. "You'll be killed. Let the money go."

Sadly, Pershing concluded she was right. He lowered his gun and watched bitterly while bushwhackers stole his goods. Their leader, Capt. Clifton Holtzclaw, harangued his captive audience, damning the abolitionists, condemning the North, and threatening to lay waste the town the next time he came. A short time later he and his raiders mounted up and rode out of town, carrying with them property estimated at three thousand dollars. When they were gone, Pershing told his wife to let young John get up off the floor where she had made him lie flat. The boy was badly frightened.[1]

Thus, at the age of three, John Joseph Pershing, future General of the Armies of the United States, was introduced to guerrilla warfare. He had been made aware that human beings kill and steal. He had been introduced to the anxiety of wives for their husbands and to the frustrated bitterness of fathers who stood by helplessly and saw their property carried off at gunpoint. He had heard the sound of bullets and, after the raid, saw what a man looks like when he is dead.

He was to know fear again in later life, although not, it seems, as much as the average man. He was to hear the crack of rifles thousands and thousands of times. He was to have experience of men taking from and killing one another. He was to see many, many men die before he himself came to die eighty-four years later.

The Pershings—they spelled it Pfoershing then—first came to America in 1749. Frederick Pfoershing disembarked in Philadelphia from Amsterdam, whence he had come from his native Alsace, that much contested territory between France and Germany. He was not wealthy. He came as a "redemptioner," which meant he had to pay off his passage in labor.[2]

Apparently the Pershings stayed put in Pennsylvania, for one hundred years later John Fletcher Pershing, great grandson of Frederick, was working a farm there. About 1857, when he was twenty-three, he developed wanderlust. Turning the farm over to younger members of the family, he set out down the Ohio River and the Mississippi to make his career in the West. Work as a logger on the rivers brought him to St. Louis, where, in February, 1858, he entered the firm of Stone, Pershing, and Jennings, which later undertook a subcontract on a railroad built from St. Louis to Macon. The route cut through a place called Warrenton and Pershing soon began to court a young girl named Anne Elizabeth Thompson who lived there. They were married in March, 1859.[3]

After the railroad was completed to Macon, Pershing needed a job. It happened that Macon lay on the route of another railroad—one running west across Missouri from Hannibal to St. Joseph—which needed a section manager for a seven-mile strip between Laclede and Meadville. Pershing took the job, moving himself and his young bride to a house near Laclede. Here their first child, John Joseph, was born, probably on January 13, 1860.[4]

In October, 1861, the family moved into Laclede where Pershing exchanged the job of section foreman for owner and manager of a general store. It was in Laclede that John was reared and that eight other children were born, three of whom died in infancy.[5]

The Pershing family occupied a prominent place in Laclede. Mr. Pershing was the leading business man in the little town. When he had moved there in 1860, the 18th Regiment, Missouri Volunteers, stationed there, were lacking a sutler; Pershing filled the job for them, and later for the 1st Regiment of the Missouri State Militia. He also ran a general store in Laclede and acted as wholesaler for smaller shopkeepers in outlying districts. In addition he served as village postmaster, locating the post office in one corner of his store, which enhanced his business. After the Civil War he bought a lumber yard, two 160-acre farms, and what was probably the finest house in town. In the 1860's Pershing was considered one of the wealthiest men in the county.[6]

He was also one of the most civic minded. He had been the driving force behind getting the new Methodist Church built, and he was one of the five men who in 1866 obtained the incorporation of Laclede as a township. Among the offices which he held were captain of the home guard, superintendent of the Sunday school, and member of the school board. Friends urged him to run for the State Legislature and for Congress, but he declined.

As a family man he was a devoted husband and a loving, if stern, father. He did not hesitate to use the rod if he thought the boys needed it. All unpleasantness, however, was forgotten when he gathered the family around the piano for their nightly song fest.

Pershing's store clerk, Henry Lomax, evaluated him thus: "He was a very active business man with wonderful energy, strictly honest, never stooped to a dishonest trick; a pronounced man in the community; the leading business man. . . . He was a man of commanding presence. He was a great family man, loved his family devotedly. He was not lax and ruled his household well."[7]

Mrs. Pershing ran an efficient household, keeping things spic and span, being kind to the help but not taking any nonsense from them in the way of laziness or slipshod work. People around the town held her in high esteem. She was educated beyond the average for a woman of those days and was very ambitious for the education of her children. Her piety was open and deep, with family prayers every night, church and Sunday school on weekends, and a sharp reprimand for the children when they misbehaved.[8]

Religion was a dominant influence with both the Pershing parents and they tried to pass this on to their children. Most of the people they associated with in Laclede were religious; just about all who had standing in the community were church members. Even the diversions and entertainments—spelling contests, singing schools, sleighrides—were church affairs, with the old well-to-do families setting the example.[9]

Records of John's attendance at Sunday school date from the time he was ten, although probably he attended much earlier. His baptism occured at eleven, and six months later, in May, 1872, he was received into the Methodist church as a full member.[10]

Townsfolk remembered him as a quiet, studious, determined lad, not snobbish, not wild, quite popular, very level-headed, and strongly dependable. They agreed that there was nothing spectacular in his boyhood, no aureole around his brow indicating future fame.[11] There was devilment in him, to be sure. Years after he left Laclede, they were still trying to figure out who had mobbed Captain Love's "Billy Goat," or why certain watermelon crops proved a failure, or why Glovers' tame turkeys were killed (in self-defense?) during John's camping trips, and a hundred other things.[12]

At the age of seven, an incident occurred in school which affected his later life. Dragooned into a public recital, John was assigned as the opening speaker. When he got up before the audience his mind went completely blank. Mrs. Pershing prompted him through the first verse, then through the second. Looking back on the incident years afterwards, Pershing recalled: "My embarrassment was so painful that the memory left with me was lasting. . . . I have rarely been entirely at ease before an audience on any formal occasion."[13] In his adult years Dorothy Canfield Fisher said of him: "He was one of the world's poorest public speakers, and never, if it was possible, accepted any engagement where he was going to be called upon to speak."[14]

At thirteen he was catapulted into adult responsibilities when his father, impoverished by the Panic of 1873, had to become a traveling salesman. John took over the family farm in his absence. He had to split rails, plow fields, and bring in the crop.[15] It was hard work. Once a plague of grasshoppers ruined the crop. On another occasion a drought came which nothing was able to exorcise, not even prayer meetings in church. When it was gone the corn was withered down to nubbins. Even success was illusory. One autumn he harvested forty acres of beautiful timothy, baled a carload, and sent it to St. Louis, expecting a substantial profit. When the returns came they were barely enough to pay the freight.[16]

Despite the disappointments, John felt that running a farm was good for him. "It was the best thing that ever happened to me. It taught me more, gave me greater confidence and a keener sense of responsibility than anything else could have done."[17]

Farm work also gave him a tough, strong body which served him well through his long life. In 1945, when he was an eighty-five-year-old patient in Walter Reed Hospital in Washington, D. C., a nurse adjusting his bedding noticed that he held himself stiffly in a very awkward posture while she worked. "How can you hold yourself like that for such a long time?" she asked. "From digging potatoes," he replied.[18]

To supplement the farm income John worked at various times as section hand on the Hannibal-St. Joseph Railroad, as janitor in the public school, as teacher in the Negro school at Laclede and as instructor in a school at Prairie Mound, Missouri.[19] Judging by his later performance at the University of Nebraska, his teaching method was prosaic. He was not too adept at explaining mathematics or making English interesting. His forte was assigning matter to be learned on the pupil's own, and inflicting punishment if it was not done.

With money earned as a teacher, John attended college at Kirksville, a small normal school about forty-five miles northeast of Laclede. His roommate recalled that he was very level-headed and that nothing ever seemed to upset him. He was "just one of the boys," added a classmate, "neither a rowdy nor a tin angel, but he was a fellow whose path it was not exactly safe to cross."[20] His language was at times pretty vulgar.[21]

In 1881 he sought and won an appointment to West Point, not because of any desire for a military career but because it was romantic, offered a free education, and would prepare him for law, his boyhood ambition. He probably lied about his age to get in;[22] even with the age he listed (22), he was just under the maximum age limit.[23]

When he reported at the Academy in June, 1882, he stood 5'9" and weighed a well-proportioned 155 pounds. His life on the farm had made him an excellent horseman. The cavalry and Pershing were made for each other.[24]

The educational system at West Point followed the pattern established by its founder, Sylvanus Thayer—a core curriculum, small classes of about ten men each, daily recitation by every cadet. The function of a teacher was not so much to instruct as to be an external pressure on the students, compelling them to do the work necessary to learn a subject on their own. Too often, he was a young lieutenant, recently graduated from the Academy and selected for the task because he had not had time to forget what he had learned as a cadet. He might know little more than the students and be only a few pages ahead of them in the textbook. "I never knew a man who taught English or history at West Point who was worth a damn," said Pershing in later years.[25]

When called upon to recite, a cadet went to the blackboard, made what notes he considered necessary, then turned and faced his instructor until called upon. "I am required to discuss the four forms of the quadratic equation," he would begin, and then attempt to recite in an orderly manner. He was graded from "3" for a maximum score (or "max") to "0" for an absolute failure. The instructor's function was to assign recitation matter, listen to each cadet in turn, grade him, and transfer him to higher or lower sections. For all practical purposes, he was simply a grading machine.[26]

In his studies Pershing was not particularly bright. He had never been. He graduated thirtieth in a class of seventy-seven—just about the same average as U. S. Grant, whom he greatly admired. (Pershing considered "the greatest thrill of my life" to have been standing at "Present arms" while Grant's funeral train slowly passed by in 1885.) Like Grant, he was pedestrian rather than flashy—a "plugger."[27] After a particularly bad showing in class recitation, a cadet found him in his room during recreation time poring over French books "with an expression of hopelessness and discouragement that indicated he felt he would sink unless he immediately started to work."[28]

But if Pershing was ill-at-ease in the classroom, it was otherwise on the drill grounds and in command of men. He was, after all, more mature—about four years older than the average cadet. "He was the leader of our class," said Charles Walcutt, his roommate, "not in his studies, but in everything else. He was conscientious, took the requirements of the Academy very seriously and gave his best in every element going to make up the sum total of life at that institution. He was a strict disciplinarian and one who observed very closely his own precepts.''[29]

Robert L. Bullard, who was one year ahead of Pershing at West Point and who later commanded the Second Army in the A.E.F., described him thus:

"Of regular but not handsome features and of robust, strong body, broad shouldered and well developed; . . . with keen searching gray eyes and intent look, Pershing inspired confidence but not affection. Personal magnetism seemed lacking; he won followers and admirers, but not personal worshippers. Plain in word, sane and direct in action, he applied himself to all duty and all work with a manifest purpose, not only of succeeding in what he attempted, but of surpassing, guiding, and directing his fellows in what was before them. His exercise of authority, was then and always has been since, of a nature peculiarly impersonal, dispassionate, hard and firm. This quality did not in him, as in many, give offence; the man was too impersonal, too given over to pure business and duty. His manner carried to the minds of those under him the suggestion, nay, the conviction, of unquestioned right to obedience. There was no shadow of doubt about it.

"Of Cadet Pershing one memory more. He was a hop-goer, what cadets called a 'spoony' man. He loved the society of women. That too, like other early characteristics, seems to have held on with him."[30]

Pershing was elected class president in his freshman year and every year thereafter.[31] Each year he held the highest rank possible for a man of his seniority: first corporal, first sergeant, first captain. He was ambitious and relished the honors that came to him, especially the first captaincy. "No military rank that has ever come to me gave me quite the satisfaction that I felt that day," he said.[32] It also gave him a sense of *noblesse oblige,* of being above the herd. "We old First Captains, Douglas, must never flinch," he told Douglas MacArthur during World War I.[33]

While at the Academy from 1882 to 1886, Pershing had the chance to look over a number of fellow cadets and to form judgments on them —both members of his own class and those in the classes before and behind him. He looked carefully, and what he saw stood him in good stead when the time came to select key men for the A.E.F. command

Pershing as a Cadet, U. S. Military Academy, Class of 1886
Photograph courtesy U. S. Military Academy Archives

Officers' quarters, Fort Bayard, New Mexico
Photograph courtesy Marie C. Cook

in 1917-18. The men he noted as cadets, the world noted years later as generals: Avery D. Andrews, Robert L. Bullard, George B. Duncan, Mark L. Hersey, Mason M. Patrick, Peyton C. March, Frank McIntyre, Benjamin A. Poore, Charles T. Menoher, James W. McAndrew, Walter A. Bethel, and others.

Pershing's class of '86 produced ten brigadier generals, fifteen major generals, and one General of the Armies—a total of twenty-six general officers. Of the forty-two American divisions in the first World War, fourteen were at one time or another commanded by '86 classmates, and sixteen others by men who had been cadets either just before or just after him. All told, the men Pershing knew during his four years at the Academy furnished over one-quarter of the 474 generals of the war.[34]

In his "Autobiography" Pershing related an incident about one of them, George B. Duncan. Invited to the superintendent's home for dinner, Cadet Duncan was asked to carve the duck in the absence of the host. Wonderfully inexperienced, Duncan wrestled with the bird for a minute when suddenly it slipped off the plate and landed in a lady's lap. Nothing deterred, he leaned over and asked in a businesslike voice, "I beg your pardon, madam, but may I trouble you for that duck?" Said Pershing of Duncan, whom he made commander of the 82nd Division in World War I: "He was as cool in the heat of battle as he had been at that supper."[35]

Cadet Pershing was in many ways a preview of Pershing the Man. Hard work, confidence, lateness for appointments, fondness for "Flirtation Walk," shyness, the concern to look good, intolerance for sloppiness, anger at being embarrassed, striving to be always in command were his characteristics.

A plebe in 1886 (Pershing's graduation year) spoke of him as "tall, dignified, self-possessed," and reported the joy of fellow cadets when they trapped him into giving a speech during a stunt night when he was sitting in the audience with his "spoon" or date. "Pershing got white around the mouth, and in response to cheers and repeated encores, had to get up, very much embarrassed, and make a speech. He is so rarely disconcerted that the audience really appreciated the joke."[36]

Guerrilla Warrior

He was a man among men but not completely one of the gang. Locker room camaraderie had its limits with him and anyone who burst out with a remark like "How are you, you old son of a bitch?" did so only once. Pershing froze up with a look straight out of Antarctica.[37]

He was a strange mixture of modesty and vanity. The modesty was exterior and would manifest itself later in striking actions such as wearing only the common Victory Medal after World War I (in contrast to other officers whose chests were bedecked with medals and ribbons) and in the simple "G.I." tombstone which marks his grave in Arlington (in contrast to the massive monoliths of some of his generals). Innately he realized that exterior modesty was really a way to stand out from the crowd, to look good, to call attention to oneself while not seeming to.

Pershing backed into West Point for reasons of expediency, but, once there, took to the life. Grant had attended the Academy; so had Lee and Sherman and other of his boyhood heroes. These halls, these rooms, had once felt the presence of these men, once cadets like himself, now world famous. He thrilled at the thought, at the heritage. Mature though he may have been, Pershing had enough boyhood hero-worship in him to take detours in order to cross Sherman's path when the old warrior visited the Academy and so be able to salute him.[38]

West Point as a military academy in Pershing's day left much to be desired. There were practically no field exercises and no tactical studies. No cadet ever had a chance to command so much as a platoon in a simulated problem of reconnaissance, attack, or defense. There was too little contact with the outside world and too much stress on discipline. Instructors, inadequately trained, left much to be desired. Basically an engineering school, West Point was remembered by one cadet as a place where everything was studied except war. There were, for example, no studies of the Napoleonic campaigns. The only war studies were drill regulations and, in senior year, a course on the Civil War.[39]

The Academy stressed formation rather than information. It sought to instill a certain attitude of mind and spirit, perhaps feeling that the actual conduct of war could be learned somewhere else (on the battlefield, for instance), whereas no amount of practical training would avail if an officer lacked certain soldierly qualities: discipline, loyalty, obedience.[40]

At West Point Pershing came to believe that loyalty and obedience are the criteria with which to predict the probable response of a soldier in battle. If a man is lazy, unruly, or disorderly in time of training, he will likely be the same in time of crisis. Hence Pershing's life-long stress on what some call the superficialities of soldiering: drill, discipline, obedience, smartness, bearing, pride of uniform, pride of service. It could be summed up in a dictum: "If they won't soldier, they won't fight."[41] This is not, strictly speaking, true, of course, and Pershing probably knew it. All wars bring instances of people who, although goldbricks and troublemakers in time of peace, become model fighters in wartime, and revert to their earlier condition afterwards. But for him, willingness to "soldier" was the best (if not the only) indication of how well a man would react in combat.[42]

Avery D. Andrews, his classmate, thought that Pershing may have been influenced somewhat by the example of Col. Wesley Merritt, the superintendent, reputed to be the strictest in West Point history. "There were many things in Pershing's attitude in later life that suggested that stern discipline of Wesley Merritt," he said.[43]

Pershing was "a champion at deviling plebes," remembered another cadet. Having been "deviled" himself when he entered, he made sure that he gave back what he got, and then some. "I hope the day will never come when hazing is abolished," he said.[44] A plebe whom Captain Pershing "deviled" wrote home: "We have an awful mean Captain."[45]

West Point endeared itself to Pershing and deeply influenced his life. To him, "Duty, Honor, Country" were more than just words. At the end of World War I, when the Superintendent of the Academy sent his congratulations, Pershing wrote back:

"No message that I have received from any source whatever has given me as much pleasure, as much gratification, as much satisfaction as the one I received from you, in which you speak of my being a representative of our dear Military Academy. What the Academy stands for has always been my guide throughout my military career, and

13

to have approached the high ideals . . . of West Point, has to me a meaning that nothing else has."[46]

In his student days, however, he had less romantic thoughts. The question, "What's good for John J. Pershing?" was never far from his mind and when people told him there would not be a gun fired in the coming one hundred years, he quickly saw that an Army career might not be too promising. "I'll graduate," he told a friend, "but afterwards I may resign and take up law."[47] Eventually, he did all these things, although not in that order. He graduated, got a law degree seven years later as a sort of safety-valve, and retired at the end of a long Army career, not, however, without thinking of it before then. In due course, he made a name for himself as a frontier cavalryman and guerrilla warrior.

It began at Fort Bayard, a small post of adobe brick in southwest New Mexico, seventy miles from the Mexican border. It was in frontier country—dry alkali sand, networks of canyons, rock-strewn mountains —the kind of country Pershing would encounter thirty years later when he chased Pancho Villa.

At the time, however, the 6th Cavalry, which Pershing joined in September, 1886, was pursuing Indians, not Mexicans. Geronimo, the great Apache leader, had surrendered three weeks before Pershing arrived, but Mangas, one of the minor chiefs, still had to be hunted down. In October, two cavalry troops, including Pershing's L Troop, went out to scout for Mangas in the Mogollon Mountains to the northwest of Bayard. On the day of departure Pershing noticed that a number of men had liberally patronized the post trader's bar. The first day out they neglected to hobble their horses when grazing so that a noise stampeded them. "It was a somewhat embarrassing situation to find ourselves," he remarked, "—cavalrymen afoot . . . with not a horse in sight."[48]

By noon the following day the horses were all collected and Pershing began to understand why men got drunk before an Indian campaign in New Mexico. The sun beat down unmercifully; the wind and dust cracked lips, ears, and faces. Many times they had to make "dry camp" and when they finally reached a water hole the horses were often so thirst-crazed that men had to beat them back with rifle butts until they themselves had drunk. Occasionally Indians poisoned a water hole by throwing in animal carcasses. The men boiled the water, but the smell and the taste were still bad, even when mixed with coffee. They were not unhappy, therefore, when someone else captured Mangas in Arizona, after a pursuit which covered six mountain ranges.[49]

Pershing was twenty-six and inexperienced. A civilian dubbed him and two others whose names began with the same initial: "The Three Green Peas."[50] On one occasion Pershing borrowed an officer's bed roll and carelessly forgot to return it. The latter, suddenly called out to the field, had to go without a change of linen, and on his return gave the lieutenant an earful: "Mr. Pershing, the first thing a man learns in the army is courtesy. It starts from the day you learn to salute."[51]

But he was learning. A senior officer said later: "In those days when a youngster joined a regiment, he was not expected to express himself on military matters until he had some little experience. But there was a certain something in Pershing's appearance and manner which made him an exception to the rule. Within a very short time after he came to the post, a senior officer would turn to him and say: 'Pershing, what do you think of this?' And his opinion was such that we always listened to it. He was quiet, unobtrusive in his opinions. But when asked, he always went to the meat of a question in a few words. From the first he had responsible duties thrown on him. We all learned to respect and like him."[52]

Pershing kept growing. He picked up Indian fighting and learned how to handle enlisted men. When occasion demanded, he settled a dispute man-to-man with his fists rather than pull rank on a recalcitrant subordinate. He treated men "straight," without trying to domineer. But they knew what he liked and didn't—as anyone could testify who was ever caught mistreating an animal.[53]

At Fort Bayard Pershing enjoyed himself immensely. "He was genial and full of fun," a fellow officer recalled. "No matter what the work or what the play, he always took a willing, a leading part. He was punctilious in his observance of post duties; always keen for detachment work; glad to help get up a hop, go on a picnic with the ladies, romp with the children, or sit in a game of poker."[54]

The remark about poker has a history behind it. Pershing's experience with cards had been limited to an occasional game of euchre or seven-up. One day an officer, suddenly called out, asked him to sit in. When the man returned, Pershing had won a considerable sum and thereafter took up the game with a vengeance, seeking to augment his $125 a month salary. "I began to see poker hands in my sleep," he confessed. This convinced him he had better taper off and in later life, if he played at all, it was for trivial stakes.[55]

On August 11, 1887, L Troop was transferred to Fort Stanton. Life was less formal, since the garrison was smaller; of the four years Pershing spent in New Mexico, he liked his stay there best. "It is unsurpassed in many things," he said, "hunting, fishing, location, and spooning."[56]

In the fall Gen. Nelson A. Miles, commanding the Department of Arizona, organized sessions in Indian fighting. While dignified with the name of "field maneuvers," they were really old-fashioned games of "cowboys and Indians," or, as the soldiers called them, "rabbit hunts."

One detachment was designated "raiders"; another, "pursuers." Raiders had an eighteen-hour head start and "raided" an Army post by coming within 1,000 yards of its flagstaff in daylight without detection. Raiders were considered captured when pursuers came within hailing distance or bugle call. The idea was to simulate Indian warfare, familiarize the men with the country, and make a game out of what was work.[57]

On September 25, Pershing set out with a detachment of raiders. He escaped capture the first and second day, covering 110 miles before he made camp in the Black Mountains northeast of Fort Bayard. The Apaches had raided that country not long before. As Pershing was eating breakfast an old prospector strolled into camp and asked if Indians were on the warpath again. Pershing said no. Almost immediately some pursuers hove into sight and let out war whoops. "Good God, Captain," exclaimed the prospector, "the Indians are on you!" and he took to his heels.[58]

Pershing liked the maneuvers and thought they were good training.

Fort Wingate, New Mexico, where Pershing was stationed in 1889
Photograph courtesy U. S. Signal Corps

Pershing as a 2nd Lieutenant of the 6th Cavalry
*Photograph taken 1886 or 1887,
courtesy Library of Congress*

His men enjoyed them, though it often meant long hours in the saddle. Once they covered 130 miles in forty hours, with seven hours in camp on the first night and only three on the second. Yet every horse and mule finished in good condition, and General Miles complimented Pershing for the accomplishment.[59]

In January, 1889, Pershing was transferred to Fort Wingate, headquarters of the 6th Cavalry, located in northwest New Mexico. "This post is a S.O.B. and no question," he said. "Tumbled down, old quarters. . . . The winters are severe. It is always bleak and the surrounding country is barren absolutely."[60]

In the surrounding country, somewhat near the fort, was a reservation of Zuni Indians. In May, word came that the Zunis, usually peaceable, were under arms and besieging white men at the [S] ranch. Pershing was ordered to take a detachment of ten men and rescue them.[61]

After a hard ride, Pershing came upon a log cabin surrounded by about a hundred Indians firing a steady fusillade. The Zunis, greatly excited, explained that the men inside were horse thieves who had killed some of their tribesmen in a running fight.

Pershing replied that his orders were to rescue the white men and take them under arrest to Fort Wingate. Only with difficulty did he persuade the Zuni chiefs to permit this action; to see thieves and killers ride off unpunished was not their idea of justice. He then walked to the cabin and got the men to surrender—an easy task, for they knew they were doomed if they stayed.[62]

The critical moment, of course, was when they had to pass through the Zunis; anything might happen if some young buck started pumping bullets. On the way in Pershing said to one of his soldiers, "We are going to take those men away and if these bucks get hostile, remember *we mean business.*" Mounting troopers on either side of the prisoners, he rode rapidly through the lines of threatening braves. No shots were fired.[63]

Col. Eugene A. Carr, commanding Fort Wingate, commended Pershing for successfully handling a touchy assignment. But Pershing may have wondered if Indian justice was not, after all, better than the white man's. Of the three horse thieves and murderers, one escaped from the guard house, and the other two were later released without punishment.[64]

A second incident with Indians was almost fatal. Pershing had led out a detail of troopers in search of an Apache raiding party which had been harassing settlers, and, riding a zig-zag course in an effort to find tracks, had become separated somewhat from his patrol. Suddenly about eight Apaches rode out of an arroyo and bore down on him. Pershing spurred his horse and drew his pistol, but it was too late. An Apache gave him a sharp crack on the head, he tumbled off his horse, and the pistol flew along the ground to rest about twenty feet away.

In the meantime, his own men saw what was happening and started to the rescue. An Apache, bending over the semi-conscious Pershing with a raised tomahawk, suddenly changed his mind. He ran over to the pistol, retrieved it, and rode rapidly off with his companions.[65]

In September, 1889, Pershing was transferred back to Fort Stanton, his favorite post, where he fulfilled a promise made to Colonel Carr. The latter was fond of hunting and, since Pershing claimed to know people at Stanton who specialized in hunting dogs, Carr asked him to buy one. Pershing spent $50.00 and shipped him "a wonder." On the first hunt the dog took one look at a bear and ran all the way back to the post.[66]

Colonel Carr bore him no grudge, giving the officer a "most excellent" rating on the 1890 efficiency report and commending him for "studious habits."[67] Pershing's first published article appeared in the *Journal of the U.S. Cavalry Association* in December, 1889. In September of that year he had asked to attend the infantry and cavalry school at Fort Leavenworth; Carr recommended him but he did not get the assignment. On his own, Pershing then undertook a reading program covering the cavalry, modern tactics, reconnaissance, topography, and the campaigns of the Civil War. He wrote a friend at Fort Leavenworth, asking him to forward the whole course as taught there "from first to last."[68]

Carr also commended Pershing's "great interest in rifle, carbine, and pistol practice." Pershing ranked as "Marksman" in the 1887 competitions, and as "Sharpshooter" the following two years. In 1890 he ranked as "Marksman" again, and in 1891, as "Distinguished Marksman" (the highest rank possible). His interest in shooting was contagious. More than once he took a group which stood low in target practice and, by his instruction and enthusiasm, raised it to the top of the regiment.[69]

On November 23, 1890, the 6th Cavalry received orders to move to South Dakota where trouble had broken out among the Indians.

Locked within their reservation, their chiefs shorn of power, their great warriors dead, the buffalo gone, their lands taken from them, the Indians had for decades lived in idleness, supported by government doles. They were a people without wealth, dignity, or hope. They drank the white man's crazy-water, made big talk, dreamed of the past, and lived in misery. But all this, so it seemed to them, was about to change.

An Indian named Wovoka had had a vision of a New Era. The land was to be restored to the Red Man again. As in the past, there would be plenty of game. The hated white man would be destroyed. "I went up to heaven and saw the Great Spirit and all the people who had died a long time ago. . . . He gave to me a dance to give to my people."[70]

This dance was the so-called Ghost Dance, executed by forming a large circle which alternately contracted and expanded. As they danced, the warriors chanted songs of promise:

Over the whole earth they are coming—
The buffalo are coming, the buffalo are coming.

Clothed in brightly colored Ghost Shirts, on which were painted bows and arrows and thunderbirds, the warriors believed that the new Ghost Dance ritual would make them immune to the white man's bullets.[71]

By November, 1890, some 3,000 Indians from the Rosebud and Pine Ridge Reservations had taken refuge in the Badlands. Well armed, they had posted themselves on a high mesa, inaccessible except by a few trails and by a wagon road, where they awaited the appearance of an Indian "Messiah," who would lead them in retaking their lands from the white man. To the north, on the Cheyenne and Standing Rock Reservations, other Indians were preparing to join their comrades in the Badlands. A full-scale Indian uprising was in the offing.[72]

The 6th Cavalry left New Mexico on December 1 and detrained in Rapid City, South Dakota, on December 9. There they got their winter clothing—heavy felt socks, fur-lined caps and gloves, blanket-lined canvas overcoats, arctic overshoes. Then they rode out to quash what was to be the last great Indian uprising in the United States. Their aim was to throw a cordon around the Badlands, prevent new bands from joining the renegades, and starve them into submission. They were "almost constantly in the saddle," Pershing recalled, "patrolling and scouting in every direction."[73]

The weather was bitter cold. Civil War veterans said the campaign was the hardest they had ever experienced. Fording icy rivers, sleeping tentless in the snow, making forced marches through sleet and gale in sub-zero temperature, riding in isolated troops with always the danger of being massacred—such was the campaign of the Ghost Dance Rebellion, as it came to be called.[74]

Pershing never forgot the freezing weather. When an officer drew a pint of whiskey from his pocket, his fingers were so numb that it fell on a rock and splattered on the snow. A shivering enlisted man chattered: "Sir, have I your permission to eat that snow?"[75]

To protect themselves against the cold, men devoured tremendous quantities of food. Breakfast was a large pie plate heaped with bacon, beans, and hard-bread and washed down with a quart of steaming coffee; lunch, whatever could be stuffed into the saddle bags and eaten on the way; supper, heaps of beef, potatoes, and other substantials. "I could not now eat in four days what I did then in one," Pershing said later. He gained twenty pounds in two months.[76]

On Christmas Day they received bad news: Big Foot's band (many of whom had been in on the kill at Custer's Last Stand) had escaped and were headed south. Could the 6th Cavalry intercept them before they united with other Indians?

A much-used trail passed down Porcupine Creek to the south. Pershing suggested to Maj. Emil Adam, the squadron commander, that Big Foot would probably come that way. Adam disagreed and posted soldiers on another trail. "But for fate," Pershing complained afterwards, "the 6th Cavalry would have captured Big Foot's band. . . ."[77]

Big Foot slipped through but was captured on December 28th by another squadron. Then, when all thought that affairs would be settled without bloodshed, occurred a clash at Wounded Knee Creek. To this day the details of how it started are still not clear, but it left over two hundred casualties, most of them Indians, including women and children. "This came like a thunderbolt," said Pershing, "as the troops thought by that time that the campaign was going to be ended peaceably." Thereafter they felt constant fear that some isolated unit would be surprised and wiped out.[78]

After several weeks the Messiah craze subsided and the Indians returned to their reservations. The troops went into camp at Pine Ridge, South Dakota, where Pershing had a pleasant reunion with eight members of the class of '86. Liquor flowed freely and Pershing poured it down. "It would have been more pleasant," he said, "had two or three or four of the boys not gotten a little too full, one of whom I am which. I never went to a reunion yet that I did not wind up full as eighteen goats."[79]

Pershing's next assignment was commanding a company of Sioux Indian Scouts, one of four such hired by the government at the regular pay for cavalry. Their job was to go wherever disaffection was suspected, watch for gun running and inter-tribal conspiracies, smooth over trouble, and act as go-between for the government and the Indians. They were to take the pulse of Indian affairs, so that an uprising such as had just occurred could immediately be detected and checked, or—better—so that discontent would never reach the revolt stage.[80]

This was Pershing's first experience in handling men not of his own race and culture. He succeeded with them, just as he succeeded later with American Negroes and with Philippine Moros, by treating them with respect and consideration. He did not tolerate them; he liked them. And almost universally they liked him in return. More than once a Sioux Scout appointed himself Pershing's personal bodyguard when they were in dangerous territory. At Wounded Knee Creek, for instance, Indians with "bad hearts" prowled about, wrapped heavily in blankets with hatchets underneath. At night a Sioux Scout had placed himself outside Pershing's tent, watching carefully that no one approached. Even in daylight another Scout, without orders, followed closely as a bodyguard.[81]

Compared to the normal army roster, the Scout muster roll was a galaxy of strange names: Thunder Bull, Red Feather, Broken Leg, Crow-on-head, Has-white-face-horse, Kills Alone, and so on. The Scouts were generally well-behaved, though some became unruly from drink. When this happened, their own non-commissioned officers disciplined them without instructions from Pershing. These officers were selected from those of highest tribal rank, lest any chief's son be subject to the indignity of taking orders from a common brave.[82]

The Sioux Scouts were enrolled for only six months and were not asked to re-enlist. Pershing always felt this was a mistake. The Sioux were natural soldiers. They instinctively sent out flankers and advance guards; they approached each hill cautiously, prepared for a possible enemy just over the top; they would never blunder into a trap. Why not enroll a regiment or two in the Regular Army, he wondered? It had been done with Negroes with good success. It would bind Indians to the government in a special way. Unfortunately, the Sioux Scouts went out of existence soon after Pershing's service with them ended.[83]

Pershing served as a frontier cavalryman from 1886 to 1891. Most of his duties were routine: an occasional Indian scare, the arrest of cattle thieves, and the like. Maj. Gen. William A. Kobbé said later: "The experience a large majority of our officers got at frontier posts between the Civil and Spanish Wars was pretty worthless."[84] Was it for Pershing?

Yes and no. Soldiering was small unit stuff, company level rather than regimental or larger, and certainly far removed from the divisions, corps, and armies of World War I. As far as experience in large units with combined arms (infantry, cavalry, artillery) was concerned, Pershing might just as well have stayed at West Point. But a certain amount of seasoning took place—necessary seasoning, which distinguished the real soldier from the textbook buff who happened to know a lot about military things. Pershing learned how to get along with people—and how to go along: with his fellow officers, with the enlisted men, with the angry Zuni and with the strange Sioux who needed special handling and who were almost a school of psychology in themselves. He discovered the value of a bold front when danger threatened and learned to live with equanimity in situations where one could never be sure death wasn't around the corner. Two months before his Sioux Scout service a fellow officer was murdered while visiting an Indian camp.

Pershing began service with what has been called the "Old Army" and it left its mark on him. Disdain for the militia, a strict caste system, pride in the Regular Army—especially the West Pointer—these were part of it. In our modern era some Old Army customs seem strange and mandarin-like. At one post, for example, a lorry customarily made the rounds of the officers' quarters to pick up wives for a trip into town; at the colonel's house, all other wives got off, the colonel's wife got on, and then everybody else re-entered. Rank had its privileges in the Old Army. Pershing imbibed this spirit from his earliest Army days.[85]

Though he might eventually resign from the Army, Pershing decided that, as long as he stayed, he might as well be professional about it. What was worth doing was worth doing well. He studied. He published. He took pride in training men well, in making marksmen as good as himself. As at West Point, he was a leader, a man who could be trusted with responsibility.

He was no tin soldier and certainly no figurine saint. A warm man, he enjoyed and matched wits with life: meeting Buffalo Bill,[86] hauling in 240 trout in six hours with two companions in fabulous fishing country,[87] shooting some farmer's pig under the misapprehension (so he said) that it was a ferocious wild boar,[88] asking to remain at Fort Stanton on the plea that it had an officer shortage, when in fact he wanted to stay there to keep an eye on some mines he had invested in.[89]

The austerity and coldness later associated with Pershing, "the cold front," was not yet in evidence. There was no need for it. He had no reputation to carry, no stereotype to live up to. He could, with a glad heart, become a poker fanatic, note good places for making love, and drink himself "full as eighteen goats." The young cavalryman was a very human gentleman.

2

Commanding Cadets

With peace reigning on the plains, Pershing looked for greener pastures. His family had moved to Lincoln, Nebraska; he applied for duty at the university there and in 1891 was appointed professor of military science.[1]

He had his work cut out for him. University of Nebraska students had no tradition of military training; they had rebelled when a previous commandant insisted that they drill in uniform.[2] By the testimony of the university chancellor, James H. Canfield, Pershing "found a few men, the interest in the battalion weak, the discipline next to nothing, and the instincts of the faculty and the precedent of the University against the corps."[3]

When the cadets met their new military instructor for the first time, they saw a lean, young officer, clad immaculately in dark blue blouse and the light blue trousers of the cavalry. His mustache was well clipped (he had grown it in New Mexico); his shoulders were as square as his jaw. His clothes were spotless, his collar was exactly the prescribed one-quarter inch above the coat collar, and his shoes were brightly shined. The brass buttons on his uniform, the buckle, and all the metal trimmings glistened smartly in the sunlight. The new lieutenant looked formidable.[4] How formidable was evident at the first inspection. He walked briskly up and down the line inspecting shoes, uniform, gloves, and rifle. Not a knot in a shoe string, not a tarnished brass button escaped his attention. "Suck up your gut!" Pershing commanded. "Pull in your butt! Cut out that farm walk."[5]

Punishments were swift; so were rewards. There were no favorites. If West Pointers used as much elbow grease, brass polish, and tar heel as Pershing demanded on belts and cartridge boxes, the Nebraska cadets wondered if they had time for anything else. They learned what was meant by a "strict disciplinarian."[6]

One day at target practice Pershing barked out the first three commands: "Load!" "Ready!" "Aim!" Then, touching a cadet lightly with his foot, he whispered so that only he could hear: "Fire your piece."

"Rrr-ip," went the cadet's old 45-70 Springfield. "RRR-IP," went all the other rifles up and down the firing line.

Pershing stormed up to a cadet.

"Did you hear the command 'Fire'?"

"No, sir."

"Then why did you fire?"

"I heard some one else fire, sir."

"Do you *always* do what you hear other people do?"

The point was made. Thereafter no cadet fired his piece without first hearing the order.[7]

Said one cadet about the annual summer encampment: "Pershing ran that camp just as though the enemy was just over the hill and no fooling about it. We had a couple of old cannons and they had to be dragged to the camp and set up ready for the attack of the enemy."[8]

One night about 1:00 A.M., one cannon went off with a terrible bang. "Pershing sure did raise hell," the sentry remembered, "as he just could not stand for any infraction of discipline. He had every man on the carpet, but did not find the culprit or culprits. I guess he had to punish someone so he put me in the hoosegow for the duration of the camp."[9]

One might expect Nebraska farm boys to resent the new discipline, and some did. But the strange thing was that, with most, Pershing had a way of making them like it, see a value in it, and actually take pride in it. It was amazing, but there was no getting around it.

"We all tried to walk like Pershing, talk like Pershing, and look like Pershing," a cadet recalled. "His personality and strength of character dominated us. . . ."[10] "Every inch of him was a soldier," testified another. "In all my life I have never seen a man with such poise, dignity and personality. Whether in uniform or not, he attracted attention wherever he went. But he was always affable and interesting to talk with, and popular with students and professors."[11]

The cadets liked their new commandant because he was scrupulously fair. He did not incline to snap judgments, but when he made decisions, he made them quickly and they stuck.[12]

He was credited with an almost photographic memory. At the beginning of the school year, Pershing lined up a company and had the First Sergeant read the roll; as the men answered, Pershing mentally connected name and face, remembering perfectly, so that during the first drill he was able to call down a cadet by name.[13]

Faculty members too thought highly of Pershing. Dr. Fred Morrow Fling of the History Department remarked: "He had a fine presence, a genial and unpretentious manner and one gained the impression that he was a man of great physical reserve with unusual driving power. His speech was incisive; he was quick in action."[14]

Jack Best, the university trainer, noticed that, despite great personal dignity, Pershing had a way of "getting next" to the new students, and added: "He was the finest man I ever worked with. It is true that he was mighty strict in his work, but the results he got were so good that everybody he worked with loved him for it. . . . I just worshipped that man and everybody around the University felt the same about him."[15]

Pershing revolutionized the Military Department at the University of Nebraska. He reorganized the entire corps, patterning it after the battalion at West Point, so that corporals were chosen from sophomores; sergeants, from juniors; and lieutenants and captains, from seniors. He got the Board of Regents to increase compulsory training from two to three years.[16] He changed the uniform, established a lyceum, improved and tripled the equipment, and generally tightened things up.[17]

"He had a really wonderful success," said a contemporary, "in transposing the West Point atmosphere briefly into those hours when the battalion was drilling or parading."[18] Even one who disdained military training had to admit, "He could take a body of cornfed yokels and with only three hours of drill a week turn them into fancy cadets, almost indistinguishable from West Pointers."[19]

Just how well Pershing succeeded in making "fancy cadets" may be gathered from Maj. E. G. Fechet, a War Department inspector, who found the marching "very steady" and movements "finely executed." Arms and accoutrements were "in excellent condition."[20] Fechet said the cadets "showed a degree of proficiency that I believe can be equalled by but few military organizations. . . . I doubt if there can be found a better drilled Battalion outside of West Point, either Regulars or Militia. I know these are high words of praise, but I feel confident that any officer of experience, after seeing the Battalion manoeuvre, would confirm my opinion. The high degree of proficiency attained is due entirely to the energy, ability and tact to organize and command, of Lieut. Pershing. Previous to his arrival, but little, I understand, had been accomplished. No special interest had been manifested in the Military Department, either in the college or among the residents of Lincoln. Now it is just the reverse. All seem to try to see who can show the most interest in the University Battalion."[21]

A high point in Pershing's work with the battalion occurred in the spring of 1892 at a national drill competition at Omaha. From 100 cadets who volunteered, he selected forty-five and put them through intensive training. As captain of the company, Pershing selected George L. Sheldon, later governor of Nebraska.[22]

The contest opened with a parade through the crowd-lined streets of Omaha. Veteran drill companies were there—the National Fencibles of Washington, the Sealy Rifles of Galveston, the McCarthy Light Guards of Little Rock.[23] The Nebraska cadets were cocky, but Pershing deflated them with a blistering talk about their poor appearance and

Pershing as Commandant of Cadets at the University of Nebraska, 1891–1895
Photograph courtesy Nebraska State Historical Society, Lincoln, Nebr.

Pershing (at center, seated) with members of the Cadet Battallion,
University of Nebraska, 1895
*Photograph courtesy Nebraska State Historical Society,
Lincoln, Nebr.*

sloppy marching in the parade. "They were too good," he explained afterwards. "They were perfect and they knew it. I couldn't let them go into a competition feeling like that."[24]

When the company assembled next day to march to the contest, Pershing again berated them. But just before arriving, he halted them unexpectedly and said, "I think you are going to win the first prize."[25]

The contest had two divisions: the Grand National (open to all) and the Maiden (open to new companies). Pershing entered both. In the former, the cadets had bad luck. Nervous as rookies, they failed to execute "stack arms" and did not place.

In the Maiden Division it was different. They swung through maneuvers with a vengeance and showed a confidence rarely seen in new companies. The regulations allowed forty-five minutes for the exercises; the cadets finished in just one half that time. They took the first prize of $1,500 easily. The Nebraska student body and a large section of Lincoln townspeople scrambled over the guard rails and carried the cadets bodily off the field.[26]

Perhaps no single event gave such impetus to the military program at Nebraska as this win at Omaha. The next school year saw a larger percentage of students in the program than ever before. A picked group of cadets organized themselves as the "Varsity Rifles" and voluntarily continued their training. By 1895 the "Varsity Rifles" had become the "Pershing Rifles," the first of scores of military companies throughout the United States to bear that name.[27]

When Chancellor Canfield first met Pershing, he suggested studying law at Nebraska. No telling when such knowledge would serve an officer handily, said Canfield. Pershing had once been interested in law; why not enroll in the university and take a course on the side?[28]

In making the suggestion, Canfield probably had hidden motives. "I think my father took his measure pretty early," said the Chancellor's daughter, Dorothy Canfield Fisher. "Pershing had a reputation for not being the most sober member of society. My father knew that a full-blooded young man of that age really wouldn't have enough to do to keep him out of mischief just with training the battalion which wasn't allowed too many hours out of the regular educational work." Hence the suggestion about law.[29]

The Nebraska Law School was new and the only one in the state. Pershing appears to have enrolled with the first classes and, if one source is to be believed, to have received some kind of advanced standing due to his prior reading of Blackstone and Kent.[30]

He did well in his studies. "He had a keen analytical mind," said Henry H. Wilson, one of the professors, "and was a diligent student of the law. No one intimately acquainted with the young lieutenant will doubt that he would have become an eminent lawyer had he devoted his life to the practice of that profession."[31]

Charles E. Magoon, a lifelong friend, later Governor of Panama and Cuba, remarked: "He has naturally a legal mind. . . . I doubt if he ever would have made a good jury lawyer. . . . But for grasp of legal principles, for power to discern the relation of one group of facts to another, I believe, had he followed the law, he would have stood in the forerank of the profession."[32] On June 7, 1893, Pershing received his diploma as Bachelor of Laws.[33]

With his cherished law degree, Pershing thought of quitting the Army, for it was woefully small and he would be only a major at retirement. He approached another young lawyer, Charles G. Dawes, suggesting they form a partnership. Dawes said no. "Better lawyers than either you or I can ever hope to be are starving in Nebraska," he warned. "I'd try the Army for a while yet. Your pay may be small, but it comes very regularly."[34]

Pershing took the advice but sometimes had second thoughts. "I am disgusted with the Army and the way it is treated," he wrote his brother in 1898. "I don't know whether you expect to stay in the army or not, but there's nothing in it,—but hope deferred."[35]

In 1906, when he became a general officer, he more or less decided to stick with the Army.[36] But even then, in moments when military life seemed to separate him too much from his family, he would cry out, "Damn the service," and speak of resigning.[37]

In addition to his duties as Military Commandant and his studies in law, Pershing undertook another assignment at Nebraska: teaching mathematics in a preparatory school associated with the university. Pershing's idea of teaching was to scare people into learning. He would pace back and forth in front of the class and fairly pounce on the students with questions.[38] One of them, Dorothy Canfield Fisher, left a vivid picture of him as a teacher.

"He taught a living subject like geometry as he would have taught a squad of raw recruits he was teaching to drill—that is, by telling them what to do and expecting them to do it. He was of the kind who said, 'Lesson for tomorrow will be from page 32 to page 36. All problems must be solved before coming to class.'

"He never gave us any idea of what geometry was all about, and I now have the impression that he didn't know himself that there was anything more to geometry than what was on page 32 and following. I particularly remember that class because one girl in it was completely bewildered by geometry. She didn't understand it at all, nor was anything ever said in class to make her understand it. But she had the quick, facile memory of a youngster. And she was also very much afraid of Pershing's harsh rebuke when somebody didn't know a lesson. So she ended by committing her lessons to memory. That is, if anybody had changed the lettering of a problem, of the different points of a triangle, for instance, she wouldn't have been able to do it. But by committing it to memory she was able to get through each day's recitation. And she was passed at the end of the year without Pershing ever having detected the fact that she didn't understand a word of what she was saying.

"And yet, the older men students got a great deal out of it. The point was, they had the motivation, and also the maturity of mind and experience, which took them out of the class of the bewildered little girl, and enabled them to need just what Pershing gave, a sort of supervision of self-education."[39]

Another student destined for the literary world sat in Pershing's class —Alvin Johnson, later editor of the *New Republic* and the *Encyclopedia of the Social Sciences*. Johnson carefully studied the young lieutenant, whom the registrar later described as the toughest teacher in the school. He was "tall, perfectly built, handsome. All his movements, all play of expression, were rigidly controlled to a military pattern. His pedagogy was military. His questions were short, sharp orders, and he expected quick, succinct answers. Woe to the student who put a problem on the board in loose or slovenly fashion! Pershing's soul appeared to have been formed on the pattern of 'Present—arms! Right shoulder—arms! Fours right! Forward march!' "[40]

Like Miss Canfield, Johnson admired Pershing—but as a soldier, not as a teacher. "Never in the whole year did he give us . . . enthusiasm for mathematics. . . ."[41]

What Pershing did give, though not right away, was an amazing demonstration of memory. At the end of Johnson's first year, Pershing appointed him cadet corporal. For some reason Johnson declined. About half a century afterwards, the two ran into each other again at a party given by Bernard Baruch.

"I think I have met you before," said Pershing.

"Certainly," replied Johnson. "You have met hundreds of thousands, who all remember you, but you can't remember the hundreds of thousands."

"Was it in Nebraska, when I was Commandant of Cadets?"

Johnson was startled. "It was."

"And you were the cadet who refused to be a corporal. I never did understand your reasoning."[42]

Another cadet, Erwin R. Davenport, later encountered Pershing after a separation of over forty years. When he introduced himself as a former cadet, Pershing put out his hand and said, "Davenport, I remember you—glad to see you." Davenport thought the recognition was trumped up and that Pershing "was lying like a gentleman." But after thinking a moment, Pershing asked what had become of Harry Oury, Phil Russell, and Bert Wheedon, all members of Davenport's fraternity. Davenport was flabbergasted. He asked how Pershing could remember such names after all those years. "Oh, I don't know," was the answer; "they just come to me."[43]

The greatest friend Pershing made at Nebraska was Charles G.

Dawes, later Vice-President of the United States in the Coolidge administration. Many times they sat down together at Don Cameron's lunch counter, where the pancakes were good and, more important, cheap. Both had to watch their pennies. When Pershing's dress suit got threadbare he saved money by having some tails cut out of old trousers and stitched on.[44]

In after years both men loved to joke about their Nebraska days. At a superb French banquet during World War I, Dawes turned to Pershing and said, "General, I know . . . our hostess will be interested if you tell her about the old Spanish nobleman, Don Cameron, who used to entertain in the same way in the old days."[45]

On another occasion, while dining in the home of Ogden Mills in Paris, which had formerly been the palace of Marshal Lannes, Dawes looked around and said, "John, when I contrast these barren surroundings with the luxuriousness of our early life in Lincoln, Nebraska, it does seem that a good man has no real chance in the world."

"Yes," answered Pershing, "Don't it beat hell!"[46]

In the spring of 1895, when Pershing's term of service at the university drew to a close, Chancellor Canfield wrote a glowing report on him:

"He is the most energetic, active, industrious, competent, and successful officer that I have ever known in a position to this kind. We have the second best corps in the United States according to the reports of United States inspectors; the first being the corps at West Point. Lieutenant Pershing has made this corps what it is today. . . . By his indomitable energy, by his engaging personality, by his unquestioned ability, and by his untiring industry, he has brought the battalion to its present position."[47]

The years at the University of Nebraska had been happy for Pershing. They were also formative. Pershing, after all, was a country boy. He spent his first twenty-two years in a small town in Missouri, his next four in the confining, almost seminary-like routine of West Point, and his next five in isolated army posts on the frontier. His only contacts had been with country people and soldiers. The Nebraska assignment brought him in contact with a more urban society, a university atmosphere, and a civilian populace.

He found it "one of the most . . . profitable" experiences of his life. He later declared that every officer should have some experience at a university, precisely because of its broadening influence. University life would teach, as in no other way, an understanding of the young men who would form the nation's citizenry in peace and her armies in war.[48]

But if the university did much for Pershing, he felt that he had done much for it. His military course taught precision, fitness, and a respect for authority. "In my opinion," Pershing told the Board of Regents in his final report, "the influence of the discipline required in the Military Department can be credited with the excellent state of affairs from a disciplinary point of view now existing in this University."[49]

How the cadets generally felt about Pershing is clear. They were utterly devoted to him. Dorothy Canfield Fisher, who knew Pershing then and later, doubted whether at any other period of his life he brought out in other people such intense personal devotion. By the testimony of her own brother, a cadet, this devotion existed throughout the battalion.[50]

When Pershing came to leave the university, the cadets wanted some kind of remembrance. A committee approached Pershing and asked for a pair of his breeches.

"What in the world do you want a pair of my breeches for?"

They explained that they wanted to cut them up into little bits of cloth, showing the yellow seam (the cavalry color) on a blue field, and wear them as service ribbons.

Pershing was touched. He said, "I will give you the very best pair I own."[51]

Pershing's next assignment was Fort Assiniboine, Montana Territory, a lonely but impressively solid frontier post thirty miles south of the Canadian boundary. It was a cold place (temperatures in January went down to -20°), situated nowhere in particular as far as civilization was concerned, but near enough to Indians to remind them of authority. Pershing reported there in October, 1895, and commanded a troop of the 10th Cavalry, a Negro regiment.[52]

Service with Negro troops was not especially sought after, for it meant more work for the officers. But Pershing's attitude towards the Negro was, in his own words, "that of one brought up among them" —a reference to the fact that a number of his playmates as a boy in Laclede had been black. He treated them with the same respect and consideration he had shown the Sioux Indians and was later to show the Philippine Moros. In all three cases he succeeded, for he had a knack for dealing with those who were not of his own race.[53]

In June, 1896, Pershing saw action when a group of Cree Indians, international vagabonds for ten years, had to be rounded up and returned to Canada. In a sixty-two-day campaign covering 600 miles, Pershing collected some 400 of them scattered over northern Montana and took them to Coutts Station on the border.[54]

An incident occurred during the expedition which illustrates one of his ways of handling men. At the Marias River, swollen and dangerous, there was a delay while wagons were converted into boats by stretching canvas tent flies over the sides and bottom. One man was continually goldbricking. While others were in the river waist deep, he carefully avoided getting even his feet wet. "Get down in the water like the rest," Pershing ordered. The trooper made no move. Pershing's fist exploded on the soldier's jaw, knocking him full length in the water.

There was no more shirking after that. A saying developed in D Troop whenever anyone began loafing: "You better git at it, fella, or 'ol Red'll knock you into the river."[55]

Pershing served at Assiniboine until October, 1896, then enjoyed a leave of several months.[56] Being a good Republican, he visited his old friend, Charles G. Dawes, already a rising force in politics, at Republican headquarters, where he met the National Chairman, Mark Hanna. In Chicago he watched a procession of the followers of William Jennings Bryan, whooping it up for the 1896 election. "It was composed, it seemed to me, of all the riffraff of Chicago," he said.[57]

That winter Pershing spent a short tour in Washington, D. C. on the staff of the Commanding General of the Army, Nelson A. Miles, whom he had impressed when the latter visited Fort Assiniboine. Miles sent him to observe a military tournament in New York where, by chance, he shared a box with Theodore Roosevelt, then serving on the Board of Police Commissioners. Both men hit it off immediately. Their host, Avery D. Andrews, a Pershing classmate who had resigned from the Army, said of the meeting: "Both were enthusiastic and expert horsemen and both had seen much of the West. Both knew the Indians and the Indian Country, and both spoke the language of the plains and mountains. They spent the evening in a lively exchange of views and stories of the West and formed a friendship which lasted through life."[58]

In the summer of 1897 Pershing reported to West Point as a tactical officer. His job was to instruct in tactics and to enforce discipline in one of the cadet companies. With respect to instruction, he favored a practical course which would give cadets training in the command of platoons, companies or higher units, instead of graduating them almost without experience, as he had been. His suggestions, however, were vetoed by the Commandant, so that the course he gave was by his own admission "somewhat monotonous."[59]

He did have a chance, however, in the classroom and out, to look over some very promising cadets and to mentally note those who might be good men for future appointments. Twenty years later, the following former cadets were in important positions in the A.E.F.: Fox Conner, Malin Craig, Robert C. Davis, Leon B. Kromer, George S. Simonds, George Van Horn Moseley, Stuart Heintzelman, Wilson B. Burtt, and Upton Birnie, Jr.

All observers agree that Pershing was a strict disciplinarian—not to say over-strict. Many cadets disliked him. True, he was a "tac" and therefore a certain amount of hostility was expected. One who is always checking up on others will never be popular. But many felt that Pershing was unnecessarily strict, even for a "tac," that he needlessly irritated sensibilities, that he was an arrogant martinet.[60] "Of all the tacs, I would say he was the most unpopular," said a cadet.[61]

One incident illustrates why. Regulations were that cadets should wear a white shirt under their jackets. But since jackets so covered the body that one could not tell without checking whether a shirt was underneath, many cadets left them off in hot weather. Pershing, however, made it a point to order jackets removed during drill. Those who had on only underwear he "skinned" for not having white shirts.[62]

Pershing further irritated cadets by disregarding long-standing customs. "His offenses," said a cadet, "were inspections at unusual hours, doubling back on his tracks for second inspections, heavy punishments and what seemed to be unrealistic standards. He was gruff and unsympathetic and made a hard life harder."[63] Not the least of his offenses, added Cadet Malin Craig, was that, having once been a cadet himself, he recalled all the old secret hiding places where upperclassmen stored their tobacco and other contraband.[64]

One day a girl visiting West Point asked Pershing why there were never any disturbances when he was Officer of the Day? "I have a bluff on the Corps," he answered. The remark went through the Academy like wildfire. Small red flags appeared and voices cried "Hurrah for Anarchy! Allah be praised and the Commandant be damned!" Several cadets marched into the mess hall with a piece of red ribbon tied around their wrists. Pershing went quietly among the tables, making a report; anyone wearing red was later punished.

"That night was one of the wildest ever staged at West Point," a cadet said. The old cannon which were off limits suddenly discharged at about 10:00 P.M. Cadets let out unearthly yells, slammed the lids of their foot lockers, beat against iron buckets, and made a terrific din for about three minutes. That was their answer to Pershing and his "bluff on the Corps."[65]

Admittedly Pershing's work as a "tac" was made difficult by the section he was in charge of—A Company. High-strung and spirited, resentful of discipline, they showed their unruliness in various ways.[66] In chapel on Sundays, whenever "Lord God Almighty" appeared in the text, they shouted it at the top of their voices.[67] With a strict "tac" like Pershing in charge of them, there was bound to be a clash.

It came February 8, 1898. A cadet in A Company, William P. Wooten, filled a water bucket and placed it atop a slightly ajar door in one of the rooms. It was an old trick, sometimes played on cadets but never on an officer. It was designed to "cool off" the Lieutenant when he inspected while the cadets were in class.

Pershing never got wet. Malin Craig, captain of A Company (and later Army Chief of Staff from 1935–1939), warned him.

"As Pershing went around my room," recalled Craig, "I said to him 'Do not enter the first sergeant's room.' He stopped and asked why and I told him to send for me afterwards, but to keep out of that room. Pershing sensed the situation after he left me and sent a janitor into the room, and the innocent janitor got the deadfall on his neck and shoulders and was somewhat drenched. In about half an hour, Pershing sent for me and asked me who placed that bucket on the door. I told him I did not know and asked him to please drop the matter, as I had taken a chance of being sent to Coventry by my class, if not by the whole Corps. . . . He told me it was too late, and in about an hour my company, including myself, was placed in arrest in barracks and we stayed there for about three months doing all-night guard duty and with all privileges suspended. An investigation by the Commandant failed to bring out the name of the culprit, though it is quite probable that Pershing knew who had done it. Wooten was quite willing to confess what he had done, but his class took the responsibility of preventing his doing so. . . . The first class in particular, and A Company felt very bitter about the matter. . . ."[68]

Matters worsened, as A Company and the authorities went out of their way to irritate each other. A company was confined either to barracks, area of barracks, or the gymnasium. When girls visited, they could not be entertained in the barracks (there were rules against that!), nor in the area of barracks (it was too cold outside). Hence they could only visit in the gymnasium. Out came an order from the authorities: Whenever members of A Company are in the gymnasium they will exercise! The result was ridiculous. All over the gym cadets slowly twirled Indian clubs as they talked with their girls.

The Hundredth Night Show (100 days until graduation)—a big event of the year—was now at hand, but since they were in confinement, A Company would miss it. The show managers persuaded the authorities that there should be at least one dress rehearsal and staged it in the gymnasium. Thus it was that A Company saw the show—again twirling their Indian clubs.[69]

When the curtain went up on the night of the performance a huge red "A" appeared on each side of the arch. The audience went wild. Then Cadet Markham, vice-president of the Dialectic Society, stepped to the center of the stage.

"Owing to the fact that the Mosaic Law still obtains at the Military Academy, which requires an eye for an eye, a tooth for a tooth, and thirty days for a water-bucket, I must speak for the President of the Society, who is in Company A."

On went the show. All portions which had been previously censored reappeared and there were severe punishments afterwards.[70]

How badly relations between Pershing and the cadets had deteriorated may be gathered from the fact that they gave him the famous "silence." This is timed for the entrance of an officer into the cadet mess hall, which, when several hundred men are jabbering amid the clatter of plates and utensils, is usually noisy. Suddenly all talking, eating, and movement ceases. Several hundred cadets sit in absolute silence to express as a corporate body their dislike of that officer. It is an embarrassing moment. It says more than a thousand words—that the officer is disliked, intensely so, not just by the members of a given company but by the whole cadet battalion. The "silence" is not often given. But it was given to Lieutenant Pershing.[71]

Cadet C. L. Maguire remembered the incident well:

"Usually after the Battalion was seated, the officer in charge that day would go into the mess hall and pass down the center aisle. Pershing made quite a feature of this passing, and one day during the passage the mess hall became very silent. He immediately called for attention and dismissed all the Companies without waiting from them to be fed."[72]

Another cadet, Gilbert A. Youngberg, pointed out how this incident indicated the widespread feeling against Pershing throughout the corps. "Silence could be pulled off only at the mess hall during meals and required the concurrence of all present, including the cadet captains, lieutenants, sergeants, corporals and privates. Company A by itself could not put over a silence if opposed by even a small portion of the cadets in the other companies."[73]

Pershing must have been deeply piqued as word of the incident spread over the post. The contrast with his popularity at the University of Nebraska was particularly galling.

"My reputation is made," he told A Company disdainfully. "There is nothing you can do to hurt me."[74]

But there was. Cadets can make life unpleasant for an unpopular "tac." They made it so for Pershing, because at the end of that year a friend said: "I wish you would tell me why you did not like the West Point detail."[75] And in his unpublished autobiography written later, Pershing said not a word about his relations with A Company and very little about this period in his life.

His unpopularity was the reason for the nickname he subsequently bore. The cadets discovered that he had previously served with a Negro regiment and, since they disliked him, began calling him "Nigger Jack" or "Black Jack."[76] While not explaining why, Pershing admitted that the name "Black Jack" originated with the cadets while he was a tactical officer.[77]

There is irony in Pershing's failure with cadets at West Point after his success with them at Nebraska, but perhaps "failure" is too strong a word. George Van Horn Moseley, a cadet under Pershing at the Academy, has stressed that the important thing is not whether Pershing was liked or not, but whether he did his job well. According to Moseley, he did. He enforced discipline and as a result was unpopular. A number of other tactical officers did not and were not.[78]

Nonetheless it is true that Pershing was more than ordinarily disliked at the Academy. After having attained brilliant success at Nebraska with civilians who had no tradition of military training, winning their affection and admiration, he failed miserably to achieve even normal rapport with men who had dedicated themselves professionally to the military life as he had. True, his work at West Point was different from that at Nebraska, for it was more disciplinary and punitive. Yet it was not necessary to fall into the trap of discipline for the sake of discipline—as in the matter of checking on undershirts at drill and doubling back on inspections. At West Point Pershing manifested a rigidity he had never displayed at Nebraska, an inability to recover when he got off on the wrong foot, a tendency to cockiness in his "bluff on the Corps," a petulance which sought refuge in his supposed reputation.

But he learned something at West Point too, bloody as the experience was. He learned that there is a point beyond which one cannot profitably push men, that the quality and amount of discipline in an organization is limited by what its members think just and reasonable and are willing to submit to, and that, beyond this, trying to impose a higher standard runs into the law of diminishing returns. Never again would Pershing make so grievous a mistake in human relationships. In the future his men may not have had affection for him as the cadets did at Nebraska, but neither did they feel the cold hate the cadets did at West Point. Men's relationship with Pershing became more neutral, ending in a balance between affection and hate, which is probably best summed up in the word *respect.*

Meanwhile events in the outside world were moving swiftly. The *Maine* blew up in Havana harbor on February 15, 1898, and war fever mounted during the next two months. On April 27, Congress declared war on Spain. Pershing asked to be relieved at West Point for field service.[79] "I appreciate fully that it is fraught with danger," he told a friend, "but I have existed all these years in the service for just this sort of thing and to tell the truth if I should accept any duty which would keep me from field service . . . I should never forgive myself. I could no more keep out of the field than I could fly. . . ."[80]

On April 29, 1898, Pershing was ordered to join his regiment.[81]

3

"The Splendid Little War"

Pershing was somewhat displeased when he joined the 10th Cavalry, at Chickamauga Park, Georgia, May 5, 1898. He was going to be in the war, and that pleased him; but he was going as a first lieutenant, and he felt he should do better than that. Promotions were made during wartime. Should this chance pass, there was no telling when another would come. He was almost forty years old and still only a lieutenant.

During May he sent off a spate of letters, applying for a vacancy in a Montana regiment, a lieutenant colonelcy in the Adjutant General's Department, a colonelcy in the Nebraska volunteers, a captaincy in one of the immune regiments, and other positions.[1] When the answers came back, they were all no.[2] Pershing went off to war as a first lieutenant.

He was regimental quartermaster and quartermaster affairs in his unit, as in others, were a mess. Although the 10th Cavalry was about to leave for Cuba, little had been done to equip it. Pershing worked far into the night on a crash program of supply, but when the time came to leave, the regiment still was not ready.[3]

At Tampa, Florida, the embarkation point, affairs were hardly much better. "Little short of chaotic," was Pershing's way of describing it. The freight yard was jammed with railroad cars and no one had any idea what was in them or to whom it belonged; quartermasters had to go from car to car, break open the contents, and find supplies as best they could.[4]

On June 14, 1898, the ill-prepared expedition left for Cuba.[5] It had been ready on June 8, and again on June 10, but was twice delayed by a rumor that Spanish warships had escaped Admiral Sampson's blockade and been seen near Nicolas Channel, through which the expedition would pass. By June 14 the rumor was definitely disproved. So after two false starts, each with much hoopla, the expedition sailed away unceremoniously. The only ones to see it off were three Negro women, three soldiers, and the stevedores on the dock.[6] It comprised some 16,000 men on thirty-two troop ships, guarded by a fourteen-warship escort, and it was scattered over seven miles of sea in three uneven columns.

The troops were not overly impressed with their commanding general, William Shafter, a fleshy old man weighing over three hundred pounds and too ill to perform his duties. Their choice would have been Nelson A. Miles, Commanding General of the Army. A successful Miles, however, might emerge from the war a political rival of the administration; there was no such danger with Shafter.[7]

Nor were the men on Pershing's ship, the *Leona,* impressed with their captain. They were not sailors, but it seemed to them that their vessel should not be sailing in as many circles as it did. "If I had been in command I should have put him in irons," Pershing said of the man.[8]

By dawn of the third day the captain had succeeded in completely losing the convoy. There was little danger, since the Spanish fleet was corked up in Santiago harbor; nevertheless Gen. Samuel Young, the Brigade commander, lined the upper deck with infantrymen under orders to shoot at any Spanish ship that appeared. To Pershing this seemed ludicrous.[9]

His diary listed suggestions for improving troop travel: "More air —hammocks for men—cooking arrangements on board should be provided—travel ration unpalatable and stale—more fruit necessary—clothing too hot. Canvas washable caps better than hats. Anxious to see landing facilities—look for a lot of confusion."[10]

There was confusion, all right, but not as much as there would have been if the Spaniards had disputed the landing. Daiquiri, where the troops were to disembark, presented a rugged shore line, backed by a low ridge about 150 feet high—an excellent defensive position, especially if supported by artillery. But the Spanish retired without offering opposition.[11]

On June 22, after the Navy had shot up the countryside for an hour or so, preparations for the landing began. Each soldier carried three days' field rations of raw bacon, hardtack, and coffee. On his back were strapped his rifle, 100 rounds of ammunition, a blanket roll, a shelter tent, and a poncho. So weighted down, it meant certain death if he fell into the water while boarding the landing craft.

Pershing watched the first boat load up. It was tricky work. The men had to drop ten or fifteen feet into a vessel bobbing and weaving in a rolling sea. No accidents occurred then, but two men drowned later when they missed the pier on shore.[12]

Each landing boat held up to thirty men and was towed by a steam launch in groups of four or five. General Shafter's old regiment, the 1st Infantry, had the honor of going in first. Near the shore they hopped out and waded through the surf, amid cheers and whistles from the warships. As boatload followed boatload in an unopposed landing, the invasion took on aspects of a beach holiday. Men shouted and laughed when their comrades were drenched by a big wave.[13]

Getting horses and mules ashore was a problem. The method used was to push them overboard and let them swim in. Some, frightened and bewildered, swam out to sea, despite all efforts to stop them. Later someone thought of tying the animals loosely together and guiding them in behind a boat.[14]

Pershing did not go ashore with his regiment. As quartermaster, he stayed with the *Leona* while she went to Aserraderos on the other side of Santiago to pick up General Garcia's insurgent army. The insurgents were supposed to number 3,000, but it seemed to Pershing they were

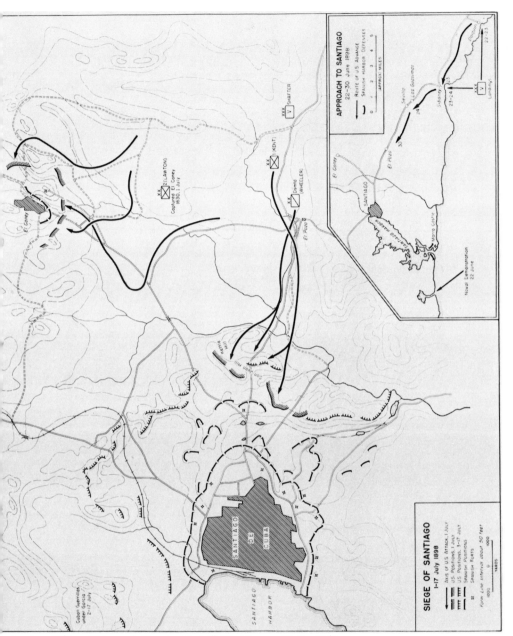

APPROACH TO SANTIAGO
22-30 June 1898

Route of U.S. Advance
Spanish Harbor Defenses

APPROX MILES

XX
V   SHAFTER

XX
2(LAWTON)
Captured El Caney
1630, 1 July

XX
(KENT)

XX
GRIMES
(WHEELER)

El Pozo

El Caney

El Caney

Sevilla

Las Guasimas

El Pozo

Siboney

V   Landing
22-23

SANTIAGO

Morro Castle

Marina Outworks

Naval Demonstration
22 June

Cuban Guerrillas
under Garcia
2-17 July

SANTIAGO
DE
CUBA

SANTIAGO
HARBOR

SIEGE OF SANTIAGO
1-17 July 1898

Axis of U.S. Attack, 1 July
U.S. Positions, 1 July
U.S. Positions, 3-17 July
Spanish Positions
Spanish Forts

Form Line Interval about 50 feet

1000   0   1000
YARDS

American Military History, ed. Maurice Matloff, Washington, D. C., 1969

Seige of Santiago

not half that. "We brought back 1,000 and a miserable lot they are," said his diary. "In my opinion they will prove of little service to the Americans."[15]

On June 23 the Americans occupied Siboney, another coastal town, and the next day fought a brief encounter at Las Guasimas on the trail leading to Santiago. The Spanish withdrew and the invaders pushed slowly on.

The American problem now was to get organized, to get supplies off the ships (which tended to run out to sea at the least danger) and up to where they could be used. The roads soon became huge gutters of mud from the rains.[16]

"Everything was in the direst confusion," said Pershing of the unloading at Siboney. "No one seemed to be in command and no one had any control over boats, transportation nor anything—and it was only by the individual efforts of the officers of the line that order was brought out of chaos, at least a semblance of order."[17]

Grumbling was inevitable. One trooper damned Shafter up and down as a fat old slob who was sitting on his rump in his tent when he should have been on the spot straightening out the supply mess. Pershing listened for a while, then told the trooper off:

"Why did you come to this war if you can't stand the gaff? War has always been this way. Did you expect to see the Old Man standing out here with a book in his hand, telling these mule-skinners how to handle their outfits? The fat Old Man you talk about is going to win this campaign. When he does, these things will be forgotten. It's the objective that counts, not the incidents."[18]

On June 27 the Spanish began digging rifle pits on the side of San Juan Hill. Strangely, no one made any attempt to stop them or even to bother them by lobbing in a few artillery shells.[19]

On June 30 the 10th Cavalry moved up to El Pozo, one and one-half miles east of San Juan Hill. American forces there now consisted of two divisions: Jacob F. Kent's and Joseph W. Wheeler's. With Capt. George S. Grimes' battery, they totaled some 7,000 men.[20]

About 8:00 A.M. on July 1, Grimes opened up on the San Juan blockhouse from 2,500 yards. His fire was ineffective. The distance was great and the heavy black powder his guns used soon enshrouded them and blocked visibility.

Immediately the Spanish returned fire. Because they used smokeless powder, their gun positions were invisible. Standing in a group of military attachés and war correspondents, Pershing watched the artillery duel and tried to locate the Spanish guns. A force of Cuban insurgents applauded each American shot, apparently on the theory that what counted was noise. When a shot from a Spanish battery suddenly crashed near them, they scattered and were not seen again until the battle was over.[21]

About 8:30 A.M. orders came to start down the El Pozo-Santiago road, with Wheeler's division in the lead (Pershing's 10th Cavalry was part of it) and Kent's following. The road was narrow, tortuous, and flanked by heavy jungle. It funneled the men down the one and one-half miles to San Juan Hill like steers going down a cattle chute. The sun was hot and the weather close; men began to drop out because of the heat. After a mile they reached the Aguadores River where the country became more open. In front of them lay San Juan Hill, and, a little before it, Kettle Hill, both blocking the way to Santiago.[22]

The plan was for Wheeler's division to deploy to the right of the road and Kent's to the left. As the first of Wheeler's men came out onto clearer ground, the Spanish opened a lively fire. The terrain was difficult and deployment slow. Back along the trail traffic began to pile up and then jam, as Kent's division came abreast of Wheeler's.

To make matters worse, an American observation balloon came down the narrow road just then. Floating above the trees, it betrayed the position of the stalled advance, and the Spanish peppered away with everything they had. The 10th Cavalry, caught underneath the balloon, received "a veritable hail of shot and shell," said Pershing. An officer in the balloon called down:

"The Spaniards are firing at you."

"Yes, we know it, you damned fool," the troops roared back, "and you are drawing the fire. Come down! Come down!"[23]

The Spanish fire grew withering. In panic, the 71st New York threw themselves down in the middle of the road, blocking the way. Other regiments had to walk over them. Deploying as best they could, Wheeler's and Kent's divisions took cover in the tall grass in front of San Juan Hill as bullets whizzed past and thudded into the turf.

Most American casualties occurred here. Lying helpless waiting for orders, the men were sitting ducks for Spaniards on the heights above or snipers hidden in the trees along the trail. The enemy's smokeless powder and the noise of so many rifles made it impossible to determine where fire was coming from. In the confusion some units were dispersed and others missing.[24] One soldier remembered vividly the sight of a young officer, fresh out of West Point, who lay sprawled on his back. "His glazed eyes were staring at the trees overhead and ants were already crawling over his eyeballs."[25]

This was Pershing's baptism of fire. In his twelve years as an officer, he had never before been shot at. Yet when Capt. Charles Ayres encountered him directing troops to their positions, he was "cool as a bowl of cracked ice."[26] A similar tribute came from Col. Theodore Baldwin, commander of the 10th, who sent Pershing to find a missing unit while others were pinned down in the grass. "I shall never forget your actions when I had you searching for that troop," said Baldwin. "I have been in many fights and through the Civil War, but on my word 'You were the coolest and bravest man I ever saw under fire in my life' and carried out your orders to the letter—no matter where it called you."[27]

Finally the order came to advance. There was no place else to go. The road behind was clogged for two miles and they were being decimated where they were.

Troop alignments were hopelessly mixed, but officers (or just plain privates) took charge of those in the immediate vicinity. Richard Harding Davis, the war correspondent, was surprised at how few the men appeared to be as they started forward. "It seemed as if someone had made an awful and terrible mistake. One's instinct was to call to them to come back."[28]

Across San Juan River they went, struggling through dense brush and over layers of barbed wire. Before them lay Kettle Hill and San Juan Hill. Pershing described the action:

"It was a hot fight, . . . the converging artillery and infantry fire made life worth nothing. We waded the river to our armpits and formed line in an opening in dense undergrowth facing our objective, the San Juan blockhouse, all the while exposed to volley firing from front, left front and left flank, and you know what it means to be uncertain as to the position of the enemy.

"Spanish small arm fire is terrible. . . . Men in the third and fourth lines were in as great danger as those nearer—indeed less casualties occurred close to the intrenchments. . . . Our losses were 20% killed and wounded—50% of officers were lost—a fearful rate.

"On the dusky troopers trudged, their number being gradually diminished until they reached the open in front of the position when they advanced by rushes almost halfway—then went the balance with a charge."[29]

Frank Knox, a young Rough Rider, later Secretary of the Navy under Franklin D. Roosevelt, became separated from his unit during the charge and joined up with the 10th Cavalry. "I must say that I never saw braver men anywhere," he wrote home. "Some of those who rushed up the hill will live in my memory forever."[30]

Atop Kettle and San Juan Hills, the victors shook hands, cheered, embraced, and jumped up and down. Said Pershing: "It was glorious. For the moment every other thought was forgotten but victory. . . ." When he asked a wounded man if he was badly hurt, the man replied, "I don't know, but we whipped them, anyway, didn't we?"[31]

The Spanish attempted to retake San Juan Hill that evening but were driven off; they retired to their next defensive line 300-500 yards away. Firing on both sides kept up until dark and then sporadically through the night.

American pack trains hurried up ammunition, rations, and entrenching tools. Digging went on all night. Maj. Gen. Henry W. Lawton's division and Brig. Gen. J. C. Bates's brigade, which had taken El Caney during the day, rushed up to fill in and extend the lines on San Juan Hill.[32]

That night Pershing helped entrench; he then accompanied some wounded to the field hospital four miles behind the lines. The quiet night with its beautiful moon contrasted with the noise and gore of the day. In the hospital the medics worked at top speed by lantern light; their facilities, Pershing noted, were "entirely inadequate."[33]

About midnight Pershing returned to the front. He was not particularly tired. On this, his first day of battle, he lay looking at the stars, wondering what the morrow would bring. Then he dozed off into a deep sleep.[34]

Reveille the next morning was sounded by Spanish small arms and artillery. "A cannon ball plunged through the line at the top of the hill, and went rolling to the bottom of the valley; bullets spattered against isolated trees or chugged into the soft earth, and covered us with dirt and fairly mowed the grass in front of the trenches."[35]

Snipers continued to be a problem. One of them severely wounded Malvern-Hill Barnum, the 10th's adjutant; Pershing took over for him. Five days later, because of the officer shortage, he took over command of D Troop besides.[36]

All the while, he retained his original duties as regimental quartermaster. The supply situation was awful. Supply ships were more interested in avoiding scratched hulls than in provisioning the troops; they stood well out to sea and practically had to be corralled to come in close enough to unload. And because no dock had been built at Siboney, the unloading was still done by the slow, awkward method of running small boats right up to the beach.

On the way up to battle on July 1, the troops had deposited blanket rolls and haversacks by the roadside, with details left behind to guard them. After the battle these guards were commandeered to carry the wounded to the hospital and materiel to the front. Left unguarded, the supplies were an open invitation to passersby to take what they wanted —and most passersby did, especially the Cubans.

Thus when the rains started on July 2, Pershing's men were short on blankets, food, and tobacco. Furthermore they were alternately hot and cold from the blistering sun and from fording streams. The sick list began to grow.[37]

A truce began on July 3 and, except for two days, was uninterrupted until the final surrender on July 17.[38] During it, both sides strengthened their positions. When Pershing examined the Spanish defenses after the surrender he found them "very strong" and said they "could not have been forced except at heavy cost."[39]

At noon on July 4 the regiments formed into line and Pershing, as acting adjutant of the 10th, read telegrams of congratulations from President McKinley and General Miles.

The next day General José Toral, the Spanish commander, evacuated foreigners and non-combatants from Santiago. Pershing described them as they passed through the American lines:

"Frail, hungry women carried a bundle of clothing, a parcel of food or an infant, while weak and helpless children trailed wearily at the skirts of their wretched mothers. An old man tottered along on his cane, and behind him a puny lad helped an aged woman; old and young, women, children and decrepit men of every class, those refined and used to luxury together with the ragged beggar, crowded each other in this narrow column. It was a pitiful sight; from daylight until dark the miserable procession trooped past. The suffering of the innocent is not the least of the horrors of war."[40]

The rainy season began now in earnest, turning roads and trails into mud canals. Men sank up to their knees; wagons to their hubcaps. At night it was not unusual to sleep with head raised just above the water and the rest of the body submerged in mud. During the day, troops stored their clothes in rubber ponchos and went about naked in the rain. When General Miles later visited one of the camps, he was amused to see several hundred men saluting him without a stitch on.[41]

With roads almost impassable and streams swollen into rivers, the supply problem became acute. Everything was scarce. Richard Harding Davis could find no takers when he offered $150 to rent a pony for a week; in peacetime one could be *bought* for $15. Paper became so scarce that orders were written on newspaper margins, notebook scraps, and the insides of old envelopes. So infrequent were linen changes that one trooper complained, "I do not at all mind other men's clothes being offensive to me, but when I cannot go to sleep on account of my own it grows serious."[42]

In such circumstances the Army rule book went to the winds. It was up to each quartermaster, using his own ingenuity, to provide for his men. Pershing borrowed four mules and a wagon, waded through the mud to Siboney, loaded what supplies he could (without requisitions), and waded back again.[43]

Returning in the dark, he heard great commotion on the trail and came abreast of another wagon mired down to the hubs. The driver "was urging his team forward with all the skill, including the forceful language, of a born mule-skinner." Years later that same driver invited Pershing to a luncheon and when the latter recalled the incident, his host asked eagerly, "Yes, yes, and what did I say?"

"That," answered Pershing, "I cannot repeat in the presence of the ladies."

The driver was Theodore Roosevelt.[44]

That Pershing kept the 10th supplied is attested by Col. Theodore Baldwin, the regimental commander. "You did some tall rustling," said Baldwin, "and if you had not we would have starved, as none of the others were able or strong enough to do it.[45]

Another officer, Capt. William H. Beck, praised Pershing for "the many wearying rides you took . . . in the tropical heat and rain, your energetic action in obtaining the tentage, personal baggage of officers and men, and clothing for the command—this too when you were suffering at close intervals with vicious disease. . . . I do not think it too much to say that the gallantry you displayed under fire and the untiring energy you evinced, were a devotion to duty exceeded by none, and equalled by few."[46]

The formal surrender of Santiago occurred on July 17. With both armies drawn up to witness it, General Toral rode out to meet General Shafter. The formalities were simple and courteous. Both sides presented arms; General Toral offered his sword to the victor.

With an escort and a regiment of infantry, Shafter then entered Santiago. The American troops lined up at "Present arms" along the six miles of trenches surrounding the city. At precisely 12:00 noon, the Spanish flag came down from the Governor's Palace and the Stars and Stripes were run up. The band played the "Star Spangled Banner."[47]

Lucky for Shafter the surrender occurred when it did. His army was rapidly being decimated by malarial fever which ran through camp like fire through dry brush. On July 12, one hundred cases appeared. By the early part of August, approximately seventy-five percent of the command was either ill or convalescent.

Originally it had been planned to withdraw to the hills five miles back of Santiago and there establish a series of camps. Fever cases would be left behind as the troops moved on to each new uninfected area. But so widely did the disease spread that, when the time came, the men had all they could do to make the first camp.

It became increasingly difficult to find able-bodied men to work. Because of the officer shortage, Pershing took command of three cavalry troops (replacing sick lieutenants), in addition to his duties as acting adjutant (replacing Barnum) and his designated work as regimental quartermaster. But by August 4, he also was down with the disease.[48]

The spread of malarial fever made immediate evacuation imperative. One sick soldier wrote his wife: "We hear that the whole V Corps is to be invalided into camp on Long Island—worse place possible unless they wish to exhibit us as horrors of war and raise revenue by the exhibit. We would be a howling success."[49]

The first contingent left August 7. A week later the 10th Cavalry embarked, just two months after it had left Tampa.[50]

A few days after the regiment arrived at Montauk Point, Long Island, President McKinley visited the camp. Most of McKinley's time, Pershing felt, "was occupied by those who had political aspirations"— like Theodore Roosevelt, who got McKinley's blessing for the governorship of New York.[51]

Years later, when penning his autobiography, Pershing devoted a paragraph to Roosevelt's war record and the political capital that resulted from it. "It is safe to say that in the history of the country no man ever got so much reward for so little service."[52] Later he added, "Without disparagement of Mr. Roosevelt's brief few weeks' military experience in Cuba, it must be said that it was the extensive publicity it received rather than the actual service that brought him such exceptional political preferment."[53] In subsequent drafts of the autobiography Pershing deleted these remarks. He was always one to tone down his words before they got into print.

Looking back on the war, Pershing had reason to be satisfied. Gen. Joseph Wheeler, commanding the cavalry division, recommended him for promotion because of his "untiring energy, faithfulness and gallantry,"[54] while Maj. Theodore J. Wint, commanding the 2nd Squadron of the 10th, praised him for his "gallant and efficient manner."[55]

Col. Leonard Wood, commanding the "Rough Riders," also added his commendation. "Any consideration which you may be able to show him will be well deserved and from what I know of his abilities, any position to which he may be advanced will be filled with ability."

Wood's letter went all the way up to President McKinley who wrote on the bottom, "Appoint to a Major, if there is a vacancy." On August 18, 1898, Pershing was made a major in the Volunteers.[56]

This satisfied, at least for the moment, his driving ambition, his insatiable desire to make a name for himself. He aspired to greatness and seemed to know, almost by intuition, he would someday attain it. He saved little insignificant records, like his monthly West Point report cards, as if he knew a future biographer would be interested in them. What Herndon said of Lincoln can also be said of Pershing: "He was always calculating and planning ahead. His ambition was a little engine that knew no rest."[57]

The Santiago campaign revealed certain qualities in Pershing that others would note in the future: a capacity for hard work, for buckling down and getting a job done even when things were in a mess, as was the case when he arrived at Chickamauga Park. By now he had considerably matured in the ways of the Army and of human life. He realized that inefficiency is inevitable where human beings are concerned. Though he would be known later as a "driver," a man who demanded perfection, he knew that complete perfection is never possible, and he was mature enough not to sulk or uncritically blame an institution for failings which are unavoidable because the institution is composed of human beings. "Why did you come to this war if you can't stand the gaff?" he cried. "War has always been this way."[58] Indeed it has. And so has life, composed of courage, imagination, energy, and foresight—but also of knavery, rigidity, sluggishness, and blindness. Pershing by now was mature enough to recognize that fact. He was not a crybaby over what could not be avoided. "Stop the world, I want to get off!" had no place in his makeup.

Engaged in combat for the first time, he stood up exceptionally well. No other regiment in the Cavalry Division had higher officer casualties than Pershing's. With death all around him he remained cool, did his work, and won the admiration of his superiors. He thrilled to the pride of victory. "It was glorious," he exclaimed.59

Victory had its thrill, but victory was bought at the price of human misery and degradation. Pershing knew this. He was no warmonger. War was horrible, as well as thrilling. George S. ("Old Blood and Guts") Patton, Jr. would later survey a littered landscape scarred by war—rubbled homes, burning fields, stiff-legged corpses—and declare ecstatically, "Could anything be more magnificent? Compared to war, all other forms of human endeavor shrink to insignificance. God, how I love it!"60

Pershing could never say such nonsense. His description of the weary Santiago refugees on their passage through the American lines sums up his basic feeling about war. "It was a pitiful sight; from daylight until dark the miserable procession trooped past. The suffering of the innocent is not the least of the horrors of war."61

Pershing had been a rigid disciplinarian as a tactical officer at West Point, just a few months before, but in Cuba he begged, borrowed, or stole whatever he considered necessary to keep his men fit and happy. When the situation called for it Pershing was as willing as anybody to disregard regulations. The Sabbath was made for man, not man for the Sabbath.

A piece of unfinished business awaited him when he returned to the United States. Nearly a million dollars of government property charged to his name as quartermaster was not accounted for. The 10th Cavalry had converged on Tampa from five different stations and then shipped out to Cuba before there had been time to verify property transfers or obtain receipts. With the war over, the property was gone and no one had any idea where it was—least of all Pershing. An irate Army auditor threatened to cut off his pay until he found it.[62]

About this time, a young lieutenant arrived at Huntsville, Alabama, as regimental quartermaster and found in the hands of the troops much property which had not been transferred to his account. He inventoried it and took it up in his returns as "found in camp." These items, when Pershing came to investigate, corresponded fairly closely to the shortage with which he was charged. The accounts were transferred, the matter happily settled, and Pershing made a new friend in the young lieutenant who had helped him. His name was James G. Harbord.[63]

Pershing's work in 1899 was with the Division of Customs and Insular Affairs. As a result of the war, the United States suddenly found on its hands Cuba, Puerto Rico, and the Philippine Islands. For want of an existing agency, the task of ruling these new possessions was dumped on the War Department, wherein a separate Division of Customs and Insular Affairs was set up. Through the instrumentality of an old friend from Lincoln, Nebraska days, George Meiklejohn, whom he had helped become Assistant Secretary of War, Pershing became its second Chief.[64]

The work was interesting and gave him a chance to use his legal education, but Pershing was restless. By temperament and training, he felt more at home in the field than behind a desk. When an insurrection broke out in the Philippines, he applied to go there. "A battle has a fascination for a soldier," he said. Besides, the Philippines was a foreign land, having about it the air of adventure and romance. It would mean new experiences, travel, a chance to see the world. It might also mean more rapid promotion.[65]

Friends urged him to stay in Washington, holding out the prospect that eventually he might be made a brigadier general as Chief of the Division.[66] George DeShon, a former West Point classmate, wrote from Manila, "Don't think of coming out here—You will be sick if you do—All Cuban malarial cases do very poorly here. . . ."[67] But Pershing felt he was born for this duty. "All my life I've been in command of troops," he said, "and now when there is a chance to get into a real campaign, I am put behind a desk."[68]

In August, 1899, after a second application, Pershing was ordered to the Philippines.[69] He went via England and France, seeing Europe at his own expense for six weeks. After a short stint as adjutant in Manila, he went to Zamboanga, headquarters of the Mindanao-Jolo area, in the southern part of the islands.[70]

The Army had occupied the district only a short time before. The area was large, so all that could be done was to occupy the more important coastal towns, turning them over to local commanders who ran them as they thought best. There were few precedents and little knowledge of local conditions. The Army was feeling its way, trying to make friends with the natives (Filipino and Moro), while opening up roads for better communications.[71]

Psychological and language problems complicated the Army's task. The Americans tended to hustle; the natives took their time. The former were impatient; the latter resented being jarred out of their leisurely ways. Few natives spoke English, and no American spoke a native language. Spanish, which might have served as a common medium, was not known by most Americans.[72]

Law was in a state of chaos.[73] A Zamboangan mayor invited a political rival to his home and shot him; he then got another rival out of prison, whom he likewise shot. This was the local way of keeping "law and order."[74]

Life was precarious for soldiers too. Soon after Pershing's arrival, supposedly friendly Moros attacked four soldiers for no other motive than that the soldiers were Christians and they were Mohammedans. The Moros had the "infidels" in their power; that was reason enough to kill them.[75]

American retaliation in such cases was rapid. An officer went to the village where the attack occurred and demanded custody of the murderers under threat of executing the village chiefs. When they were surrendered, an American detachment summarily executed them. The official report stated that the prisoners had tried to escape.

Pershing approved such tactics. "All the Moros have heard of this act, and it is said to be current among them that the life of an American will cost them 10 Moros. It is fortunate that such ideas prevail among them."[76]

He also approved of keeping the natives under American rule for a long time. Independence "would result in anarchy. To whom would we turn over the government? . . . There is no national spirit, and except the few agitators, these people do not want to try independence."[77]

For the Democratic party and for anti-imperialists Pershing felt only contempt. "If the facts could be known by the men who are condemning the war," he said, "there is not the shadow of a doubt that expansion would carry almost unanimously. The cost of this war can very properly be laid at the door of the Democratic Party not to mention the cost in lives of men who have come out here not only to preserve the country's honor and to uphold her flag but in the equally worthy causes of spreading enlightenment and civilization among a horde of Oriental barbarians. As a matter of fact it makes our blood boil when we sit down and talk it over."[78]

In late 1900 Pershing saw field service as adjutant in a campaign against an insurrectionist named Capistrano. "The country was indescribably difficult," he narrated, "mountainous inland, heavily wooded here and there, and cut by rivers and precipitous ravines."[79] Friendly natives gave them information and American columns were constantly on the rebels' trail, pushing them ever deeper into the interior. Combat was usually at long range, the insurgents firing down on the troops from heights or from ambush. Pershing took part in one engagement but generally saw no hard fighting.[80]

Apart from this single campaign, most of Pershing's first two years in the Philippines was spent as Adjutant General of the Department of Mindanao-Jolo. This meant he was an executive officer for the commanding general and handled supply, transportation, and quartering.[81]

Promotion in the Regular service came in early 1901 when Congress passed a bill increasing the size of the cavalry.[82] "Fifteen years to go from lieutenant to captain," Pershing groaned, "and this during the time of a foreign war."[83] The promotion, however, shifted him to a

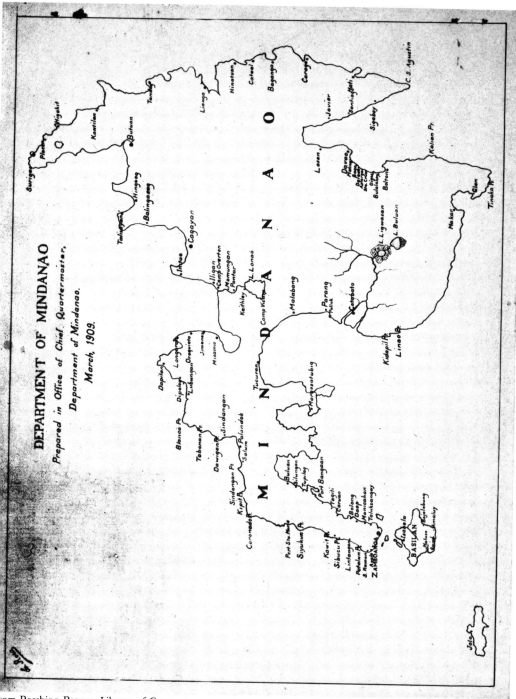

DEPARTMENT OF MINDANAO

Prepared in Office of Chief Quartermaster,

Department of Mindanao.

March, 1909.

Department of Mindanao

unit stationed in the United States. Because he desired to remain in the Philippines he transferred to the 15th Cavalry,[84] then under orders to proceed to the Philippines, and stayed where he was. When a troop of the 15th arrived, Pershing asked a major about its quality. The latter replied, "It has a hundred horses who never saw a soldier, a hundred soldiers who never saw a horse, and a bunch of officers who never saw either."[85]

After June, 1901, there was a great shakeup in Philippine military personnel. As a result of this, Pershing was one of the few experienced officers left in Zamboanga and for a time took over a number of jobs: Acting Chief Engineer Officer, Ordnance Officer, Chief Signal Officer, and Collector of Customs.[86] Then opportunity knocked.

Brig. Gen. William A. Kobbé, commanding the Department of Mindanao-Jolo, made an inspection trip, taking along Pershing as his adjutant. At Iligan, a remote coastal station on the north coast of Mindanao several hundred miles from Zamboanga, they found everything in disordered, tumbledown condition: buildings dilapidated, troops listless and sloppily dressed, the town plaza overgrown with weeds. Clearly the heat and the Orient had made a shambles of military discipline; a few minutes conversation with the post commander made it clear who was responsible.[87]

Some time later, Kobbé asked Pershing which station he would choose if he could.

"Iligan," was the answer.

Surprised, Kobbé asked why. Iligan was such an isolated place.

"The officer who commands Iligan will have a rare opportunity for important service," explained Pershing. "The most warlike people in Mindanao are the Moros of Lake Lanao. So far they have been left alone; we know little about them, except that the Spanish made several attempts to subjugate them and failed. But someday, perhaps soon, it will be necessary to bring them under control, if American rule is to be effectively extended in Mindanao. And the place from which any movement to get in touch with them will start is Iligan."[88]

Nothing more was said of the matter. Shortly afterwards General Kobbé was replaced as commander of the Department by Brig. Gen.

George W. Davis. The latter called on Pershing frequently for consultation and relied on his advice in dealing with the natives. One day in September he tossed out a bombshell.

"Pershing, as you are the only man left here who knows anything about the Moros, I'm going to send you to Iligan."

Pershing was surprised and delighted.

"I'll give you two troops of your regiment and three companies of infantry," Davis continued. "Do everything possible to get in touch with the Moros of central Mindanao and make friends of them."[89]

4

Iligan: Making Friends With the Moros

November, 1901. The first inspection at Iligan by the new commander, sent there to restore discipline in an outpost made flabby by the tropics. First Sergeant Bill Heffner described what happened:

"I followed Pershing around with a pad and pencil. He wore a mask the whole time that froze up the boys who faced him, and I knew he was playin' the game right. We came to the mess shack. The Captain was in a new uniform and white gloves. At the far end, Levi—a little Jew cook about five feet high—was standing like a grown-up gargoyle staring at a knot hole. Pershing glanced at Levi and then at the pots and pans that hung on nails along the sides of the shack. He reached up and grabbed a frying pan off its nail. He drew one finger in its new white glove across the bottom. . . . The smudge on the Captain's glove looked like he had found a lump of coal and was balancing it on his finger. . . . He never said a word, but he swung back his arm and sent that pan sliding and banging along the floor toward cookey. He was reaching up for the next pan so he didn't see his little scared trained animal give a jump at just the right second to let the projectile keep on without collision by his feet, but the cook's eyes never left the knot hole."

Pershing did the same with the next pan and the next and the next.

66

At the end his gloves looked like he'd been cleaning a chimney and the floor like a junk shop. The only things that had not changed were Pershing's stone expression and Levi's ramrod posture.

Next Pershing moved on to the knives and blades. His eyes fell on a meat cleaver, with a edge like a razor. Not a word was spoken. He picked it up, felt its edge, and gave Levi an ice water look, then he gently laid the cleaver down on the table.

A week later Iligan was markedly improved at inspection. Chins were smoother, bunks neater, shoes shinier. When the captain came to the mess shack, the pots and pans were in a neat double row, shining like mirrors. Pershing walked through fast, ignoring Levi staring at the knot hole. Outside he turned to Bill Heffner.

"Sergeant, did you see any knives or forks in there?"

"No, sir."

"And no cleavers either?"

"No, sir."

"But the pots and pans looked clean, didn't they?"

"Yes, sir!"

That was how Capt. John J. Pershing began to restore discipline to Iligan.[1]

He had a knack of commanding respect, of making the slacker feel ill at ease. The captain "froze up the boys" as Sergeant Heffner put it. When he issued orders, you knew that they were *orders*.[2]

He had his own way of cutting a man down to size. Once when he saw a soldier galloping a horse on a hard surfaced road, he brought him to a halt with a thunderous "Stop!" followed by a peremptory "Come here!"

"Who are you?" he demanded.

"I'm Lieutenant F— of the 19th Infantry," replied the soldier.

Pershing eyed him, then spoke in mock apology.

"Oh, that's different. That changes the matter. I thought it was one of those ignorant cavalrymen of mine, who doesn't know enough not to gallop a horse on a hard road."[3]

After putting backbone into the command at Iligan, Pershing set about tackling the Moro[4] problem. He had to convince these suspicious, semi-savage people that he was their friend. His ultimate goal was to reach the Lake Lanao Moros in the interior, to enter the Forbidden Kingdom. He could fight his way in, but that was costly and a last resort. His job was to make friends out of enemies. It was not a military problem. "It was a human problem," Pershing told Frederick Palmer later,[5] and Pershing had one solution for the problem. He treated the Moros as humans.

Saturday was market day at Iligan. Pershing made it a practice to visit the market and move about among the Moros, asking through an interpreter about their crops, their carabaos (water buffalos), their government, and their leaders.[6] Theirs was a tribal society, like that of the American Indians. Win over their leaders—their sultans, their dattos, their panditas[7]—and you won over all the Moros. Win over the leaders of the Malanos (the Lake Lanao Moros) and you made the interior relatively safe for Americans. But first you had to get them to come to Iligan. And then you had to get them to invite you to the interior, to Lake Lanao.

The Number One Moro on the north side of Lake Lanao was Ahmai-Manibilang. Rich and powerful, a former sultan who had abdicated in favor of his son, Manibilang was still the power among his people. He had visited Iligan only once, when the Spanish controlled the country. He was remote and aloof, but he had never opposed the Spaniards. Could Pershing get to him?[8]

He worked at it. He got to the son, the reigning sultan. The sultan liked to talk; all Moros did. Pershing indulged his liking, listened to him, made him feel important. When the sultan left Iligan, he carried away a good impression of the new captain—and also an invitation to his father, Manibilang. Letters were exchanged. The son visited Iligan again. More letters were exchanged. Then Manibilang said he would come.[9]

When he arrived, he came in style. A tall, swarthy Moro, well built, clean shaven as most Moros were, Manibilang entered with a personal retinue of thirty men. He sat astride a fine looking stallion, beside which trotted slaves, carrying red and white umbrellas. Another slave carried Manibilang's gold-mounted kris, a fierce-looking Moro weapon

which did not have to be unsheathed because in combat it cut right
through the thin cords that bound it in its two-part scabbard. Bodyguards surrounded the dignitary; each carried a campilan, a two-
handed Moro sword about three-and-a-half feet long. One slave carried
a highly polished brass box containing betel nut, the favorite Moro
"chaw," which left the inside of the mouth a hideous red. In the
entourage were minor chiefs, relatives, and slaves—all bedecked as if
for an Easter parade.[10]

Manibilang obviously viewed himself as a person of quality, a prince.
Pershing treated him as such. His instructions were that Manibilang
should receive "every attention." He personally lodged the potentate
in one of the rooms of his own quarters, furnishing other quarters for
the retinue nearby.[11]

When Pershing and Manibilang sat down to conference, the latter
was very diplomatic. He was a Moro; it was impolite to come immediately to what was on one's mind. Pershing understood and let his guest
take his time. Much depended on the impression Manibilang took away
from this meeting.[12]

Finally Manibilang came to the point. Would the Americans try to
make Christians out of them? Would they leave the country soon?
Would they try to impose American laws and customs? Would they
overthrow the sultans and dattos?

Pershing assured Manibilang there would be no interference with
religion, offering as proof that the Sultan of Constantinople ("Stam-
boul" as Manibilang called it), to whom the Moros owed spiritual
allegiance, exchanged representatives with the President of the United
States.

He explained that the Americans were not going to leave the Philippines. Unlike the Spaniards, Americans were "a different and more
friendly people." They would help Moros get rich. They would build
roads and buy products at good prices.

They would also support sultans and dattos. Although the Americans
would hold them responsible for any crimes their people committed,
the Moro rulers might govern their people in their own way.[13]

Two topics Pershing carefully avoided: slavery and polygamy. He knew they would eventually have to be stamped out, but this was no time to raise the question. The job now was to quiet fears and establish good relations.[14]

When Manibilang left, Pershing was sure the visit had been a success. Soon after, more and more Moros began to visit Iligan. Manibilang spread the word that the Americans were friendly, that Moro religion and customs were safe, and that there was money to be made at the market.

Pershing made it a point to welcome personally other important dattos and sultans. There were many of these, for no single ruler controlled the whole area, though Manibilang had the greatest single influence. In the back of his mind was always the question: would the Moros invite him to Lake Lanao? Would Manibilang return the favor?[15]

The Spanish had tried to force their way to Lake Lanao once. They had thrown four to eight thousand men into Iligan and for almost a year had fought their way south and finally reached the lake at Marahui, less than twenty miles away. There they built a few gunboats and shot up some Moro villages along the lake, but they never advanced farther on land. When the war with America came, they withdrew.[16]

Then the first Americans arrived under Capt. R. S. Stevens. He called a conference of dattos along the route from Iligan to Marahui, asking permission to visit the lake. He would take no soldiers, only interpreters. The Moros flew into a mighty furor. They demanded presents for such a permission and said they could not be responsible if Stevens were waylaid on the trail. He did not go to the lake and the Forbidden Kingdom remained forbidden.[17]

Pershing put his hope in Manibilang. He knew that Moro dattos and sultans were prejudiced and suspicious. American or Spaniard—it was all the same to them; they were both foreigners, and Moros killed foreigners who moved into the interior. Manibilang would need time to prepare the ground for his coming.

Pershing waited. Eventually the invitation came. Now there was only one question: Should he accept?[18]

"No white man will ever go up into those forests and hills and come out alive," warned Padre Tel Placido, an old Spanish priest. "The Sultans got fed up [sic] on all white men when they had the Spanish here before. These Mohammedans are waiting every day and every night to kill *you!*"

If Pershing went up to Lake Lanao, the priest insisted, he would stay there forever—pushing up bamboo. "They say up there that Americans grow nice bamboo."[19]

Others said the same—Filipinos and Spaniards, soldiers and civilians, people who had been there for years. What would happen to Pershing up there alone, surrounded by hundreds of Mohammedan savages, and he not even armed! What if Manibilang betrayed him—or if a fanatic ran amuck and waylaid him on the trail? The Moros had it down to an art: a sharp diagonal down-thrust right between the neck and the shoulders![20]

That, said Pershing, was a chance he would have to take. He had worked for this invitation. Now it had come. What did his friends expect—that the Moros would invite the whole United States Army? He wanted to open the Forbidden Kingdom; to do that he had to have Moro friendship and trust. You obtain trust by showing trust. You show complete trust by going unarmed. It was a chance, certainly, but he had confidence in Manibilang. If it was justified, he would do something no American had ever done. If not, well, maybe he would push up good bamboo.[21]

Pershing, an interpreter, and three native scouts left Iligan on Sunday morning, February 16, 1902. Accompanying them was the Sultan of Madaya, Manibilang's son, about twenty-eight years old and very intelligent. They headed south on the old Iligan-Marahui road that the Spanish had built during their year's campaign.

Marahui was reached early Monday morning. An old barracks, an old church, a small fort, and a trench—that was about all there was to show that the Spanish had ever reached this far. The pier for the gunboats was still in good condition and the Sultan pointed out where the ships had been sunk.

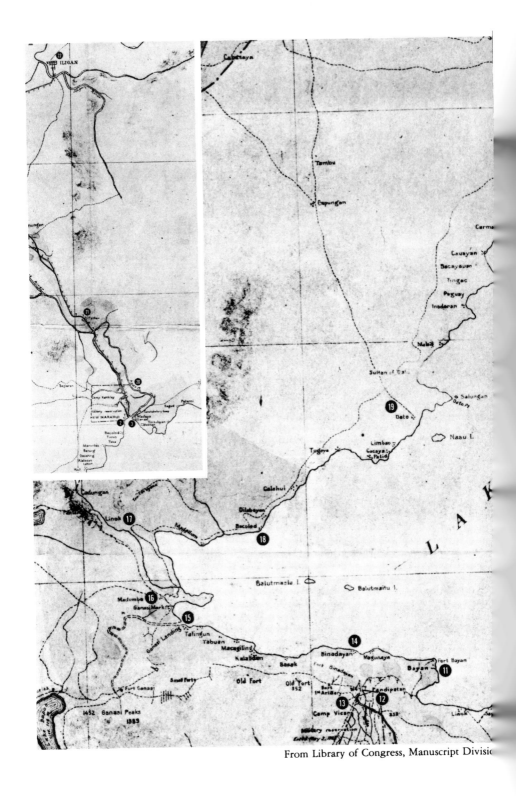

From Library of Congress, Manuscript Division

The Lake Lanao Region

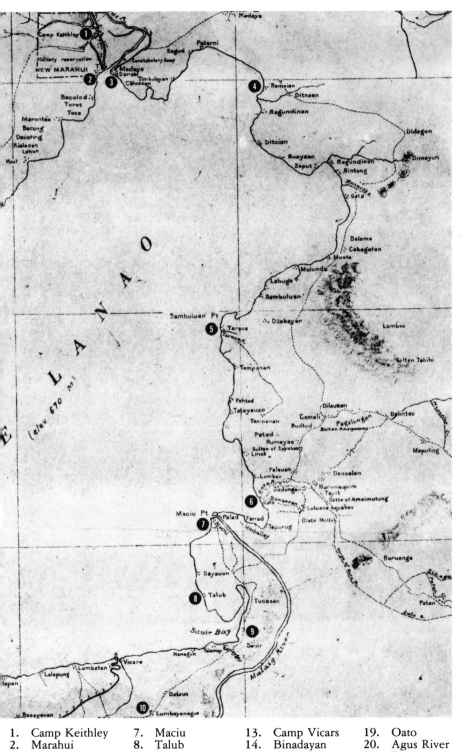

1. Camp Keithley
2. Marahui
3. Madaya
4. Remein
5. Taraca
6. Gata
7. Maciu
8. Talub
9. Sauir
10. Lumbayanague
11. Bayan
12. Panolapatan
13. Camp Vicars
14. Binadayan
15. Ganassi
16. Madumba
17. Linok
18. Bacolod
19. Oato
20. Agus River
21. Pantar
22. Iligan

In the afternoon they boarded a vinta (a small boat with bamboo out-riggers, capable of tremendous speed) and went to Madaya. There Manibilang, the old sultan, waited.

He welcomed Pershing at the door of his home, a large frame structure of hewn timbers with a heavily thatched roof—an elegant building as Moro houses went. A steaming hot meal awaited them, served Occidental style, with knives, forks, and chinaware. Whatever were Moro faults, poor cooking was not one of them; Pershing had never tasted better chicken.[22]

They talked about Moro-American relations until far into the night. Manibilang wondered again about freedom of religion and the right to manage their local affairs. He said Moros seldom raised anything beyond what was absolutely necessary for fear Americans would confiscate it. Pershing set his mind at rest on these points.[23]

On Tuesday Manibilang took Pershing by vinta to some of the other rancherias (a term used for a district ruled by a sultan or datto). The Moros were friendly, but Pershing noticed that Manibilang was nervous and kept an eye flitting over his compatriots. Evidently there had been some hostility beforehand.

At one rancheria it was market day and Pershing asked permission to address the crowd. He opened with strong professions of friendship and closed by answering questions. The people had many fears and misapprehensions but he felt he had corrected a number of them.[24]

On Wednesday Pershing returned to Iligan. Manibilang's son, the Sultan of Madaya, accompanied him with some forty of his followers, ostensibly as an escort of honor but really, Pershing knew, as a bodyguard. They also expected a free meal and a present. They received both, plus a lecture by Pershing who had lost his personal mount at Iligan: they must not steal horses any more.[25]

The trip to the lake had been eminently successful. Pershing had gone in and come out—alive. He had been the first white American to enter the Forbidden Kingdom and bring back information about its size, character, and people.[26] "As a result of my visit," he wrote in his official report, "I may say that I was very favorably impressed with these people and am of the opinion that much can be done with them by appealing to their reason and to their desire for riches."[27]

But there were some Moros who came to an altogether different conclusion. They reasoned that it was much easier to get rich by stealing and killing than working.

On March 9, 1902, Pvt. Frank Morris was murdered within a mile of the post at Parang; on March 20, six Moros jumped two soldiers, hacked one of them to pieces with a bolo, and stole the rifle of the other. On April 15, 200 Moros ambushed Lieutenant Forsyth and seventeen soldiers, killing one and stealing the horses of the rest. All this happened outside Pershing's jurisdiction, across the peninsula at Malabang and Parang, on the south coast. It was done by Moros over whom Manibilang had little influence.[28]

Early in April, 1902, Brig. Gen. George W. Davis, commanding the Department of Mindanao-Jolo came to Iligan with word that he was sending in an expedition from the south towards Lake Lanao to get the murderers and recover the guns and horses. He asked Pershing to keep the Moros quiet on the north side of the lake, while he moved to punish the guilty ones on the south.[29]

Pershing did not foresee much trouble. When Moros came to Iligan for the Saturday market, he told them what was in the wind. All responded that what Americans did in the South would not affect peace in the North. Pershing was able to report on April 21: "If punitive expedition on South coast is limited to punishment of these [Moros] who have committed overt acts, friendly feelings [of Moros on the North] will probably not be materially altered. Have lost no opportunity to reassure them that our friends will not be molested."[30]

On the next day Gen. Adna R. Chaffee, supreme commander in the Philippines, issued a proclamation announcing the expedition. He assured Moros that their religion and property were secure, but insisted that the murderers and stolen property must be surrendered within two weeks or the American army would move inland toward Lake Lanao.[31] Pershing received a copy of this proclamation on April 16, with instructions to have it translated and circulated among Moros on his side of the lake. This he did, writing a covering letter in which he asked to visit the lake again to clear up any misunderstandings.[32]

Misunderstandings there certainly were. Nothing could erase from the Moro mind the fact that about 1,200 American soldiers, all with guns (Moros had mostly swords and spears), were planning to march inland toward Lake Lanao, which had been and was the traditional Moro stronghold. They had not been invited; they were not wanted. Was this to be another Spanish affair all over again?[33]

Even a staunch friend like Manibilang was shaken by the extent and rapidity of the American march, for he wrote to Pershing, April 26, 1902: "I am very much distressed as I have heard that the Americans have arrived at Ganassi. . . . If it is true that we are friends, think before you do us any harm."[34]

Such was the situation when Pershing set out for the lake again on April 27—again unarmed, and trusting in Manibilang. But this time it was different. American troops were headed for the lake from the South; Moros were firing on them and streaming into cottas (Moro forts) to oppose them at key points. Could he trust Manibilang? And could Manibilang control the Moros? They were savages, and an excited savage is unpredictable, just about as unpredictable as Pershing's chances of coming back alive.

But he went. The Moros needed personal reassurance: not a document sent from a military post miles away, but a fellow human being standing in their midst, explaining things and answering questions. The Moros were frightened—"think before you do us any harm"—and frightened men sometimes do desperate things.[35]

He caught them just in time. When he arrived at Marahui they were talking wildly and were just one step removed from going on the warpath. The air was heavy with rumors: 1,500 American troops were in Iligan ready to sweep down on Manibilang's people; American gunboats would soon be shooting up villages again. Moros were packing their household goods and preparing to evacuate. Women and children scurried out of Marahui to take refuge in cottas or at other rancherias. They were angry and excited and terrified—all at the same time. And they were ready to fight.[36]

When they saw Pershing they seemed to hold him personally responsible for what had happened: "You have invaded our country with your troops!'' One fiery datto walked directly up and, in a threatening, overbearing manner, berated him for his talk about friendship, helping Moros get rich, and not interfering with their religion or their property. "You lied to us!" he cried.[37]

Pershing did not know the details of what the man was saying, for he spoke in Moro. But his attitude and tone conveyed the meaning, and a look at José Infanta, the interpreter, left no doubt. The blood was draining from José's face and his eyes were wide with alarm. Pershing knew the danger. He quickly warned José in Spanish, which the Moro did not understand, that any display of fear might be disastrous.

Then a voice spoke up in the crowd, a voice welcome as the sun breaking through a storm. Manibilang! He spoke in Pershing's defense, the datto calmed down, and the people agreed to hear American explanations at market day on the morrow.[38]

Everyone was there the next day—leading sultans and dattos of the North Lake Moros, leaders of other rancherias (Linek, Bayan, Ganassi, Taraca, Aremain). Pershing spoke for an hour and a half, explaining Chaffee's proclamation and answering questions, especially about religion and property. Always he reassured them, over and over and over:

"You have nothing to fear," he said in effect. "Nothing is happening in the South except what I told you in advance was going to happen, that the murderers must be punished. You have nothing to fear from us. On the other hand, we are not going to live in fear from you. We are going to explore and open roads. These roads will help you. We are going to go where we please."[39]

At the end, they expressed themselves satisfied—most of them. Some declared they would fight if Americans entered their rancherias, but these were mostly from the southern part of the lake where the troops were closest. Manibilang said that the North Lake Moros would remain friendly. This was Pershing's own judgment.[40]

In the South a fight soon developed. Chaffee's proclamation had no effect except to harden the hostile Moros; they increased their defenses and blocked the American line of march. At Pandapatan, near the south coast of Lake Lanao, the first pitched battle with Moros took place on May 2, 1902. The Moros fought from their cotta or fort, behind walls twelve to fifteen feet high and equally thick. Their defenses were surprisingly strong. The Americans took the cotta, but at the cost of sixty men.[41]

Worse than that, there was ill will after the engagement, with the prospect of more fighting, and perhaps an extended guerrilla war. This was not what General Chaffee wanted. He felt that Col. Frank D. Baldwin, who led the American advance from the South, had been too quick to pull the trigger, too slow to parley.[42] Was there someone, Chaffee wondered, who could handle Moros without killing them? He thought of the captain at Iligan, the first white American to penetrate to Lake Lanao, alone and unarmed. He seemed to have a way with Moros. He had prudence and tact. Chaffee sent for him on May 13.[43]

When Pershing reported, Chaffee explained that after the Pandapatan fight American troops had withdrawn about a mile and established temporary camp at a place named Vicars. They were up in the Lake Lanao region now and intended to stay. But they did not want any more fights, unless absolutely necessary. Peace and friendship were the watchwords.[44] Then Chaffee came to the point.

"You have been successful in handling the Moros on the North. I want you to go up to the Lake for station and do what you can to pacify the Moros on this side and prevent another clash."

Pershing pondered for a moment and saw a difficulty.

"How can I prevent anything? Colonel Baldwin is in charge at Vicars."

"You will be in charge of Moro affairs," answered Chaffee. "Orders will be given that no move will be made without your approval."[45]

5

Camp Vicars

In Pershing's own words, his relations with Col. Frank D. Baldwin were "somewhat unusual."[1] Baldwin was a colonel and in charge of Camp Vicars; Pershing was a captain (three grades below Baldwin) and his subordinate. Yet the colonel could make no move against the Moros without the approval of the captain.

Pershing had known Baldwin since they were both on General Miles's staff in Washington in the winter of 1896-1897. "He was a fine soldier with a long experience in handling Indians," said Pershing, "but he was inclined to be impetuous."[2] "[He] was disposed to use force instead of diplomacy."[3] This was brought out when Baldwin observed the Moros of Bacolod strengthening the defenses of their cotta.[4] He favored an immediate move against them, compelling them either to give in or to fight.

Pershing felt otherwise. Patience would reduce the number of ir-reconcilables to a comparative few, who could then be dealt with as Baldwin suggested; the opposite policy might provoke even friendly Moros and precipitate a war.[5] As he said on another occasion:

"I feel that we can well afford to wait and exhaust every effort to establish friendly relations with them by fair treatment and by example. . . . We should I think realize that they have held this country as their own for centuries without molestation. Being savage, they are slow to understand our motives. They cannot be measured by our standard and held strictly to account for difference in opinion. To move against those who are so-called enemies would force the hand of many who would like to be friends and cause them to take sides against us."[6]

Baldwin did not accept this view and grew impatient at inaction. "My present position is embarrassingly unsatisfactory," he complained, "scarcely a day passing without some person of my command being fired on. We have progressed as far as possible with Lake Lanao Moros until Maciu and Bacolod are reduced. I am prepared with troops and munitions of war to proceed against these places as soon as I get an order that it will be approved."[7]

The order never came. Pershing replaced Baldwin as commander of Camp Vicars on June 30, 1902,[8] and put into practice his policy of "waging the peace," resorting to arms as a last recourse. Maciu and Bacolod were indeed irreconcilable, as Baldwin had said, but Pershing did not move against them for a long while. He gave Maciu three more months of grace and Bacolod almost a year. In the end he compelled the submission of Lake Lanao Moros with only three short military engagements lasting less than a month.

"One of the reasons why I was especially pleased with this officer's behavior," said Pershing's commanding general later, "was that he seemed to enter fully into the spirit of my instructions, that the smaller the loss and the sacrifice, not only of our own men but of the Moros, the greater would be his merit. He carried out those instructions to the letter and I was especially gratified."[9]

When Pershing took command, the Vicars force consisted of two troops of cavalry, three companies of infantry, and a battery of field artillery—about 700 men, equal at that time to a regiment.[10] It normally was, and had been, commanded by a colonel. Its command then by a captain led Brig. Gen. George W. Davis to explain to the War Department:

"The situation in one respect has been anomalous—the assignment of a captain to so large and important command as that of Vicars—but it was in my opinion absolutely indispensable that the man to command on the spot should possess certain qualities not easy to find combined in one man: capacity for command, physical and mental vigor, infinite patience in dealing with these fanatical semi-savages, wise discretion, a zealous desire to accomplish the work set for him and knowledge of the Moro character.

"It was easy to find field officers possessing some of the characteristics and qualifications above mentioned, but there was no available officer of rank known to me in the 7th Separate Brigade[11] whose endowments embraced all the requisites."[12]

Pershing faced a formidable task. He had been sent as a trouble shooter, to keep the lid on a boiling pot that might blow sky high if wrongly handled. Lake Lanao Moros were extremely jealous of their freedom, and suspicious of the outside world. Fighting was in their blood. At a wedding reception that summer a local feud erupted, krises and campilans whipped out, and when the melee was over forty corpses lay hacked and bloody.[13]

No central Moro government controlled the various rancherias; no single Moro could negotiate for all. So many groups existed—each independent and under its own arbitrary, often despotic, chief—that to win the allegiance of one meant little towards winning the others.[14] Even friendly Moros rarely used their influence to make others friendly; their whole tradition of independent living precluded it.[15]

To restore good relations after the Pandapatan fight, Pershing used his Iligan tactics: personal contact, fair dealing, appeal to Moro self-interest.[16] At the Vicars market he greeted Moro leaders and offered their people work building sheds for horses and mules. He bought Moro wood and grass, rented Moro ponies, and hired Moro drivers to bring supplies up to Vicars from Malabang.[17] He visited any rancheria which invited him, though he did not feel it prudent to go without an escort of infantry.[18]

His most important work was accomplished in conferences, which, because of Moro loquaciousness, were often interminable. "A conference with Moros is a matter of hours, not of moments," said the surgeon at Vicars. "I cannot conceive anything requiring more tact, patience and courage than is requisite to deal properly with the Moros of Mindanao, and to extract the truth from people who pride themselves on their ability to lie and deceive."[19]

In the conferences Moros raised the same difficulties over and over. "You Americans will want to make us eat pork."[20] It took constant assurances and the test of experience to change their minds. "Hereafter the echo of my voice will always be for peace," exclaimed a Moro leader, finally convinced. ". . . I will be a friend of the Americans because you tell me that in America one can have any religion he desires. But do not bring hats here and make us wear them nor compel our women to wear skirts."[21]

A second difficulty concerned motives. "They are wild and untamed," reported Pershing, "and it is difficult to make them understand that you have no ulterior motive in being friendly to them. They are accustomed to being deceived by people of their own race, who rarely if ever desire to benefit them in any way unless prompted by selfish motives. Deception is a Malay characteristic and so deep-seated is it that they can hardly comprehend the motive for fair dealing."[22]

Another difficulty was Moro understanding of government. For centuries they had been accustomed to strictly personal rule. If a Moro was your friend, he helped your friends and fought your enemies, without bothering about the merits of the case. His allegiance was personal. Abstract government baffled him; he saw only its agents. They did not represent the government; they *were* the government. Consequently, a rapidly changing personnel, such as existed under the Army, was to the Moro equivalent to a rapidly changing government.[23]

"We believe what you tell us," Moros told Pershing, "but what will happen when you leave? We do not know who will come next or what he will do or if we can trust him as we can trust you." To this Pershing could but reply that he would be among them for a very long time (actually it was only a year). In his heart he had to admit that Army rotation policy confused the Moros and complicated government.[24]

That Pershing was skillful in conferences with Moros, that he had a feel for just what to say or do, is certain. "The Moros trust him, love him and believe in him," an officer reported to Washington. "Certainly

A Moro leader with his retinue. The flag held up behind him symbolizes his
submission to the authority of the U. S.; his importance is measured by the
splendor of his clothes and the number of his attendants.
Photograph courtesy Mrs. Elizabeth Daley, Arlington, Va.

no one understands the Moro character better, or is more competent to deal with them as a people."[25] "I have many very strong personal friends among the Moros," Pershing informed his mother. "Some of them will do anything for me. If I should say: 'Go and kill this man or that,' the next day they would appear in camp with his head."[26]

Once a leader was won over, he usually stayed won. Moros served as Pershing's secret service, warning him who was plotting or trying to deceive him. It was a Moro, the Sultan of Ganassi, who suggested the idea of giving friendly Moros an American flag instead of a pass to identify themselves to soldiers on the trails. Hostile Moros, pretending that a blank piece of paper was a pass, could get within striking distance; the American flag put a stop to this.[27]

As time went on, certain hostile Moros became increasingly belligerent. They interfered with telegraph lines, sometimes carrying off a mile of wire. Lying in wait in the tall, dense grass which was heavy enough in places to hide a mounted man, they attacked lone soldiers passing down the trails or pack trains bringing supplies to Vicars from Malabang.[28]

On June 21, 1902, ten Moros jumped two soldiers, wounding them both and carrying off a rifle.[29] Moros were particularly anxious to capture modern weapons, realizing that only thus could they conduct the contemplated fight on equal terms. Through his secret service Pershing discovered that the attackers were from Binidayan, a rancheria near Vicars, and had been led by a datto named Tangul. The Sultan of Binidayan was a powerful chieftain who had declared himself friendly. Pershing went to see him, demanding Tangul and the rifle.

The sultan acknowledged that the attackers came from his rancheria, but said he was powerless to control them. While pleading good will, he said he could do nothing regarding Pershing's request.[30]

"American policy," Pershing said flatly, "is to uphold the authority of the sultan in his own rancheria. On the other hand, we hold the sultan responsible for the acts of his people, i.e., you cannot be sultan and receive our support and recognition of your authority and at the same time deny your responsibility for the acts of your people."[31] Warning the native leader to find both Tangul and the gun, Pershing left.

A week passed and nothing was done. On July 19, Pershing went again—with troops. The sultan was arrested, brought to Vicars, and put in irons.[32]

Word of the arrest went around like wildfire and had a salutary effect on many Moro leaders. They said to their people: "See here, if any of you molest the Americans in any way, off comes your head, for I do not intend to be held responsible for your foolish acts."[33]

But this did not hold for rancherias where the leader himself was hostile. These openly clamored for war. Now that the crops were in, they sought to provoke a fight, or to make life so unpleasant that Americans would withdraw. Not only did they make the roads and trails unsafe; they began to move against Vicars itself.

One night during a rainstorm, a Vicars sentry saw in a flash of lightning a crouched figure moving toward the line of tents. In the next flash, he fired. The following morning a Moro was found dead on the ground, a heavy, wavy-edged kris strapped to his wrist.[34]

The Moro was after American weapons. Where he failed, others succeeded. Soldiers began to wake up in the mornings to find their rifles and ammunition gone. "In stealth of movement," said Pershing, "these [Moro] warriors were more crafty than even American Indians."[35]

Moros crept into Vicars at night, cut the tent ropes, and stabbed at those trapped inside.[36] Other Moros made the night hideous by beating drums, firing into Vicars, and yelling.[37] When Adm. Robley D. Evans visited Vicars he noticed several bullet holes through the sides of his tent. An orderly reassured him: "Don't mind them, sir. The Moros shoot at the tents at night, sir; but they won't hit you, sir."[38]

About 12:15 at night on August 11, 1902, twenty Moros surprised an outpost at the quartermaster corral, killing two and wounding two. One had his skull split open by a campilan from top to bottom. On August 12, about midnight, thirty Moros fired into Vicars for about twenty minutes. On the fifteenth, there was a call to arms at 9:00 P.M., with firing at intervals until 4:00 A.M.[39]

To discourage such attacks, Pershing relocated the outposts nightly to prevent their being spotted. So they might have complete freedom to fire in any direction except immediately to their rear, Pershing ordered the officer making the rounds to move from camp to outpost to camp to outpost, instead of taking the shorter way of going directly between outposts.[40]

One night Ben Lear, the officer making the rounds, took the short cut and was fired on by an outpost. The bullet passed through his sleeve. Next morning when Pershing overheard him narrating the experience, he growled:

"Well, it's a damn shame they didn't kill you."

"I don't agree with you, sir," Lear replied.[41]

On September 1, 1902, Moros attacked American troops at Mataling Falls, seven miles southeast of Vicars, killing one and wounding two. That made a total of four killed and twelve wounded during four months at Vicars.[42] Pershing decided the time had come to strike back. He summed up the situation to his superiors:

"We are losing influence with our friends who continuously ask, why do you Americans not punish some of those people? Datto Grande and his people [who have been friendly] have been threatened by the Bayan hostile element and I loaned him two carbines for his protection. Nightly prowlers come about in search of outposts' guns, and my secret service Moros report much talk of hostile intent and all that. The rice crop is now gathered and most Moros have nothing to do.

"My own conviction is that a good sound drubbing will be necessary and sufficient and it may be administered at Bacolod or summarily at some rancheria whose people have more recently attacked us. . . . I believe at the same time that we have made and are making material progress towards pacification, the situation is not critical in any sense and no uneasiness need be felt. We should however without further hesitation punish some of these renegades, it will help us very much in the pending peace negotiations and bring openly to our support many Moros who yet cling to what appears to them to be the stronger side —Moro side. I can handle it if permitted to do so."[43]

Approval for the attack came forthwith. It was to be against Maciu, since, with one exception, all attacks appeared to have come from there. Bacolod too had been guilty but, as General Chaffee said, "We are after effect—not revenge for wrongs done, so if Bacolod takes warning from your movements on Maciu, your purpose is accomplished."[44]

Pershing was glad. "The men," he said, "had become weary of the constant night attacks by bands of yelling demons, who beat their tom-toms and shouted defiance, daring us to come out and fight, until our nerves were on edge. . . . No enemy ever more deserved retribution than did the groups of Moros we were about to punish."[45]

Brig. Gen. Samuel S. Sumner, now commanding the 7th Separate Brigade, came to Vicars to take personal charge of the Maciu expedition. He ordered additional infantry companies sent up from Malabang and from Mataling Falls.[46]

In this, as in all subsequent expeditions, Sumner always took care that no officer senior to Pershing was included in these reinforcements. Senior officers were either delegated for temporary duty on other assignments and their companies sent up under junior officers or, if senior officers came, they were always domiciled next to, but not in Vicars—Pershing thus retaining command of the camp. Since Pershing was only a captain, and a junior one at that, juggling reinforcements often took some doing. But it *was* done, and conspicuously enough so that people talked about it.[47]

On this occasion, General Sumner sent out two columns: one under Capt. Eli Helmick, the other under Pershing. The latter's column consisted of four companies of infantry, a troop of cavalry, and a platoon of field artillery under Capt. William S. McNair—close to 550 men in all.[48] Maciu had 400 men. Most of these were armed with primitive weapons (krises, campilans, spears), but thirty had rifles and there were twenty lantacas (Moro cannon loaded with slugs and very effective at short range).[49]

General Sumner's orders were to march in, give the hostiles one last chance to accept American sovereignty (to be shown concretely by returning stolen property), and destroy any force that resisted. Friendly cottas were to be permitted to stand.[50]

Some Moros asked to join Pershing in the fighting. They wanted, they said, to settle scores with the hostiles who had "been giving us a bad name." But Pershing, wary of having armed Moros in his rear as well as on his front in this first test of strength, prudently declined. He did, however, take some leaders along as guides.[51]

Their services were important. In order to avoid antagonizing hostiles, Pershing had not sent exploring parties into their territory and consequently had little knowledge of the terrain. What he gleaned from friendly dattos was often inaccurate, made still less reliable by translation into Spanish and then into English.

The "road" to Maciu was a narrow footpath through the woods, in many places impassable. Pershing soon learned why Maciu Moros felt that they were immune from retaliation. The terrain was on their side: impassable trails or no trails at all, swamps and heavy overgrowth blocking off the path.[52]

Pershing's column left Vicars with four days' rations on September 18, 1902. They established a base camp at Pantaun, ten miles southeast of Vicars, and then set out for the first of several rancherias that had declared themselves hostile. This was Guaun, on Lake Butig, where they encountered three cottas which opened fire: one straight ahead, the others on either side of the trail.

Caught in a crossfire, Pershing thanked his lucky stars that Moros lacked modern artillery and were too far away for effective rifle fire. He ordered McNair to unpack the artillery and go to work. McNair banged away first at the cotta on the right, then at the one straight ahead.

The Moros appeared greatly surprised at the artillery. It exceeded anything they had ever seen—certainly their own short-range, slug-loaded lantacas—and they had no defense against it. As Pershing showed no inclination to charge the forts and as they were being pounded to pieces by the guns, there was nothing to do but flee.

This was exactly what Pershing intended and was to be his tactic repeatedly in fighting Moros: work their cottas over at long range with artillery, give them a chance to escape, send troops against cottas only when there was no other way. Always it was effect Pershing sought, never revenge. He was out to convince Moros of the futility of resistance, not out to spill blood. After each American victory, there was always a pause to let the lesson sink in, an opportunity for Moros next on the list to submit gracefully.[53]

There were no American casualties in this encounter at Guaun; indeed, there were few on any of Pershing's expeditions. The three cottas were reduced by artillery and set to the torch, thus advertising American victory to the countryside.[54]

On September 19, Pershing again left Pantaun, this time against Bayabao. Here the same tactics were repeated and with the same results. On the way back to the base camp that evening Pershing passed the rancheria at Lumbayanague. It flew a white flag. A good omen.[55]

Pershing had now been in Maciu country for two days, destroying five cottas. Moros had seen the smoke and flames billowing up over the treetops. Would this have an effect on Maciu itself? Pershing determined to find out right away.

At dawn on September 20 he abandoned the base camp and marched the whole command toward Maciu. At 11:00 A.M. they came out on a plateau about seven hundred feet above Lake Lanao. Below them, situated on a corner of the lake and on the south side of an inlet that separated them from the Maciu peninsula, was Sauir. Off in the distance, on the other side of the inlet, was Talub, and beyond that, Maciu.[56]

As directed by General Sumner, Pershing sent a messenger ahead to the two sultans of Maciu, Guanduali and Tauagan, inviting them to confer. Back came the answer, curt and ominous: "We do not want to meet you anywhere but at Maciu. We shall be waiting for you at Maciu. Do not send us any more messages."[57]

Pershing turned his attention to getting across the inlet. The quickest way was by boats, which he lacked. Barring this, he would have to troop down the inlet and around the tip of it. It would mean a good hike, even if the trail was passable.

In fact it was not. After two vain attempts to cross the inlet by raft, Pershing abandoned the attempt to take Maciu.[58] It was obvious that half the job of beating the Moros was getting to them. There was irony in the Moro challenge: "We will be waiting for you at Maciu."

They had spoken truly; they never expected him to get there.

American withdrawal began on September 22. As the soldiers left, Moros on the other side of the inlet jeered at them. Protected by water on the one hand and by an impassable trail on the other, they felt confident and exultant. Tight-lipped, Pershing ordered McNair to drop some scattershots on the Moros to spoil their fun; then he led his command back to Vicars.[59]

On September 28, he led them out again—virtually the same command with one important addition: a detachment of engineers and equipment for building a road around the inlet.[60]

By October 1, after good work by the engineers, the American force drew up before the fort at Maciu. Red war flags flew from the parapets and warriors jumped up and down on the walls, yelling challenges. But apparently fewer Moros were ready to fight to the death than the sultans boasted. Of the two hundred who were supposed to be waiting, half had lost their nerve and run away.[61]

McNair's artillery and the infantry's sharpshooting soon reduced firing from the cotta. The American lines moved progressively closer, making it constantly more dangerous for a Moro to poke his head up. Four smaller cottas, abandoned during the fight, were fired during the day. The smoke and flames from the fires, the din of gunfire, the yells of the Moros, the chanting of their panditas (priests), the beating of the metallic war drums—all gave a macabre, satanic setting to the battle.[62]

In the afternoon Lieutenant Loring volunteered to fire the main cotta. He came back after an unsuccessful attempt with a sobering report on Moro defenses. "The walls are twenty feet high from the bottom of the ditch," he said, "and straight up." It would be impossible to scale them without heavy losses.[63]

As Pershing surveyed the situation, a reporter from the *Manila Times* came up and sat down beside him.

"Are you going to storm the cotta tonight?" he asked.

"No, we would lose too many men."

"But aren't you afraid they'll sneak out in the long grass during the night and get away?"

"That is exactly what I expect them to do."[64]

When darkness fell, the American lines drew tighter. Sporadic firing continued by both sides.

At 3:00 A.M. some Moros made a rush to break through the American lines. Pershing knew that other Moros were taking advantage of the diversion to escape through the cogon grass. The cotta would be empty in the morning.[65]

It was. Troops went in, explored, and then set fire to the buildings. Others went through the tall grass around the cotta, flushing out die-hards.

The command returned to Vicars on October 3, having destroyed nearly ten cottas, killed fifty Moros, and wounded an unknown number.[66] The effect on the Moros was twofold. They were chastened to think that Americans could destroy supposedly impregnable cottas; hence there were fewer attacks on soldiers.[67] They were also surprised that, with a demonstrated power to defeat them, Americans did not embark on conquest, but rather sent out new friendship letters, inviting Moros to come to Vicars and visit.[68]

Many began to come. Pershing estimated that approximately two-thirds of the Lake Lanao Moros were now friendly. Certain rancherias still were hostile (Bacolod, on the west coast, and Gata and Taraca, on the east), but he was unwilling to move against them immediately. Let them visit the ruined cottas and see what American artillery could do; let friendly Moros try to change their minds. Pershing was willing to trade time for Moro lives.[69]

During the winter of 1902–1903 a problem with the Moros at Bayan was resolved in a totally unexpected way. The Bayan people lived on the south shore of Lake Lanao a little below Vicars, and had harbored resentment ever since their defeat at Pandapatan in May, 1902. Their leader was an old pandita (priest) named Sajiduciman.[70] He told his people that, since the Americans ate pork and practiced a different religion, any Moros who lived alongside them would go to hell.[71] He constantly increased his cotta fortifications, allowed hostile Moros from Gata (near Maciu) to use his rancheria as a base against Vicars, and forbade Moros to cut grass near Bayan for sale to Americans.[72]

In December Pershing wrote a strong note to the pandita, saying that he had carried his resistance far enough. Unless he was prepared to acknowledge American sovereignty, there would be trouble.[73]

An invitation came to visit Bayan on February 10, 1903. Pershing readied some cavalry and some field artillery ("just in case") and set out. On the way he encountered several hundred Moros from neighboring rancherias, all dressed up and heading for Bayan. Something was in the air.[74]

As the Americans approached the pandita's cotta, Sajiduciman came out, threw his arms about Pershing, and kissed him on each cheek. Surprised, but rising to the occasion, Pershing unflinchingly returned the favor.[75] Sajiduciman then gave him a guided tour of the cotta and ended by allowing an American flag to be raised over it, a formal acknowledgment of his submission.[76]

Next Sajiduciman indicated that he had something special to say. He and Pershing squatted on their heels while attendants set down a rare copy of the Koran, the Moslem Bible. An old Mohammedan priest performed incantations under a red parasol, symbol of Moslem authority. Beautifully engraved silver boxes of betel nut were handed around and each took a chew. Then Sajiduciman leaned over, betel-nut saliva trickling down his beard. Embracing Pershing, he said with the utmost solemnity, "You have been made a Moro datto."[77]

Pershing was thunderstruck. To his knowledge, this was unprecedented. He had never heard of a white man being so honored by Moros. Solemnly he thanked Sajiduciman. In a concluding ceremony, both men placed their hands on the Koran and swore allegiance to the United States.[78]

Pershing was to be in many ceremonies in his life—before kings, presidents, emperors, educators, and churchmen. But this ceremony in the wilds of Mindanao above shimmering Lake Lanao, squatting on his heels and chewing betel nut, swearing fealty on the Koran, was "the most unique ceremony in which I . . . ever participated."[79]

When word of Pershing's new honor got around, some of the more reserved rancherias began to thaw.[80] But there was one exception, and that was Bacolod.

Implacable, stubborn Bacolod had been a problem since the Americans first marched up to Lake Lanao. After the Maciu expedition General Sumner had written them a friendship letter. Back came the answer:

"The Sultan of Bacolod desires war at once as we wish to maintain religion of Muhamet. Cease sending us letters. What we want is war as we do not desire your friendship."[81]

Two factors delayed an expedition against Bacolod. One was a cholera epidemic which broke out in the lake region, killing an estimated 1,500 Moros.[82] The other was Pershing's feeling that the majority of Bacolod Moros did not want to fight. They had built their cotta right after the battle at Pandapatan when their blood was up, but had now had time to cool down. Part of their hostility was simply their savage pride. Thinking initially that the Americans came to enslave them, they had taken all sorts of oaths never to cease fighting; although they now saw that this was not the case, many felt they were still bound by these oaths. All in all, it was his judgment that if it came to a showdown, the Bacolod Moros would run away rather than fight.[83]

Pershing was wrong. Bacolod Moros fired into Vicars and made other hostile moves. In March, 1903, Pershing confessed that "any further effort to secure friendship of the Bacolod Moros except by force would be construed by other Moros as weakness on our part," and asked to move against them.[84]

Permission was granted on April 2.[85] Orders were to make an exploratory expedition up the west coast from Vicars to Marahui. Bacolod was on the route and hostile, but if actually confronted, might yet back down. Said General Davis, who had replaced General Chaffee as supreme commander in the Philippines: "It is hoped that Captain Pershing with his well known tact and discretion will be able to overcome this hostility."[86]

6

The March Around Lake Lanao

Pershing sent letters ahead to all rancherias on the west coast. "We are coming exploring," he said in effect, "and we are coming peaceably. But do not try to oppose us."[1]

His command left Camp Vicars early on April 5, 1903. It consisted of four companies of infantry, two troops of cavalry, two batteries of artillery—about 600 men in all, and a pretty big outfit for the Philippines.[2]

Each man carried one hundred rounds of ammunition, a haversack, and two canteens—the extra canteen because of cholera in the country. Pershing ordered no water drunk unless boiled. During the expedition he saw a civilian packer ride out into the lake, scoop up a tin full of water and drink it. He put the man under arrest and fined him $50.00. The packer raised a terrible howl, arguing that as a civilian he was not subject to military orders. Months later higher authorities ruled that he was right, but by that time he had moved to another post and never got his money back.[3]

Two soldiers also drank water without boiling it and died of cholera. When told that they were sick, Pershing exclaimed angrily, "Damn it, let them die! They disobeyed my orders!"[4]

Marching over narrow trails, the command strung out like a long snake. The artillery caused some trouble, as the mules were overloaded and went down hills very slowly, with the artilleryman holding them back by the tails. Occasionally a mule got out of control and went precipitously down a hill, profanity following in his wake. On the other hand, in going uphill mules proved a godsend to weary artillerymen, who took a good "tail-hold" and let the mule do the climbing. Many a mule returned from the expedition with a very thin tail.[5]

The troops camped that first night at Madumba, about ten miles from Vicars. Camp was made frontier style: a hollow square, with infantry and cavalry on the sides, and horses, mules, and baggage in the middle. The early part of the night was beautiful: there was a bright moon and Lake Lanao was like silver. About 1:00 A.M. the moon set and shortly afterward Bacolod Moros glided up silently in vintas and fired into the outposts. Two soldiers were hit at close range, one of whom later lost his arm. The camp got little sleep the rest of the night.[6]

They were back on the march at 6:00 A.M. Across a corner of Lake Lanao they saw Bacolod's red war flags flapping in the breeze. The Moros, sighting the troops, shot off lantacas, waved their swords, and yelled.

About 10:00 A.M. the trail passed a small Moro cotta called Linok. Pershing's Moro allies told him that he might be fired on here, and, in fact, as they passed, the cotta began shooting. Pershing ordered one volley fired in return, then hustled his men on, disregarding the attack. He discovered later that this was the most humiliating thing he could have done to the Linok Moros. They were chagrined to think that he did not consider them important enough for a battle.[7]

Approaching his objective, Pershing planned his tactics. Bacolod was situated on the end of a great ridge which ran down from a mountain to Lake Lanao. The trail ran up to its west side and ended beneath the fort. Evidently the Moros expected that attackers would come along the trail, where they would be hemmed in by the lake on one side, the woods on the other, and be under fire from the cotta in front.

Pershing's plan was to flank Bacolod—to approach by another trail higher up the mountain. He planned to gain ground on the ridge which ran down to the cotta, and pour in fire from above.

There were serious difficulties here. The terrain above Bacolod was all ridges and ravines—and running the wrong way. Their sides were very steep and the ravines filled with dense tropical growth. Pershing's plan entailed going up one ridge, down another, up a third, and so on, for the ridges ran north and south, and he was approaching from the west. Furthermore, the Bacolod Moros had foreseen just such a maneuver, for they had dug a deep trench from their cotta straight up the side of the ridge on which it was built and from which they commanded all higher approaches to it from the west.[8]

In mid-morning, the command turned off the lake trail and took one leading up towards the mountain on the left. After much labor, they gained a ridge approximately 600 yards west of the Bacolod ridge and 1,000 yards higher. By now a sizeable force of Moros had taken position on the Bacolod ridge and were firing with old flintlocks and Remingtons.

About 1:00 P.M. the Americans found a little trail connecting their ridge with Bacolod's. They moved down into the ravine below, then pushed up the other side, artillery meanwhile clearing the enemy ridge with shrapnel. They took the Bacolod ridge about 500 yards above the cotta, driving the Moros there either farther up the ridge on the north or over to the next ridge to the east.

Just at this time a tremendous downpour of rain cut loose. Pershing pushed his men on through the storm, throwing troops around the cotta on the east and west, with the main body on the north on the Bacolod ridge. The cotta was now entirely surrounded except for the south side on the lake, with artillery commanding it from the Bacolod ridge.

Here Pershing obtained his first good look at Bacolod. It was about 100 feet square, on a high bluff overlooking Lake Lanao. The parapet, twelve feet high and fifteen feet thick, was revetted with stone and bamboo. The entire cotta was roofed over, making it impossible to estimate the number of the defenders, but friendly Moros placed it at 200. Around the cotta ran a ditch thirty feet wide and almost forty feet deep, with a trench running out to the lake for the Moros to fetch water without being detected.

Pershing set a mortar to work lobbing shells into the cotta. As darkness came on, he ordered the force on the east side to join the troops on the north. This left one side open during the night, in case the Moros wished to escape.[9] A number did, but when morning dawned on April 7, many remained inside. Again, Pershing threw his cordon around the cotta, while artillery battered its earthworks. The Moros replied with small arms and lantacas, but their embrasures and portholes became so battered that they could not fire through them; and any Moro who stuck his head up above the parapet took his life in his hands.

Pershing later called Bacolod "the best fight of the Moro campaign." He told George Meiklejohn:

"Not so many Moros killed as at Bayan or Pandapatan, but fought according to some sort of system. Of course I have worked on this fight as I foresaw long ago that it must come, and the whole thing from the beginning worked out as planned. First, we got behind them, much to their surprise, and could post our guns above and drop projectiles down into their fort, so that the artillery fire in this case was not all noise. We had some work and some fighting to gain this position. Once there it was only a question of sitting down deliberately and waiting to see what the Moros would do. Many got away before the place was invested thoroughly.

"The fight began in a flood of a rainstorm that lasted till dark and reconnoitering was difficult. So we did not find all the avenues of escape until the next day and I am glad now we did not, they had such confidence in this fort, that they took many women and children inside and these escaped during the night. The next day and night we held them fast, however, tried to get them to surrender, had two talks under flag of truce, no they would fight it out. . . . "[10]

A touch of comedy occurred when the panandungan[11] sent out word that his enemies were not observing the rules of war. "If the Americans want to fight us," he complained, "let them fight. But tell them to fight

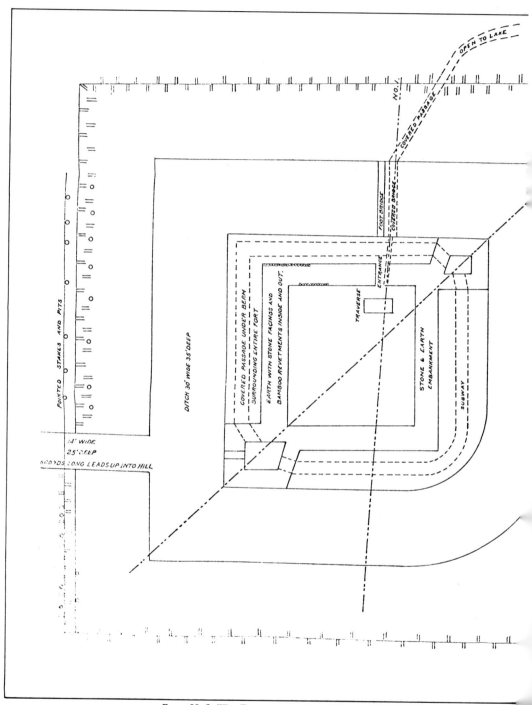

The diagram contains the following labels:

OPEN TO LAKE

NO.V.

COVERED PASSAGE

FOOT BRIDGE

COVERED BRIDGE

ENTRANCE

TRAVERSE

POINTED STAKES AND PITS

DITCH 30' WIDE 3.5' DEEP

COVERED PASSAGE UNDER BERM SURROUNDING ENTIRE FORT

EARTH WITH STONE FACINGS AND BAMBOO REVETMENTS INSIDE AND OUT.

STONE & EARTH EMBANKMENT

SUBWAY

14' WIDE 25' DEEP 600 YDS. LONG LEADS UP INTO HILL

From U. S. War Department, *Annual Report, 1903*, Washington, D. C., 1903
Volume III

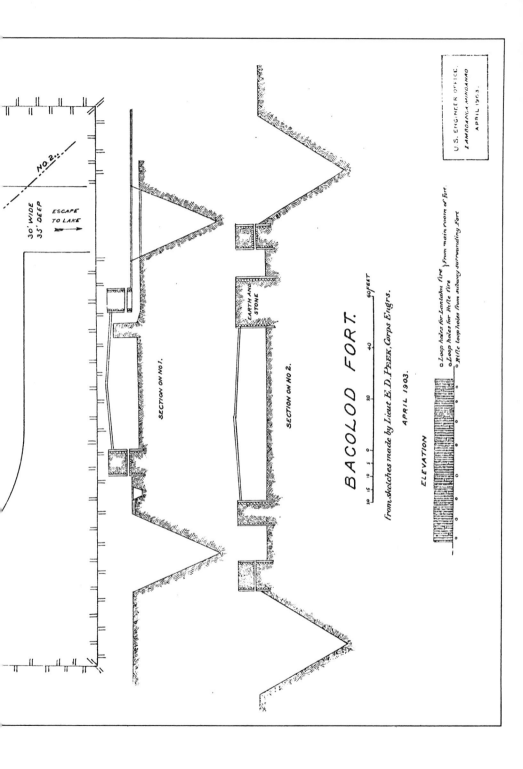

BACALOD FORT.

From sketches made by Lieut. E. D. PEEK, Corps Eng'rs.

APRIL 1903.

SECTION ON NO 1.

SECTION ON NO 2.

EARTH AND STONE

ESCAPE TO LAKE

30' WIDE 3.5' DEEP

NO. 2

ELEVATION

o Loop holes for Lantaka fire } from main room of fort
o Loop holes for Rifle fire
o Rifle loop holes from subway surrounding Fort

U. S. ENGINEER OFFICE.
ZAMBOANGA MINDANAO
APRIL 1903.

Bacalod Fort

like men. While my fort is being besieged, I see American soldiers down by the water side eating up all my cocoanuts. This is infamous and is not war!"[12]

On the evening of April 7, Pershing sent Lts. Ben Lear and George Peek to reconnoiter the ditch. They recommended filling in a short section with trees and brush, throwing a light bamboo bridge across, and sending in an assault party.[13] After the failure of the second truce talk, Pershing called his officers together and announced that he had decided to storm the cotta, using the plan suggested by Lear and Peek.[14]

At 1:00 P.M. on April 8 the Americans advanced to the edge of the ditch on all sides, pouring in a heavy fire to keep the Moros down. At the same time two companies of infantry filled the ditch with trees and shrubbery as fast as possible. Thirty minutes later an assault party swung across, formed line on the berm, and clambered up to the top of the parapet. Here Lt. George C. Shaw, who led the party, saw Moros coming on "like bees from a hive, in single file, swords in hand, each man close to the man in front."[15]

"It was as a whole a scene never to be forgotten," said Pershing.[16] The first Moro up on the parapet "sprang out as though shot from a gun," his kris uplifted, hair on end, face contorted in fury. Lieutenant Shaw shot him from two feet away; he stopped, stood bolt upright (Shaw thought he had missed), then dropped where he stood. The second Moro leaped at Sergeant Hafer, who fired point-blank, but his gun jammed. Down came a kris, almost amputating Hafer's arm; down came a rifle butt, making a bloody mash of the Moro's skull.[17]

The fight was short and bloody. Once he determined that there were no more defenders inside, Pershing called back his troops and set fire to the cotta. Because of cholera, he did not wish to examine the inside until it had burnt. When the fire reached the powder magazine, Bacolod blew up with a great cloud of smoke. Friendly Moros shouted, "No mas Bacolod!" (No more Bacolod).[18]

"Bacolod is fallen," Pershing wrote a friend, "and I am gratified to say without loss of life to us. We had nine men wounded in the fight and all will recover. Two of them will, however, lose an arm apiece.

The rest will not be maimed in any way. Of the Moros killed there were many dattos, the Panandungan in particular—all told about 120. We could have killed more but what's the use? They have learned their lesson, and I think will be good. We pounded them, and then penned them up and took the fort at our leisure. Of course we could have taken it earlier but would probably have lost a lot of men. As it is, it is better, although possibly not as brilliant. Quite brilliant enough however was the final assault, with its hand-to-hand fights on the parapets."[19]

Pershing's wisdom in holding off the assault until the third day was confirmed by Dr. Robert U. Patterson, surgeon on the expedition and later Surgeon General of the Army. Had Pershing assaulted on the first or second day, said Patterson, "the casualties would have been terrible on our side." By pounding the cotta with artillery and giving its people a chance to escape, "he so intimidated the Moros, that when he finally assaulted on April 8th, there only remained in the fort the really desperate characters who were determined to die fighting. . . . How much different would have been the result had he listened to the impetuous advice of his officers?"[20]

During the rest of the trip north to Marahui, Pershing counted "more United States flags displayed in the road and in rancherias than I supposed existed in all the country."[21] It was amazing what effect blowing up Bacolod had on public relations. Moros came in from all over, some recently hostile, to tell Pershing they wanted to be friendly. The expedition picked up a great following, all wanting to be in the victory parade.[22]

At Oato, Moros brought their legal cases to the "Commandante," as they called Pershing. He held court in a rice field, and when he gave his decision it was accepted without a murmur. It must be right, Moros concluded, if "Commandante Per-Shering" said so.[23]

At Marahui Pershing conferred with the representatives of important rancherias. They all manifested two feelings, undoubtedly related: 1) surprise at the American success at Bacolod, 2) desire to be friends in the future.[24]

After a few days' rest at Pantar, where Maj. Robert L. Bullard's infantry was working on the Iligan-Marahui road, Pershing led the command back home. He sent word ahead: "We will do no damage to any Moro property unless we are fired upon. But if we are fired upon, we will burn everything in sight."[25]

No trouble occurred. The cotta at Bacolod was still smoking as they went by and many newly made graves could be seen—large mounds with stone walls, covered by great white umbrellas. On April 16 they marched back into Vicars, rather amused to find their own camp quarantined against them, since they had been exposed to cholera. Pershing fixed that by moving all the stay-at-homes into a separate camp and putting expedition troops in the regular quarters.[26]

In Pershing's mind the campaign had been "the largest single success that had been made in the islands. One year ago nobody but me had seen the Moro in his native Laguna. . . . Now we have crossed the lake and practically marched around it."[27]

But they had never *completely* marched around it. No one had. They had explored the south, west, and north coasts, but not twenty miles or so on the east. On April 19, 1903, General Sumner asked Pershing to undertake this assignment.[28]

Pershing planned to make the march deliberately, letting the Moros know he was out to explore and not to fight.[29] But he was prepared for anything. On May 1, 1903, General Sumner telegraphed him: "You had better take all the Cavalry you can. . . . Dispatch from Bullard says that the Sultan of Marahui says there will be fighting at Taraca and at Dilamo where the Sultan of Bacolod and his people, who escaped from Bacolod, are strengthening a big fort. . . . According to Bullard most of the Sultans and Dattos north of Taraca have accepted American friendship."[30]

Pershing left Vicars on May 2, 1903, on this expedition which was to catch the Moro fancy and make a name for himself in the United States. His command was the usual one—infantry, cavalry, artillery— 500 men and 340 animals; also six large Moro vintas to carry sick and wounded back to Vicars. They marched east to Talub, around the inlet there, and passed Maciu where they had fought the previous September, now quite peaceful.[31]

Many Moros were now visibly friendly, selling fences for fuel, and camotes (a kind of sweet potato) for food. Pershing's policy was to pay liberally, sometimes even a little more than goods were worth. But if people fought against him, he took everything he wanted without giving them a dime. As Moros were usually keen businessmen, they began to see that it paid to be friendly.[32]

On the afternoon of May 3, Pershing reached Gata and passed it without incident. That he did so was a tribute to his forbearance. Several months before he had encountered it with war flags flying and had chosen to disregard the provocation. Since then Bacolod had fallen and Gata had had second thoughts. There were no war flags flying that afternoon.[33]

On May 4 they began to get into hostile country. In the distance they saw a great fort about three miles away, covered with red battle flags. Friendly Moros cried, "Taraca! Taraca! Mucho combate!!!" [34]

On the way there they crossed an open rice field, so marshy that the whole command bogged down. All the mule packs had to be unpacked and the contents carried by hand. Machetes and axes, brought along for just such purpose, cut down shrubbery and trees to build a makeshift causeway. By noon all were across and on solid ground, with Taraca one mile away.

On their right were various Moro cottas, but all flew white flags. People were sitting on the walls like spectators at a sports event, waiting to see the fight and all set to make friends with the winner. Hostile Moros began to spring up in front, fire, and then run for the cotta at Taraca.

The fight was almost anti-climactic after Bacolod. The cotta was not as strong, the ditch not as deep, and the defenders not as die-hard. It surrendered the next morning. Pershing forced the captured to bury the dead and to take an oath of allegiance to the United States. Since no Koran was handy, each Moro swore while holding with Pershing a piece of bejuco which was bent under pressure and then cut with a sword—this was considered binding. Pershing then released them.[35]

The march was resumed on May 6. Pershing pushed the men, for the rainy season was approaching which would make parts of the trail virtually impassable. But he pushed himself too, judging from the remark of an observer on this trip : "[He] was untiring in his work and had been all day on foot well ahead of the main column with two or three men and a few Moro guides, picking out the best trail. His first thought was to save his men unnecessary marching and his next, to nurse his stock."[36]

The next day the command passed Remein where the sultan sat on the wall counting the soldiers. Concluding that they were too many, he decided to be friendly and paid a courtesy call. He was a very sullen man and extremely ugly, but his clothes were luxurious and his slaves carried beautiful silver-mounted weapons and solid silver betel-nut boxes. When the troops, born souvenir hunters, saw his wealth, they regretted he had not elected to fight.[37]

On May 8 Pershing reached Marahui. He had explored the east coast, and there was now no place on Lake Lanao he had not visited.

Maj. Robert L. Bullard met Pershing and told how Moros had brought him day-to-day reports of the march up the coast. "After the fight at Taraca," he said, "a Moro, all excited, rushed into my camp and told me, 'Quick, raise the white flag! Captain Pershing and his warriors have all gone *juramentado* and are coming round the lake killing everybody they see!' He could not understand why I was not afraid of you."[38]

His mission accomplished, Pershing elected to return to Vicars by the west coast. The men had had enough of wading through bogs, unpacking mules, and corduroying trails. The west coast was shorter and familiar; they had used it on the Bacolod expedition. Besides, it would be much more impressive to make one single march all the way around the lake, demonstrating American power, than to make two half-marches covering the same distance.[39]

Pershing expected, and encountered, little resistance. People en route flew white flags. On May 10 he marched back into Vicars—the first white man to lead an expedition around Lake Lanao.[40]

Congratulations awaited him. The department commander, General Sumner, telegraphed: "Please accept for yourself and express to your command my appreciation of the soldierly manner in which they behaved during the recent expedition around Lake Lanao. They are the first Military Force that ever encircled the Lake and have accomplished a feat that has generally been deemed impossible. They have had to meet the savage foe, to overcome great natural obstacles and to face a deadly disease.[41] This was done cheerfully and manfully."[42]

From Washington, D. C., several days later came this message: "Express to Captain John J. Pershing and the officers and men under his command the thanks of the War Department for their able and effective accomplishment of a difficult and important task. Root. Secretary of War."[43]

The march around Lake Lanao caught the Moro fancy; it became an event from which to date things. About eight years afterwards, when Pershing was commander of the Moro Province, he asked a boy how old he was. "I don't know, sir," came the reply, "but I was so big [holding out his hand to measure height] when you marched around the lake."[44]

Pershing's handling of Moro affairs and his successful expeditions brought him to the attention of superiors. On June 26, 1903, Brig. Gen. George W. Davis, supreme commander in the Philippines, advised the War Department:

"When the time comes for the Department to make selection of general officers for promotion from the grade of captain, I hope that Captain Pershing may be selected for brigadier general. I have frequently brought his merits to the attention of the Department, in routine and in special communications, for gallantry, good judgment, and thorough efficiency in every branch of the soldier's profession. He is the equal of any and the superior of most."[45]

Guy H. Preston, who arrived in the Philippines in 1903, wrote a friend:

"Upon arrival I find the whole army here agog with expectations as to whether Pershing will be made a brigadier general as a reward for solving the great problem of Moro subjugation and saving the Administration the serious embarrassment which threatened it in that quarter. . . . I have had two notes from him. . . . I am going to tell you, *entre nous,* and at no suggestion from him, that he has confided to me his intention, in case he pulls off the coveted promotion, to apply at once to be sent back to Mindanao as Department Commander and to acquire at the same time the Governorship, to work in harmony with the Taft government. . . . Pershing's interest in the Moros amounts to a mania, if it were possible for such a man to have a mania. . . . I do not believe he is seriously broken in health but that just now he is making a home run before the ball is brought back to the infield. You know that ball has been long kept within the diamond of seniority and senility."[46]

About this time Secretary of War Elihu Root encountered one of Pershing's classmates at a social function and spoke of him "with unstinted praise and satisfaction." Said Root: "If your friend Pershing doesn't look out, he will find himself in the brigadier general class very soon."[47] When Pershing later became a brigadier in 1906, the charge was made that he owed it all to "pull," to the fact that his father-in-law, Sen. Francis E. Warren, was chairman of the Senate Military Affairs Committee. The charge seems unsubstantiated in view of the fact that Pershing was already being recommended for the rank as early as June, 1903, almost six months before he met the Senator or his daughter.

Meanwhile Pershing was making ready to leave the Philippines. He had been there three years, the climate had taken its toll of his health, and he had lost a good deal of weight. After helping General Davis organize the Moro Province, he sailed for home.[48]

His Philippine tour (the first of three) began the "making" of Pershing. His work at Vicars, his expeditions against Maciu, Bacolod, and Taraca, and his march around Lake Lanao had attracted comment of editors and officials as far away as Washington; he was being seriously considered for general officer rank.

Certain qualities were in evidence that justified his progress. One was discipline, which for Pershing was the backbone of a command, without which it degenerated into a spineless mass such as he had encountered at Iligan under a weak commander. The business of a soldier is war, and victory in war demands men and equipment that are ready for action. Levi, the unsanitary cook at Iligan, learned that; so did the soldier who galloped the horse on a hard road; so did (too late) the troopers who drank the cholera-infected waters. The ultimate rationale of discipline is that it saves lives and brings victory. That is why Pershing insisted on it.

Perhaps he insisted on it too much. Perhaps, due to a certain shyness, he felt that discipline, to be maintained, required aloofness in the commander, lest familiarity breed contempt. Lt. Ben Lear, who reconnoitered at Bacolod, found him "a very cold one-man individual. He seemed to have no admiration or friendly interest in any of his officers. He talked to us only on official occasions and on official matters. We missed his kindly interest and friendly advice. There was no assembly of officers for an explanation of the situation and an explanation of our missions; there were no assemblies of officers after an operation, for criticisms or compliments. No individual was ever personally praised for doing a good job,[49] unless it was in an official report covering some operation and we never learned of that."[50]

Another quality, one which not all great commanders possess, might be called his "economy with life." Casualties, both friend and foe, were low under Pershing. This was the result of forbearance (as at Linok and Gata); of delaying assaults (as at Bacolod); of giving Moros a chance to call off a fight, or, if they insisted, of giving them a chance to escape once they saw they were licked. "We could have killed more but what's the use?"[51] he said after Bacolod, and the remark sums up his combat philosophy. The operation at Bacolod was well planned and executed, a fact which in itself held down casualties.

Pershing's military accomplishments in the Philippines must not be overrated. He won all his battles, but it is hard to see how he could have lost them. The Moros were outgunned and outdisciplined to an extreme degree. Campilans and spears against rifles and artillery was hardly a fair match. His accomplishment in the Philippines was not in the battles he won, but in the battles he avoided fighting. Given American firepower, once an engagement took place, the outcome could hardly be in doubt. Pershing couldn't lose. Yet Col. Frank Baldwin who commanded at Pandapatan had the same advantage—and he had been removed from command.

Captain Pershing replaced Colonel Baldwin because, in the judgment of superiors, he inspired a confidence that Baldwin and others did not. Pershing was level-headed and gifted with prudence, that quality that weighs any given situation in delicate balance and judges correctly what it calls for: forbearance or reprisal.

He judged correctly time after time. He established American sovereignty in the Lake Lanao district with a minimum of friction and a low loss of life. American firepower notwithstanding, a guerrilla war waged by a fanatical people in an underdeveloped nation can be a very costly thing, as many colonial powers have discovered. Pershing kept guerrilla war to a minimum.

There was yet a further reason why he had been placed in command of the crucial station at Vicars and in charge of key expeditions. As his friend and classmate, Avery D. Andrews, said: "From a military standpoint the circumstances were most remarkable. All available troops in the department were ordered into the field under the command of a junior captain, while all officers senior to him were either temporarily detailed on special duty or kept idle at their posts. It would be difficult and probably quite impossible to find a comparable case in the history of our Army."[52]

That such extraordinary action was taken was due to Pershing's demonstrated success in dealing with Moros. Not for nothing did they make him a datto. It was the reward of "going in the other man's door," even when he is a barbarian, mixing with him, being considerate, flattering his ego, appealing to his self-interest, establishing a climate of trust and putting one's life on the line to maintain it. One does not learn these things out of a book. Some men never learn them, but Pershing did, and it was not necessarily easy.

At Iligan, according to Robert L. Bullard, Pershing was "almost the only one of the officers" who became interested in Moros "and by associating with them and studying them won their confidence and admiration. He became, in fact, very influential with them locally. These things I saw or learned for myself on the spot, often by the adverse criticism of men who were jealous or who disapproved of his thus occupying himself."[53]

Later, after Bullard had had some experience with Moros himself, he said:

"The more I see of this unusual work the more I know that few men are fit to manage it, and the more I am of the opinion that General Davis did right to keep Pershing in charge of these Moros instead of placing in charge some fool officer who ignorantly supposed that he could come and in an off-hand manner manage these savages."[54]

The Moros liked Pershing. When he told them something, they felt they could believe it. Their only concern was that he might be moved away and that someone strange would take his place. To this he always responded that he would remain at Vicars a long time,[55] and this, strangely enough, was the one promise that he did not keep. But neither he nor the Moros had any way of knowing that then, and, in the meantime, a real friendship developed that boded well for Moro-American relations. No less than three Moros asked Pershing to honor them by becoming the adopted father of their children.

Five days after the march around Lake Lanao George T. Bowman, Pershing's adjutant, reported to the Assistant Secretary of War:

"He [Pershing] is today the one great American to the Moro minds. They regard him as a supernatural being and the great mass of Malanaos[56] are now his fast friends. He always treats them justly and fairly, never makes a promise which he cannot fulfill and at the same time he has shown them that he can punish wrongdoers swiftly and well. I know that his success is not the result of chance. It's due to his own personality and nearly four years of study and labor on the Moro question."[57]

Moros liked Pershing because he liked them. They were not just savages, they were human beings, and his secret lay in treating them as such. He was patient with them. Their lawless habits extended over generations and would take generations to change. The way to change them, Pershing knew, was "by the tedious process of education. It should not be accomplished by extermination."[58] In January, 1903, he told Charles Magoon that his work with the Moros was "the most interesting work I have yet had in the army. . . . I hope to remain here and be permitted to work out the problem, as I have . . . a knowledge of conditions here, especially of Moros, that qualifies me to do good work."[59]

Pershing was competent and he knew it. A. H. Sunderland, a Vicars man, was repelled by "his extreme self assurance."[60] Kelton L. Pepper, who participated in the Maciu campaign, thought him "self centered," the type of man who "was out to make a name for himself so he could be made a general."[61] Frankly, he was out to be a general; his ambition was always controlling, always driving him on. It produced a professionalism, a competence. C. C. Booth, an old Philippine hand, found him arrogant, but he also ranked him as "a soldier without peer."[62] Ben Lear, who thought Pershing "a very cold one-man individual," also considered him "a remarkably fine soldier."[63] And George T. Bowman, who knew Pershing at Zamboanga, Iligan, and Vicars, remarked:

"I cannot refrain from testifying to my great admiration and respect for him. To me he seems the *beau ideal* of the American officer. He's the kind of man who always insists on everyone in his command doing his very best on all occasions and at the same time is absolutely fair to all. Always faithful, loyal, conscientious and hard working, he is certainly a magnificent example for the many young officers of what a true soldier should be."[64]

7

Love and Marriage

Pershing disembarked at San Francisco on July 30, 1903.[1] He called on Gen. Arthur MacArthur, commanding the Department of California, and MacArthur introduced his son, Douglas, who had just graduated from West Point as First Captain of Cadets and with the highest academic average in history. "I was favorably impressed," Pershing recalled, "by the manly, efficient appearance of the second lieutenant."[2]

After serving briefly on the newly formed General Staff in Washington, D. C., and in Oklahoma City as Assistant Chief of Staff of the Southwestern Division,[3] Pershing returned to Washington to attend the first classes of the Army War College. Established to prepare war plans and to train officers for higher command, the College opened for students on November 1, 1904. Pershing attended for less than two months, as a later assignment took him out of the country and made it impossible for him to graduate.[4]

Meanwhile, the movement to make Pershing a brigadier general had gained momentum, as recommendations poured into the War Department. A key figure in the movement was Pershing's old West Point classmate Avery D. Andrews, a close associate of Theodore Roosevelt.

On November 16, 1903, Andrews asked the President to raise Pershing "to the rank corresponding to the service which he has already actually performed in the field [i. e., a brigadier general]."[5] Roosevelt answered:

"Just recently I asked for Pershing to be sent here so that I might talk with him. The trouble is that I could only make him a brigadier general and thus jump him very high—much higher than any one else has been jumped. I should have to put him over Mills, of West Point, who served with me at Santiago and did just as gallant service as Pershing. I would have to put him over many other men. I would be delighted to give him a colonelcy if it were in my power; but at present it hardly seems to me that I could jump him to brigadier general."[6]

Pershing's promotion got nowhere. He was faced with a system based on seniority in which, in exceptional cases, the President could promote to the rank of lieutenant or to brigadier general, but to no ranks in between. Roosevelt would have had to jump him over hundreds of senior officers. The solution to the problem was to change the promotion system, and allow the President to promote to the in-between grades. As Roosevelt said in his 1903 message to Congress:

"When a man renders such service as Captain Pershing rendered last spring in the Moro campaign, it ought to be possible to reward him without at once jumping him to the grade of brigadier general."[7]

Meanwhile Pershing was taking to heart the advice of Gen. George W. Davis: "Now go home and share your embraces with a good woman while you are young enough. An old bachelor doesn't make a good General officer. He needs to dangle something on his knee, first the wife and then the babies. Success to you in this. . . ."[8]

It all began on the evening of December 9, 1903. Fond of dancing, Pershing attended a weekly hop at Fort Myer, just outside Washington, where he met twenty-three year old Frances Warren, daughter of the wealthy senator from Wyoming. His life was about to change.[9]

Frances Warren had a bright smile, a ready laugh, and a contagious gaiety. "I don't remember that she was ever blue or discouraged or out of sorts," said an acquaintance.[10] Recently graduated from Wellesley College, Frances had come to Washington to be with her father for the opening of Congress. On the train she had read a newspaper article about Pershing's Moro work.[11] In the Senate galleries on December 7 she heard President Roosevelt's message to Congress conclude with a reference to Pershing and the promotion system.[12] Then came December 9 and the dance. "Went to a hop at Fort Myer . . . ," she wrote in her diary. *"Perfectly lovely time.* Met Mr. Pershing, of Moro and Presidential message fame."[13]

Recalling this evening Senator Warren said later: "I see now it was love at sight. They sat together, Jack and Frances, and for the most part they were oblivious of the rest of us."[14]

Frances' diary for the week following reveals how completely she was swept off her feet:

"December 11, 1903: Had dinner with the Millards to see Capt. Pershing. . . . It was *just great.* Have lost my heart.

"December 12: Capt. Pershing told Miss Millard that I was a very 'jolly' girl—and that he thought I could keep up with the procession. Oh, joy!

"December 18: Very elegant dinner. . . . Afterward, went to dance at the Navy Yard. . . . Danced every dance but one—and have lost my heart to Capt. Pershing irretrievably. Perfectly elegant dancer."[15]

If Frances was lost "irretrievably," the feeling was mutual. Charlie Magoon never forgot the night Pershing rushed in and woke him from a sound sleep.

"I've met the girl God made for me!" he exclaimed.

Then he sat down and talked endlessly, asking a thousand questions: Was it right for an "old man" like him to think of marrying a young girl? Could he support her in the manner to which she was accustomed on just a captain's salary? What did Charlie think?

What Charlie thought was that Pershing should go to bed and leave him alone. "Look, John," he said sleepily, "maybe you're in love and can live without sleep. But I'm *not!*"[16]

On December 22 Pershing learned that he was to be transferred to the Southwestern Division, so he stepped up the pace of his courtship. He sent Frances orchids with a request that she save the cotillion for him on December 29.[17]

It snowed that night and the sidewalks were slushy. Frances had come to the cotillion alone, so Pershing saw her to her carriage; he turned to leave. Frances noticed that he had no rubbers or galoshes and faced a walk home in the snow.

"Get in," she said. "I'll drop you off at your place."

Pershing demurred. "I don't think it would be proper."

Frances insisted. Pershing looked around at people coming out of the dance. What would they think?

"All right," said Frances. "Walk ahead down to the corner. I'll pick you up there."[18]

Nothing illustrates better the contrast between the two—John, concerned with convention and propriety; Frances, a freer spirit, caring little what people thought. They complemented each other well.

On his arrival in the Southwest, Pershing took up by mail where he had left off in person. His letters to Frances are interesting. He felt strongly about her right from the start, yet hesitated to say so openly. The salutation of his letters was a very formal "Dear Miss Warren" and his closing an equally formal "John J. Pershing." Frances was similarly restrained.[19]

After a month Pershing took a gamble. After writing and tearing up three attempts to say what he felt, he went out on a limb and stated frankly that he had certain grave financial difficulties which she ought to know about:

"We, you and I, have become friends almost from the very first moment we met, and it continues to grow stronger, that tie of friendship—yes, and it seems that there is possibly something just a shade deeper than ordinary friendship. So that I can see no other course for myself than to tell you what I have told you [about my finances]. . . . I trust that I have not written more than I should have nor that you fail to understand me."[20]

She did not fail.

"I understand why you wrote to me as you did, dear Captain. . . .

You were enough afraid of something more than friendship to want me to know that you were not in a position to ask me to be something more than a friend. . . . You wanted me to know that you could not ask me now to love you or to marry you. Time will show us whether there is anything more than friendship. But if there should be I want to tell you something. If you should love me at all, I want you to love me so much that you will ask me to marry you in spite of anything in the world. . . . I am trembling a little as I let this letter go from me."[21]

Pershing responded:

"Don't think me in the least conceited when I say that I know and *knew* that you liked me. . . . You must know too, Dear, that you have become more than Miss Warren of Washington, . . . more than an attractive girl. . . . Have you ever thought that it were perhaps best that a woman should marry a man near her age? Or, did it ever occur to you that a soldier's profession is a jealous mistress? That he is subject to the will of others? That an army wife has no permanent home? That her children have little chance for an education? That she may be separated from him for years . . . ?"[22]

Thereafter their affection grew with each letter. By April 3 Pershing was openly confessing that he loved her and she said the same, yet strangely—perhaps it was a holdover from the Victorian Age—they both mixed warm expressions of love with a certain formality. Pershing would write movingly of his love, call her "dearest," speak of her "dear arms about me," yet sign the letter "John J. Pershing"—almost as if writing a business letter to a stranger. She did the same.[23]

Throughout the spring of 1904 both planned to see each other when Frances returned to Cheyenne with her father after Congress adjourned, but something always seemed to come up to prevent it. Finally in mid-August a meeting was arranged and Pershing visited for two days.[24] They rode horseback over the broad, fresh sweeps of the Senator's ranch, so vast that people called him "the greatest shepherd since Abraham."[25] Coming in from the ride Pershing took Frances in his arms and she "felt all through my being, 'He loves me.' "[26] Pershing said, "I never kissed your lips until we both said we loved each other. I should not have done so under any other circumstances. That kiss, as all others have been, was attended with feelings that to me are divinely sacred."[27]

In the winter Frances returned to Washington to be with her father, and John to attend the War College. It was now definitely assumed they were to be married, the only question was when. Gone was any formality. They addressed each other in their letters now as "Frankie" and "Jack."

Pershing, however, still felt that a marriage proposal would be unfair until his financial condition was better. In 1902 his brother Jim had failed in business, involving the whole family. John sent over $6,000 from the Philippines to help. When he returned he found that the money had been totally lost.

From August, 1903, John supported the family, paying $2,000 out of his salary for their debts. Even after this, family liabilities still totalled $1,500, his own were an equal amount, and those of his sister Grace, who died in 1904, almost $1,200. His sister May's health broke and she had to go to Europe to recover; John paid for it. Grace's children were being brought up by a relative and John had to guarantee their support.[28]

When John told Frances all this, she offered her own bank account of $10,000 to pay off the debts; what was left would serve them to live on. John said no. His self respect demanded that he delay marriage until the debts were paid off, or at least reduced, and by himself.[29]

Frances understood. "You have the right to a reasonable amount of time to straighten out your affairs so that you can take me with the sense of pride in yourself which I want you to have." But, she added, "beyond a reasonable amount of time, I have the right to your life— to your youth—the most precious years of your life for me."[30]

When John spoke of his financial troubles as a marriage "obstacle," Frances reacted vigorously.

"Let me tell you right here, you dear old Jack Pershing, that you might just as well stand in the middle of a field and wave a red flag at a bull as to flaunt that word 'obstacles' at me. . . . Here I am just urging and urging you to marry me again. It seems to me I have done nothing else since last February, and I am just getting discouraged with you. . . . I am going to bend all my efforts to fall in love with every attractive man I meet. . . . Please may I kiss your nose?"[31]

To Frances it seemed unreasonable to postpone a marriage too long because he would not let her help out. Pershing would at times agree, then have second thoughts.

"You are incorrigible," Frances wrote him once. "Next time you get on the verge of taking my view of things, stay there till I come. One can get a fine ring for one dollar ($1.00), or if worst comes to worst, one can be procured along with a stick of candy for one cent—and I'll loan you that much. Of course, Jack, you will succeed, but I want you ready to marry me any way. Pish, tush! . . . Consider yourself made fun at."[32]

By Christmas, affairs had evolved to the point where Pershing felt he could take the plunge. On December 25 he asked the Senator for his daughter's hand. It was given him willingly and warmly.[33]

The wedding was set for June, but at once complications developed. The Russo-Japanese War was on and Pershing had asked to go as an observer. On December 27 he was ordered to sail for Tokyo on February 15.[34]

A June wedding was now impossible. A further complication was the War Department's decision that all military observers must be single.

On Senator Warren's suggestion, Pershing decided to lay the matter before the Secretary of War, William Howard Taft. Unknown to him, a friend alerted Taft ahead of time.[35]

The interview opened strangely.

"Do you play bridge?" Taft asked. "Lloyd Griscom [American Minister in Tokyo] wants a bachelor to play bridge with him."

Pershing answered that his game was poor. He then blurted out his difficulty: "There seems to be a decision by the Staff that no married officer can have a post in Tokyo."

Taft smiled. "That's right."

"Well, Mr. Secretary, I'm engaged to be married."

Taft roared with laughter.

"You're not married now are you?"

"No."

"You have the appointment, don't you?"

"Yes."

"Then go ahead and get married. What you do after you have the appointment is your business. I know of no Army regulation which forbids a man to marry. No Army board or court will revoke an appointment because of marriage."[36]

This hurdle cleared, John and Frances decided to get married right away. The newspapers announced the engagement on January 11, 1905. After a dance that night Pershing wrote in his diary, "She was certainly divinely lovely and I am simply crazy about her."[37]

To those who might have missed the announcement, Pershing wrote privately. In one instance, "Here is a piece of news that will startle you, . . . I have at last decided to join the army of benedicts."[38] And in another, "You can probably guess the young lady's name from what you saw and heard in Colorado Springs last summer."[39]

They planned initially for a simple wedding, just the families and a few close friends, but one name led to another until the invitation list grew interminably long. The couple then threw up their hands and decided to make it a real splash. They ended by sending out 4,500 invitations.[40]

Practically all official Washington attended the wedding: President and Mrs. Roosevelt, Cabinet members, Supreme Court justices, Congressmen, the diplomatic corps, Army, Navy, and Marine Corps officers.[41]

The ceremony took place in Washington on Thursday, January 26, 1905, at the Church of the Epiphany (Episcopal). Frances' maid of honor was Miss Anne Decker Orr, a Wellesley classmate. John's best man was Charles Magoon. Pershing was in full dress uniform, as were the ten ushers—among them Archie Butt, the White House aide, and Generals William Crozier and William Lassiter.[42]

"Everything went off in first rate fashion," Pershing noted. "Church packed. I saw no one but Dearest Frances. Was not a bit excited but rather weak kneed. . . . I am the happiest man in the whole world and have the dearest, loveliest wife. —The bravest, the truest and the best."[43]

For the honeymoon they headed west—to Chicago first, where Jim
Pershing lived and also Charles Dawes. John's father came up from St.
Louis to see his daughter-in-law and, unknowingly, to say a last goodby
to his son, for he died in less than two months.[44]

On February 7 they arrived at Cheyenne and the Warren's ranch.
"Love Frances more every minute," John confessed. "Ours is destined
to be one of the happiest marriages that ever was. Do not conceive of
anything that is possible to happen to make it otherwise."[45]

At Cheyenne Pershing encountered a little eight-year old girl named
Marcella Tallant in circumstances which she remembered vividly over
fifty years later. Pershing came across her after she had been thrown
from her horse and was being dragged along the hard roadbed with her
foot caught in the stirrup. He rescued her. She was bloody, bruised, and
tearful, but not seriously injured. After satisfying himself of that, he
said, "I'll help you on your horse and you ride home. I'll be following
and keep an eye on you."

"No," she pleaded. "I can't ride him again. I can't. I'm afraid.
There's room in your carriage. Please drive me home. *Please!*"

"No. You'll either ride back, or walk. Come, I'll give you a hand
up."

"I'll walk. I won't ride him." She began to cry.

"Up," said Pershing, lifting her bodily into the saddle. Then he
climbed into his carriage and followed her slowly all the way home. On
arriving, he lifted her down, then held out his hand to say goodby.

"If I hadn't made you ride home you might always be nervous about
horses. It wasn't his fault, you know. He's a fine beast, but you should
not ride him around here alone.

"Now for a word of advice, and don't forget this. If you have a fall
—mental, moral, or physical—pick yourself up and start over again
immediately. If you do, in the long run life won't beat you."[46]

The Pershings took ship for Tokyo on February 15 and Frances
almost immediately became seasick. Pershing's diary for the trip is filled
with expressions of sympathy and affection for her.[47]

A stop at Hawaii enabled Frances to get her feet on solid ground again and to keep some food down. Now the newlyweds had "the time of our lives." In his diary Pershing (always the cavalryman) told of a dance at which Frances, having difficulty keeping her slippers on, "cast a shoe" every now and then.[48]

The sea was calm as they left Hawaii.

"Frances and I hung over the railing all afternoon and on into the evening—watched the twilight come and go. Oh, so sweet and how I love this dear wife of mine. It seems that we must go on for ever passing beautiful landscapes, and, watching the days come and go, be happy, forever. The cool breeze whispers messages of love that are inarticulate and we understand their meaning—messages from the future, here and in the great beyond. They bid us be happy and to be happy we must love with a pure and a whole heart, and to do that we must trust and confide in each other. We must live for each other unselfishly, absolutely devoted to the well-being of each other.

"And oh! another sweet thought came over the waters on this same evening breeze—the voices of sweet childhood, those that are coming to us—to have Frances for their mother and me for their father—so glad were they and so glad it seemed we would some day be when they come. Yes, and the sound of voices long silent came, those we had heard in our own childhood, where we dimly remembered nestling at a dear mother's breast and then wondered, as we wonder tonight, how the great being who directs all things could have planned so well for our happiness. It was this night that of all nights I felt how great was my love for Frances, and how great she is whom I thus love."[49]

It is hard to read the above and still think of Pershing as "the great stone face," all spine and no heart.

8

Promotion and Scandal

The Pershings arrived in Japan on March 5, 1905. Four days later, having entrusted Frances to the friendly care of Mrs. Lloyd Griscom of the American Legation, Pershing headed for the theater of the Russo-Japanese War, then in its last stages.[1]

At Moji, in Southern Japan, he got his first look at Russian soldiers, prisoners of war; they were not at all the large, hulking men he had expected. At Dairen, the principal Japanese base in Manchuria, there was much hustling and noise, but no confusion. "The capacity of the Japanese for organization," Pershing commented, "had brought order out of what would otherwise have been Chinese chaos."[2]

Pershing reached Mukden, Manchuria, scene of a recent Japanese victory, about March 20, 1905. Evidence of the battle was still visible —shattered artillery, broken down transport, ruined homes. Yet the Chinese were already back at work, repairing their hut-like dwellings and clearing their fields for the spring crops.

At Mukden Pershing saw at first hand the supply problem imposed by modern war. Mile after mile was clogged with army carts, taking every bit of space on the road north; anything moving south had to bump across open fields.[3] Thirteen years later the same difficulty would face the A.E.F. in France.

From Mukden Pershing went north to join the First Army of General Kuroki, who commanded the right wing of Japan's advance in Manchuria. Like other military observers he found himself confined mostly to the backwash of the war, stuck among the supply trains and ammunition dumps, and only occasionally permitted to see a skirmish, even at a distance. As one Japanese officer explained: "We are paying for this information with our blood."[4] In exasperation Pershing penned a strong letter to Washington saying that he was not allowed to see anything and might just as well be elsewhere. The censor spotted this, as Pershing intended; the next day he was allowed to join a cavalry regiment at the front.[5]

What he saw impressed him. The Japanese soldiers were tough, eager, and disciplined. Straggling was unknown and they went forward without commands. They were not afraid to die.[6] Because of this, some military observers rated the Japanese infantrymen as the best in the world. Pershing felt differently. "The American is the best soldier—the best material if well trained," he maintained.[7] His contention, reflecting an understandable national pride, was based partly on a certain racism, partly on a vision of future trouble with Japan. "The white race made [a] mistake in permitting the Japanese-Russo War," he wrote in his private notebook in 1905.[8] And, thirty-six years before Pearl Harbor, he speculated: "While today there may not be even a remote intention on the part of Japan to acquire the Philippine Islands, . . . yet there is no telling what in the years to come in Japan's rise to power may be regarded by her . . . *as manifest destiny.*"[9]

The Russo-Japanese War was the first major conflict in the twentieth century which called new weapons into play. When a friend asked if he were learning much, Pershing replied, "A great deal. I'm getting bits here and there, and patching them together. All invaluable if I am ever to command in the field."[10]

He noted, for example, the importance of telephone and telegraph for front-line communications. "No longer is it possible for even Brigade commanders to observe their entire command, much less for Division and Army commanders, and the day for brigadier generals to rush forward in the firing line waving their hats and yelling 'Come on boys' is in actual warfare at least a thing of the past."[11] He noticed too the increased use of artillery—"the most striking change in our time."[12] Machine guns, which were just coming into use, he considered primarily an offensive weapon. He would learn otherwise in the Meuse-Argonne. "Too much reliance in machine guns [is] dangerous," he ventured; "artillery can do about all machine guns can do."[13] Again he was wrong.

The most important lesson Pershing learned in Manchuria, one he was to harp on again and again, was the need for preparedness. "Lack of preparation beforehand," he warned, "cannot be remedied by the publication of long letters of instruction, nor by any other means, within a reasonable time, after war begins."[14]

All his life this lesson went unheeded.

In Manchuria Pershing made new acquaintances. One was Frederick Palmer, a top American war correspondent, who remembered the day he was sitting miserably in a stifling tent listening to rain drumming for hours on the roof. Suddenly the flap opened and Pershing, in a wet slicker, stuck his head inside.

"Come on, I dare you," he challenged. "See me back to quarters. It's no farther for you to go than I have come to see you. I have done half my stretch and will do the other half on my way back to camp, but I prefer not to walk back alone. You'll feel a lot better for it."[15]

Pershing was right; he did feel better. And it was incidents like this which led Palmer to consider Pershing "the most pleasingly human and companionable" of all the people he met in Manchuria. They became good friends and eventually Palmer published a life of Pershing.[16]

Other new contacts were the military observers: Major von Etzel and Captain Max von Hoffmann (German), Major Bela de Dani (Austrian), Colonel Charles Corvisart (French), and Major Enrico Caviglia (Italian). Von Hoffmann was destined to become the most prominent of the four. Pershing said of him: "He is a wild eyed German—Bloody Dutch

—I call him, but a good fellow and apparently a good friend of mine. At any rate I like him. . . ."[17]

Save for the two Germans, everyone got along well. At a banquet Major von Etzel explained that his companion was ill and could not come. The following day Frederick Palmer encountered Hoffmann, who looked quite well, and congratulated him on his quick recovery. "I was never sick," said Hoffmann, and stomped off. Mystified, Palmer asked Pershing to explain.

"You are not up on the social relations of my German colleagues," he answered. "Your invitation went to von Etzel as the senior in rank. So he accepted it for himself. Hoffmann would not have gone, anyway, not with von Etzel or von Etzel with Hoffmann. Can you beat it? The two are living in that little room, sleeping in beds across from each other, and they have not spoken for weeks except when officially necessary. What a life! You'd think they'd have a good 'bawling out' and make up for convenience's sake if not their Emperor's."[18]

When World War I came, the former military observers were pitted against one another. Hoffmann succeeded Ludendorff as Chief of Staff on the Russian front. Dani and Caviglia were on opposite sides for Austria and Italy, respectively. Corvisart commanded a French Corps in August, 1917, in the attack near Verdun; opposite him, commanding a German division, was von Etzel. And Pershing commanded the A.E.F. Of the six military attachés who had good times together in Manchuria, three fought for the Allies, three for the Central Powers.

Pershing was in Manchuria but his heart was back in Japan—with the young bride he had left after less than two months together. He missed her terribly. He remembered her bravery when they said goodbye and he could still see her at the station, waving and calling, "Banzai, Jack."[19]

The first few days away were especially hard. "I am most fearfully lonesome for her and unable to pull myself together. I must come to realize that we are to be separated for some time, but it is going to be the most difficult piece of self-discipline that ever I undertook."[20] Twenty days after leaving Japan he was thinking about returning, partly because of Japanese secretiveness, but partly too because of love-sickness. "I miss her so!" he lamented. "She is making me love her to distraction."[21]

After about six weeks of separation, he wrote in his diary: "No letter from Frances. No answer to telegram. Damned lonesome and more or less unsettled. . . . If she could know tonight how I love her. . . . Her love is the greatest inspiration of my life and all my efforts shall be devoted to her. My life is now hers and I owe everything to her, not only because I have vowed to do this, but because she has given me her love and confidence. . . ."[22]

During a lull in the fighting, Pershing returned to Tokyo for a month. Afterwards, on the first day back in Manchuria, he complained: "I hope this blooming war will soon end. . . . I am just about as forlorn as I can be, and there's nothing to do but work. I am glad for Frances' sake that she has something to do in fixing up the house. . . . What lovely times she and I had together buying things. Only symbolical of a life, a whole life, of such happiness. She is certainly an angel and I love her to very madness."[23]

He was glad, therefore, when the Russo-Japanese War ended and he returned to Tokyo permanently as military attaché at the consulate. Life with Frances was idyllic, especially the summer of 1906, which they spent at the beach at Hayama. In the fall, on September 8, she gave birth to their first child, Helen Elizabeth.[24]

That same month more good fortune came: President Roosevelt named Pershing a brigadier general.[25]

Pershing had jumped 257 captains, 364 majors, 131 lieutenant colonels, and 110 colonels—a total of 862 senior officers! There were only fourteen brigadier generals in the Army and Pershing, yesterday a lowly captain, was now one of them![26] So startling a promotion was bound to cause comment. "Is not the Pershing case," asked the *St. Louis Post-Dispatch*, "an excellent example of promotion by selection—selection in marriage? A social pull, service in Washington, good luck in an adventure of doubtful value, as in Pershing's case, and perhaps 'selection in marriage' these are the steps of the ladder of promotion. Is efficiency to be attained by such gross favoritism?"[27]

Washington scuttlebutt had it that Senator Warren, chairman of the Military Affairs Committee, had hinted that, unless his son-in-law was made a general, Army appropriation bills would have difficulty getting through that year.[28] Continuous talk about "pull" eventually brought Theodore Roosevelt to publish a letter he had written Senator Warren:

"The promotion was made purely on the merits, and unless I am mistaken you never spoke to me on the subject until I had announced that he was to be promoted. . . . To promote a man because he marries a senator's daughter would be an infamy; and to refuse him promotion for the same reason would be an equal infamy."[29]

On December 10, 1906, the Senate confirmed Pershing's appointment. Senator Warren offered to absent himself during the voting, but his colleagues insisted he remain. The confirmation was "without a vestige of objection," according to newspaper accounts.[30]

Was Pershing raised in rank simply on his merits? Certainly he had made a name for himself in the Philippines. Commendations, as we have seen, were being sent to the War Department while he was still there and a definite movement for his promotion was under way before he became Senator Warren's son-in-law and before he even met his future wife.[31]

On July 16, 1903, while Pershing was still in the Orient and five months before he met Frances Warren, Secretary of War Elihu Root penned the following to President Roosevelt concerning the promotion of Thomas H. Barry and Pershing to brigadier general. ". . . Barry ought to be put into the August vacancy, leaving Pershing to be taken up in January when Young goes out. . . . I assume that the same view of Pershing's ability which led Davis and Sumner to put him into the Mindanao situation, to the exclusion of old officers who ranked him, will lead them to recommend him. . . . I find Barry to be considerably older than Pershing, . . . and while I am strongly in favor of the promotion of Pershing, I do not think he is entitled to go ahead of Barry."[32]

By 1906, with one exception, every general in the Army had recommended Pershing for promotion to brigadier general.[33] Nor was such a jump unprecedented. Albert L. Mills, Leonard Wood, and J. Franklin

Bell had all jumped from captain to brigadier general, the last over 1031 seniors.[34]

Theodore Roosevelt once told Frederick Palmer that there were two outstanding men in the Army, Leonard Wood and John J. Pershing, and "by George" (T. R.'s words) he intended to see their abilities used.[35] If Palmer is to be believed, Roosevelt had intended to promote Pershing all along—to a lesser grade if he could get the promotion system changed, but, if not, then to brigadier general. Senator Warren was important, not for getting Pershing promoted, but for seeing that the promotion went through.[36]

In 1916, when Pershing's next promotion came to major general, he wrote Senator Warren that he was glad the latter had absolutely nothing to do with it. Said Pershing: "I think that the question of my first promotion [1906] is well understood and believe that everybody today has all the facts in the case, which are that Roosevelt made the appointment on his own initiative and on his own responsibility."[37]

The Senator replied that he was glad that the new promotion came at the hands of a Democratic President and at a time when he and other Pershing friends were out of Washington "because this puts the 'kibosh' on all of the talk heretofore indulged in regarding your former promotion—i.e., that it was all on account of your father-in-law being in the Senate and at the head of the Military Affairs Committee."[38]

Perhaps the key words in the previous quotation are "all on account." Having a Senator for a father-in-law did no harm. Even taking Pershing's merits into account, his family connection weighed in the balance, causing him to receive promotion in 1906 rather than later. Pershing later admitted as much. As an old man in Walter Reed hospital his sister came across a newspaper item alleging that he had been promoted because of the Senator's influence. She read it; then expressed indignation that anyone should say such a thing.

"Well, it's true, isn't it?" Pershing answered.[39]

Hard on the news of Pershing's sensational rise to brigadier general came assertions that he had been involved in scandal. On December 18, 1906, the *Manila American* published a story it claimed to have investigated and verified: Pershing, while stationed in the Philippines, had lived with a Filipino woman, Joaquina Ygnacio, and had had two children by her. One died in the cholera epidemic of 1902. The other, Petronilla, now four-and-one-half years old, lived with her mother at Zamboanga.

According to the newspaper, Pershing commenced relations with Joaquina, one of four attractive sisters who ran a canteen, in 1900, when he erected a cottage in Zamboanga in which they lived almost openly. Petronilla was born July 11, 1902. The woman's present husband, a Mr. Shinn, reported that a Pershing emissary approached Joaquina in the spring of 1906, offering fifty dollars "hush money." She refused, saying that Pershing had always been kind to her and that she would not expose him.

Certain Army officers, the newspaper continued, had communicated the facts to some U.S. Senators, hoping to delay confirmation of Pershing's appointment as brigadier. Further charges against him would be forwarded to the United States. Col. Jasper Morrison, Capt. Thomas Swobe, Capt. Sidney Cloman, and others knew details and their names would be used against Pershing.

Thus said the *Manila American*.[40]

This story did not take the War Department unawares. In March, 1906, the White House received an anonymous letter suggesting an investigation of Pershing's private life before promoting him since, it said, he had lived almost openly with a native woman and fathered several children.[41] Secretary of War Taft then questioned Gen. George W. Davis, one of Pershing's old commanders, about the matter. Davis responded that he had had little contact with Pershing in the Philippines, since the latter was just leaving to take command of Iligan when he arrived. Still, he added, if there had been any rumors or suspicions he would have heard them. He hadn't. "I heard nothing . . . that could justify anyone to cast a stone."

This response pleased Taft and a short time later he told Davis that Pershing's appointment as brigadier had definitely been decided on.[42]

Nevertheless the charge kept cropping up. Oswald Garrison Villard, editor of the *New York Evening Post*, sent Taft a letter from one C. H.

Clark which repeated the story about the two half-breed children. "Does this come in under the order of the Square Deal?" he asked.

Villard declared that his own brother-in-law, Capt. C. M. Sandford, had actually seen the woman involved. "Captain Sandford says I may tell you that he not only saw the woman but a child, and that the woman declared in the presence of himself and three other persons in the government service that Pershing was the father of the child. Pershing's picture was in her possession at the time—on her bureau."

An officer of the 23rd Infantry confirmed Captain Sandford's statement, said Villard. Others reported that enlisted men hung woolen socks on Pershing's tent for his "cold feet" during an expedition. The editor concluded: "The intense bitterness over Pershing's promotion, in the service, surpassing that against Wood and Mills combined, with Funston thrown in, . . . makes me feel that the charges will yet be aired. . . . I call them to your attention, confident that you would not for a moment wish a general of this kind . . . on the roll of the army."[43]

The charges were indeed aired. After December 18, 1906, when the *Manila American* published them, they were widely circulated in reprints in American papers. The *New York Evening Post* ran its own version, based on an unnamed source, on December 20. Secretary Taft sent Pershing a sample newspaper requesting an answer.[44] Rumors flew around Washington that Mrs. Pershing was thinking of a divorce.[45]

Actually she was thinking no such thing. On first hearing rumors of the accusation, she wrote her husband, who happened to be away at the time: "Dear baby of mine, why must I be away from you now when you most need to put your head on my shoulder and feel my arms around you? Dear Husband, you will know, of course, where I stand, won't you? I love you wholly, devotedly, with all my strength, for always and always and always. You will know that my love is the same whether it is true or not—only that if they should be able to substantiate their charges against you, I would love you more than ever because your need of me would be greater. Oh, Husband, I love you until I am mad with love. Oh! I want you so! I want to take you on my breast and hold you—and love you, and love you, and love you!"[46]

Meanwhile, the *Washington Herald* reported that no Senator could be found who had received letters against Pershing, as the *Manila American* had suggested. Col. Jasper Morrison, one of the alleged witnesses, had been dead four years and two other witnesses, Capt. Sidney Cloman and Capt. Thomas Swobe, issued public denials.[47]

"For two years," said Swobe, "I was the constant daily almost hourly companion of Pershing at Zamboanga Mindanao. . . . We messed at the same table, our rooms were in the same building and very close to each other. We walked together, rode together—drank from the same bottle, and I know Pershing as well as any man living knows him. And no more honorable upright, manly and soldierly man than Pershing ever wore Soldier [*sic*] straps. And I stand ready to defend him against any charge his enemies may bring, and if necessary am ready and willing to go to Washington and appear before the Senate committee for that purpose."[48]

Swobe attributed the attack on Pershing to "those who are jealous of his rapid rise in army circles, and their desire to prevent his confirmation."[49]

Pershing denied the charges, not only publicly but—what is more significant—in confidential letters to his friends. One such, Guy H. Preston, had doubts. When Pershing cleared them up, Preston confessed himself relieved:

"I am frank to say I had not been sure that you would repudiate the matter and in terms that can leave no doubt in my mind as to the character of the libel. You know the course of our lives in the old days was such as to suggest the possibility that the statements rife might have some foundation in truth. It was simply a case of the pot and the kettle, the one not recognizing that the other might not be black, you see. . . . I am now assured, and while my letter must have troubled your mind greatly, your own, in denial, places mine in perfect ease regarding the outcome."[50]

Pershing had returned to the Philippines, meanwhile, and gathered material in his defense. On February 2, 1907, he sent Secretary of War Taft several affidavits, with a covering letter stating he was "very glad to have the opportunity of . . . presenting to you proof of the falsity of these reports."[51]

The key affidavit was by Joaquina B. Ygnacio, dated January 18, 1907:

"It has recently come to my knowledge that one John J. Pershing, formerly residing at Zamboanga, is alleged to have lived with me openly and that I was his mistress, and that the said John J. Pershing constructed a house in the said town of Zamboanga, and otherwise provided for my support and keeping, and, furthermore, that the said John J. Pershing is alleged to be the father of two children by me. I do hereby solemnly swear that each and every one of the above allegations is wholly untrue and false in each and every respect."

Another affidavit, dated the same day, was by the woman's husband, Zellar H. Shinn. He swore "that any and all statements printed in the *Manila American* of Tuesday, December the eighteenth, 1906, purporting to have been made by me relative to one John J. Pershing are false, malicious, and wholly devoid of truth in each and every particular, and that such statements so purporting to have been made by me relative to the said John J. Pershing were never made by me in whole or in part to any representative of the *Manila American*, or to any one else at any time or in any place."[52]

With the affidavits went an endorsement by Gen. Leonard Wood, commanding the Division of the Philippines: "The . . . declarations of the woman and her husband establish in my opinion the falsity of the charges published against Gen. Pershing and should end the matter."[53]

Undoubtedly it should have. But such charges, once started, do not easily die. In 1912, when Pershing was rumored as the next superintendent of West Point, they were resurrected and used against the appointment.[54]

A year after that Pershing commissioned an attorney, James Ross, to clear him once and for all. Ross arrived in New York in June, 1913, with a bundle of affidavits by Frank P. Helm, Richard M. Corwine, William T. Page, Ira L. Frendendall, Thomas Garley, Henry Rodgers, C. F. Bader, and others—all testifying to Pershing's innocence.[55]

Summing up the evidence, one must conclude that the charges involving him with Joaquina Ygnacio, triggered by his sensational advancement to brigadier, must stand as "not proved." Pershing and his friends attributed them to "certain featherbrained soreheads."[56]

Meanwhile new work awaited him, new challenges, to test whether he was worthy of the bright new silver star that shone on his shoulder.

9

Fort William McKinley

Pershing's new assignment was command of Fort William McKinley, located outside Manila. It comprised two regiments of infantry (a brigade), two squadrons of cavalry (two-thirds of a regiment), a battery of field artillery, a company of engineers, and a medical unit. The whole outfit was known as a "reinforced brigade" and was the only one in the Army at the time. It was also the largest concentration of troops outside the United States. Pershing commanded it from January, 1907 to July, 1908.[1]

He was glad to be back in the Philippines and especially at McKinley, for he hoped to put in practice his ideas on training troops in large units. For years the Army personnel had been scattered in isolated posts along the American frontier, or in the Philippines as protection against small marauding bands. Parceled out in driblets—in companies, or at most in a regiment—they had no experience in large commands such as would be necessary in modern war. World War I was less than a decade off, yet "so backward was our preparation," said Pershing, "that we were just beginning to have field training of a brigade as such for the first time."[2]

When one considers that a brigade was only half a division, and that in World War I Pershing would have to create, train, and command not only divisions, but whole corps and armies, one has some idea of the magnitude of the task he later accomplished in rush-order fashion. The seeds of success were planted at Fort McKinley, where he pioneered in troop maneuvers on a comparatively large scale.[3]

"It was amazing to find how many officers and non-commissioned officers there were," he said, "with little conception of their duties and responsibilities in the conduct of actual operations."[4] To remedy this he turned the troops loose on maneuvers. He insisted that the men know how to make long marches, live in the field, draw maps, follow trails, reconnoiter, and attack positions. He also gave attention to the problem of combined command (infantry, cavalry, artillery) and to simulated problems of defense.[5]

During one of these maneuvers he had an opportunity to show his leadership. Heavy rains had swollen a river across which an attack was to be made. Pershing told a young lieutenant in the Corps of Engineers to construct a bridge so the troops could cross. After a time the lieutenant returned, saying he couldn't execute the order because the water was so high he couldn't get the first rope across.

"I never ask the impossible of any officer or soldier of my command," said Pershing. "When you get an order you must find a way to execute it. Now come with me."

He rode rapidly to the river. The water was indeed high. But Pershing fastened a rope to his saddle, spurred his horse into the waters, and in a few minutes was across. Shortly afterwards the bridge was under way.[6]

The rainy season at McKinley lasted from mid-June to mid-November. During this time, when outdoor activity was curtailed, Pershing inaugurated a system of schools for both officers and men. The former had the regular garrison schools prescribed by the War Department, plus advanced courses in map exercises and in recent wars as prescribed by Pershing. The enlisted men had instructions in scouting, rifle and revolver firing, riding, swimming, gymnastics, as well as schools for mule-packing, bread-baking, carpentry, blacksmithing, horse-shoeing, clerical work, and typing.[7] Pershing was "an early advocate of army schools," said one of his former classmates, "and was among the first to establish schools for the instruction of officers and men of his own command."[8]

So enthusiastic was Pershing that on October 9, 1907, he wrote his superiors about the exceptional advantages offered by McKinley for training troops, especially the combined arms. He proposed "to make this post a brigade and school of practical application for the Island and to give regiments a year's tour of duty here. The regiments selected should be sent here about June 15th each year. They could then all start at once and carry through an established course of theoretical and practical training, ending in say a month's brigade maneuvers."[9]

Maj. Gen. Leonard Wood, commanding the Philippines Division, disapproved.

"The question of changing the garrison each year, with a view of affording brigade instruction to a large number of regiments and other units, is one that must be governed largely by the military demands of the time [i.e., 1907]. . . . It involves too frequent moves and imposes too great hardships."[10]

Perhaps true, but Wood did not properly read the future. The immediate problem in 1907 was maintaining American authority against isolated groups of Filipinos and Moros, an assignment for which companies or regiments sufficed. But within a decade America would have to fight a war against a highly industrialized, thoroughly trained foe whose force numbered in the millions. Pershing would face the overwhelming task of training troops almost under fire.

He liked life at McKinley. With a good Officers' Club and a large contingent of officers, it furnished a social world all its own. Pershing made it a point, however, to avoid concentrating on Army friendships. "We Army people tend to stick together too much and become clannish," he said. "It's good to know civilians. It helps them appreciate what the Army is like and it's good for us to know what they're like."[11]

When Pershing came to McKinley, Col. Henry P. Kingsbury was in charge. He had graduated from the Military Academy fifteen years before Pershing, and had been a captain in the 6th Cavalry when the latter joined it as an inexperienced second lieutenant. Now Pershing outranked Kingsbury and was superseding him in command. There were grounds for ill feeling.

Kingsbury's phone rang one day. A voice said, "How are you, Colonel?"

Kingsbury recognized it immediately.

"I'm all right, General. How are you?"

"May I come over and see you?" (Army etiquette requires that the subordinate officer shall make the first call on his superior.)

"I'd be highly honored if you did, sir."

When Pershing arrived they had a long, pleasant talk about old times in the 6th Cavalry. It didn't make being outranked any easier for Kingsbury, but it helped to soften the blow.[12]

Yet Pershing felt acutely the awkwardness of his situation. An Army wife said of him, "He was very nervous and ill at ease in the company of colonels, lieutenant colonels, and majors who were senior to him and whom he had passed over. Outside of their company, however, he was relaxed and comfortable."[13]

At McKinley Pershing had a good reputation with the enlisted men. "There was absolutely no high hatting in or about General Pershing," recalled one. "He was not comfortably settled in his quarters before he began lightening our duties, such as reducing the number of sentries for guard duty, eliminating a great deal of fatigue by substituting civilian labor, visiting our mess rooms, and improving our food, improving sanitary conditions, tearing up summary court charges of trivial offenses made by some over-zealous younger lieutenant just out of the Point, and all other conditions necessary to encourage members of his command to be clean, healthful soldiers.

"[I recall] one incident when a forced march was ordered. General Pershing invariably inspected all animals and equipment before the march was undertaken and during such inspection took notice of the worn out and rusty condition of my canteen. I was asked by the general why I was using this canteen. I replied that the supply sergeant declined to issue me a new one. He immediately called the supply sergeant and warned him in the future to be more careful of the equipment he issued and incidentally delayed the march some fifteen minutes until a replacement was made."[14]

As the largest American post in the Philippines, Fort McKinley was a showplace for visiting dignitaries. One of the most outstanding was Secretary of War William Howard Taft, who came in October, 1907, to open the new Philippine Assembly. Pershing planned a magnificent dinner in his guest's honor, but found he had a problem. "My valet forgot to pack my waistcoat," announced Taft; "do you have one here I can borrow?"

Pershing scurried about trying to find a waistcoat which would fit Taft's 300 pounds. Anything he found was too small and no amount of stretching made any difference. Finally Pershing borrowed a waistcoat, split it up the back, and gave it to Taft, who wore it pinned to his shirt front.[15]

The centerpiece at the dinner that night was a floral model of the White House so arranged that the front door faced directly opposite Taft. The Secretary remarked that his entrance was "a long way off."[16] Pershing judged otherwise, and wrote to a friend:

"Mr. Taft is received on all hands as the probable candidate for President and is making friends where before he had enemies. I hear nothing but praise for him and his broad-minded views, and feel that the impression that he has made here will, in a large measure, influence his campaign at home."[17]

Pershing's only extended absence during his command of Fort McKinley was from October to December, 1907, when he went to observe Japanese military maneuvers. He found them highly interesting, but saw little new to record except an increased use of artillery and machine guns. His observations, duly reported, made no impact at home. At the start of the First World War, the United States had not even adopted a machine gun.[18]

Japan's army impressed Pershing[19] and in the final paragraph of his report he suggested that its very large size revealed "the magnitude of the Japanese ambitions."[20] Their ambitions, he well knew, extended to the Philippines. One day at Fort McKinley he received a phone call from Capt. Martin Crimmins who had noticed two men dressed as Filipino laborers walking around with heads down as if saying their prayers. Crimmins judged they were counting their steps and measuring distances. He took them into custody and under questioning discovered they were Japanese naval officers in disguise. When Crimmins telephoned for instructions, Pershing asked if the prisoners were carrying surveying instruments; if not, they must be released, since people had a right to walk around the fort. It turned out they had none and therefore went free. But the incident was not lost on Pershing.[21]

On July 31, 1908, Pershing's tour of duty at Fort McKinley ended and he prepared to return to the United States. He and Frances routed themselves through Russia and Europe for sight-seeing.

Making a quick calculation of the necessary funds, Pershing took only that amount for the trip. Like many travelers, he found costs greater than expected. Tips ran up, an extra berth cost sixty-seven rubles, and charges for extra baggage ran ninety more. As the train pulled out of Vladivostok, Pershing counted the money he had left for the 3,000 mile trip to Moscow. Exactly two rubles! "I am sure my wife thought me hopeless," he confessed.[22]

The trip was memorable for two "battles." The first was over baggage, which they had in abundance because it was cheaper to carry than to ship. It consisted of three large-size containers, three smaller ones, three suitcases, one carpetbag, two handbags, one basket full of books ("heavy as lead"), one roll of rugs, one basket full of bottles, and several umbrellas—not to mention various souvenirs such as ikons, tea urns, etc. Frances described the porters' reaction when they saw the aggregation:

"Everywhere the heathen rage, Porters gesticulate wildly, point to our baggage, wave their arms in despair & pour out torrents of Russian. But Jack, with a fierce mien, pours out an even more voluble torrent of English mixed with Spanish & Japanese for the words he really wishes them to understand (it being his invariable habit to shout 'Abandi' to a cochero and 'Cuidado' to a rickishawman & a mixture of both to one of any other nationality. His voice gradually drowns them out, & they retire sadly & leave him victorious on the field of battle."[23]

The other struggle concerned accomodations. Frances recalled later: "We had bought 1st class tickets expecially for the use of the washrooms which they assured us we had. When we arrived on the car we were enraged to find no washrooms, &, as we suspect, second class accommodation. The conductor had 1st class compartment with toilet room. We insisted on having that instead, sat ourselves down in the room, & told him 'Hier willen wir bleiben.' I expostulated with him some time in German with no effect. But when Jack got into the game with some vigourous English punctuated with gestures of ejection for the porter and immobile fixity for ourselves, he caved and gave us two apartments—*both* with washrooms!"[24]

In Berlin the American military attaché took Pershing to the German War Office where he found, as expected, "every sign of smartness and efficiency." Later he visited an artillery regiment at Potsdam and listened while its colonel explained arrangements made for rapid mobilization. "I had never seen such perfect preparation," he said.[25]

The Germans made a strong impression, all in all. "The discipline of the German people was evident at every turn. All things seemed to be done in military fashion. The army, so to speak, was the nation. This was especially noticeable to one who had just come from Russia. There the army seemed a thing apart from the people; here it was a model which they were proud to emulate. In Russia there were murmurings of discontent and there had recently been a revolutionary outbreak which had included a mutiny in the Black Sea fleet; here the people were proud of their Kaiser, confident in his administration and apparently glad to perform what they believed to be his will. The men who ran the railroads and those who cleaned the streets went about the duties exactly as if under military direction."[26]

Leaving Berlin, the Pershings went to Belgium so that John could see Waterloo, then to Paris which they found in the grip of a war scare because of Austria-Hungary's annexation of Bosnia-Herzegovina. The War Department cabled Pershing to mark time in Europe. "In case any actual hostilities ensue in the Balkan situation you will be designated by the War Department as a military observer. . . ."[27]

While waiting at Tours, Pershing took a course in French which would come in handy nine years later. During his stay he met Wilbur Wright, the pioneer aviator, who was giving flying lessons to French officers. The airplane was still so primitive that it took off by catapulting down an inclined plane, but Wright already predicted great importance for it in future wars. There is no evidence that Pershing was so prescient. Certainly the U.S. War Department was not, for as late as 1916 it had only thirteen planes in commission, eight of which were used up in the first months of the Punitive Expedition into Mexico.[28]

When the Balkan kettle simmered down Pershing returned to America. He served for a while in the office of the Chief of Staff in Washington, but his heart was back in the Philippines, in the Moro Province which he hoped to command. Orders had, in fact, already been drawn up directing him there.[29]

Before he could leave, a health problem arose. He had been five years in the enervating tropics, during which he had developed a heart palpitation. This proved to be nothing serious and a rest and treatment at the Army-Navy Hospital at Hot Springs, Arkansas, quickly restored his health.[30] It did, however, change Pershing's habits with tobacco. Previously he had smoked, but when he suspected heart trouble he swore off and took up chewing, using a wad of cigar or a regular plug. He kept the "chaw" habit throughout later life, using as a spittoon whatever potted plant happened to be handy in his office. "Some of those plants looked pretty sick when the General got done spitting on them," a secretary remembered.[31]

Meanwhile, Pershing's family was growing. Anne, his second daughter, had been born at Baguio in the Philippines in March, 1908. In June, 1909, Frances gave birth to a boy at Cheyenne, whom they named Francis Warren Pershing in honor of the Senator.[32]

When Pershing sailed for the Philippines in the fall of 1909 he was a considerably different man than when he had left the islands in 1903. Something new had come into his life—Frances. For forty-five years he had lived as a bachelor, despite an interest in women which gained him the reputation of being a "ladies' man." Most women found him attractive. Frances Warren's initial thought on their first meeting was that he was the strongest, most vital man she had ever seen, and that she could trust him until death.[33]

Marriage seems never to have seriously entered his mind until he met Frances. Given American sexual practices in the Philippines around the turn of the century, he may well have fathered some native children, as Guy Preston thought,[34] although he did quite well in clearing himself of the 1906 charge that he openly kept a mistress. Yet whatever Pershing's habits may have been as a single man and a widower, he was a faithful husband.

It is significant that he married a woman utterly unlike him in temperament. Adjectives which people used to describe Frances—joyous, bright, gay, friendly, sunny[35]—would never come to mind in describing her husband. He was not morose, but years of Army command had left him reserved. Frances complemented her husband, filling his life with qualities he lacked and serving as the perfect counterpoise for the man whom Dorothy Canfield Fisher once described as a "rather stiff West Pointer."[36] She brought out a side of Pershing that few people knew he had: his tenderness. "And oh! another sweet thought came over the waters on this same evening breeze—the voices of sweet childhood, those that are coming to us—to have Frances for their mother and me for their father. . . ."[37] Those were his own words, and they expressed a different Pershing from the conqueror of Moros.

This woman, by no means physically stunning or overpoweringly beautiful,[38] could move him deeply. "Frank, I am not going to stay in the service away from you," he exploded once. "Damn the service. Damn everything, and everybody that takes from me or ever has taken from me one minute of your time or one thought of your mind. I'm sick of it and just want you."[39] And again, "Oh, Frances, I need you every moment. I cannot live without you. And I shall not try. It is only a half a life. It's so incomplete, so aimless."[40]

His wife was good for Pershing. She loosened him up. People described her as "a complete extrovert"[41]—something they would never say about Pershing. "Nothing ever bothered her in any way, no matter what," said an acquaintance. "She was not at all punctilious about the things the General made much of."[42]

Pershing had been punctilious about time; in this respect Frances loosened him up too much, so that in later years he became oblivious of it. At Fort McKinley, the Pershings were perennially late for social functions.[43] The General would pace up and down the veranda balcony outside his quarters, dressed and ready to go, stopping periodically to ask, "Frances, are you ready? Frances, are you dressed yet?"[44]

Pershing had left the Philippines a captain; he returned a general, his ambition realized. Those whom he had admonished to look out for his interests with Theodore Roosevelt—"Jog his memory a little 'lest we forget!' "[45]—had done their work well. Still, many people had hard feelings about his sudden rise, and long memories.[46] Friends of Pershing, although glad of his success, felt it fostered a bad precedent. Skyrocketing a captain to a general was a "damn bad principle." Said one of them: "If the Colonels of the U.S. Army are not fit to be Brigadier Generals, then they should all be fired out in some way and other men promoted colonels, from among whom a Brigadier General can be selected."[47]

Pershing returned to the Philippines in 1909 a better soldier than he had left it in 1903. His horizons had been broadened. His professional training had been furthered. Assignment on the General Staff in Washington, attendance at the Army War College, duty in Manchuria during the Russo-Japanese War, service as military attaché in Japan, command of the largest foreign troop concentration at McKinley, travel across Asia, observation of the German war machine, contact with men like Arthur MacArthur, Theodore Roosevelt, George W. Goethals, Senator Warren, Max von Hoffmann, Leonard Wood, William Howard Taft, Wilbur Wright—it all added up to quite an education for the shy farm boy from Laclede, Missouri.

Pershing was a professional soldier with the pride of his profession. He had been a good field officer, now he sought to be a good general. He maintained the same solicitude for the enlisted man that he had as a junior captain. At Fort McKinley he stressed active field maneuvers

—something not always emphasized by "stay-at-home" commanders. He pioneered in the use of Army schools. And he had no false modesty. Later he wrote to Maj. Gen. Leonard Wood, who had been his superior in the Philippines and who was then Army Chief of Staff: "You are entirely familiar with how the Brigade post and the Brigade were managed by me at McKinley and how well trained it was."[48]

10

Governor of the Moro Province

On November 11—a date which would have additional significance for him and many Americans nine years later—Pershing began his new duties. The Governorship of the Moro Province was, strictly speaking, a civilian position, but, because of the presence of the Army and the lack of capable civilians, the policy since the founding of the Province in 1903 had been to appoint Army generals who served in both military and civil capacities. Pershing, ruling from 1909 to 1913, would be the last military governor.[1]

The Moro Province embraced the islands of Mindanao and Jolo and was divided into five districts: Zamboanga, Sulu, Davao, Cotabato, and Lanao. The population numbered approximately 520,000 of whom about 325,000 were Moros (Mohammedan), 85,000 Filipinos (Christian), and 105,000 wild tribes (pagan). Province headquarters was at Zamboanga, a city of 20,000 on the south-western coast of Mindanao. Here in his dual role as civil governor and military commmander, Pershing had two offices entirely independent and located in separate buildings. He usually spent mornings in one and afternoons in the other.[2]

Surveying the work done since he had left Mindanao in 1903, Pershing was critical. "It does not seem to me that we have made much impression on the native mind," he told the new Governor-General of the Philippines, William Cameron Forbes. "I do not believe that we get out among these people enough. We have been sticking too close to the coast and to the military posts. We must branch out and let all the people of the Moro Province know there is a government which is looking after them and which proposes and intends to encourage and protect them."[3]

To do this, Pershing stationed members of his troop companies, especially the Philippine Scouts who were native soldiers under American officers, in small detachments in areas previously unreached by the government. He believed that crime and lawlessness would decrease where soldiers lived, and that law-abiding people, hesitating to farm because marauders plundered their crops, would settle nearby. "No influence can ever reach these people except the influence that comes by direct contact," he told Maj. Gen. J. Franklin Bell, the supreme U. S. commander in the Philippines, "and the only means of obtaining direct contact is by sending among them, for longer or shorter periods, detachments of troops stationed in their vicinity."[4]

That Pershing was correct was borne out in time; by their mere presence, troops did reduce crime and promote agriculture and trade. But the splitting of companies into minuscule detachments did not make for military efficiency or advance troop training—a fact which General Bell soon noted. He confessed some impatience at Pershing's scattershot methods. But when the latter explained his aims and showed good results, Bell changed his mind. "I saw that he [Pershing] had . . . good reasons in every case," he told the Army Chief of Staff, Maj. Gen. Leonard Wood. The question was whether they wanted to emphasize the military training of the Philippine Scouts or their civilizing influence. Bell concurred in Pershing's choice of the latter.[5]

Another point which Pershing criticized on his return was abuse of the natives. Six weeks after assuming command he complained to Forbes that white planters in most cases were not dealing fairly with their workers. They expected a man to work from eight to ten hours a day for fifty cents, and then to take out his pay in trade at the owner's store which made up to 100 percent profit.[6]

The military, too, had abused their authority. Where patience and forebearance would have brought results, they had imposed their will forcibly, even violently, thus alienating the people and their chiefs. When one of the Philippine Constabulary, hiding under the cloak of authority, killed a man against whom he had a personal grudge, Pershing commented, "Such acts . . . set us back many years, and after a wholesale killing of that sort, it is very difficult to make the Moros think we are at all friendly with them."[7]

In the Lanao district, especially significant to him because of his earlier work there, Pershing was "not at all satisfied" with the military's conduct. "There has been entirely too free a hand given to young officers of both the Army and the Constabulary," he informed Forbes, "and as a result I am prone to believe a great many innocent people have lost their lives. It is a case of very bad management. I met all of my Moro friends and spent an entire forenoon talking with them, and it was more or less pathetic to hear their recital of events during the last six years."[8]

He laid down as a guiding principle during his administration, therefore, respect for Moro feelings. Frank Lanckton, Pershing's orderly for twenty years, later noted that Pershing always took pains to observe the little courtesies which Moros thought important. "It never made much difference . . . ," said Lanckton, "whether he was talking to a half-naked semi-civilized Moro chieftain or to the King of England. He was always courteous and polite. He has a way of making anyone certain of his good will. It is not so much what he says, because he does not talk very much, but his ability to say the right thing at the right time and in the right way."[9]

Early in his administration, Pershing visited all five districts of the Province, assembling native leaders and listening to their complaints. Some of these were merely personal (the Sultan of Jolo spoke about his wives' infidelity), but many were well founded and concerned everyone.[10] At such assemblies Pershing repeatedly assured Moros of his friendship. "I wish to impress upon the Moros here," he said at a meeting at Marahui, "that this country is the country of the Moros; that they are a strong race of people, in fact, the strongest race that I have seen in the Island. . . . Again I wish to state that this is not the country of the Americans, but is the country of you Moros, and we are not going to bring here Americans to push you out."

At the Marahui meeting he encouraged the natives to build roads, attend schools, and learn English. To bring more land under cultivation, he urged them to have lots of children. "It is true that some of my old friends are a little too old to do much along this line, but they should give this advice to the younger men," Pershing said with a smile.

He also spoke a word of warning. Moros practiced sacopy, a form of indentured servitude in which a datto furnished support and protection while the sacopy furnished labor in return. Pershing was willing to recognize sacopy if it was voluntary; he would not permit slavery.

On the touchy subject of religion Pershing took a bold stand, attempting to end the perennial Moro fear that the government would force them to become Christians. "I believe that the Moros should live according to the teachings of the Koran," he said, "because I think that the Koran is the best book that they can follow." He promised to donate government land for Mohammedan houses of worship and reminded them that he had personally given a copy of the Koran to one of their leaders in 1903. When they had made him an honorary datto that year, he had sworn friendship on the Koran.[11]

At such conferences Pershing's personal bearing, perhaps more than his words, made a favorable impression. His whole manner seemed to say, "We are friends, I trust you. Look, I place myself into your hands."

Frank Lanckton, his orderly, gave an example of this. The General on one occasion informed him that a conference was scheduled with a Moro datto; he and Lanckton would be the only ones to attend. "Don't take any arms," Pershing ordered.

Lanckton, a prudent man, procured a revolver and stuffed it in his pants, concealing it with his shirt. After they had started along the trail to the Moro village, Pershing suddenly stopped.

"Lanckton, what have you got under your shirt?"

As he spoke he tugged at the shirt. Out fell the gun.

"Throw it away," Pershing commanded. "A soldier's word counts for more than his gun."

Lanckton obeyed, but he confessed that he spent the rest of the morning in constant fear, with every ripple of the waves or rustling of the leaves raising the hairs on his head. And Pershing's reaction? "The Old Man moved along as if he were taking in the morning air at the Presidio of San Francisco."

The sight of two unarmed Americans made quite an impression on the datto when they reached him. Pershing had spread it far and wide that he was the Moros' friend and friends had no need to be armed. —Here then was a man who practiced what he preached.[12]

In Lanckton's recollection Pershing never showed any fear of Moros. The only time in twenty years that he could recall apprehension in Pershing's voice came not with Moros but with his own men. It was while Pershing was commanding a detachment sent out to run down six juramentados (Moros who had taken an oath to kill Christians). Some new recruits, detailed as sentries, saw Moros everywhere—in bushes swaying in the wind, in animals prowling in the dark. Throughout the night they kept calling for the corporal of the guard and it was not long until the whole camp was on edge. Particularly near Pershing's tent were they diligent in detecting figures or noises—being more alert to notice them there. Inside Pershing tossed fitfully, a nervous "Corporal of the guard!" interrupting his slumber whenever he started to doze off. Finally he called Lanckton.

"Get those damned sentries away from my tent! One of them is liable to shoot before the corporal of the guard arrives, and there's no telling what would happen. I'll take my chances with the Moros. "[13]

Once renegade Moros were captured, they stood trial; here Pershing introduced a reform in the Province legal system. The old practice was to try Moros in a Court of First Instance, an Insular court which convened every six months. Appeal lay to the Supreme Court in Manila, which often took a year to decide a case. Hence between the time of a crime and the ultimate decision there was a long delay— several months before the trial and a year on appeal.

There was added confusion too, because even before the case came to the Court of First Instance a preliminary investigation was held in the ward courts. To the Moros this investigation looked like a real trial; they could not understand why no prompt decision was given. In Pershing's words, "They are game and are ready to take what is coming, but they are impatient at delay."[14]

To remedy this situation Pershing put through a law enlarging the jurisdiction of the local ward courts, which were presided over by the district governors and secretaries. Henceforth the ward court became a real trial court, capable of handling all criminal cases except death penalty offenses and most of the civil cases likely to occur. Appeal was to the Court of First Instance whose decision, in both criminal and civil cases, was final.

This form of justice appealed to the Moro. It was quick and simple; he knew where he stood. It also accorded more with his own legal traditions, in which executive and judicial powers were not separated but united in one man—formerly the sultan or datto, now the district governor or secretary. These latter liked the change because it enhanced their prestige among the Moros. Even the judges of the Court of First Instance approved it, for they knew little of Moro customs and had no time to learn. All in all the change was a good example of adapting Western legal customs to Moro traditions, instead of compelling the natives to adopt practices foreign to them.[15]

Another example of adaptation was the labor contract law, passed in 1912. Henceforth failure to fulfill a contract on the part of worker or employer was not punishable unless it could be shown that it sought to defraud or injure. This avoided much legal complication. One could not sue for a simple breach of contract (often a Moro's failure to show up for work meant nothing more than that he felt like sleeping that day), but only a breach resulting from maliciousness.[16]

Coupled with legal reform was prison reform. During Pershing's administration the Province obtained San Ramon, a 2,500 acre farm located thirteen miles northwest of Zamboanga. The provincial prison was established there and became an experiment station combining both farm and prison work. The idea was to teach men useful occupations and at the same time make the prison self-supporting through their labor. In 1911 the seventy prisoners cleared the land, helped build the prison structure, and planted nearly 75,000 coconut trees which were said to constitute the best coconut grove in the islands. By the time the trees became productive in 1922, San Ramon was self-supporting and maintained about 700 prisoners without cost to the government.[17]

In its rehabilitative work the prison taught all kinds of farming, the care of stock, and other industries useful to the inmates after their release. The authorities appealed strongly to the prisoners' self-respect, encouraging them to become "trusties," who gave their word of honor not to run off and who were allowed to go about without a guard. They lived in their own cottages outside the prison and were usually given work near their quarters. In 1913 Pershing reported that about one-sixth of the prisoners had become trusties, many of them serving life sentences. In very few cases had they betrayed their word; occasionally they even apprehended and returned escaped prisoners.[18]

During Pershing's four years as governor the Province constructed 200 miles of telephone lines and 500 of roads. The latter were especially appreciated by the Moros, who depended on them to get their products to market. Often, in fact, when the government initiated a road project, Moros gave hundreds of days of free labor to complete it. Once Pershing asked a datto from the back country what he considered the most wonderful thing he had seen. "The fine road the Americans have built from Lanao to Iligan," was the response.[19]

Another public service much appreciated by Moros was medical care. By 1913 some thirty-seven dispensaries were established, distributing medicines at cost to indigent persons and at a nominal fee to others. Even hostile Moros took advantage of the medical center! Pershing felt that no other public service did more to change enemies into friends.[20]

About one-sixth of the annual Province revenue went into education during Pershing's administration. In 1913 school enrollment reached 7,500—up fifty percent from 1909. The people were reasonably eager to learn; lack of teachers was the big problem. Moros objected to being taught by Filipinos, whom they considered fit only to be slaves, and vice versa.[21]

To obtain teachers the government conducted a normal school at Zamboanga, paying the transportation there of anyone who desired to come. Instructors emphasized domestic and industrial work rather than "book learning." They did, however, encourage the people to learn English.[22]

Whatever was built—roads, dispensaries, schools, bridges, wharves—was usually financed by revenue raised within the Province, without troubling the Insular government for help. Governor-General Forbes, who from Manila watched with interest the work of the Province, found only one thing to criticize. "Pershing is putting up his public buildings without any design, which makes me peevish . . . ," he noted in his journal.[23]

Much of Pershing's work as governor was devoted to promoting the economy. In 1913 a law prohibited pagan tribes from selling their land without the governor's permission. These tribes, backward and ignorant, had been easy prey to unscrupulous traders who got them to sell their property at a fraction of its worth.[24]

The Province also undertook a homestead project. It encouraged the propertyless to settle on government land, cultivate it, and obtain title to it. Even squatters could obtain a permanent legal title which would stand up in court.[25]

Over and over, Pershing urged the Moros to better themselves financially, appealing to their enlightened self-interest. In the very first number of *The Sulu News,* a monthly which was begun in 1911 to explain government policies, he said: "The government does not desire riches for itself, but it desires the people to be rich. And I am sure that when the Moros understand this, they will heartily cooperate with the government. Indeed, they can hardly do otherwise, since when they help themselves in the proper way, they are carrying out the wishes of the government."[26]

By the third year of Pershing's administration the value of the three most important Province exports (hemp, copra, and lumber) had risen from 1,850,000 to 4,860,000 pesos—a gain of approximately 163%. For the first time in history, Moros began to make deposits in a bank.[27]

Another opportunity for financial betterment was trade. An earlier administration had established "Moro Exchanges"—places where the hill people could bring their products to trade with buyers from the lowlands. A government agent was on hand to see that the hill people were given a fair price. One effective method was simply to inform the people what the current market prices were and what the traders would ask for the products when they resold them down on the coast.[28]

Pershing left the Moro Exchanges intact, but added three improvements through his "Industrial Trading Stations," established June 8, 1911. At these the government bought everything not perishable which any Moro offered for sale; thus no Moro faced a long journey over difficult terrain with no buyer at the end. Secondly, the government went into the business of selling, at a reasonable profit, everything Moros needed and couldn't get except from private parties at extortionate prices. During a famine, for example, it prevented unscrupulous merchants from jacking up the price of rice—thus saving many Moros from starvation and/or financial ruin. Thirdly, the government located the new industrial trading stations far in the interior, sometimes three or four days journey from the coast, where the ordinary trader did not penetrate or, if he did, where he usually cheated the people.[29]

A sideline of the new system was the government-operated general store in Zamboanga, where goods bought in the outlying stations were sold to troops stationed there and to visitors passing through. It had fabulous success. Such was the demand for native ornaments, utensils, weapons, and clothes, that the administration had difficulty keeping the store stocked.[30]

The industrial trading stations worked well. Amazed at the high prices they received, natives in the back country made journeys of twenty-five miles or more to market their products.[31]

Pershing also worked to interest American investment in Mindanao. The Province, he said, could "make millionaires out of men who have the courage to judiciously invest a few dollars." In 1910 he sent his fellow officer, Clarence Edwards, 200 copies of the *Mindanao Herald* commemorating the tenth anniversary of U. S. occupation, asking him to spread them around among American investors. He also sent copies to leading chambers of commerce in the United States and to various journals.[32]

"Why don't you come down here and look over things for yourself?" he asked Martin Egan, managing director of *The Manila Times.* "I think we have a few eye-openers down here that will pay you to look into." He then described a budding cattle business in Mindanao which could be expanded to raise all the cattle needed in the Philippines. "I am putting you next to one of the biggest things in the Philippine Islands today . . . ," he said enthusiastically. "I will undertake to provide labor for any enterprise desiring to locate in the Moro Province. . . ."[33]

An interesting event in the economic life of the Province was the Zamboanga Fair of February 7–14, 1911. Pershing had district governors bring large delegations of their people to Zamboanga, carrying with them their industrial products for sale. Some 20,000 people attended.

Financially the natives made a killing. General Bell, who came for the event, estimated that Jolo's sale of brass work "sent the whole tribe back rich." The Bagabos, who had the reputation for being the best dressed people of their area, went home almost naked; their picturesque costumes of multicolored shell work were in the hands of admiring American buyers. Commenting on native reaction to the fair, Bell said, "To say they went home enthusiastic is to put it mildly."[34]

The fair also had educational values. It made natives acquainted who had heretofore been ignorant of one another or hostile. "The thing which impressed me most," said Bell, ". . . was the remarkable effect of bringing so many wild antagonistic tribes together."[35]

What Bell meant was well illustrated in the stirring opening day parade. Leading it was the District of Zamboanga—Chinese and Japanese merchants, Filipino school children, Moros, Samal fishermen, Subanos from the highlands, long-haired Yakans from Basilan. Following them was the District of Jolo, Moros almost to a man, fierce warriors, marching behind their head man, the Sultan of Sulu. After them came the District of Cotabato, led by the American district governor and his two bronzed and muscular Moro bodyguards, naked except for a bright loin cloth and turban. From the Cotabato hills came the Tirurais contingent, sporting tinkling anklets and bracelets which ran from wrist to elbow.[36]

Next came the Lanao group—the people with whom Pershing had worked as a captain in 1902–1903. As they passed the reviewing stand they cheered wildly and threw turbans in the air. "I could hardly keep back my tears," said Pershing. "I had fought them but not without fair warning, and I had served them but not only as a duty. They had first thought of me as the leader of their enemies; now they regarded me as first among their friends. And I had a sincere affection for them."[37]

Last came the Davao district: wild savage Mandayan, whose chiefs took rank by the number of enemies slain, Manobos carrying long fifteen-foot spears, Mansakas with ruffles on their trousers, and others.

The strange procession gave visitors vivid ideas of what it meant to be governor of the Moro Province.

In staging the fair, the largest in the Philippines up to that time, Pershing had hoped to show the people something of Western civilization. Wide-eyed, they spied an American warship in the harbor with its big ten-inch guns, contrasting it with their own little vintas—tiny canoes with outriggers, propelled by the wind. They marveled at the change from the jungle to the hippodrome, from earth trails to modern roads. They were thrilled to ride on a merry-go-round.[38]

From a human interest viewpoint, one of the highlights of the fair was the wedding of Diki Diki, a midget from Jolo. Less than three feet high, he wedded a nine year old girl and created a sensation when Pershing, as host, invited the couple into his car and toured the grounds with them. It was hard for Moros to decide which was more marvelous: the car, which was a novelty to them, or Diki Diki, who sat puffing a cigar almost as long as his arm.[39]

A problem peculiar to the Moro Province was Moro-Filipino antipathy, centuries old. As Pershing said in his annual report in 1913: "Although they have always lived as neighbors, they have never mingled, and know practically nothing of each other. It is a rare thing to meet a Filipino who speaks Moro or vice versa. . . . The Filipino regards the Moro as a barbarian or a savage, while the Moro thinks the Filipino inferior, fit only to be his slave. They are in no sense brothers, but are irreconcilable strangers and enemies in every sense. . . . The actual relations are such that any attempt at Filipino government would lead only to rebellion and disaster."[40]

This view was emphasized by an incident which occurred during a Zamboanga visit of Secretary of War Jacob M. Dickinson on August 23, 1910. In the theater where they met to honor him, Moros and Filipinos sat on different sides of the aisle, as if to represent their mutual feelings. Even their clothing bespoke differences. The Filipinos wore white coats and derby hats; the Moros, bright-colored jackets and gaudy turbans.[41]

Although outnumbered by Moros more than three to one, the Filipinos asked Dickinson for representation in the Manila Assembly, pointing to their superior education, culture, and property holdings. A toothless old Samal warrior summed up the Moro position when he rose stiffly, unwound his turban to show his white hair, and said: "I am an old man and had hoped that my fighting days were over. But if it should come to pass that Filipinos are set over us, my people will all fight and I will lead them."[42]

Pershing knew that the old warrior accurately represented Moro feeling. He deplored Filipino efforts to dominate Moros or to effect a premature American withdrawal from the Philippines. "Peace in the Moro Province can be maintained only by continuance of American control."[43] Basic to Pershing's contention was his conviction that Filipinos were not even ready to govern themselves, much less the Moros. "Outside of the few important sea ports and commercial centers," he asserted, "three-fourths of the population are yet under the spell of ignorance and superstition, while the Moros and wild tribes must still be classed as barbarians or savages."[44]

Throughout his administration Pershing faced a major problem in finding suitable governors for the five districts of the Province. "The question of district governors is one that is giving me much concern," he said in 1909, "and I feel that this question is one upon which the success of the Government down here depends. . . . It is my purpose to secure men who may be detained for a period of years or who are likely to be stationed here for a lengthy time. . . . Just how far I shall be able to carry out this plan remains to be seen."[45]

It turned out that he could not carry it very far. Because competent civilians were lacking, district governors were usually Army officers and these were constantly subject to change. Pershing had hoped to keep them in office for four to six years; in point of fact, they stayed considerably less than that. The average tenure for a district governor was fourteen months.[46]

The bad effects of such short term rule were evident. To govern Moros it was necessary to know and understand them, and this took time. Acquainted only with personal rule, the Moros saw a change in officials as a change in government rather than in mere personnel.[47] To remedy the situation, Pershing recommended that the term of military service in the Philippines be increased from two to four years. Such a long stay would normally be enervating, but he believed that six months spent at either Lake Lanao or Baguio, both of which had temperate climates, would recoup a man's strength.[48] Later he lowered his recommendation after he himself had gotten sick, despite excursions to Baguio and elsewhere.[49]

By 1913, Pershing knew that the basic difficulty was not the short term for Army service, but the continuance in office of military men whose places should be taken by civilians. The solution was basically to transfer the Province to civilian control.

Apparently he had not seen this point initially. Col. James G. Harbord, Assistant Chief of the Philippine Constabulary, told Maj. Gen. Leonard Wood on October 7, 1910: "General Pershing has certainly departed from the idea of getting civilians into places as fast as practicable, and making the government as civil as possible, calling on troops only when absolutely necessary."[50] Until 1911, half-way through Pershing's administration, every district governor and every district secretary, who acted as second in command, was a military man. Beginning that year, however, Pershing began to appoint civilians. By November, 1913, shortly before he left the Moro Province, only one military man remained in office—himself. The following month a civilian whom he had recommended, Frank Carpenter, took his place.[51]

Pershing's administration had its share of criticism. General Wood, who had governed the Moro Province from 1903 to 1906, deplored Pershing's initial policy of making local military commanders the district governors. "They are changed too often," he observed.[52]

Charles Brent, an Episcopal bishop, later Chief of Chaplains in World War I, inspected the Province schools and reported them to be "pitiable, both in personnel and work." The blame was not wholly in the superintendent Pershing had appointed, Brent admitted, but also in a lack of money to work with.[53]

Colonel Harbord, later to be Pershing's Chief of Staff in France and one of his strongest supporters after World War I, told General Wood in 1910: "I feel that the Moro Province has been practically a blank since you left there, and that its future is being hazarded more or less as a tail to the Pershing kite."[54]

Harbord also reported that Pershing warned the people before the visit of Secretary of War Dickinson not to make any complaints which were not first cleared with him; otherwise they would feel "the heavy hand" of the governor. When Pershing was confronted with the charge, he denied it, but not without "se puso colorado" (becoming red).[55]

Other Harbord reports charged Pershing with excessive expenditure on the Zamboanga Fair in February, 1911, which cost the government 50,000 pesos and "was not a success financially."[56] He said that Pershing's decision to disarm the Moros in September, 1911, which brought on two major military engagements, Bud Dajo and Bud Bagsak, was made without consulting, or even informing, General Bell, the supreme U.S. commander in the Philippines.[57]

"I think affairs in the Moro Province are in a lamentable condition," Harbord wrote on July 2, 1912. "The Constabulary are absolutely shot to pieces. Men were transferred from one company to another without reason; officers were picked up and switched from company to company; companies were taken from regions where they were acquainted and where their friends and families lived and have been shot off for a year at a time into unknown regions. There has been no discretion used at all in this most delicate matter of keeping officers with companies that they know, and companies in places that they know. I believe that it is a wonder that we have not had more mutiny and desertion there than we have had. Pershing pays no attention to the district director [of Constabulary], as far as giving his orders through him is concerned; at least that is the way it appears on the face of it. Promises made the companies are not kept and, generally, things are in a bad state."[58]

As Harbord was Acting Chief of the Philippine Constabulary at this writing, he may be presumed to speak with authority. Pershing himself, in an undated jotting, admitted the lack of close connection between the government of the Moro Province and the Philippine Constabulary, whose headquarters were in Manila. It "always has been that way," he commented, "except perhaps during General Wood's time, due to close personal relations between himself and Colonel Harbord. . . ." Co-ordination would be better, he felt, if the same man were both Provincial Secretary and Constabulary director.[59]

Pershing's work as governor of the Moro Province added a new dimension to his life: administration. For the first time he had in his charge some half million oriental people, most of them savage or semisavage, ignorant and superstitious. He was responsible for their welfare, for peace in the area, and for bringing them along the path of civilization. Most of them were Moros and to them he devoted most of his attention, although he was not unmindful of the Filipinos and the pagan tribes.

To a remarkable degree he sought to understand the Moro mentality. He was open-minded. He took their side against the military when Moros complained—justifiably in his opinion—of military high-handedness. He respected their feelings and he did the leg work that was necessary to get around the Province and find out how they felt. He did not share the fear which others felt for his people. Courage was part of his makeup and the Moros respected courage.

As the Lanao Moros paraded by at the Zamboanga Fair they had cheered him and Pershing said he had trouble keeping back tears. He was not being sentimental. Rather he was rejoicing in a hard-won success against great odds, success in public and personal relations where others had failed and would fail. Ten years later, in 1921, Pershing cabled a message of greeting to inmates of the San Ramon prison farm. They responded with loud cheers and the cry, "He is of our family."[60]

As an administrator Pershing was noted for hard work. He was not just putting in time; he served his people. Sometimes it was by innovation, as with San Ramon Prison and the Industrial Trading Stations. Sometimes it was by imagination and adaptation, as with the changes made in the legal system. Whatever it was, the results were impressive and visible: roads, schools, dispensaries, bridges, services.

A strong man, he tended at times to ride roughshod over others. Harbord noted Pershing's "heavy hand" on dissidents, his tendency to act unilaterally. As governor he fragmented his troops and parceled them out in driblets among the natives—a policy he had criticized at Fort William McKinley when he wanted to concentrate troops there (under *his* command) for training in larger bodies.

Overall, his work as governor was successful. This was attested by the commendations given by the two men who had supreme authority in the Philippines and under whom he worked: Bell, the military commander, and Forbes, the Governor-General.

On November 24, 1913, three weeks before Pershing left the Philippines, Bell wrote this: "I know of nothing connected with the service of General Pershing and the Army in Mindanao during the past three years which merits anything but praise. Much hard work has been done and most remarkable results have been brought about. Conditions in Mindanao have improved in every possible way . . . and conditions of peace, prosperity and industry are no better anywhere in the [Philippine] Department than they seem to be in the District of Mindanao."[61]

Forbes also spoke highly of Pershing's work—and of Pershing too, for they became warm personal friends. "He is big, able, responsive, and sensible," Forbes said of him. "I like him the best of all the generals of the army that I have yet dealt with."[62]

After an inspection trip of the Moro Province, Forbes noted in his journal: "General Pershing is a whirlwind, and I told him how much I appreciated his work."[63] To the Secretary of War he wrote: "The change there is most startling and enheartening; the result of General Pershing's arrival, and his work there is something magical. Every one of the things which I found to criticise with the administration of the Moro Province had been remedied and with a firm hand."[64]

In December, 1911, Pershing threw over 1,000 men in the field to break a Moro revolt at Bud Dajo; Forbes called Pershing's management of the affair "masterly."[65] In June, 1913, after another military campaign at Bud Bagsak, Forbes commended Pershing for handling the situation "with sagacity and skill."[66] Both these military expeditions arose out of a key decision during Pershing's administration: the disarming of the Moros. To this we must now turn.

11

Disarming the Moros

A young American woman, wife of an officer who was stationed in the Moro Province, wrote home about life there. "Last December," she said, "a Moro attacked a captain, who fired six .38 caliber shots into him. The Moro didn't stop running for a second; he came right on, cut the captain to pieces with his bolo and started on his way rejoicing, when a guard finally finished him with a .45 caliber bullet."[1] What the woman related was simply an echo of what Pershing had described to Governor-General Forbes, six weeks after assuming command of the Province: "There is a laxity in the enforcement of law and order. . . ."[2]

This laxity was one of the major problems of his administration. It took many forms. Sometimes a Moro "ran amuck," i.e., went on a killing spree. Swinging his blade wildly, he struck down whoever crossed his path—enemies, strangers, friends, even his own family. At other times a Moro "went juramentado," i.e., killed only Christians. This was more common. It consisted of taking an oath (the Spanish word for an oath-taker was juramentado) and going through an elaborate preparatory ceremony. Early in the morning the juramentado visited a Mohammedan priest and received absolution. Having shaved his head, eyebrows, beard, and armpits, he bound his body tightly with cloth, so that, if wounded, he would not bleed to death before killing his Christian. He donned a white robe and turban, attached a charm to his waist to ward off blows, and then sallied forth to murder.

The Koran prescribed that the Mohammedan exhort the Christian to conversion and warn him before attacking. But the Philippine Moro disregarded this prescription, and sometimes also the above ceremony, if he thought it would make his mission more difficult. He killed without warning. Sauntering down the street as if for a stroll, he waited until a Christian's back was turned. Then out came his blade and terror followed in his wake.

"He cares no more what Christian he kills," remarked Hugh L. Scott, "than you care which one of a bunch of railway tickets you receive, any one of which will take you to your destination and he has no more animosity against the Christian than you have against the ticket; he is simply a means to an end."[3]

The end, of course, was the Mohammedan paradise, his reward for killing a Christian. That he himself would be killed in retaliation meant nothing; he had died for the faith and Allah gave him a martyr's crown. He entered a land of crystal streams and unalloyed pleasure, where the Tree of Life, its branches laden with every kind of delicious fruit, bent to his touch. Christians were his slaves. Women gratified his passions; his wives, restored to their youth, vied with the dark-eyed houris.[4]

The juramentado practice was widespread. It occurred so often, especially on the island of Jolo, that American troops went armed at all times. Yet even this was not always enough—witness the incident related by the young American woman. "I am just beginning to go around without feeling scared to death," she said. "Joe says I will give him nervous prostration if I don't stop grabbing him and saying, 'What's that?' . . . I suppose I shall look back on this as a great experience, but just at present I spend my time hoping and praying that I won't have cholera or be boloed by a Moro."[5]

To combat the juramentado, Pershing tried burying him when caught with a pig, thinking that this was equivalent to burying the Moro in hell, for pigs were impure animals to a Moslem. General Bell, the

American military commander in the Philippines, thought it worth a try. "This is a good plan," he said, "for if anything will discourage the juramentado it is the prospect of going to hell instead of to heaven. You can rely on me to stand by you in maintaining this custom. It is the only possible thing we can do to discourage crazy fanatics."[6]

A nice theory, but it was not true and did not discourage anybody, at least not for long. Hugh L. Scott, who had been governor of Sulu, noted that when one of his predecessors buried pigs with juramentados the only people who got angry were some humanitarians in the United States. The Moros? They "did not care enough about it even to discuss it among themselves."[7]

But juramentados were only part of the problem. Ever since its establishment in 1903 the Province had been notorious for murder and lawlessness. A Moro outlaw gave this example: "I used to see a Moro fishing in his boat and would draw up alongside and offer to trade rifles, and when his was handed over for examination I would shoot him through the belly with his own gun, and after that it was just the same as if you were picking up your own property."[8]

Capturing outlaws was often a real problem. Policemen were inadequate; on running down a criminal they frequently found a host of his followers, all armed to resist. Arrests, in fact, required sending a detachment of troops, with pitched battles sometimes resulting. To avoid continual fighting, which was risky because it might trigger a general uprising, known criminals were sometimes left unpunished.[9]

There was also the problem of slavery. In November, 1909, to take just one example, Moros from Lake Lanao descended on the Subanos, timid, ignorant people living in the hill country of the Zamboanga peninsula, and made them virtual slaves. Saying that a great fire and flood would destroy all mankind, they persuaded the Subanos to flee to a remote territory in the Bukidnon Strip, there to await the end of the world on a high mountain.

Once there, they organized the Subanos into work camps, established a slave trade, and confiscated the homes the Subanos had left behind. When the latter, disillusioned, sought to get away, the Moros resorted to imprisonment, terror, and murder. A government expedition finally rescued the Subanos and ended the slavery. But the incident brought out clearly what could be expected as long as the Moros owned arms.[10]

For these reasons—juramentados, murder, robbery, and slavery—Pershing decided that the Moros must be disarmed. "The Moro Province has long been considered a lawless locality," he told General Bell. "Moros have run amuck in groups or as individuals from time immemorial, and yet they have been allowed to go on carrying arms."[11] By disarming them, Pershing hoped to place the weak on an equal footing with the strong, thus safeguarding personal rights.

He knew there would be opposition, not only from Moros but from some Americans. The question of disarming them had been discussed for years. Every one of Pershing's predecessors had concluded it would be impossible without bringing on a war.[12]

"You cannot disarm the people," said Maj. Gen. Leonard Wood, the first governor of the Moro Province and, in 1911, the Army Chief of Staff. "It means they will bury their best arms and turn in a few poor ones, especially some who want to make a show of obedience."[13]

General Wood regarded disarmament as "an extremely ill-timed move. . . . It is going to bring on a very embarrassing situation at an unfortunate time. Moreover, it is wholly uncalled for. . . . It seems to be rather ill-judged and ill-timed, although apparently well-meant."[14]

Although Pershing had decided on his course, he was careful not to be precipitate. Many sections lacked good roads. Until these were built, and until troops could reach all parts of disaffected areas and protect cooperative Moros, disarmament would merely throw good Moros on the mercy of the bad.[15] He was careful also to consult Moro leaders, urging the wisdom of disarmament. Most agreed that it was wise, provided that everybody be disarmed.[16]

Pershing was sure that they could be. Six weeks before issuing the disarmament proclamation, he informed Governor-General Forbes:

"I have little doubt that this can be accomplished if undertaken quietly and resolutely and without publicity or ostentation. Much can be done through the leading Moros by appealing to their reason and by taking them into one's confidence. My own personal experience in this regard leads me to believe that the plan will work. Some force or show of force may be necessary in a few cases, but even so, disarmament must come and I desire to have it accomplished under the present insular and provincial administration."[17]

Forbes replied:

"I am pleased with your disarmament scheme. I think it to be absolutely necessary, and the fact that thirteen years of American occupation have gone by without our having the districts of Lanao and Jolo in such shape that a man can walk about with any degree of personal safety is a good deal of commentary on our administration and makes it necessary that some different measure be adopted. I have been coming slowly to the conclusion that disarmament is a proper thing, and I think your plan of going at it slowly to be extremely wise."[18]

On September 8, 1911, Pershing issued Executive Order No. 24– the formal disarmament order which made it unlawful to possess a gun or to carry a cutting weapon.[19] In hopes of avoiding bloodshed, Pershing visited various districts, explaining it. The better Moros again admitted its wisdom, but doubted that it could be achieved without a fight. Especially in the District of Jolo was resistance strong. There even friendly Moros predicted a general uprising if the order was seriously pushed.[20]

Pershing used every argument and medium to win the Moros over. An editorial in the government newspaper, *The Sulu News*, presented disarmament as something any enlightened Moro should want:

"You do not know when some misguided person will run amuk (juramentado), or who he will be. He may be your own father, or brother, or son, and in his madness, he may kill you or some member of your family. What, then, could be a better protection against amuks than to forbid every one to carry arms? If the amuk, when the murder-madness comes upon him, has no arms at hand, the search for weapons will cause delay and may permit of his capture, or even recovery from the obsession, before he actually commits any crime."[21]

December 1, 1911 was the deadline for turning in guns and receiving payment. Long before that, however, it was clear that many Moros were not going to comply and that the government must fight or back down. Pershing's "friendly persuasion" had failed. Even he admitted this. In his correspondence he no longer spoke of "appealing to the Moro's reason" or "taking them into one's confidence." Now he said flatly: "We shall disarm these people without much *fighting.*"22

"The fact is," he told General Bell, ". . . that the Moros should have been disarmed some time ago. A state of peace can never exist in Jolo or elsewhere in this Province as long as the people are allowed to bear arms without question."23

Trouble broke out on the island of Jolo. Moros rushed an American camp at Seit Lake at night, killing one and wounding three.

Pershing decided to take action. "We shall not submit to that sort of thing any longer," he said. "The time has come now to settle this thing once for all."24 He left for Jolo to take personal charge of operations.

Pershing divided the Jolo Field Forces into two commands. One went east to Seit Lake; the other, west to Taglibi, eight miles west of Jolo City. As the Taglibi area had always been a hotbed of anti-American sentiment, Pershing suspected that an incident would not be long in coming there. To prevent surprise attack, the troops dug entrenchments, strung barbed wire, and cleared away the jungle about two hundred yards from camp.

On the night of November 28, just as the moon was going down, Moros hit the camp, throwing themselves recklessly against the barbed wire.25 Although there were no American casualties, Pershing's blood was up. "They must now have a lesson or two. They have fired on U.S. troops—and they have not been punished for it. I intend to give them a drubbing."26

Yet he acted with reluctance. "I would give anything to end this business without much fighting," he wrote his wife, "but the Taglibi Moros seem vicious. They have shown their teeth and even snapped at us. Reed thinks he can talk them around but you can't talk a fellow around to much of anything if he is shooting at you all the time. I stood this sort of thing for a year once27 and I have always said it was an error to sit idly by and let these savages shoot you up without going after them, politics or no politics, and I do not intend to stand for it or permit it."[28]

On December 3, Pershing sent out three columns in the Taglibi area. About 800 yards from camp the Moros attacked. The troops drove them back, then scattered them helter-skelter.

Two days later Pershing stepped up the offensive. He sent out five columns simultaneously from equidistant points along the Taglibi boundary, combing it thoroughly. The columns met little organized resistance; the Moros seemed dazed by the appearance of so many soldiers in so many different places.[29]

To his wife, Pershing wrote exultantly:

"I have moved so swiftly and so secretly so far and have covered so much country that the Moros are reported scared to death. They seem to be willing to do almost anything if we will keep soldiers out of the country. That is what I wanted. They have hitherto been accustomed to having people (Scott for instance)[30] sit around and allow them to build cottas up in the hills and wait for them to get all ready. No[t] so this time. They were hit from five directions at once and each column did good work. They say the Moros are confused."[31]

They were. So confused that on the afternoon of December 5 an influential Moro came into camp with news that they had had enough and were willing to turn in their arms. Pershing suspected a ruse to gain time, since Moros had pulled this trick before, but suspended operations pending negotiations.[32] To foster good will, he wrote their leaders, urging them to cooperate. A sample letter, quoted in part, shows Pershing's manner of writing and his desire to win them over without a fight.

"I write you this letter because I am sorry to know that you and your people refuse to do what the government has ordered. . . . I am sorry the soldiers had to kill any Moros. All Moros are the same to me as my children and no father wants to kill his own children.

"Now, I am writing you this letter that you may know that I want my children to come in and stop fighting. We do not want any more killing. Too many Moros and their women may be killed. I ask you to tell me why the Moros are fighting. Their guns are old and they have very little ammunition and these guns are not worth fighting for so Moros are certainly not fighting to keep these old guns. Your people are better off not to have these guns as we can then have peace in the island. The government will pay for all guns.

"I do not want to punish you and your people any more. If you turn in your guns, no one will be arrested and your people may return to their homes to cultivate their fields. If your people need rice to eat, the government will give it to them. The soldiers did not destroy your houses nor any of your property.

"If you leading men do not stop fighting, you will be responsible for the lives of many people under you who want to give up their guns. You will be responsible for the lives of your women and children. You have no right to lead all these people to follow you into a fight. You had better give up the guns and save your own lives and the lives of your people."[33]

Certain remarks in the letter call for explanation. Several times Pershing spoke of innocent non-combatants being endangered: "Too many Moros *and their women* may be killed. . . . You will be responsible for the lives *of your women and children.*" He was referring to the Moro practice of taking their women and children into their cottas or fortresses. In an attack, using shrapnel from artillery and mortars, many of these non-combatants would be slaughtered.

That Pershing dreaded this is evident from his letters to his wife during this campaign. Five years before, in 1906, the Moros had holed up with their families in a cotta at Bud Dajo; Gen. Leonard Wood had stormed the place and killed many women and children in the process. Said Pershing to his wife: "I would not have . . . [that] on my conscience for the fame of Napoleon. . . ."[34] Yet he could not be sure that, in the last resort, he would not have to order the very same thing. "You can never tell what Moros are going to do," he complained. "All these people are crazy to fight."[35]

The negotiations dragged on. "I should dread to think of having to kill women and children," Pershing informed his wife. "If they do not come to terms soon I shall make a quick night movement across the mountain behind them and get between them and the top of the hills they intend to occupy.—Then I may save their women and children. I want to keep them out of it if possible."[36] But it was not to be. On December 13, 1911, Pershing left Jolo for his headquarters at Zamboanga to catch up on some back work. The next day a telegram arrived from Jolo: the Moros were occupying Bud Dajo, their sacred mountain, in force.[37]

Pershing left for Jolo at once. On board the *Samar* he penned a note to Mrs. Pershing: "I am very sorry those Moros are such fools—but then Dajo will not mean the slaughter of women and children, nor hasty assaults against strong entrenchments. I shall lose as few men and kill as few Moros as possible."[38]

When Pershing arrived in Jolo on December 15, Col. Frank West, commander there, reported an estimated 500 to 800 Moros atop Bud Dajo, inside an extinct volcanic crater. They had between 150 and 250 rifles, plus cutting weapons. They had already constructed rather formidable entrenchments. [39]

This was bad news. Bud Dajo was the highest mountain in Jolo with a crater able to hold abundant food and water. Hugh L. Scott, who had a run-in with Moros in 1905, said of it: "Bud Daho [sic] was a very difficult nut to crack, and I did not want to be obliged to assault it. . . . I did not want them to learn how difficult it really was, and have to contend with it more than once. It was plain that many good Americans would have to die before it could be taken. . . ."[40]

On the morning of December 16, 1911, a squadron of cavalry reconnoitered the terrain, looking for possible camp sites and estimating Moro strength. Friendly Moros stated that the movement to the crater had been precipitate; they doubted if the hostile Moros had had time to take up sufficient supplies.[41]

At this point Pershing took personal command of operations and ordered an immediate investment of the mountain. He explained the situation to General Bell as follows:

"No one who is familiar with Moro character is at all surprised at any turn affairs may take. The more foolish and asinine the thing is, the more likely a Moro is to do it. They make a sudden resolve to die and try to get as many people to die with them as they can. If they are given some time to think this over it is often possible to bring them out from under the influence of the spell. More patience is required in handling a situation of this sort than any other I can think of. Of these Moros who are reported to have gone to Mount Dajo, there is no one man of any prominence whatever. They all belong to the tao class.

"I am strongly of the impression that they can be induced to come down, or if that is impossible, they can be starved out or will escape in time of their own accord. It is not my purpose to make any grandstand play here and get a lot of soldiers killed, and massacre a lot of Moros, including women and children."[42]

More troops arrived on December 17—three companies of American infantry, three companies of Philippine Scouts, one machine-gun platoon. Pershing personally inspected camp sites and trails near Bud Dajo.[43] "Have sent Infantry out to invest Dajo," he wrote his wife. "We must never have a big killing at Dajo or elsewhere."[44]

On December 18, reconnaissance revealed that there were three main trails leading up the mountain. Pershing established three camps at the base of the mountain, one along each of the trails. Thus he cut off reinforcements and supplies to the top.[45]

At dawn on December 19, troops surprised Moro cargadores attempting to sneak in supplies and drove them off. In the afternoon reconnaissance parties pushed up the mountain, looking for side trails along which Moros might escape or be supplied. About 300 yards from the top of the crater other troops began to cut lateral trails around the mountain side, connecting up American outposts. They discovered minor trails, unknown at the start, along which Moros had escaped earlier. These were entirely sealed off.[46]

Pershing now had over 1,000 men in the field. By December 22 he had thrown a circle around Bud Dajo like a noose around the neck of an enemy, which, slowly constricting, made it ever harder to resist. "I think we have got this place so thoroughly closed in that a cat could not sneak out," he told his wife.[47]

Early stories about Moros being short on food and supplies were confirmed. Despite desperate Moro efforts to break through on dark nights, Pershing was squeezing the fight out of them—and without needlessly risking the lives of his men,[48] nor of the Moros. From the start, Pershing's intention had been to avoid a fight if possible and, if unavoidable, to keep Moro losses at a minimum. "Have no outposts nearer than 300 yards to summit of mountain," read one of his orders. "Avoid contact if possible. Do not return fire but keep hidden."[49]

So much did Pershing seek to save enemy lives that one officer actually considered him a pacifist! Robert Lee Bullard, an A.E.F. division, corps, and Army commander in World War I, said in his diary, "General Pershing is not a fighter; he is in all his history a pacifist and, unless driven thereto . . . will do no fighting. . . . I have had some (perhaps better than others) means and opportunity, in the Moro country in the Philippine Islands, of observing and judging him. He is . . . not a warrior."[50]

Pershing had sent some friendly Moros to try to convince the hostiles of the folly of resistance. Nothing could come of it save starvation or death, he told them. Neither was warranted. He wanted only guns, not lives. If they would merely surrender their guns they could go home in peace.[51] Some Moros responded. On December 19, twenty surrendered. During the following four days they came in sporadically, in groups of fifty to two hundred. It was evident that at the start there had been about 800 people atop Bud Dajo.[52]

On December 23, Pershing informed Moros still holding out that after the next day they would be given no chance to surrender, except unconditionally. He then spent the entire day visiting outposts, giving directions about positions and changes to be made during the night.

Next morning, about eleven o'clock, Pershing again sent up friendly emissaries. They returned, announcing that the crater was deserted. The hostile Moros, estimated at sixty to one hundred, had hurriedly evacuated, probably that very morning. Rushing up two companies of Philippine Scouts (145 men), Pershing occupied the crater immediately. He now had the Moros caught between two circles—a ring of Philippine Scouts in the crater and a ring of troops about 300 yards down the mountain. The Moros were in the woods somewhere in between.

Pershing knew that they were hoping he'd go away. He had no such intention. He fortified all points of the line where they might try to break through; then waited. Without food and water, it was inevitable that they would try to escape that night.[53]

"Fighting last night was terrific," Pershing wrote his wife the next day, December 25. "Estimate at least seventy-five Moros tried to rush the lines at one place."[54]

Only a few were successful. When Christmas day dawned, most were still penned up between the crater and the cordon of troops encircling it.[55]

A Moro datto[56] who had surrendered asked permission to go into the woods to see if he could persuade the hostiles to come in. It would save lives; Pershing let him go. But any surrender must be unconditional, he insisted.

The datto returned in the afternoon with forty-six men, one woman, and one child. They brought with them several rifles and a large number of cutting weapons. Many other rifles, Pershing believed, had been cached in the woods, hidden in hollow logs or in the branches of trees. When the Moros were released, they would return and retrieve them.

Pershing released the woman and child. But since the forty-six men had surrendered after the deadline, he sent them to Calarian Prison on the mainland of Mindanao to await trial for insurrection. Later he decided to drop the trial and use the prisoners as hostages instead: so many prisoners for so many guns. When a prisoner's friends had collected enough cached arms, he was released. This they speedily did. Thus the Moros got their freedom and Pershing got their guns—which is exactly what he wanted.

Meanwhile, the Bud Dajo operation was almost over. Prisoners dropped the information that some hostiles were still out, hidden along the southwest side of the mountain. On December 26, a company of Philippine Scouts formed a skirmish line to flush out the die-hards. Their right end touched the crater rim; their left, the line of outposts 300 yards down. They moved to the left along the mountain side, the crater and the outposts penning in the Moros at the top and bottom of the line. It was slow work, taking some three hours, but it was sure. They flushed and killed six Moros.

Casualties for the whole campaign were, on the American side, three wounded; on the Moro side, twelve killed and a few wounded.[57]

On December 27, his work finished, Pershing sailed on the *Samar* for Zamboanga. That same day Governor-General Forbes telegraphed the American Secretary of War: "John J. Pershing reports 300 Moros surrendered. Opposition to disarmament Jolo practically ended. Consider his management has been masterly."[58]

Indeed it was. Hugh Scott had predicted that "many good Americans would have to die" before Bud Dajo could be taken.[59] Pershing captured it with only three wounded. Furthermore, he did it without wholesale slaughter of his enemies; he saved Moro lives in spite of themselves. As he said in his report on this campaign:

"It should be fully understood that there was never a moment during the investment of Bud Dajo when the Moros, including women, on top of the mountain would not have fought to the death had they been given the opportunity. They had gone there to make a last stand on this, their sacred mountain, and they were determined to die fighting. Their former experience on Bud Dajo [against General Leonard Wood in 1906] did not deter them from taking this step, and it would not have deterred them from fighting to the death had an attempt been made to dislodge them by force. It was only by the greatest effort that their solid determination to fight it out could be broken. The fact is that they were completely surprised at the prompt and decisive action of the troops in cutting off supplies and preventing escape, and they were chagrined and disappointed in that they were not encouraged to die the death of Mohammedan fanatics."[60]

The Bud Dajo campaign highlighted certain characteristics of Pershing. One was resolution. The Moro Province since its inception had been lawless. Pershing resolved to stop the lawlessness by disarmament. His proposal ran contrary to the judgment of his predecessors, one of whom was the current Army Chief of Staff, who flatly asserted: "You cannot disarm the people."[61] Pershing went ahead and did it.

Not without some miscalculation, however. Pershing had great—at times overgreat—confidence in his powers of persuasion with the

Moros. His letter to Moro leaders, while conciliatory, was also paternalistic. One wonders how rebel Moros received the news that Pershing considered them his "children?" They resisted more than he hoped or expected. He had had to fight—but it was only a campaign and not a war.

And here another Pershing characteristic was revealed—restraint. He was a moderate man. He was slow to escalate. He tried burying pigs with juramentados and, when that didn't work and he decided on disarmament, he sought to effect his will by persuasion, appealing to Moro self-interest by personal contacts and by written word. He readily suspended troop operations in Taglibi in favor of negotiations. When negotiations broke down he reluctantly took to the field, so reluctantly that Robert L. Bullard considered him a pacifist. He surrounded the Moros on Bud Dajo and then sat it out, ordering his troops to avoid contact and not to return fire. Leonard Wood had had a slaughter at Bud Dajo. Hugh Scott had called it "a difficult nut to crack" and dreaded to assault it.[62] Pershing took Bud Dajo without loss of an American life and with only twelve lost by the enemy. It was indeed a masterly campaign.

12

"The Good Old Days at Zamboanga"

In his later years, Pershing looked back on the Moro Province days as the best in his life. "My first love" he called it.[1] The work was satisfying and, by and large, successful; his health, except near the end, was good, and the physical set-up at Zamboanga was ideal. In 1919 he smiled happily as the 4th Division passed in review with the band playing "No Te Vayas de Zamboanga" ("Don't Go Away from Zamboanga")—one of his favorite songs. James G. Harbord said on one occasion, "Come what may, the good old days at Zamboanga . . . were the best." Pershing certainly agreed.[2]

Frances had already given him three lovely children and a fourth, Mary Margaret, was born at Zamboanga on May 19, 1912. In their correspondence his wife was "Frank" or "Frankie"—he, "Jack" or "Jackie."[3] During the Bud Dajo campaign he punctuated his letters with phrases like "Darling Mine," "Sweetheart," and "Dearest."[4] With rifle bullets whining in the background he would write "Yours with soul," "Kiss those dear Kiddies for me—their papa," and "I love you to death."[5] A visitor in the Pershing home once noticed a message which Pershing had scribbled for Frances when she should return: "I just stopped by, Darling, to tell you that I love you."[6]

Once during a separation he wrote a poem to her entitled "Since You Left Home." Here is part of it:

> The place looks, well! I'd say like hell
> The grass is overgrown
> The orchids droop, the roses fade
> Since you left home.
>
> The floors are covered with thick dust.
> The walls no better done,
> The cobwebs come and never go
> Since you left home.
>
> The moon is pale, the night is gloom,
> The days drag slowly by,
> There's nothing in this life for me
> Since you left home.[7]

They both loved this home, so filled with happy memories. A large structure, with numerous guest rooms and a dining room that could seat sixty, it had windows of delicately colored translucent sea shells, and walls covered with spears, krises, and other Moro weapons. Save for Ogden Mills's house in Paris and the famous chateau at Chaumont, where he stayed during World War I, it was the finest residence Pershing ever occupied.[8]

Twenty paces from the back door were the waters of Basilan Strait. Hardly a day passed without a morning dip. A strong swimmer, Frances would dive in and head straight out for Borneo; Pershing was never at ease when over his depth.[9]

At 4:00 P.M. they usually went riding. Frances was accustomed to horses from Wyoming and Pershing was born on horseback. They taught the children to ride as soon as they could sit a pony; Warren learned before he was three.[10] Warren's earliest lessons were on a hobby horse which he rode with spurs on his little moccasins; later Pershing bought him a tiny Filipino pony. The first time Warren mounted, the animal was sulky and unresponsive. "Bad boy!"

Approach to the house on Zamboanga where Pershing lived while Governor
of Moro Province. The dining-room seated 60, the windows were made
of delicately colored, translucent seashells.
Photograph courtesy Mrs. Myrtle
Montgomery, Bethesda, Maryland

The Pershing family "at home" in Zamboanga
Photograph courtesy Mrs. Myrtle Montgomery

cried Warren disgustedly, and that became the pony's name.[11]

One afternoon Pershing returned home just in time to see his son tumble off the pony into the canal which ran by the house. Hauling him out, Pershing put him to bed. He "gave me a large dose of castor oil," recalled Warren, "which was his sovereign remedy for any and all the ailments of childhood."[12]

Of all the children, Pershing probably loved Warren, his only son, most. Busy as he was with his work, he found time to spend hours playing with him, down on his hands and knees like a child. Frank Lanckton, Pershing's orderly, taught Warren the military courtesies almost before the child was out of the cradle. He remembered Pershing's reaction when Warren first surprised him with a salute. "I never saw the Old Man so pleased . . . and I never saw him . . . return a snappier one."[13]

Bishop Charles Brent suggested one evening that the children be baptized. "We must think of these things," Pershing said in agreement; "we must do all we can to start children on the right road."[14] Not long afterwards, Pershing himself was baptized in the Episcopal Church. On January 23, 1910 both he and Frances were confirmed by Bishop Brent.[15]

From December 28, 1910 to January 12, 1911, Pershing was temporary commander of all U.S. troops in the Philippines. Gen. William P. Duvall, who was retiring from that position, hated his replacement, General Bell, and left the Philippines early to avoid meeting him. Pershing filled in until Bell came.[16]

During this time an embarrassing incident occurred with the Japanese. Duvall believed that they were engaged in espionage and, on his own initiative, raided the homes of prominent Japanese in Manila, confiscating their papers. Having lit the bomb, he then went out of office, leaving things to blow up in Pershing's face.

When the latter discovered what Duvall had done, he was "greatly perturbed" and immediately informed Governor-General Forbes. The Japanese consul called, demanding an explanation. Forbes felt that the Japanese would never believe that the seizures had been made without his own knowledge or that of Washington. So, after a few delays, he replied that secret service reports had come in—to which he personally gave no credence—which had forced him to undertake the search purely as a formality. He was happy to report that nothing subversive had been found.[17]

That is Forbes's version of the story, recorded in his journal for 1910. But Henry J. Reilly, the officer in charge of Military Secret Service in Manila, said that there actually was Japanese espionage at the time. Two spies named Kawodi and Sugunami were arrested and deported with Pershing's approval for attempting to steal plans for the Corregidor fortifications. When the Japanese consul kicked up a fuss, Reilly uncovered enough personal scandal ("wine and women stuff") to quiet him. "Less than a year later," added Reilly, "under General Bell, who didn't believe much in secret service work, the Corregidor plans were stolen. They were probably used by the Japanese in 1942."[18]

In February, 1912 Pershing was offered command of the Mounted Service School at Fort Riley, Kansas. Although tempted, he declined, giving his reason that he had come to the Philippines with the understanding that he would remain at least three years.[19] Later that year a rumor that Pershing would be the next superintendent of West Point brought a revival of the scandal story of 1906.[20] By now he felt he knew who had instigated the original attack on him in the *Manila American*: several disgruntled colonels who had resented his promotion to brigadier general. "That crowd of sneaks" was what he called them. "I have always regretted that I did not shoot the editor and sue the paper for slander."[21]

When several American papers again printed the bastardy allegation, Pershing wrote Senator Warren, "I am getting very tired of having this old-exploded and often refuted scandal reprinted and propose to go after anybody else who prints it in the future. I am of the opinion now that we should start in on the *New York World*. . . . Whoever is at the bottom of it ought to be made to pay the penalty, either personally or through the courts."[22]

In 1913 Pershing brought suit for libel against the *World* and forced it to print a retraction.[23]

The decision to disarm the Moros in 1911 was the work of Pershing, Governor of the Moro Province. But its enforcement was the work of Pershing, Commanding General of the Department of Mindanao. He had two separate jobs: one civil, the other military. A word should be said now about the latter, for soldiering, after all, was Pershing's profession; being a civil governor was purely temporary.

He considered himself a strict, hard-working commander. "Notwithstanding my civil duties," he told General Bell, "I devote more time to my work than any other brigadier general in the army. I see more of my command, visit the various posts oftener and exact a stricter enforcement of instructions and discipline than any other officer I know of, except yourself. It is now and always has been a part of my creed."[24]

Pershing's description fitted the facts. William H. Oury, the Department Quartermaster, remembered "the great demands for work" which Pershing made on his subordinates.[25] Another commented that "Pershing never seemed to get much pleasure out of life unless he was working hard."[26] A third, noting that the General's work took him all over the islands, added: "The Old Man did not know what fatigue meant. I, a generation younger, had a hard time keeping up with him. He almost lived in the saddle."[27]

Wherever Pershing visited, he carefully noted the discipline of the men. It might be 120 degrees in the shade, yet he insisted that clothes be pressed and shirts buttoned up at the throat. "He was everywhere and he saw everything," reported his orderly. "And believe me, he knew his soldiers. There was no trick tried by any of them that he didn't get on to real soon."[28]

Yet he was human and had a sense of humor. On inspection once, he encountered a man who needed a haircut standing next to a man almost bald. "It's too damn bad these two can't be divided up," he commented.[29]

On another occasion Pershing met a Philippine Scout with his shirt unbuttoned.

"Button up that blouse and double time back to your company area," he ordered.

"Yes, sir," the Scout answered. He gave a snappy salute, buttoned his shirt, and stood still.

"Do you understand me? I told you to double time!"

"Yes, sir, I am waiting for you to give the command *March.*"

Pershing paused for a moment, thoughtful.

"That's one on me, soldier. You return to your company area, but you need not double time."[30]

More than discipline, Pershing valued efficiency. Was the work done and was it done well? "God help the fellow who failed to produce results," declared a subordinate. "No excuses or alibis were accepted and he was relieved at once."[31]

Although strict with subordinates, Pershing willingly listened to their opinions. Once he ordered his judge advocate, Capt. Allen J. Greer, to prefer charges against a captain for illegal use of government transportation. Greer argued against it.

"If we try him by court martial, there's a good chance he'll be acquitted. If not, the most he'll get will be a reprimand. Wouldn't it be better if I just write a letter of reprimand and have it signed by the adjutant general?"

"Write the letter," said Pershing. "We'll do it your way."[32]

After he had given an assignment Pershing's policy was to let a man have a free hand accomplishing it. "He did not bother about giving any details as to how he wanted the job done," one commented; "that was up to the individual. If you produced results that was all he asked for and he did not care what method you used."[33]

One of Pershing's dicta about military life stressed concern for the enlisted man. "There are plenty of candidates to be officers," he said; "but it isn't so popular being a private. Look after the privates."[34]

His anger flared when they were not being cared for. The enlisted man's uniform was poorly made as a rule and ill-fitting. "This clothing is as poor an excuse for a military uniform as can be imagined," he grumbled. "Instead of offering soldiers some inducement to enter and remain on foreign service by giving them good-looking and well-fitting clothes, we force upon them these unbecoming, hot, heavy, ill-fitting uniforms. The best khaki cloth is an English manufacture, and should be prescribed for the army."[35]

In 1911 Pershing recommended that the post exchange be allowed to serve beer and wine; this would give enlisted men a club of their own and save them "from the grog-shop and the brothel."[36]

He also recommended improvements in training. Recruits should be accepted at stated times and all trained together, instead of taking them in dribblets and teaching the whole group the same thing over and over again for the benefit of new men. Everyone loses interest, he observed, and no one is ever "well-instructed."[37]

G. F. Edwards related a 1913 incident when Pershing led sixteen men over the old "O.K. Trail" from Camp Overton to Camp Keithley. It rained on the way and the men arrived "dirty, miserable, wet, tired and hungry." The local commander met Pershing and told him his quarters were ready. "What have you done for my men?" the General responded. "Before I go anywhere myself I want you to see that these men are quartered and fed and that the post quartermaster issues them dry clothing which is not to be charged against their clothing allowance."

Said one of the troopers: "That little incident showed clearly that the Old Man always thought of those under him and saw that their comfort was arranged for before he would let anything be done for him. And believe me it went a long way to endearing him to the enlisted men."[38]

Pershing's work as commander looked not just to handling Moros, but to the defense of the Philippines against an aggressor. He was sure one would come. "Universal peace is as far away as the Millennium," he told the editors of *Life* in 1913. "Human nature is such that there has always been, and will always be, extreme views on any particular subject. These extreme views lead to extreme action. . . . A nation which is not ready to fight is at the mercy of the 'bully' nation, and there are 'bullies' among nations just the same as there are 'bullies' among men. . . . With different languages, different interests, different traits of character, different instincts and customs, different religions, Universal Peace in the world, even among the leading powers, is impossible."[39]

When war came he wanted Mindanao ready. In 1912 he recommended transferring department headquarters from Zamboanga to Camp Keithley on the north coast of Lake Lanao, where a last-ditch stand could be made. In 1913 he drew up a defense plan for Mindanao and headed a board to prepare a general defense of the Philippines.[40]

Should war come, Pershing predicted that the Philippine people would stand loyal to America.[41] That the prediction stood the test in World War II was in part "due to the good work of Pershing himself." That was the opinion of James L. Collins, who served as his aide in Mindanao and knew his work there and his influence on the people. "Pershing's achievements in pacifying the Moros and in building up a program of public works (schools, roads, dispensaries, etc.) was to a great extent responsible for the loyalty of the people to America when the test came."[42]

Pershing knew that America would not be ready for war, whenever it should break out. She never was. In 1910 he had called national defense "deplorable," pointing out that the Army, "unorganized and scattered over an immense territory at home and abroad, is almost negligible for anything but police purposes."

Two or three major powers, he said, had the capacity to land on American soil in six weeks a trained army as large as the whole American volunteer force in the Spanish-American War. In 1898 it had taken the United States longer than that just to assemble volunteers in instruction camps!

"There is no time to organize armies and train soldiers after war has begun," Pershing said in 1910. "We lose sight of this fact, and foolishly continue to depend upon that slender reed, the raw recruit. Time was when this might be done with impunity, but it is not so today. We are no longer secure in our isolation because we are no longer isolated. Something more than untrained numbers is imperative for self-defense. As a great nation we have obligations to meet. If we expect to have a voice potent for peace we must be prepared to do more than make declarations of policy. No people have ever kept a leading position in the world who were not prepared for war. Our country cannot hold her place among nations unless she supports a sufficient force to compel their respect."[43]

Comparing the armies of Europe with America's, he remarked: "It is not the number of men and guns that appeal to one, but it is the perfect organization behind it all; it is not the actual standing army but the consciousness of latent force pent up in the hundreds of thousands of trained soldiers returned to civil walks who stand ready to take up arms again. We have no such force. We have no such organization."[44]

As a minimum Pershing suggested a trained force of 300,000 men: two-thirds for defending the coasts and one-third in reserve. Nothing came of it. Nine months before the United States entered World War I, the Regular Army totalled only 100,000[45] and in the 1920's, when Pershing was Chief of Staff, it numbered little more.[46]

Several things may be noted in a characterization of Pershing at this stage of his career. "Affectionate" is not a word usually associated with him, but affectionate he was, as anyone could testify who saw him with his wife and family. "What gave the Old Man his happiest moments in Mindanao was the presence of his family," said his orderly.[47] "In his home," said an acquaintance, "he threw aside all the worries and cares that fall upon a commander, and seemed to banish all thought of them while he entered into the amusement and games of the children. . . ."[48] A third remarked: "He loved his family and did everything necessary to make them happy. . . . He was a family man."[49]

As a commanding general, he was strict, hard working, open to suggestions, but utterly intolerant of bungling, sloppiness, and inefficiency. Some people felt at ease in Pershing's presence and others didn't; some found him warm and human and others cold and aloof. The explanation may well lie in nothing more complicated than whether a person was doing his job or not. If he was not, Pershing could be hell on wheels.

Pershing was aggressive, at times unreasonably so. He realized the importance of a good staff and, when he found a good man, he would move heaven and earth to have him transferred to his command. "Great God, Pershing!" exclaimed General Bell in exasperation, "is there no work outside the Moro Province that is of any importance whatever?"[50]

Pershing was large-minded. He gave a man a job and let him work it out his own way. Sometimes the results could be pretty bizarre, as when two of his officers chopped off a dead renegade's head for identification to save lugging the whole body back over a long trail. No matter. "They had the right head," said Pershing.[51]

He was large-minded too in planning for the future, in realizing that America was not always going to be able to get by with a small army suitable only for police purposes. A professional soldier par excellence, he distrusted reliance on raw recruits who were supposed to spring to arms overnight in an emergency. Such a military policy would collapse under stress. He was outspoken in favoring a larger professional army and universal military training.

Finally, throughout life he was concerned for the welfare of the enlisted man, striving to improve his lot and instill pride of service. "Look after the privates," was one of his maxims.[52] It would be hard to have a better one.

13

The Bud Bagsak Campaign

On August 23, 1912, Pershing wrote to his superior, General Bell, that things were going quite well. Ever since they had decided to disarm the Moros the year before, lawlessness had decreased. Human life was now worth something. Criminals were easier to catch. "Never in the history of the Moro Province has [*sic*] there been such peaceful conditions as at present."[1]

His optimism was not entirely justified. The disarmament order, promulgated September 8, 1911, had brought in thousands of guns, but Moros on the island of Jolo were still rebellious. The Bud Dajo campaign in December, 1911, had quieted them for a time, but a few months after Pershing wrote so glowingly to Bell, there was again trouble on Jolo.

Moros fired on American troops on the trails or even into American camps. In Lati Ward especially, an area of about twenty square miles under the leadership of a chieftain named Amil, the Moros steadily collected arms and men until they numbered between five and eight thousand. They made no secret of what they had in mind. Amil sent a message to Lt. William W. Gordon who served as governor of the area: "Tell the soldiers to come on and fight."[2]

Two skirmishes occurred in late January, 1913, and Moros were the aggressors in each. Immediately afterwards, some five to ten thousand of them stampeded to Bud Bagsak, where they had a series of fortified strongholds built on top of an extinct volcano. As was the Moro custom, they took their wives and children with them.[3]

Pershing preferred as before to go slow, to let the Moros stay up on top of their mountain until they ran out of provisions or until it was time for them to plant their crops. He said to Governor-General Forbes: "My avowed and announced policy with reference to these Moros has been to disarm them by any means except by fighting. I have been and am especially anxious to avoid a big fight. I have been trying to scare, bluff or tire them out, and am willing to do anything, except run away, to avoid shooting them up."[4]

Soon rumors circulated that things were getting out of hand in Jolo. Colonel Harbord told the Army Chief of Staff, Leonard Wood, that Moros were firing into the city of Jolo to such an extent that Army wives and children had been evacuated to Zamboanga.[5] Worried, Forbes cabled Pershing: "Constant rumors from various sources indicate bad conditions in Jolo growing worse." He heard that the Lati Ward Moros were pillaging and murdering those who had surrendered their guns to the government. "It is my belief," said Forbes, "that there are times when as many men as are thought necessary should be sent in so as to absolutely smother any difficulty. I will support you in whatever action may be necessary for public order. Send me report as to conditions."[6]

Pershing's reply was born of his years of experience in dealing with Moros. "[The Moro] is not at all overawed or impressed by an overwhelming force," he answered. "If he takes a notion to fight he will fight regardless of the number of men brought against him. You cannot bluff him."

Already there were more than enough troops on the island of Jolo, said Pershing. Reports indicated that Bud Bagsak held five or six times as many women and children as Moro warriors. "While I do not believe . . . that the Moros who are openly opposing us will all yield without a fight, yet I am not prepared to rush in and attack them while they are surrounded by women and children."[7]

By the middle of February the Bagsak Moros were willing to talk. Their supplies were running short and government troops at the base of the mountain prevented them from being resupplied. Pershing wanted to talk too. Planting time was coming on and, if the Moros did not return to their fields, the Province would soon find itself with thousands of starving Moros on its hands. Yet as long as troops stayed in Lati Ward the Moros would not return.[8]

Lieutenant Bill Gordon, on the spot in Jolo, recommended that they pull back the troops. Three-quarters of the people atop Bagsak were women and children, he told Pershing in late February. He asked permission to negotiate—the Moros to surrender their weapons, and the government to withdraw its troops.[9]

Pershing approved. On March 7, 1913, Amil led 1,500 Moro fighting men to Taglibi for a conference. Representing the government was the Sultan of Sulu and Datto Mandi of Zamboanga, both Moros cooperative with Pershing. After three hours an agreement was reached. Government troops would be pulled back as far as Jolo City. The Bagsak Moros would return to their homes and take care of their planting. For the time being they would be allowed to retain their cutting weapons and guns, but they promised to do whatever Pershing would later ask of them through the Sultan of Sulu.[10]

Several months later the Moros reneged, declaring they would never lay down their arms. The most desperate were atop Bagsak. Those who worked their fields held themselves in constant readiness to bolt for the mountain again at the first indication of troops coming to enforce disarmament. Others, as a gesture of defiance, crept up at night and fired into the army barracks at Jolo, the capital city.[11]

Here was a test of Pershing as governor of the Moro Province. In 1911, when rebellion flared and had been extinguished at Bud Dajo, the Lati Ward Moros had stampeded to Bud Bagsak and prepared for a fight. His policy then had been to ignore them, hoping they would cool down. Dajo, like Bagsak, had been considered impregnable, yet he had made short work of it.[12] But these Moros never learned the right lesson. In early 1913, when they had again stampeded to Bagsak and troops had moved into the area, the withdrawal of the soldiers according to agreement had given the impression that they were afraid to fight.

Now the Moros openly defied the government and were threatening the capital city. Pershing could not ignore this. Ninety percent of the task of governing this unruly province lay in convincing the natives that he was strong and brave, and that he could crush anyone who tried to rebel. Once let the idea get abroad that he was weak or cowardly, and the whole provincial government would disintegrate.

The slightest move against Lati Ward would send men, women, and children scrambling towards their mountain stronghold. The death of the men did not particularly bother him, but killing women and children did. His only hope lay in somehow segregating the noncombatants, in attacking Bud Bagsak before the rebels had a chance to bring in their families. To do so he would have to get their guard down, make them think that the government was retreating even more. In early June, 1913, he cabled the commanding officer in Jolo, calling off all field operations and reconnaissance.[13]

Four days later he cabled that he was leaving his headquarters at Zamboanga to visit his wife and children, then summering at Camp Overton, Mindanao. That evening, taking with him his aide-de-camp, Lt. James L. Collins, he embarked on the transport *Wright* which pulled out of Zamboanga and headed northwest—the usual route to Overton. But once out of sight of Zamboanga the *Wright* changed course, heading south for Jolo. Pulling in at Isabela, Basilan, the party (which by now everyone realized was a "war party") embarked Capt. George C. Charlton and his 51st Company, Philippine Scouts.[14] About noon on June 10, they docked at Siasi, where they took on Capt. Taylor A. Nichols and his 52d Company, Philippine Scouts. They sailed for Jolo City, arriving at 8:00 P.M. with lights out.[15]

The secret had been well kept. When Lieutenant Collins arrived at the commanding officer's house with orders to assemble the men for an attack on Bagsak at dawn, he found practically all the officers on the post in dress white, paying a social call with their wives.[16]

Neither had the enlisted men any inkling of what was planned. There had been rumors of an expedition against Bagsak, but everyone said it wasn't scheduled before June 20 at the earliest, when there would be a full moon and good conditions for a night attack. The story around the barracks was that there would be another try to win over Amil without a fight. Everything seemed to confirm this. Hadn't Pershing left Jolo on June 9 and returned to Zamboanga? Hadn't he then taken ship for Camp Overton, several hundred miles up the coast? And hadn't all the troops brought to Jolo for the expedition recently been sent away by boat, including practically all the white troops composing the Jolo garrison?[17]

One soldier in Jolo was not so sure. Maj. George C. Shaw had served under Pershing in 1903 and knew something of his methods with Moros. "I felt he would talk for a while and win over the wavering ones but in the end there would be one big fight in which all the bad ones would be finished." So Shaw kept his Philippine Scouts in readiness. "[We] got our field kits where we could grab them at once as we soon learned that Gen. Pershing moved things quicker than ever and he was always some[what] swift."[18]

Things moved with speed that night. By 11:00 P.M. two companies of Philippine Scouts (24th and 31st) were on the march to invest Bud Bagsak on the south and prevent entrance or exit by that direction. They were to arrive there by daylight. A detachment of fifty men of the 8th U.S. Cavalry, together with the pack train and the mules which would carry the mountain guns in the field, left to march seventeen miles along the coast to Bun Bun, which was to be the base camp for the attack on Bagsak, three and one-half miles inland. The rest of the force—the main body—comprising six infantry companies, two mountain gun detachments, a medical detachment, and a demolition squad, left at 1:00 A.M. to go by water aboard four launches: the *Wright*, the *Jewell*, the *Geary*, and the *New Orleans*. All together the expedition numbered about 1,200 officers and men.[19]

At 3:30 A.M. on June 11, they made an unopposed landing at Bun Bun; they had not dared hope that the surprise would be so complete. Rendezvousing with the pack train, they established a base camp, transferred the mountain guns from the launches to the mules, formed two columns and by 5:15 A.M. moved out for the attack. Major Shaw

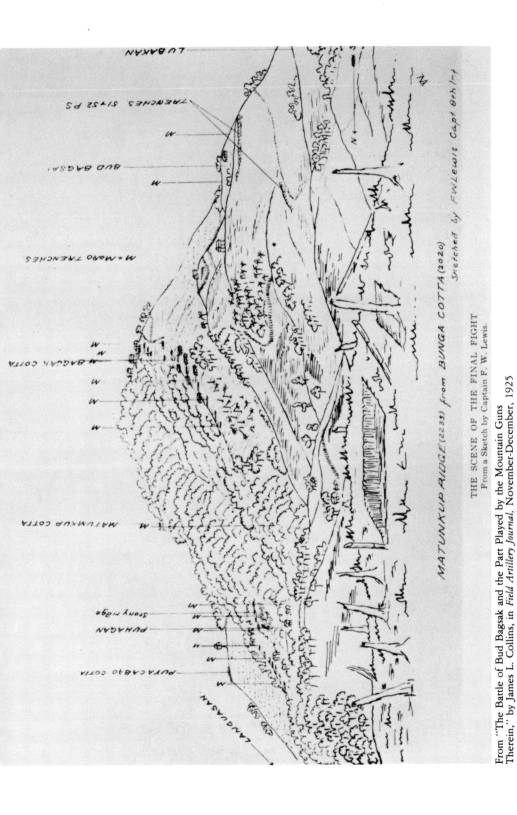

LUBAKAN

TRENCHES 51+52 PS

BUD BAGSAI

M = MORO TRENCHES

M BAGSAK COTTA

MATUNKUP COTTA

Stony ridge

PUHAGAN

PUYACABAO COTTA

LANGUSAN

MATUNKUP RIDGE (2233) from BUNGA COTTA (2020)

Sketched by F.W.Lewis Capt 8th Inf.

THE SCENE OF THE FINAL FIGHT
From a Sketch by Captain F. W. Lewis.

From "The Battle of Bud Bagsak and the Part Played by the Mountain Guns Therein," by James L. Collins, in *Field Artillery Journal*, November-December, 1925

Mount Bagsak

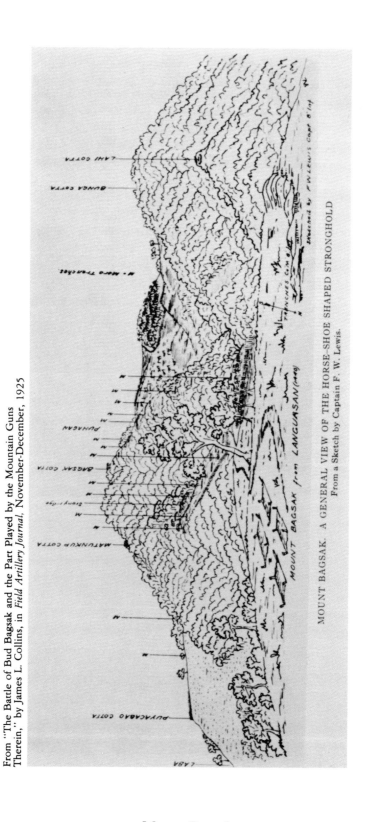

From "The Battle of Bud Bagsak and the Part Played by the Mountain Guns Therein," by James L. Collins, in *Field Artillery Journal*, November-December, 1925

MOUNT BAGSAK. A GENERAL VIEW OF THE HORSE-SHOE SHAPED STRONGHOLD
From a Sketch by Captain F. W. Lewis.

Mount Bagsak

commanded the right column and Captain Nichols, the left. Each column had a mountain gun detachment, plus two and three companies of infantry respectively. Held in reserve at Bun Bun were the cavalry and one infantry company. A dressing station for the wounded was also established.[20]

As they advanced, the troops understood why the Moros believed Bud Bagsak impregnable. Bagsak was a great volcanic cone rising some 2,200 feet above the sea. About half way up it became quite steep, and thereafter rose more and more vertically. In most places the last 100 feet was almost perpendicular, while in some places it went quite literally straight up and down.

At the top was a crater about 800 yards wide and 1,000 yards long. It was shaped like a gigantic warped horseshoe with cottas or forts at all prominent points and fortified trenches along the rim. Part of the rim had broken down where lava had poured out and this section (between the heels of the horseshoe) served as main entrance to the crater. Here Amil had constructed a heavy defensive trench and fortified it with a cotta called Pujagan. Flanking it were two other cottas, Puyacabo and Bunga; both were on the part of the rim that had not broken off and could fire down on Pujagan if it were captured.

Leading into the entrance at Pujagan was Languasan Hill, a bald knoll of volcanic ash about 200 yards distant and separated from it by a valley 100 feet deep. Commanding this knoll were the guns of Pujagan, Bunga, and Puyacabao, as well as those of a fourth cotta (Matunkup) situated still higher up on the left side of the rim, halfway between Puyacabao and the toe of the horseshoe.

Occupying the toe was still another cotta, Bagsak, strongest of them all, on the highest point of the rim. It looked directly across the crater to Languasan Hill and could also reach it with its fire.[21]

Against Languasan Pershing sent Shaw's right column, consisting of M Company, 8th U.S. Infantry, and 40th Company, Philippine Scouts, with orders to seize it and cut the main escape route. Shaw's men struggled up the steep hill covered with upland rice and grass. Carl F. McKinney's mountain gun (attached to Shaw's column) banged away at Pujagan and Bunga, while 1st Lt. Thomas F. Van Natta's gun (attached to the left column) opened fire on Puyacabao, trying to relieve pressure on the infantry.[22]

At 11:45 A.M., Shaw's men took Languasan. They then dug in as fast as they could since bullets were coming at them on all sides—from Pujagan in front, from Puyacabao and Matunkup to the left, from Bunga to the right, and from Bagsak across the crater. The Scouts lacked entrenching tools (a fact which Shaw bemoaned in his report on the operation) so his men had to dig in with their table knives and mess kits. They lost two killed and five wounded before they could get covered up; the wonder is that they did not lose more.[23]

Straight in front of them and on their level was the Pujagan cotta. Shaw had McKinney's mountain gun brought up the hill (the last 500 feet had to be by hand because of the steepness) and put in the foremost position, where it spent the rest of the day shooting at Pujagan.[24]

Meanwhile the left column under Captain Nichols had been doing good work. The 51st Company, Philippine Scouts, scaled a sheer cliff hand-over-hand on bejuco vines for 100 feet and captured Matunkup. The 29th and 52d Companies, Philippine Scouts, took Puyacabao. To do this Nichols had led his men up the side of the mountain at a point between Puyacabao and Matunkup, gained the inside of the crater, then worked his way down and around until he finally came up against Puyacabao from behind and on higher ground. The garrison was completely surprised and wiped out. Nichols lost only five men wounded.[25]

The capture of Matunkup and Puyacabao—both by 12:20 P.M.—was a severe blow to the Moros. These cottas had been considered impregnable and their loss rendered untenable several other strong cottas inside the crater which Matunkup and Puyacabao looked down on. The only cotta, in fact, which was substantially higher was Bagsak itself, destined to be the last to be taken. Another advantage of the capture was to take pressure off Shaw's right column, dug in across Languasan, which had been under considerable fire from the two fallen cottas.

Shaw's position, in fact, was of great tactical importance, blocking as it did the mouth of the crater and preventing the entrance of friends or families of the defenders. The Moros now seemed to realize this and concentrated upon it the fire of their remaining major cottas: Pujagan, Bunga, and Bagsak.[26]

At 4:00 P.M. on June 11, Pershing reinforced Shaw with Van Natta's mountain gun. Shaw placed it in the front line with McKinney's gun and a short time later a good shot knocked out one end of a Moro trench near Bunga which had been molesting them. There was no more firing from that point thereafter.[27]

Before dark Pershing sent word to Shaw to drop back down the hill for the night if he thought his position too dangerous to hold. Now that the U.S. forces held Matunkup and Puyacabao, they had superior ground from which to fire down on the Moros, should they occupy Languasan during the night. Shaw sent word back that they would stay where they were.[28]

It was a very black night until the moon rose at 2:00 A.M. The mountain guns were loaded with shrapnel with the fuse set near zero, so they could fire a sort of canister shot if the Moros came on in the dark. Shaw entrenched his men in a circle, every man in a trench, every other man awake while his neighbor tried to sleep. "It was a very dangerous place," said Shaw afterwards, "as there were Moros all around us and we did not know when they might take a notion to rush us. . . . There were alarms during the night probably from animals but while there was some firing nothing happened and we were very glad when daylight came."[29]

In the morning firing resumed early. At 9:00 A.M. Pershing reinforced Shaw still further with two more companies of Philippine Scouts. These were the troops who had marched to the south side of Bud Bagsak on the night of June 10-11 to cut off approach from that direction. Shaw's seizure of the main entrance meant they were no longer needed there.[30]

Meanwhile the position of the Pujagan Moros was becoming intolerable. They were being hit at 200 yards by Shaw's two mountain guns and by the withering fire of four companies of infantry (over 300 men) stretched across Languasan Hill. In addition, they were under fire from Matunkup and Puyacabao.

During the night the Pujagan Moros beat tom-toms and made a lot of noise shouting. In the morning this increased. Soon they could be seen in the trenches all dressed up in their best finery, wearing the bright, gaudy costumes saved for special occasions. Old timers in Shaw's trenches nodded knowingly to one another. "They're going to charge," they told the younger men. "They've gotten themselves all dressed up to die."[31]

At 9:30 A.M. Moros poured out of Pujagan with blood-curdling yells and screams, waving spears, krises, barongs, and daggers. Shaw's men opened fire, dropping a number almost immediately.

The others disappeared in the deep valley which separated Pujagan from Languasan and for a minute were lost from sight. Then they appeared—less than fifty yards away—screaming like banshees and coming straight on. Shaw's men stood up in their trenches and fired as fast as they could. The two mountain guns belched flame and shrapnel. It was a slaughter. Not one Moro reached Shaw's trenches.

That took care of Pujagan. "This rush," said Shaw afterwards, "was a most exciting and spectacular affair and is an illustration of the fanatical bravery of the Moros."[32]

Soon after, Captain Nichols came over from Puyacabao. "There's a sharpshooter on Bagsak," he warned. "He has a high powered rifle and he's a good shot." A moment later, Shaw saw a little puff of white smoke near the Bagsak cotta. He heard a queer sound beside him—a pop like a cork being pulled from a bottle. Nichols slumped to his knees, doubled over, with blood pouring from a hole under his right eye like water from a pitcher. He died on the spot.[33]

Pershing meanwhile had given orders that no one was to go to Pujagan. Five hundred feet lower than the rest of the rim, it would be subject to fire from the remaining Moro cottas, Bagsak and Bunga.

To the conquest of these, Pershing now set his mind. Bagsak was the strongest; it was 300 feet above the rest of the rim and most heavily defended. Pershing's closest position was Matunkup, only 600 yards away, but an attack from there was out of the question. The path ran along a very narrow ridge, only wide enough for one man at a time. When ten Philippine Scouts had attempted a dash across it, everyone had been killed or wounded.

That left Bunga. It was farther away than Bagsak, but it provided a better route for the attack. On the morning of June 13, Pershing detached the 24th and 31st Companies from Shaw's command and sent them around to the right to take Bunga. With them went Van Natta's mountain gun detachment. The other companies from Captain Nichol's former command (51st and 52d, Philippine Scouts) were sent from Matunkup and Puyacabao to work up to Bagsak from the south side.[34]

It was difficult reaching Bunga, for the place was accessible only by two hog-backs, with sheer up and down sides. Once they scaled the heights, the troops found the cotta loaded with Moros, armed mostly with cutting weapons and a few guns. It fell about 1:30 P.M. with minor losses: one soldier killed and one wounded. The one killed was almost cut in two with a barong.[35]

Taking advantage of the fight at Bunga, Pershing, with his aide, James Collins, and ten men, made a reconnaissance of Bagsak. Crawling along the edge of the crater rim, they advanced to within seventy-five yards of the position, where they could see the Moros watching the Bunga fight and talking excitedly. "It was an extremely dangerous reconnaissance," said Collins afterwards, "and I have often thought since, that a single volley from the Moros on Bagsak that day might have changed considerably America's part in the World War."[36]

On the way back they caught a wig-wag signal from across the crater, announcing the capture of Bunga. But the sides of the mountain were too steep for the mountain gun, the message added. It would have to be taken apart and carried up by hand, delaying use of it until at least 10:00 the next day.[37]

During the days of the battle the weather had been fearfully hot, with frequent showers. By June 14 the stench from the dead at Pujagan had become overpowering; therefore Shaw, despite Pershing's orders, advanced a detachment, gathered up the corpses, and buried them in one of the large trenches. Turning over one of the bodies, they found Amil, leader of the rebellious Moros. He had been killed as he led his men out of the Pujugan defenses on their last desperate charge.

By 12:30 P.M. on June 14, Van Natta's mountain gun had been set up on Bunga. It banged away at Bagsak all day, softening the position up for the assault on the morrow. Meanwhile the 51st and 52d Companies, accompanied by the cavalry, had reconnoitered the rim of the crater between Bunga and Bagsak. About 600 yards from the latter, and on the south slope of the hill, they found a favorable position in which to concentrate for the final attack.[38]

June 15 dawned with a heavy fog. By 7:30 A.M. it cleared and Van Natta opened up on Bagsak, taking up where he had left off the day before. At 9:00 A.M. the signal was given for the advance of the infantry.

The attack was to be made by the 51st and 52d Companies, Philippine Scouts. Both were Moro units commanded by American officers. They moved out from a grove about 450 yards from the Bagsak cotta, at the bottom of a steep ridge. To their right was a heavily wooded section, more or less untraversable, channeling their advance to the left along a sharp incline which was open and heavily fortified. Some eight to ten bamboo blockhouses interspersed with trenches dotted the heights up which they must charge.

The last hundred yards below the Bagsak cotta were particularly strong. Here the ridge narrowed and turned sharply to the left. Across the whole length of the ground the Moros had constructed three successive standing trenches, faced on the front with logs and heavily occupied. All along this area, to the right and left, they had cleverly constructed bamboo fences, preventing an enemy from flanking. The attack must be head-on.[39]

At the start the shrapnel fire from the mountain gun and the small arms fire from other troops in the vicinity kept the Moros down, and the 51st and 52d, commanded by Capt. George Charlton, made good progress. But when they began to hit the trenches, their movement slowed. "The resistance was very tenacious," said Pershing in his dry, colorless official report on the battle.[40] Privately, in a letter to his wife, he said, "The fighting was the fiercest I have ever seen."[41] The Moros fought like devils. More than ever before, in this last major stand they were to make against American authority, in this cotta which they considered impregnable, they justified the observation Pershing had made of them: "They are absolutely fearless, and once committed to combat they count death as a mere incident."[42]

The battle lasted nine hours. At 10:20 A.M. Pershing reinforced Charlton with the 24th Company, Philippine Scouts, under 1st Lt. Ralph G. Craven. At 2:45 P.M. a demolition squad attached to Shaw was also sent. It was not used. Such a squad was new in the Army and the hand grenades furnished by the War Department lacked "punch." The troops preferred homemade grenades (four sticks of dynamite with a fuse in the middle), which did a good job against Moro earthenworks. The only trouble was that sometimes the Moros threw the dynamite back.

By 1:30 P.M. Charlton's men had reached within one hundred yards of the Bagsak cotta and begun to traverse the difficult area defended by the three final trenches. There was no room to maneuver. The Moros, reconciled from the start to losing their lives, fought with abandon and skill.[43] The situation was "desperate," according to Captain Charlton.[44]

During the battle Pershing came up to the very front line. "I think it was largely due to his coolness and courage that the soldiers did such effective work," said a participant afterwards. "General Pershing stood so close to the trench, directing operations, that his life was endangered by flying barongs and spears which were being continually hurled from the Moro stronghold."[45]

Up until now Pershing's instructions had been for the American officers to stay behind the lines and direct the advance through the non-commissioned Moro officers in the front. The battle thus far had been Moro against Moro and the Scouts had done well, but when Pershing arrived they had lost six killed and ten wounded, the fight was particularly fierce, and the Scouts were beginning to hold back. Pershing therefore reversed his order, sending the American officers into the front lines to lead the attack personally.[46]

"The effect was electric," said Collins. A wave of energy seemed to sweep over the attackers and they pushed the assault with vigor and speed. Disregarding flying barongs and spears, they began to tear down the bamboo fences on the right. Soon they flanked the Moros on that side, firing at them through the fences. As fences were torn down, more and more attackers enfiladed the defenses; the end was only a matter of time.

Their trenches flanked and useless, the remaining Moros dashed out and threw themselves violently against the troops. Collins saw one soldier struck full in the chest with a long spear. He fell backwards into a trench, the spear quivering crazily in his body.[47]

The end came quickly. At 4:40 P.M. Charlton's men overran the remaining trenches and took Bagsak cotta.

Government losses in the five-day engagement were fifteen dead and twenty-five wounded—almost half of these on the last day against Bagsak. Total Moro losses were over 500 killed and unknown number wounded. A number of others escaped in the course of the battles.[48]

Despite Pershing's attempt to isolate non-combatants, five to ten percent of the Moro dead were women and children. This was inevitable, given the Moro policy of taking their families with them when they fought.

Pershing won, but as in the case of his earlier operations in the Lake Lanao region as a captain, it is hard to see how he could have lost. The odds were unbalanced. The Moros charged out of Pujagan, not with rifles and pistols, but with spears and krises. The Moros in Bunga had few guns, mostly cutting weapons. As Pershing told General Bell before the campaign, "There has not been a single moment . . . when we could not have gone on top of Bagsak and cleaned up this bunch of Moros with small loss to ourselves. . . ."[49]

On the other hand, that the odds were unbalanced did not stop the Moros from forcing a contest. Before the campaign, troops in the capital city slept on the floors in their barracks, mattresses propped up against the walls to stop Moro bullets during terrorist attacks.[50] The tragedy of Bud Bagsak was that the Moros brought on a battle they could not possibly win. They construed kindness and leniency as weakness. Pershing had offered complete amnesty to Amil and his followers if they surrendered their guns.[51] The Moros treated such an offer with contempt.

200

Scene at top of Bud Bagsak, Island of Jolo,
Philippines, after the June, 1913, battle
Photograph courtesy Col. Adelno Gibson

Amil, Moro leader at Bud Bagsak, with his son
*Photograph (circa 1913),
courtesy Mrs. Elizabeth Daley, Arlington, Va.*

Pershing's accomplishment at Bagsak lay not in winning the battle but in the way he won it and in his conduct beforehand. He knew Moro character as few others did. He knew that overwhelming force meant little to a Moro. As he had told Forbes: "If he takes a notion to fight he will fight regardless of the number of men brought against him. You cannot bluff him."[52] But you could trick him, and that, essentially, is what Pershing did. Moros were people who made a sudden resolve to die and then tried to get as many people to die with them as they could. Pershing's accomplishment was in saving the Moros from their own foolishness. A lot fewer Moros died than had planned to.

He delayed his campaign until the Moros had tended their crops. He also exercised that habitual restraint which we have noted in other campaigns. "I am willing to do anything, except run away, to avoid shooting them up," he said.[53] His secret move by ship and land on the night of June 10 was well planned and executed. One American officer found it so unexpected that he was drunk when orders came and had to spend the night being ducked in the *Wright's* bathtub to sober up.[54]

Pershing's tactical disposition of troops about Bagsak was excellent, as was his fighting of them during those June days. But his great accomplishment was the speed and secrecy with which he invested the mountain, blocked up the entrance at Languasan, and kept the deaths of women and children to a minimum. When the Moros had stampeded to Bagsak in January, 1913, estimates of non-combatants present ran as high as 75 percent. When the battle was finally fought in June, their casualties ran 5-10 percent.

The U.S. public was sensitive in 1913 to any killing of women and children. Hence American papers readily picked up a story by one John McLean in San Francisco on July 30, 1913, to the effect that Pershing at Bud Bagsak had killed 196 women and 340 children whom the Moros had held up as shields. Just back from Manila, McLean stated that the story had been censored and that threee newsmen in the Philippines were in danger of being jailed for trying to release it.[55]

Denials were not long in coming. "The statement . . . is untrue, and was undoubtedly circulated with malicious intent," said Pershing.[56] "McLean . . . was at [Fort] McKinley [in Manila] when the Bagsak fight took place and knew nothing about who was killed there," said an old Philippine hand. "In fact he was reading the papers about the fight one day at our mess, which incidentally, he beat out of a big board bill."[57]

Although McLean's account can be discounted, Pershing did kill women and children at Bagsak, and this fact eventually cast the operation in a bad light. In 1938, in an article on chemical warfare, an officer cited Bud Bagsak as an example of how gas could have achieved victory without loss of life on either side. When he submitted the article to *The Military Engineer*, it was rejected. The editor quoted a letter from the Chief of Chemical Warfare Service, disapproving publication "because it is believed that the actions at Bud Dajo[58] and Bud Bag Sak [*sic*] represent incidents which should not be unduly publicized. This discussion of these actions may revive public attention to military operations that might well remain forgotten."[59]

It is easy to find fault, especially from hindsight. Pershing had honestly tried to avoid killing *anybody*. General Bell, reporting to the War Department on Bagsak, said that Pershing had been subjected to "much criticism" by other Americans for his efforts to avoid an armed clash.[60]

Neither of Pershing's immediate superiors criticized him in 1913. Governor-General Forbes told the War Department that Pershing's attack on Bagsak was necessary, that he had exhausted patience, and that he managed the operation well. "The officers who were present have been loud in their praises of the way the thing was handled. They say it seems incredible that the thing could have been done with the small number of casualties that actually occurred."[61] General Bell, in endorsing Pershing's report on Bud Bagsak, stated: "I know of nothing which has taken place in the Department in the wisdom of which I do not concur. The policy of disarmament also had my cordial concurrence."[62]

Pershing himself had no doubts about his conduct. "They were given a thrashing which I think they will not soon forget," he told his superiors in Washington. "The backbone of outlawry and resistance in Jolo is broken. . . ."[63]

Indeed it was. Edward Bowditch, former Acting Governor of the

Moro Province, wrote from the Philippines one year after the battle of Bud Bagsak: "Conditions appear quiet throughout the Department. Sulu [i.e., Jolo] is very peaceful."[64]

For his courage in the front lines at Bagsak on June 15, 1913, Pershing was recommended for the Medal of Honor. Capt. George C. Charlton, who wrote one of the five testimonial letters which were forwarded to the War Department, said that Pershing "personally assumed command of the firing line when matters looked desperate for our side and by his personal presence, encouragement, and example in the firing line" brought about victory. His action "was entirely voluntary, and was way and above the call of duty."[65]

Pershing would not hear of it. "I do not consider that my action on that occasion was such as to entitle me to be decorated with a Medal of Honor," he wrote the War Department; "I went to that part of the line because my presence there was needed."[66]

The War Department agreed. In fact, the decorations board had voted against the recommendation even before receiving Pershing's letter, sent through channels.[67] Around 1922, after Congress authorized the Distinguished Service Cross, the decorations board again reviewed Pershing's action at Bud Bagsak and recommended him for the D.S.C. Pershing said no. He was Chief of Staff at the time (with automatic control over the decorations board) and did not feel it proper to receive the honor.[68]

In 1940, twenty-seven years after the event and sixteen after he had retired from the service, Pershing was awarded the D.S.C. for Bagsak. President Roosevelt called him to the White House on his eightieth birthday and personally presented the medal. "For extraordinary heroism in action against hostile, fanatical Moros . . ." read the citation. "His encouragement and splendid example of personal heroism resulted in a general advance and the prompt capture of the hostile stronghold."[69]

14

Tragedy at the Presidio

By and large, Pershing's health held up well in the Philippines. He lived a vigorous outdoor life, scarcely a day passing without his riding one to three hours. "Rain, heat or typhoon mattered little," said his orderly—"he rode."[1]

During Pershing's fourth year, however, trouble began. In August, 1913, he was admitted to the Manila hospital for indigestion, sore mouth, and diarrhea; two months later he asked to leave the Philippines "immediately." In December the War Department ordered him home.[2]

His new assignment was command of the 8th Brigade at the Presidio in San Francisco. He did not stay there long. In April, 1914, trouble broke out in Tampico, Mexico, over the arrest and imprisonment of American sailors; later that month U.S. forces bombarded Vera Cruz and seized the city. War seemed imminent.

With feelings running high, rumors flew about that Francisco (Pancho) Villa, a Mexican insurgent, was planning to cross the border and raid El Paso. On April 24, 1914, the 8th Brigade, 3,500 strong, entrained for Texas under rush orders.[3]

"It looked as though we were going right on into Mexico and eat them up at once without any further discussion," Pershing said. "We fully expected to be in the city of Mexico before we again drew rein."[4]

Arrived at El Paso, Pershing found that the rumors had little foundation.[5] He remained there under orders which put him in charge of all troops in the city and on the Fort Bliss military reservation just outside it. He was entrusted with the defense of the border from Columbus, New Mexico, to Sierra Blanca, Texas.[6]

In August, 1914, Pershing met Pancho Villa, his later adversary in the Punitive Expedition, when the latter passed through El Paso on route to a conference at Nogales. Pershing invited him to Fort Bliss to watch a troop review, then to his quarters for drinks.[7] Although Villa wore civilian clothes, the bulge in his coat revealed a brace of pistols in his hip pockets. He seemed shy and bashful. When his bodyguard, Rodolfo ("The Butcher") Fierro, forgot to remove his hat, Villa jabbed him in the ribs and growled in a stage whisper, "Take off your hat, you brute, you animal!"[8]

Villa impressed his host as "a strong man,"[9] certainly better than Venustiano Carranza, whom Pershing later termed a "charlatan."[10] When someone subsequently described Villa as "head and shoulders" above other Mexican leaders and "a remarkable man in many ways," Pershing responded: "My impression of the general corresponds to your own. I think he will yet do great things for his beloved Mexico."[11]

When World War I started, Pershing asked to go abroad as an observer, but nothing came of it.[12] He was pro-Ally and after the Germans sank the *Lusitania* on May 7, 1915 he reacted violently against what he considered Wilson's soft policy.

"What do you suppose a weak, chicken-hearted, white-livered lot as we have in Washington are going to do?" he asked his wife. "When asked their policy, they say it is to do 'whatever seems best for human welfare'—a fine, strong aggressive answer for what purports to be the greatest nation on earth! Good God, deliver us from the disgrace of the present administration. It makes me ashamed to be in its service. . . . We need strong and courageous men at the head of affairs and not meek sops."[13]

Three days after the *Lusitania* disaster, President Wilson in an address to a large gathering in Philadelphia said: "There is such a thing as a man being too proud to fight. There is such a thing as a nation being so right that it does not need to convince others by force that it is right."

Pershing approached apoplexy when he read the words.

"Isn't that the damnedest rot you ever heard a sane person get off? The idea of a President saying such nonsense as that. It is truly hopeless. I suppose he is trying to outdo Bryan in idiocy. . . . Deliver us from theorists and sophists and psalm singers. I had rather die on the field of battle supporting the right than live a thousand years in dishonorable peace. I should be ashamed to look my wife and children in the face. Oh, Lord, all this makes my blood boil. It's too pitiful for words."[14]

Time dragged on and it seemed likely that Pershing would be stationed at El Paso for a long period because of uncertain relations with Mexico. He decided to bring his family down. "I'm tired of living alone," he told a friend. "I'm having my quarters fixed up so that my wife and children can join me."[15]

Then tragedy intervened. During the night of August 26-27, 1915, fire broke out in the Pershing home at the Presidio. When it was over, Frances and the three girls were dead; only Warren survived.

The tremendous shock to Pershing can be imagined. Reading the correspondence between him and Frances in 1915, one is struck by the depth of their mutual love. It had not decreased since the days of their courtship over a decade before; indeed, it had grown.

Recalling his first letter to Frances in 1904, which was very formal and reserved, Pershing told her in 1915: "I have wished a thousand times that I had written you as I then felt. But I have you and love you *more* than then even if it were possible. You beautiful thing—Sweet—Darling—Mine—Angel—Wife."

To this letter, signed "Jack," he added a postscript:

"Millions of kisses from the craziest lover that ever wrote a line to his sweetheart. Wife and sweetheart in one—and that one—MINE."[16]

Frances felt the same. Her letters would open "Darlingest" or "My darling Boy" and be signed "Your Frankie."[17] About two weeks before she died, she wrote: "Oh my heart is so full of things to say to you tonight, darling. All day I have felt so near you and I have been so filled with a sense of your nobility and of your dearness—and with a desire to kneel at your feet and adore you. I wish there was no such thing as time, or beds or going to bed. I feel as if I could fill the night loving you. . . .

"Dearest, really I am wound up to run all night—but I must go to bed. Went to a great 'At home' at the Darracks this afternoon. Everyone there had . . . written or done something of note. My only claim to be present was for having tamed a wild hero.

"Jack, I'm homesick for you as can be. Shall I stay and be a suffragette & attend the National Convention—or shall I be plain me & come home soon? I wouldn't give ten cents to be a suffragette with individuality when I could crawl into your shadow and be a slave."[18]

How poignant are these final letters of Frances, so filled with love and sunshine. "The world is so clean in the morning," she wrote, "—there is the sound of meadow larks everywhere. And God be thanked for the sunshine and the blue sky! . . . Do you think there can be many people in the world as happy as we are? I would like to live to be a thousand years old. . . ."[19]

At the Presidio on August 26, 1915, Frances had as an overnight guest Anne Orr Boswell, her old college chum and maid of honor at her wedding. In the early hours of the morning of August 27, Mrs. Boswell was awakened by fire. Rousing her children who were staying overnight too, she called to Frances and tried to reach her room. She received no answer and the smoke drove her back.

Retreating through a window to the porch roof, Mrs. Boswell threw her children into the arms of soldiers one floor below, then descended. Someone then led them away to the Officers' Club for shelter and recovery.[20]

By this time the reveille gun had fired and a siren had awakened the post. Soon a large crowd converged on the Pershing residence, as huge clouds of heavy smoke poured out of it. The post fire department arrived and played streams of water on the flames.[21] But during this time no one attempted to reach the Pershing family, lying helpless in the upstairs bedrooms. No one thought they were there. By a tragic error someone mistook Mrs. Boswell for Mrs. Pershing when she and her family were led away to the Officers' Club. In the fog, smoke, and darkness it was easy to do. Word went around that the family was safe, no one knowing that two families had been in the house that night.

"Thank God there's nobody left in there," said one bystander, watching the flames. "The damned old firetrap might as well burn right down."

Suddenly a wave of shock swept through the crowd. Someone back from the Officers' Club reported that Mrs. Boswell and her family had been rescued. The crowd gasped in horrible realization: Mrs. Pershing and her children were still in the house!

Immediately volunteers went to the rescue. Three men climbed into the upstairs back bedroom and groped their way across the room until they ran into a door. It was stuck or locked. After vainly trying to open it, they were forced back to the window for air. The smoke in the room was terrific.

As they crawled back one of the men bumped into an unconscious child lying on the floor. It was a boy. Carrying him to the window, the rescuers called to those below: "Here, take this kid!" Someone came up the ladder and took him from their arms.

The men returned again to the back bedroom, but found no one else. They made a second attempt at opening the door—all in vain. The smoke finally drove them out for good.[22]

By this time other rescuers had gotten up on the front porch and into the front bedroom window, where they found Mrs. Pershing and the other three children. All were still in their beds, unconscious. The only sign of movement was Mrs. Pershing's arm which dangled over the edge of the bed, probably an involuntary motion caused by restlessness from the smoke.[23] The rescuers carried them out through the window. A sudden hush came over the crowd as they appeared.[24]

All five members of the Pershing family were carried to the parade grounds on which the house fronted and given emergency treatment.

Every effort was made to revive them. Only the boy Warren responded.[25] None of the victims was burned; death was by suffocation. Their facial expressions were those of a deep sleep. This fact seemed to give some consolation to Pershing when he learned it afterwards, for it meant that they probably had not suffered.[26]

Years later one of the men who rescued Warren was asked to give his recollections of the fire. He did so reluctantly, fearing that the rescue might be played up as heroic. "I do not feel that it deserves any special recognition," he said, "as my feeling about the whole episode has always been one of deep regret that owing to a misapprehension (the statement by some one that the family was not in the building) no more desperate effort was made *at the time* to get into the bedrooms. Perhaps Mrs. Pershing could have been gotten out in time. *No one at the fire felt like a hero afterwards.*"[27]

Meanwhile in the office of the *El Paso Herald* two newsmen were running through telegram copy. One was Norman Walker, an Associated Press correspondent; the other was Hubert S. Hunter, news editor of the *Herald*. At first the story came over the wire that there had been a fire at the Presidio which destroyed the Pershing residence. Later the "wrap-up" story came: except for Warren, the whole family was dead.

Thinking that Pershing must know the news by now and that the dispatch might have some details he would appreciate learning, Walker phoned Fort Bliss and asked for General Pershing's quarters. A voice came on and Walker, thinking he was speaking to an aide, said: "Lieutenant Collins, I have some more news on the Presidio fire."

"What fire?" came back the voice. "What has happened?"

Sickeningly, Walker suddenly realized two things: (1) He did not have an aide on the other end of the line, but Pershing himself. (2) The General had not yet heard the news.

"What fire?" the voice repeated.

Caught and unable to do anything but go on, Walker hesitatingly informed Pershing that a fire had occured at his Presidio home and that a dispatch had come in about it. He read him the wrap-up story about the death of all but Warren.

"Oh, God!" exclaimed Pershing. "My God! What's that? Read that again!"

Walker repeated the dispatch, then listened agonizingly as Pershing caught his breath. Like a heavy blow in the stomach the full import of the message struck home.

"My God! My God! Can it be true?" Pershing was stunned, his whole world crashing down around him.

After a pause Walker apologized for his mistake in thinking he was talking to Lieutenant Collins and expressed his condolences. Just as he was about to sign off, Pershing spoke again:

"Wait a minute. Who is this? Who am I speaking to?"

Walker identified himself.

"Thank you, Walker," said Pershing gravely. "It was very considerate of you to phone."[28]

This is one account of how Pershing learned the news. A different version was related by James L. Collins, Pershing's aide, who lived in the General's quarters in El Paso.

Collins remembered that August 27 very well. It was usually his custom to ride with Pershing early every morning, taking a two-hour horseback tour of Fort Bliss. But that morning Pershing did not ride. He had taken a dose of castor oil and told Collins to go out alone.

After about an hour Collins saw a horseman riding towards him at a gallop. It was Pershing's orderly, who ordered his immediate return. When Collins saw Pershing, the latter was excited and distraught.

"My God, Collins," were his first words. "Something terrible has happened at the Presidio! There's been a fire at the house!"

According to Collins, that was all that Pershing knew at the time: there'd been a fire. He did not yet know of anything worse. "He did not know that any of his family had died."

How Pershing received the news of the fire, Collins never knew. He insisted, however, that the Presidio disaster came to Pershing in two stages: first the fire, then the deaths.[29]

Two days after the fire, at 8:30 A.M. on August 29, Pershing arrived in San Francisco. En route he had been met at Bakersfield, California, by Frank A. Helm, an old friend. "He was in terrible distress," Helm recalled. "The first thing he said to me was, 'I can understand the loss of one member of the family, but not nearly all.' "

According to Helm, Pershing put his arms around his neck and held him that way repeatedly from Bakersfield to Oakland—almost 300 miles. Helm became so worried about his friend's condition that he sent word ahead to have a doctor meet the train with a sedative. "I really believe that if Warren had also been lost, Pershing would have lost his mind," he said.

In San Francisco Pershing went at once to the funeral parlor. He stood in front of his dead for a few moments, then asked to be left alone. His worried friends went out but kept an eye on him through the heavy drapes. They saw him get down on his knees and stay there for about ten minutes before each casket.

When he came out, head bowed, he asked to go to the Presidio. Helm remonstrated, then gave in. Pershing, he knew, would never be satisfied that his family could not have been saved until he actually saw the burned house for himself.[30]

At the Presidio they reconstructed the fire. The cause was the corner grate in the dining room from which live coals had rolled out on the highly polished floor. (After the fire someone recalled that the same thing had occurred several days before, but during the daytime and while someone was present.)[31] Three or four holes were burned in the wood in front of the fireplace but, with this exception, the floor had not burned through. What had done the damage was not flame but smoke —heavy, death-bearing fumes which billowed forth as the fire travelled across the floor and up the stairway.

Mrs. Pershing and the baby, Mary Margaret, had been in the front upstairs bedroom, Helen and Anne in an adjoining room, and Warren in a back bedroom separated from the other rooms by a bathroom.

As the baby had a cold, Mrs. Pershing had closed the windows in her bedroom and in the adjoining rooms where the children were sleeping. For ventilation she had opened the door of her room (which was at the head of the stairs), the connecting doors to the children's rooms, and thence to the back stairs. Inadvertently she formed a perfect draft for the fire.

That night the flames and smoke came up the stairs, through the open door into Mrs. Pershing's room, then into the adjoining room, asphyxiating the mother and the three girls. Mrs. Boswell, sleeping across the hall with the door closed and the windows open, escaped; so did Warren, whose room was farthest from the head of the stairs. Even so, smoke blackened the ceiling of his room and the wall six inches from the top.

Ironically, it was Army "spit and polish," so characteristic of Pershing, which was responsible for the catastrophe; the highly polished floors—recently waxed and oiled—carried the fire and smoke rapidly upstairs and killed his family in their sleep.[32]

After visiting the house Pershing said, "I am now satisfied that nothing could have been done. They had no chance. I wanted to see that for myself."[33]

Leaving the Presidio, Pershing went to the Letterman Hospital and picked up Warren who had been taken there after the fire. On the way to the Hotel Stewart he held the boy on his knee.

"Have you been to the fair?" Pershing asked as they drove past the Fair Grounds.

"Oh, yes," replied Warren, "Mama takes us a lot."

This unnerved Pershing. His body began to shake so much that Frank Helm had to hold Warren for the rest of the trip.[34]

The funeral was later that same day, Sunday; the services were conducted by an Episcopal clergyman. Head down, Pershing emerged from the chapel wearing black civilian clothes. "He bore himself with dignity, but he was clearly moved," said Nellie Tayloe Ross, later the first woman governor of Wyoming. "I shall never forget the look of grief on his face as he came out the door."[35]

The bodies were shipped to Cheyenne and buried in the Warren plot. That same week the government announced plans to raze the house at the Presidio.[36]

The period immediately after the fire was a difficult one for Pershing. When a trunk was shipped to him containing some personal effects of the family he broke down.[37] Friends tried to distract him from his sorrow; an overwhelming number of acquaintances (including Pancho Villa) wrote letters of condolence to ease the pain.[38] But mostly he had to fight his battle alone. A year after the event he said of Frances: "The anniversary of her tragic death has just passed—August 27—and it has been so bitter—so difficult to get over. Now our eldest little girl's birthday, September 8, is approaching—she would have been 10 years old."[39]

To his friend, Bishop Charles H. Brent, he remarked still later: "I have been able to get so little consolation out of life since that time. About the only respite I have known is by keeping every minute occupied."[40]

Religion was some help. Pershing believed in Providence; he thought that life, even its tragedies, must have meaning. "It is hard at times of course to bring one's self to believe that there is any Great World Plan," he admitted, "but there must be a plan, else everything would be chaotic."[41]

In 1915, a few months before Frances died, he had written to her about a matter which was bothering him: "I have prayed over this thing. . . . In all my life I have never come to a hard place like that without going to God in secret and getting down on my knees as I did Sunday afternoon and asking Him. . . . Ask Him in all sincerity—and *Faith*—what to do. . . ."[42]

In 1918 when there was a death in the family of one of his staff, he took the man aside. "I know how you must feel," he confessed. "All one can do is to go on with life. One must get over the sorrow or it will break you. What happens is God's will."[43]

Biographers of Pershing in later years inquired of his friends whether he talked about the fire? "Incessantly," answered James H. Frier, Jr., whose father was on the border with Pershing in 1915. "He blamed himself for the highly polished floors which caused the fire to travel. He talked so much of the fire that my father became bored hearing about it."[44] Later, however, it was otherwise. Warren Pershing never once heard his father mention the incident.[45]

When Pershing wrote his autobiography, he treated the fire in the briefest way. After stating that his family had remained in San Francisco because "life seemed to be safer and better for them" there, he said: "But on the night of August 26, 1915, the house took fire and only our

John J. Pershing, and his son, Warren
Photograph courtesy Mlle. Micheline Resco,
Paris, France

son was saved."[46] That was all. He was never one to make a display of his emotions.

Yet he had them; he was no "iceberg," despite what people thought. From time to time, like a cork bobbing to the surface, the memory of that night at the Presidio forced its way into consciousness and revealed how deeply he was moved. Mrs. J. Borden Harriman remembered the time Pershing visited her and seemed "all down in the mouth." When she commented on his look, he explained. "Today is my daughter's birthday."[47]

Charles G. Dawes, his old friend, related an incident which occurred on August 31, 1917, when he and Pershing were riding together in an automobile. "Neither of us was saying anything," said Dawes, "but I was thinking of my lost boy [Dawes's son had drowned in 1912] and of John's loss and looking out of the window, and he was doing the same thing on the other side of the automobile. We both turned at the same time and each was in tears. All John said was, 'Even this war can't keep it out of my mind.' "[48]

Did the tragedy change Pershing much? Some said yes, exteriorly. "Pershing was never a morose man," commented Henry J. Reilly; "he was a silent man. But after the fire he was even more silent."[49]

Maj. Gen. Leon B. Kromer, a Philippine campaigner, said he never saw such a changed man as Pershing after the fire. His wife agreed. "Pershing withdrew more into himself," she explained. "He became more frosty on the outside. It was still true that once you got to know him he was warm and human. But he became harder to know."[50]

Others felt differently. "I don't think there was any great change," said Dorothy Canfield Fisher, whom he had taught at the University of Nebraska.[51] "Pershing's reaction," said James L. Collins, his aide, "was simply that of *a normal man* in such a tragedy. He took the news neither with exceptional stoicism nor exceptional emotion. It hurt him terribly at the time, as it would any man. He was utterly crushed in San Francisco. In later life it did not change his character in any radical way, any more than it would be expected to change any strong character. He felt saddened by the incident and the memory of it stayed with him, just as it would with any normal man, but no more or no less."[52]

15

Chasing Villa

March 9, 1916. In the dead of early morning, Francisco (Pancho) Villa, "the Lion of the North," crossed the American border with 485 men. At approximately 4:15 A.M. he struck Columbus, New Mexico, in a sneak attack. "I was awake; they were asleep," he said later of this raid which took American troops stationed there by surprise, ". . . and it took them too long to wake up."[1]

Like much of what the flamboyant Pancho said and did, this was an exaggeration. True, he had surprised Columbus. Eighteen lay dead and eight others were wounded (about equally divided between soldiers and civilians) when he scampered out of town again. But his own losses were far heavier: between one and two hundred. The gringos woke up quicker than he expected.[2]

Villa's raid was the culmination of a series of events "South of the Border" which Americans found disquieting. Since 1911, when the longtime dictator Porfirio Díaz had been overthown, Mexico had been in the throes of a series of revolutions and counter-revolutions which led to murder, banditry, and general insecurity. Díaz was replaced by Francisco Madero, who was murdered, in all probability, at the instigation of his successor, Gen. Victoriano Huerta. Huerta, in turn, was

ousted by a combination of foreign diplomatic pressure and internal
revolt led by Emiliano Zapata, Álvaro Obregón, and Pancho Villa, each
with their private revolutionary armies. By 1916, Venustiano Carranza
had risen to the top of the heap, proclaiming himself "First Chief" of
the "de facto" government. Conditions, however, were still unsettled.
Villa in the North and Zapata in the South were in revolt; life and
property were precarious, including that of Americans.

In January, 1916, in the state of Chihuahua where Villa held sway
as a war lord, seventeen American miners were murdered in cold blood
by his men at Santa Isabel. Two months later Villa himself led the raid
at Columbus against American territory.[3]

Villa's motive in making the raid is disputed. He badly needed
supplies, especially horses, to replenish his stock.[4] He bitterly resented
American recognition of his rival, Carranza, and may have thought to
embarrass him by provoking American armed intervention which the
First Chief would be powerless to stop.[5] He may even have been an
agent of German intrigue which sought to preoccupy the United States
with Mexico.[6]

Whatever the reason, the raid was the latest of depredations against
American lives and property which had been going on for years, and
Americans were thoroughly angered. Juan Sanchez, one of the Villistas
captured at Columbus, was condemned by a federal court and hanged.
He was pronounced dead and taken down, but through some strange
circumstance began to revive. "Hang him again," ordered Sheriff Matt
Gallagher.

"You can't do that," protested Sanchez's lawyer. "This man has
been pronounced dead."

"Mister," replied the sheriff coldly, "my orders from the judge were
to 'Hang him by the neck till he is dead, dead, dead'; I've got two more
shots at the sonovabitch!"

The next time Sanchez was taken down there was no question. He
was dead.[7]

Voices everywhere demanded an expedition to hunt down Villa.
Senator Ashurst of Arizona summed up sentiment when he said that

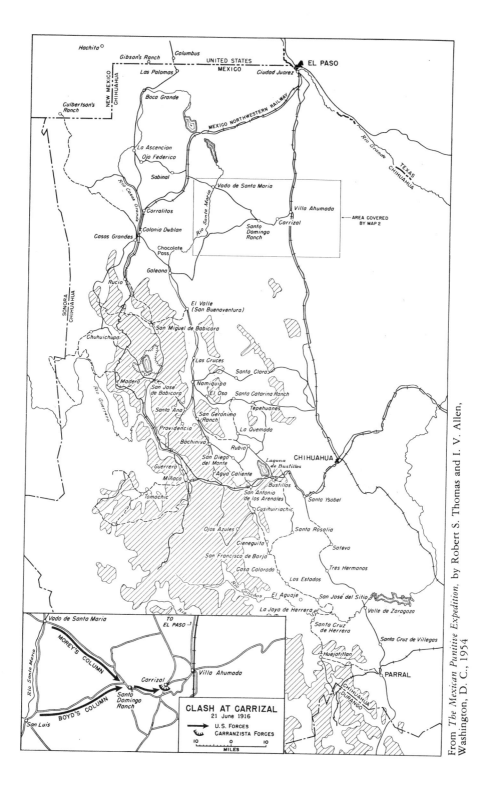

Mexican Punitive Expedition, 1916: Area of Operations

what America needed was less "grape juice" (a reference to the teeto-taling of Secretary of State William Jennings Bryan) and more "grape shot."[8]

The demand for an expedition took the War Department by sur-prise. Plans on file made no provision for chasing a single guerrilla. All plans were based on the assumption of a full-scale war, with seaborne operations at Vera Cruz and Guaymas. Any expedition hunting Villa would have to "play it by ear."[9]

On March 10, 1916, Maj. Gen. Frederick Funston, commanding the Southern Department at Fort Sam Houston in San Antonio, cabled Washington that Villa was at Boca Grande, about fifteen miles south of the border. He recommended sending two columns after him—one from Columbus, the other from Hachita, forty-three miles to the west. He assumed that the Mexican government under Carranza would grant permission to use Mexican railroads to transport troops and supplies.[10]

That same day Secretary of War Newton D. Baker, who had taken office only the day before, authorized the expedition: "The President has directed that an armed force be sent into Mexico with the sole object of capturing Villa and preventing any further raids by his band, and with scrupulous regard to the sovereignty of Mexico."[11]

On the recommendation of Major Generals Hugh L. Scott and Tasker H. Bliss, Chief of Staff and Assistant Chief of Staff respectively, Pershing was selected to command.[12] Why him? "The reason is not far to seek," he explained; "I was simply on the ground and more available than anyone else."[13]

This was unnecessarily modest. True, he was on the ground. But so was Funston, who outranked him by a grade and who itched to com-mand.[14] Furthermore he was five years younger than Pershing and might be supposed to be more fit for an arduous campaign. But reports had been coming in to the War Department about his drinking—something never charged against Pershing. This may explain why the latter was chosen.[15]

Another reason was mentioned by Newton D. Baker in a lecture he gave later to the Army War College. "I had never seen General Persh-ing, but they [Generals Scott and Bliss] knew him and he was represented to be an officer who was absolutely loyal to the policy of the civil authorities under whom he was serving."16

From the start, the expedition was plagued with difficulties. The Carranza government vetoed use of the two Mexican railroads which connected Mexico with El Paso, which meant that supplies would have to go in the hard way—by horse and buggy, or by the primitive Dodge trucks just coming into use.17

Both had their difficulties. The animals required food and would eat up more and more of what they carried, the farther the expedition got from its home base. The trucks were in short supply and would not have been available at all but for the Chief of Staff flagrantly violating the law. When the Quartermaster General said there weren't enough trucks for the expedition, Scott asked how much it would cost to buy enough.

"About $450,000," replied the Quartermaster.

"All right," said Scott, "send right out and buy those trucks. . . ."

Later, when Scott told the Secretary of War that he had committed a penal offense by spending money without Congressional authorization, Baker told him not to worry.

"If anybody goes to jail, I'll be the man."18

Carranza's refusal of the railroads made Columbus, New Mexico— a quartermaster's nightmare—the base of operations. A small town of about 300 people out in the middle of the desert, Columbus had not even recovered from the Villa raid before men, animals, and supplies began to pour in. By March 15 the single siding was logjammed with freightcars. No one had any idea of their contents because, in the rush, they arrived before their bills of lading.19

Chihuahua—the land over which Pershing and Villa were to play cat and mouse—was a nightmare too. "The country itself was an enemy," said one student of the campaign, "wrinkled and tawny as the skin of a dead lion, searingly hot by day, freezingly cold by night."20 "Carrion land," another called it.21 Pershing's aide, James L. Collins, was convinced that Chihuahua was connected up with the Sahara Desert by some subterranean passage "or other hellish manner," because he could not imagine there being so much sand and dust in two different parts of earth. No rain had fallen since the previous July, nine months before, so that inevitably men on the march choked on clouds of alkaline dust kicked up by moving feet and hooves.[22]

One officer put it this way: "If God had set out to mold a country as a stage for a cavalry campaign, he would have made . . . Chihuahua. This was a stage . . . across which snow, sandstorms, tropic heat and sharp cold added to the misery of the actors."[23]

To make matters worse, the terrain was unknown. "There is no part of Mexico which is more poorly mapped than the northwest section of Chihuahua," Funston reported.[24]

From what was available and could be rushed to the border quickly, Pershing selected his men for the Punitive Expedition. The initial strike force consisted of the 7th, 10th 11th and 13th Cavalry, the 6th and 16th Infantry, and two batteries of the 6th Field Artillery. The 10th Cavalry had been his old regiment. The 6th and 16th Infantry had comprised the 8th Brigade which he had brought down to El Paso from the Presidio in 1914; later they would form half of the First Division, his favorite, in World War I. The 6th Field Artillery also would go to France later as part of the First Division.[25]

On the night of March 13 Pershing arrived at Columbus to take charge. He was immediately presented with bad news. Word came from Palomas, the small town right across the border, that the Mexican commander planned to resist his entry.[26] Pershing waited a day, pending orders. Then at noon on March 15, the time given for moving unless he heard otherwise, he crossed the border. Meanwhile the War Department had cabled: "In case you have crossed border, under no circumstances return and, if necessary . . . , strengthen force there."[27]

There was no fight at Palomas. The town was deserted; the Mexican garrison had pulled out that morning. But the incident was an earnest of what was to come. As Pershing said afterwards. "At the very gate we met something which was symbolical of the Mexican attitude. . . . From then on, we met but more or less disguised ill-will."[28]

The Columbus column, mainly infantry, moved slowly. Pershing left

Pershing leading cavalry during Mexican campaign, 1916.
Actually most of his travelling in the
pursuit after Villa was by automobile.
Photograph courtesy National Archives

it at Palomas and joined the other column at Hachita, which crossed after midnight on March 15–16. Mostly cavalry, they moved at a good clip—fifty-five miles that day and sixty-eight the next, arriving at Colonia Dublán the night of March 17. Three days later the slower moving Columbus column came in.[29]

By now Villa was reported gathering supplies and mounts at San Miguel de Babicora, some fifty-five miles south. Pershing sent out three parallel columns, hoping to block a move west toward Sonora or east towards the Mexican National Railroad, with the added hope of cutting Villa's trail or getting south of him before he could move into the mountains back of Guerrero.[30]

At 3:00 A.M. on March 18 the first column rode out: approximately 675 officers and men of the 7th Cavalry (Custer's old regiment) under Col. James B. Erwin. Pershing strictly commanded them, and all other columns, to treat Mexicans with every consideration. "Make the utmost endeavor to convince all Mexicans that the only purpose of this expedition is to assist in apprehending and capturing Villa and his bandits."[31]

Colonel Erwin carried a copy of a proclamation by Álvaro Obregón, the Mexican Secretary of War and Navy, stating that the U.S. and Mexico had entered an agreement which mutually permitted crossing the border in pursuit of bandits. But unknown to Pershing, the two countries interpreted the document differently. The United States understood that the agreement was retroactive; Mexico did not. Concluded after the Villa raid, the agreement was interpreted by Mexico to authorize expeditions if there were *future* raids; by the United States to authorize Pershing's expedition because of the *past* raid. A long exchange of diplomatic notes was to take place before the United States finally admitted, on June 20, 1916, that it had, rather conveniently, misinterpreted Mexico's intention and sent Pershing into Mexico without authorization. By that time, however, the expedition, for all practical purposes, was just about over.[32]

No student of diplomacy, Pershing considered the Mexicans in bad faith—as allowing his entry (which they never did) and then doing everything they could to hinder him (which they certainly did.)[33] But whether he realized it or not, the Mexicans had a case. Americans had robbed them of Texas and California in the previous century; who could say that a similar aggression was not now being attempted? Pershing's force comprised cavalry, infantry, and artillery, and, as the Mexicans pointed out in one of their diplomatic notes, swift-moving mounted guerrillas were not usually pursued with artillery and infantry. What then were these forces for?[34] No wonder Colonel Erwin found that every Mexican he met questioned his right to be there.[35]

On March 19 two more columns left Colonia Dublán: one under Col. William C. Brown (2nd Squadron, 10th Cavalry, about 275 officers and men) and the other under Maj. Ellwood W. Evans (1st Squadron, 10th Cavalry, about 210 officers and men). They embarked on a special train brought to Colonia Dublán from El Paso—one of the rare instances of a use of the Mexican railroads. Five times in ten hours the engine ran out of either water or fuel. Everything stopped while troops scrounged the countryside for mesquite, wooden corrals, telephone poles, and water. It took a whole day to reach Rucio where Brown detrained on March 20, rode east, and surrounded San Miguel de Babicora. He found that Villa had not been within miles of the place.[36] This was the first instance of a false rumor. Before the campaign ended troopers got their bellies full of them. Major Evan's column detrained farther south, near Musica, and began to beat the countryside. They were no more successful than Brown had been. [37]

At Colonia Dublán, Pershing got his first taste of Chihuahua weather when a storm hit camp on March 23. Men staggered through driving sand like awkward swimmers under water. Inside tents the troopers lay on their stomachs, sand goggles over their eyes, handkerchiefs wrapped tight about their mouths. After the storm, when they went to wash, the water was frozen solid in the buckets. What a godforsaken country![38]

Soon after, Pershing held his first press conference. He summarized the movements of the roving columns and Villa's line of retreat, which now appeared to be through Namiquipa.

"Our troops seem to be pressing him," he ventured. "But I won't hazard any predictions. Villa is no fool. It may be that campaigning has just started."

The newsmen jotted it down. Nearby a red-shirted bronc buster from Arizona named Tracy, who doubled as a scout, sat on his haunches, pensively munching a piece of straw. Glancing up, he spoke—a slow Will Rogers sort of drawl, straight out of the movies.

"As I figure it, General, we've got Villa entirely surrounded . . ." He paused.

". . . on one side."[39]

Actually, Tracy was right. On March 18, the day Pershing entered Colonia Dublán, Villa arrived at Namiquipa, ninety miles to the south. On March 20 Villa left Namiquipa; the first Americans, Col. William C. Brown's squadron of the 10th Cavalry, did not reach there until four days later.[40]

Hoping to wear Villa down, Pershing sent out four new columns on March 20, 21, 24, and 30 respectively:

Maj. Elmer Lindsey, 5 troops, 13th Cavalry, about 300 officers and men.

Maj. Frank Tompkins, 2 troops, 13 Cavalry, and 2 troops, 10th Cavalry, about 175 officers and men.

Maj. Robert Howze, provisional squadron, 11th Cavalry, about 265 officers and men.

Lt. Col. Henry T. Allen, provisional squadron, 11th Cavalry, about 300 officers and men.[41]

The "provisional squadrons" were picked men from the twelve troops of a normal regiment. Forming such squadrons fragmented the regular units and was criticized after the campaign, but it was probably necessary. Many mounts had been driven hard—first to reach the border and then to Colonia Dublán. Some were weak and ailing. Hence the decision to cut through normal units and skim off the cream; only the fittest horses could stand the arduous campaign ahead.[42] And arduous it was. Howze rode out in a snowstorm without even shelter tents and with five days' rations. He was gone twenty-two days, covering nearly 700 miles on half rations for both men and animals. When he returned, not a leather stirrup hood remained; they had all been used to make half soles for men's shoes.[43]

A truck train which resupplied the 7th Cavalry (Erwin's column) hardly recognized them. "The men were a nondescript looking crowd.

Their faces were caked with gray alkali dust and they had been without regular rations for some days. Coffee, salt and tobacco were beyond price."[44] Another trooper commented: "When I first saw some of these fellows of the 7th coming toward me, I thought we were in the center of a Mexican camp where each man chose his own uniform. Some of the men wore large Mexican sombreros, their own hats having been lost, others were clad in the loose jacket of the Mexican laborer."[45]

"On this march," said one commander, "the men were so weary that orders were issued that every one would remain standing during the short halts, otherwise men would immediately drop off to sleep, and there was much difficulty and delay rousing them."[46]

So mountainous was the terrain that one cavalry outfit spent ten out of twelve hours leading the horses on foot.[47] So meandering was the Santa Maria River that in five hours Colonel Allen's command had to cross it 120 times![48] One troop which started with sixty horses was down to thirty-three two weeks later, and, of these, two dropped dead of exhaustion during a charge.[49]

Said one old veteran later: "I have been in three wars, and for unmitigated hardship, the Punitive Expedition was the worst of all."[50] There was truth in Pershing's remark: "I do not believe that the cavalry in all its experience has done as hard work as the cavalry with this expedition. . . ."[51]

By March 25, one week after the first column had left Colonia Dublán, Pershing was still in the dark about Villa. The country was destitute, communications bad, and natives unfriendly. He was unable to hire them as messengers and, because of the danger, feared to send soldiers, except in detachments. As Herbert Mason, Jr., has remarked: "Going into Chihuahua to lay hands on Villa was like the Sheriff of Nottingham entering Sherwood Forest expecting the peasants to help him hang Robin Hood. Pershing could not count on idolaters to help him catch the idol."[52]

Nor were Carranza troops of much help. When they met bandits, they either did not fight or came off second best. "If this campaign should eventually prove successful it will be without the real assistance of any natives this side of [the] line," Pershing predicted.[53]

On March 27 Pershing packed up headquarters and moved south. He traveled light: a few enlisted men, an aide, an orderly, a cook, and a few newspaper men who tagged along. New headquarters were established on March 29 at San Geronimo Ranch, almost 200 miles from the border.[54]

"It was 7,500 feet up in the Sierras and snowing," Frank Elser of the *New York Times* recalled. "The wind-driven sand and snow cut like a knife. The horses stood miserable and dejected at the picket lines like cattle drifting before a blizzard. Pershing had no tent, no table, not even a folding chair. To build a fire and not have it blow away we stretched a sun-dried bull hide between two poles and squatted in its lee. All the available cavalry was afield; the general had as a headquarters guard possibly thirty men. This included scouts, guides and correspondents. . . ."[55]

The newspapermen just mentioned were under strict control. Pershing told Maj. John L. Hines, his adjutant, that he didn't want anything derogatory to the expedition or anything that might be useful to Villistas sent out by the reporters. Hines served as press censor and wielded a very heavy blue pencil, much to the consternation of the newspapermen.[56]

One of them, either by design or accident, hurried up to Pershing with what he claimed was an urgent story that he would like to send off right away in order to make a deadline. Would the General mind quickly glancing through it and approving it, he asked? This would save the time of waiting for it to be censored by Hines.

In a genial mood, Pershing took a quick look at the story, wrote "O.K. J.J.P." at the bottom, and returned it to the reporter, who took it to Hines's tent with the request, "Please send this off right away." When Hines began to read it, the reporter interjected: "You don't have to read it. Look and you will see there that it has been okayed by General Pershing."

Hines read it anyway, got up and went to Pershing's tent. He read several paragraphs aloud and then asked: "Well, General, is that what you would like to see published in the newspapers back home?"

"Good God, no!"

"Well, look here it says, "O.K. J.J.P. You've already cleared it to be sent."

"Don't pay any attention to what I approve," replied Pershing. "You're the censor here. Only what you approve is all right to be sent. You censor all these dispatches the way you see fit and don't pay any attention to what I may write on them."[57]

One reason why Pershing was so sensitive about censorship was that he was pushing his command unmercifully, going to extremes in an attempt to bag Villa. William B. Cowin, a captain in the 7th Cavalry, surmised that Pershing didn't even want mail to go out because "he is afraid that they will get after him for the way he is treating the troops. His abuse of men and horses has been simply awful. Old Indian campaigners say that they have never seen men or horses treating [treated?] as Pershing is treating them. . . ."[58]

On March 27 Captain Cowin informed his wife: "This is the first day we have had to rest since we left U.S. We have broken all the records in the world for long distance marches and in this short time. Everybody is rather dazed over what we have done. . . . We have done so much night work that my body has been dead for loss of sleep, and yesterday I was actually hungry and thirsty for the first time in my life. One day I had three crackers for three meals. . . . I have never been so dirty in all my life. Some days have not washed all day and hardly ever had enough water to wash my mess outfit in."[59]

Thirteen days later he added: "Some of our men are bare footed— and I am going to be in the same shape pretty soon. I started with a good pair, but the mountain work cut them up like a razor."[60]

Meanwhile Villa had come within a hair of being captured. Col. George A. Dodd, whom Pershing had placed in charge of coordinating the three advance columns and who was riding with Erwin's 7th Cavalry, arrived on March 28 in Bachiniva. There he received confirmation of a report that Villa had clashed with Carranza troops at Guerrero, had been wounded, and was recuperating. Guerrero was only twenty miles away. Convinced for once that his reports were true, Dodd rode all night, hoping to surprise Villa at dawn.

His command was tired. Since March 23 they had been continuously in the saddle, living off the country on very reduced rations. Furthermore, his Mexican guide, forcibly impressed, led him by a circuitous route, virtually doubling the distance and wearing out the command still more. When they approached Guerrero at dawn, they had been on the go for seventeen out of the last twenty-four hours.

The Guerrero terrain made surprise practically impossible. The ground was corrugated and Dodd had to approach along precipitous bluffs, cut by deep arroyos which ran the wrong way—at right angles to the march—and had to be headed. Thus when Dodd appeared on the bluff overlooking Guerrero about 7:00 A.M. on March 29, the Villistas had time to scamper out while he negotiated the arroyos. One group escaped by ruse. Riding calmly out behind a leader carrying a large Mexican flag, they passed themselves off as Carranzista cavalry.

Nevertheless Dodd killed at least thirty and wounded many more. Since most Villistas were Yaqui Indians who were accustomed to carry off their dead, the total was probably much higher. Dodd's casualties were four wounded, none seriously.

The wounded Villa, his right leg in splints (a bullet had gone through his shinbone), had left Guerrero sometime after midnight, just hours before Dodd arrived.[61]

With cavalry drumming the country and with Villa hurt, people were sure the end was near. An undertaker in Lynnburg, Tennessee, wrote Pershing requesting Villa's body for embalming and exhibition.[62] "An airplane has just come now, ..." wrote Frank Elser on March 31. "It has lighted, and the aviator is coming to report to the general. When he takes flight again, he will carry this dispatch, which may or may not reach New York before Villa is dead or a prisoner."

Pershing censored this, frowning. "You fellows mustn't be too sanguine. It may require weeks, perhaps months. It's like trying to catch a rat in a corn-field."[63]

It sure was. On the night of April 1, Pershing went to Bachiniva, where Tompkins was camped with his 13th Cavalry, and confessed his ignorance.

"Tompkins, where is Villa?"

"General, I don't know, but I would like mighty well to go find out where he is."

"Where would you go?"

"I would head for Parral and would expect to cut his trail before reaching there."

"Why?"

"The history of Villa's bandit days shows that when hard pressed he invariably holes up in the mountains in the vicinity of Parral. He has friends in that region."

Pershing sat silent, thinking. Tompkins pressed his case.

A small command, he said, could move faster than the regular squadron, conceal itself better, live off the country easier, and might even tempt Villa to give battle because it is so small. Besides, if Villa had actually been wounded, he would certainly head south where he could hole up and recover.

The next day Pershing gave Tompkins twelve pack mules, five hundred Mexican silver pesos, five days rations, and these instructions:

"Find Villa."[64]

Tompkins had guessed correctly; Villa was headed for Parral, going by way of San Antonio de los Arenales, Cienégita, San Francisco de Borja, and Santa Cruz de Herrera. A Mexican peasant named Modesto Nevares, whom Villa had forcibly impressed into his "army" and who served as driver of the wagon on which the wounded man was being carried south, described the painful flight.

"The legs of his pants and drawers were cut away nearly to the hip, leaving his leg bare, and after some days it turned very black for about twelve inches above and below the wound. I noticed that after that he nearly lost his courage, and at times seemed to be unconscious. He would cry like a child when the wagon jolted and curse me every time I hit a rock. After we passed San Antonio and started south through the mountains, he got so bad that he could not stand the wagon any longer.

"They then made him a litter by cutting four small poles . . . and placed his bed on it. They detailed 16 men to carry it in turn. . . . [T]hey had me drive the wagon close behind them, and they traveled almost day and night. When they wanted to stop General Villa would not stand for it. He was the worst scared man I ever saw."[65]

Pershing, however, did not have the consolation of knowing this. Where was Villa, he wondered? How ferret him out in this elusive country where contradictory rumors were as numerous as dry water holes and sunbaked canyons! He had pinned great hopes on the airplanes, which would be his eyes and ears. They would roam far and wide, discover Villa, and direct the columns to converge for the kill.

But it did not work out that way. One plane (out of a total of eight) cracked up on the first flight from Columbus to Colonia Dublán. The other seven were plagued by bad climate which split the wooden propellers, by wind currents which drove them down to treetop height, and by lack of maps, lights, and instruments.[66] "We had a lot of very interesting experiences down there . . .," commented Capt. Benjamin Foulois, who commanded the 1st Aero Squadron. "We had to try to get over 12,000 foot mountains with 10,000 foot airplanes, and we couldn't do it very well. . . ."[67]

In late March, Pershing complained: "The aeroplanes have been of no material benefit . . . either in scouting or as a means of communication. They have not at all met my expectations."[68]

The General's complaints, however, were as nothing compared to those of the flyers, who, unlike him, risked their lives in the rickety "Jennies." As one of them, Lt. Edgar S. Gorrell, said later, the aero squadron "was in horrible shape. . . . The airplanes were not fit for military service, especially along the border. Hunsaker, who was then in charge of aeronautical engineering at the Massachusetts Institute of Technology, had just reported that these airplanes had only four horsepower over and above the amount necessary to fly at sea level, that they were not stable, that they were liable to go into a spin or do a number of other highly undesirable things."[69]

Willingly then did the pilots pour out their woes to Byron C. Utrecht of the *New York World*, who accompanied the expedition. Utrecht dutifully wrote it all down and sent it off to his paper, wisely neglecting to submit the dispatch to the censor who would have surely killed it. On April 3, the *World* printed the story under a subhead: "Risking Lives Ten Times a Day, but Are Not Given Equipment Needed" and quoted Lt. Herbert A. Dargue as saying it was "criminal to send the aviators up under such conditions." The Jennies were "suicide busses," the pilots alleged, and blamed "politics, personal ambition and utter lack of knowledge of aviation" on the part of military superiors for the condition.[70]

Reaction to the story was immediate and strong. Secretary Baker descended on Funston who descended on Pershing who descended on his inspector general who descended on the pilots, demanding to know if they had ever said the things Utrecht reported them as saying. They piously denied that they had and Utrecht was later sent home as a *persona non grata* with the Punitive Expedition. He had, however, brought the plight of the flyers to the public's intention, which undoubtedly was what they hoped would happen. Congress passed the Urgent Deficiency Act which provided $500,000 for the Air Service to buy twenty-four new airplanes. None, however, arrived in time to be useful.[71]

On April 3, in the absence of any news, Frank Elser asked Pershing if he'd care to make a statement on Mexican-American relations. The General smiled and dictated the following, slowly and carefully:

"After having progressed 350 miles into the interior of Mexico it is very gratifying to be able to state that our relations with the Mexican people, both military and civil, have been exceptionally cordial and friendly. From the military forces of the de facto government we have received hearty co-operation."[72]

This was an attempt at public relations, not warranted by facts. Several days later when Lt. Herbert A. Dargue landed his plane at Chihuahua City he was stoned and shot at.[73] Even as Pershing spoke, a Carranza general, José Cavazos, was obstructing Tompkins, telling him to move no farther south until the Carranza government authorized it. When Tompkins did not stop but advanced on San Borja, Cavazos sent a note:

"As I have just received knowledge that your forces are advancing in accordance with the itinerary which I have prepared for the troops under my own command, I would esteem it very much if you would suspend your advance until you receive the order to which I refer, by which means there can be avoided a conflict which may occur by reason of your advance. . . ."[74]

To avoid a clash, Tompkins went to see Cavazos. The Mexican said that Villa was dead; therefore Tompkins had no reason to go farther. He tried to be friendly—he gave Tompkins a drink from his bottle—but was adamant against his moving farther south.[75]

Taking Cavazos at his word about a clash, Tompkins turned back to Cienéguita, headed east to Santa Rosalía, then turned south again, giving San Borja and Cavazos a wide berth. By April 10 he was at Valle de Zaragosa and almost as far south as Villa, who was at Santa Cruz de Herrera, somewhat to the west and on the route which Tompkins would have taken had he not been opposed at San Borja.[76]

On April 6, Col. Henry T. Allen, recently arrived at San Geronimo, moved out in the direction of Bachiniva. In the van was Peter, a black burro, who bore on his back 500 dollars in silver. "First American Bank of Mexico" was his nickname, and rightly so, for he was Allen's means of living off the country.[77]

Allen's departure reduced headquarters camp to virtually a skeleton, alone and isolated. The following day several hundred horsemen appeared. They were not American and Pershing looked them over carefully as they approached. He had under thirty fighting men at most, including the newsmen. The situation had its possibilities—none good.

They were Carranza troops, heavily armed, commanded by General Luis Herrera. Pershing met him with a show of courtesy, found him formal and reticent, and also somewhat surly.

How large a force did the Americans have afield? questioned Herrera. Where were they? How far south were they going? How long were they going to stay in Mexico?

Pershing shrugged. How many men did Herrera have? he asked. Where was he going? How many government troops were hunting Villa and where were they?

Frank Elser wrote of the incident: "Seeing that it was a case of dog eat dog, and possibly divining that the general was not a garrulous sort of person, Herrera bowed with Latin courtesy, mounted a pacing roan and rode away. . . . Stripped of its urbanity, his speech was a warning that the Americans had gone far enough in Mexico."[78]

Such warnings were becoming increasingly frequent. On April 5, General Funston reported to the War Department a growing impatience on the part of certain Carranzista generals to Pershing's presence and mounting pressure to demand his withdrawal. Mexican troops were moving by rail towards northern Mexico. Cover stories put out to explain the movement were obviously false, for they claimed to be moving against an outlaw who, Funston knew, was in the south of Mexico—if he was in Mexico at all!

Said Funston to General Scott, the Chief of Staff: "We might as well . . . prepare for the gravest possible eventualities. . . . It is my opinion that unless we should get Villa quickly, a not likely outcome, and consequently be able to withdraw gracefully and victoriously, we are going to have to fight, and fight hard."[79]

By now rumors of Villa's death were everywhere. As such stories continued to circulate and grow, an American newspaper reported sarcastically:

"Since General Pershing was sent out to capture him, Villa has been mortally wounded in the leg and died in a lonely cave. He was assassinated by one of his own band and his grave was identified by a Carranza follower who hoped for a suitable reward from President Wilson. Villa was likewise killed in a brawl at a ranch house where he was engaged in the gentle diversion of burning men and women at the stake. He was also shot on a wild ride and his body cremated. Yet though all these experiences which, it must be confessed, would have impaired the health of any ordinary man, Villa has not only retained the vital spark of life but has renewed his young and strength."[80]

Pershing put no faith in rumor's of Villa's demise. "I'm from Missouri," he said.[81] He did, however, send an intelligence officer to exhume the body at a supposed grave. "It's not Villa," the officer reported. "Just some little bit of a runt."[82]

On April 7, Howze almost clashed with Carranza troops. Ten miles south of San Borja his advance guard encountered Cavazos, the general who had obstructed Tompkins two days before. "Cavazos was in a very ugly mood," recounted Lt. Sumner M. Williams, who commanded the leading riders, "and . . . evidently thought he had come upon a very small force of our troops, as we were well strung out and only the advance guard, about eight men, were in sight at the time." The Mexicans suddenly drew their rifles, gave a battle cry, and came on at a gallop. Williams quickly put his men in an arroyo for cover and, at the same time, the rest of Howze's command, about 175 men, began to come into view. Howze quickly took in the situation and dashed towards the onrushing Mexicans, waving his hat and yelling at the top of his lungs, "Americanos! Americanos!"

Within the last fifty yards Cavazos reined in. Howze was sure he would have wiped out half the Mexican force in one volley had he given the order to fire. Cavazos attributed the charge to a mistake (some of Howze's men wore sombreros which give them a "Villista" look), but Howze was not so sure. "General Cavazos was seeking conflict," he felt. "His manner and tone were quite offensive."[83]

Meanwhile, with columns penetrating ever farther, the supply problem was becoming acute. Colonia Dublán, which had been the advanced depot, became an intermediate one on April 5, when the advanced depot was moved to Namiquipa, about 175 miles south of Columbus.[84] Railroads would have eased the problem, but use of them was forbidden. Yankee ingenuity got around that somewhat by consigning goods to Mormon merchants living at Casas Grandes, who, by gentlemen's agreement, turned them over to the quartermaster at nearby Colonia Dublán. Later the United States worked out a system whereby it sold supplies to the Mexican government at El Paso and bought them back again at Casas Grandes and Colonia Dublán.[85] But this did not really solve things, especially in the early days of the campaign, when the situation was fluid and the advance columns were consistently outrunning supplies.

Captain William Cowin's wife remembered receiving letters from him in Mexico written on telegraph blanks, leaves from a pocket note book, or part of a cracker box.[86] "The Supply Department has fallen down awful," he told her on April 7. "Our maps furnished by the War Department are very poor. Lt. [Emil] Engle bought a Rand & McNally pocket map for 15¢ which is much better than any map we have. Think of that."[87]

For supply work the Quartermaster Corps used, besides horse and wagon, an entirely new mode of transportation—motor trucks. Heavily laden, they sank deep into the soft, alkali soil, cutting great furrows. During the rainy season they mired to their hubcaps and stuck fast. One group of trucks, the four-wheel-drive Quads, were called "man-killers" because of the brute strength needed to control them.[88] "Along roads that were not roads, but a series of sandy ribs and high centers, strad-dled and restraddled, the truck trains smashed their way," wrote Frank Elser.[89]

By August 31, 1916, American engineers had bulit 157 miles of new roads and repaired 224 miles of old. Eventually the expedition had twenty-two companies, each with twenty-five trucks, shuttling over these roads from Columbus to the advance depots. When asked later what monument the Punitive Expedition left, Pershing replied: "A practicable automobile road 200 miles into Mexico."[90]

By April 10, Funston was calling the supply line "preposterous." Only the advance cavalry, driving towards Parral, was having any effect on the chase. The other troops were engaged in getting supplies up to the front, and not doing too good a job at that. "The line of communi-cation is so long," Funston told the War Department, "that the troops in rear guarding it consume nearly everything that can be brought up along it. . . ."[91]

Meanwhile Pershing had pulled up stakes and headed south again. His advance columns were simply moving too fast for him to stay at San

Geronimo and direct operations. Tompkins's 13th Cavalry was streaking for Parral. Brown's 10th was about a day behind to the east and Howze's 11th the same distance to the west.[92]

The move south was not without incident. They passed a camp of Carranza troops—dirty, ragged, bare-footed, indistinguishable from Villistas, except that they appeared friendly. But soon afterwards someone shot at the rear trucks which were carrying fuel for the airplanes.

Who did the shooting? The trucks were rolling through heavy mesquite in which vision was obscured. In his *New York Times* account, Frank Elser speculated that the attack came from Villistas under General Tarango. Perhaps. But Elser had to get his dispatch through the hawk eye of the censor. The shooting had occurred within rifle shot of the Carranza camp. That Villistas would be so close to them is unlikely.[93]

On April 11 Pershing established headquarters in a corn field at Satevó, 285 miles south of Columbus and about 75 miles north of Parral. That night the headquarters contingent did something it had never done before. It dug in. Fifty miles north was Chihuahua City, full of Carranza troops. Almost within rifle shot of camp was the Carranza detachment which had probably fired at the aero squadron. Somewhere —God only knew—General Herrera was roaming the countryside. Here at Satevó was the commander of the American Punitive Expedition, isolated almost 300 miles within Mexico, his only escort about twenty men—and that was counting mechanics, cooks, and newspapermen.

The trucks were formed into a square, Indian-fighting style, with stray baggage packed between the wheels—bags, boxes, bedding. Inside the square the men dug a shallow skirt trench.

Pershing walked about inspecting the firearms, including those issued to the five correspondents: Floyd Gibbons of *The Chicago Tribune,* Robert Dunn of *The New York Tribune*, H. W. Blakeslee of *The Associated Press*, Byron C. Utrecht of *The New York World*, and Frank Elser of *The New York Times*. The last correspondent confessed that he had lost his rifle.

"Soldiers don't lose their rifles," Pershing frowned.

"No sir, they don't, soldiers," Elser replied.[94]

The night passed without incident. Most of the men bedded down inside the square, but Pershing slept outside and alone, some fifty yards away. Elser noted his breathing, deep and regular.

With the campaign almost a month old, Pershing took stock. Thus far Carranza troops had been little help, and the prospects were not better for the future. They not only failed to give accurate and timely information, but they obstructed the march south (e.g., Tompkins at San Borja) when speed was imperative.[95]

Chances of catching Villa were slim. The expedition operated in unfamiliar country, which was sparsely settled by ignorant people who feared reprisals. For information it depended on frightened, unwilling natives or on untried American employees. With Villa exactly the opposite was true. He knew every foot of Chihuahua and could depend on natives for reliable information on every step Pershing took. Villa traveled light, lived off the country, rode his mounts hard, and replaced (or stole) them whenever he needed fresh stock.[96]

On April 12, Pershing cabled his superiors: "Now evident capture Villa will require many months difficult work by small columns and well organized secret service. . . ."[97]

Actually one column had just missed capturing him. On April 10 Villa arrived at Santa Cruz de Herrera, still nursing his leg wound. In accord with his custom of never staying overnight inside a pueblo, he made camp outside of town. At 3:00 A.M. that night Major Howze reached Santa Cruz and surrounded the town. While Howze searched it, Villa was not more than one kilometer away. "It was the closest call to capture I have ever had in my life," he was quoted as saying later. "I was actually in very great danger."[98]

Communication between American units was by now becoming a problem. Wireless sets, in their infancy, were small and their range limited to twenty-five miles. With cavalry often making fifty miles a day, they were next to worthless.[99] Nor was the telegraph much better. Lacking field wire, the signal corps used uninsulated iron wire for telegraph lines; when wet, it did not work. Often too, horses, mules and wagons spread out on the line of march, got tangled up in the wire, and broke it. In a single day one wire broke thirty-three times.[100]

On April 12, Funston must have wondered if Mexico had not opened up and swallowed the expedition. A report came in that 8,000 Carranza troops were moving east from Sonora through Pulpit Pass, heading for U. S. lines of communication. Try as he might, Funston could reach neither Pershing at Satevó nor his Chief of Staff, Lt. Col. De Rosey C. Cabell, at Namiquipa. He therefore put the northern part of the line under separate command—under Maj. William R. Sample at Colonia Dublán.

Eventually Pershing's Chief of Staff hurried up to Dublán, assumed command and directed defense for an attack which never came. For two days he sent telegrams twice daily to Pershing through El Paso and Chihuahua City, reporting the situation. None of these ever reached him.[101]

What did reach him, however, was word from another quarter. On April 14 Captain Foulois returned from Chihuahua City where he had gone to wire messages. When he landed his rickety biplane at Satevó he carried news that was hot as hell. American and Carranza troops had clashed at Parral.[102]

16

Parral and Carrizal

On April 10, Maj. Frank Tompkins, with his two troops of the 13th Cavalry, had made camp at Valle de Zaragoza, forty miles north of Parral. Tompkins, a rough-riding, no-nonsense type of cavalryman, knew how to get things done. "Shortly after our arrival," he related, "I had a conference with the head official of the town. When this talk was over, I asked him to have enough beans cooked for the command for breakfast to be delivered by daylight. He assured me there was not a bean in the community, and besides there was nothing to cook them in. I told him we would have nice hot beans for breakfast or his house would burn. The beans came at the time ordered and were paid for in Mexican silver. There were enough for breakfast and luncheon too."[1]

That night Tompkins had a visitor from Parral who informed him that Gen. Ismael Lozano, the Mexican commander, would have some men meet Tompkins when he arrived, help him be reprovisioned, and show him a suitable camp site on the south side of the town.

Tompkins reached Parral on the morning of April 12. No one was there to meet him. Taking an advance guard, he rode to General Lozano's headquarters. The latter disavowed any promises that Tompkin's visitor had made, and warned that entering the town with troops, as the Americans had done, might be highly provocative. Nevertheless he agreed to help them resupply and to lead them to a camp site.

Meanwhile a crowd of townspeople, in an ugly mood, had gathered in a small plaza where the American troops waited for Tompkins. Urged on by a woman named Elisa Griensen, who some later claimed was working for the German government, they began crying, "Viva Villa! Viva Mexico!"[2]

Someone sent a mule with a heavy cart bolting down the street towards the cavalry, evidently with the intention of scattering them. "A big Yank grapped the mule by the bit and stopped that little act," Tompkins noted. "This incident was so indicative of treachery that I slipped my holster in front in anticipation of immediate need."[3]

With Lozano leading them, the Americans left the plaza. The crowd followed, hurling insults and imprecations. "As we approached the outskirts of town the rabble was pressing us pretty close," said Tompkins, "so I dropped back to the rear of the column to keep an eye on the situation. . . . I noticed a small, compactly built man, with a Van Dyke beard, riding a fine looking Mexican pony, who seemed to be trying to stir the people to violence. He was well dressed in grey clothes and looked like a German. He would ride into the crowd and yell 'Todos! Ahora! Viva Mexico!' I watched this bird very closely and made up my mind to fill him full of holes should the break come as he evidently wanted it to."

In an attempt to ease the tension, Tompkins shouted, "Viva Villa!" The crowd laughed.[4] The mood changed quickly, however, when a shot rang out, probably fired by Elisa Griensen. Other shots followed, all by Mexicans aimed at the American rear guard. A few moments later Carranza troops began to take position on a hill flanking the American line of march, which, Tompkins noted with dismay, appeared to be towards a perfect cul-de-sac. He hurried forward to tell Lozano at the head of the column that they were being shot at. Lozano ripped out an oath and started back on the gallop. American soldiers reported later that he tried to beat the people back with his saber and that another officer shot down four of the crowd trying to disperse them.[5]

More and more Carranza troops began appearing on all sides of Tompkins' force, firing at them. Lozano sent word that he could control neither the people nor the troops; he asked Tompkins to withdraw.

By now Mexican soldiers were crossing the road and attempting to turn the American left flank. Tompkins, who had dismounted and was lying down, rose and waved for them to go back. The Mexicans fired a volley. Sgt. Jay Richley, who had been lying next to Tompkins, received a bullet in the head, killing him instantly.

Tompkins got his command under control, organized it, and changed the line of march out of the cul-de-sac. He headed towards Santa Cruz de Villegas, about eighteen miles north. The Mexicans kept at his heels all the way, pursuing in the fields or along the road. Tompkins made the retreat leisurely and in good order, halting his command on occasion to dress a wound or to pour forth a fusillade when the attackers seemed to be getting too close.

"As we passed over a ridge and dipped down out of sight, I told Captain [Frederick G.] Turner to dismount 20 men, deploy them across the road and kill as many Mexicans as they could, for they evidently were getting ready to make one desperate charge to cut us off from the shelter that was just ahead. In a minute or two they came, without formation, hell-bent-for-election, firing in the air, yelling like fiends out of hell, and making a most beautiful target. When they were about 200 yards off Turner's men fired one volley; ponies and Mexicans rolled in the dust, some of those in rear tripped over the fallen, the balance checked their ponies quicker than any polo pony ever stopped, wheeled and raced to the rear."[6]

At Santa Cruz Tompkins fortified his position and waited. Mexican cavalryman hesitated for a moment about a half mile off, then began to advance slowly. On one of the roofs, Capt. Aubrey Lippincott, known as one of the best shots in the Army, especially at long range, took a rifle, carefully calculated the wind and distance, and squeezed off a shot. The leading Mexican fell out of his saddle. "I got one at 800 yards, Major," Lippincott shouted down to Tompkins. The Mexicans, amazed and frightened by such incredible fire, turned and galloped away, breaking off the engagement. Casualties for Tompkins were two killed and six wounded; for his assailants, forty killed and an unknown number wounded.[7]

Hearing of the fight, Pershing sent armed couriers by car to obtain more information. He also ordered all cavalry to consolidate, ready to defend themselves if Parral should be the overture of a large-scale attack. Two pack trains with supplies and ammunition were rushed south from San Antonio towards Parral.[8]

Consolidation was easy, thanks to Pershing's arrangement of columns in the strike through Chihuahua. Colonel Brown's 10th Cavalry reinforced Tompkins at 7:30 P.M. on April 12, just a few hours after the clash; Tompkins felt that this prompt reinforcement dissuaded further attack on his small (ninety men) command.[9]

Actually Brown came to Tompkins' rescue even before receiving orders. Three stragglers from Tompkins' command, fleeing north, encountered Capt. George B. Rodney of the 10th Cavalry late in the afternoon of the Parral fight and told of the ambush. They were "scared almost beyond speech," Rodney recalled. "Boots and Saddles," the emergency cavalry call, was sounded, and in fifteen minutes Brown's regiment was in the saddle and riding hard. It was dark when they got to Santa Cruz de Villegas and Brown took the precaution of halting while buglers blew two peculiarly American calls, "Attention" and "Officers' Call," to signal who they were. Back came an answering call, and Brown's men rode through the American barricades.

When Tompkins saw the 10th Cavalry, he exclaimed to one of its Negro officers, Maj. Charles Young: "By God! They were glad to see the Tenth Cavalry at Santiago in '98, but I'm a damn sight gladder to see you now. I could kiss every one of you."

"Hello, Tompkins!" Young called back, grinning. "You can start in on me right now."[10]

By the morning of April 15 Colonel Allen had ridden in with 90 men and Major Howze with 175 more. The total American force at Santa Cruz de Villegas was now over six hundred men.[11]

His fighting blood up, Pershing called Parral "an act for which immediate reparation should be insisted upon, by force if necessary." American troops "should not be moved one inch backward if it can be avoided," he told Funston, "because such a move is certain to be construed as a retreat and would possibly bring upon us the combined attack of all factions."[12]

On Saturday, April 15, headquarters packed up and prepared to move north. The Punitive Expedition, whether they knew it or not, was nullified. Never again would an American column go as far south as Parral, nor headquarters be as far south as Satevó.

In the afternoon Pershing climbed into his Dodge and gave the word to move. He sat grim and silent, taking the bounces from rocks and holes. He was suffering from indigestion, a complaint frequent in the "hard-tack" days of the campaign. After an all night ride they reached Namiquipa at sunrise, covering 115 miles. Pershing conferred with his staff and sent a report on Parral to his superiors via field radio. Elser brought him a dispatch for censorship which he had written for *The New York Times*. It read as follows:

"The United States Punitive Expedition directed against Pancho Villa and his followers has come to a standstill. Whether the halt is to be permanent or not depends on circumstances beyond the control of General Pershing. But from a military standpoint he has for the time being come to the end of his line. . . ."

Reading, Pershing stroked his chin, his pencil raised to blue-pencil the copy. A stubborn look passed over his countenance.

"Is that your deduction?" he asked.

Elser nodded.

"All right, send it!" he snapped.[13]

To Pershing, Parral was the turning point of the campaign. But for it, he believed that Villa would have been taken. Already four cavalry columns were south of where the fugitive was convalescing at Santa Cruz de Herrera, and his movements would perforce have slowed because of his wound.[14]

"With the Parral incident, the expedition came practically to a stop." That was Pershing's comment to James Hopper, who interviewed him in June, 1916. "The pursuit of Villa ceased for fear of a clash. It ceased, not because of our inability to go further, not of any lack of wish of ours to go further, not because of any want in us of confidence that we could capture Villa; it ceased because Carranza stepped between us and our government and insisted that we should retire."[15]

Until Parral Pershing censored news dispatches which mentioned Mexican uncooperativeness. Now the lid was off.

"Nothing now should be kept from the public," he told reporters. "You can go the limit."

When Robert Dunn of *The New York Tribune* called Parral "an ambuscade," Pershing leaned over his typewriter to write in "treachery."

"How's this, sir?" said the mischievous Dunn, punching out a mock headline:

"ARMY IN FULL RETREAT TO SALT LAKE CITY. PERSHING DECLARES ALLEGHENY MOUNTAINS AT ANY COST MUST BE DEFENDED."

Pershing failed to see the humor in it; he shook his head and walked away. "Just a chuckle, to my mind, would have made him a great man," thought Dunn.[16]

To his friend in Washington, Gen. Enoch H. Crowder, Pershing lamented: "I . . . feel just a little bit like a man looking for a needle in a hay stack with an armed guard standing over the stack forbidding you to look in the hay. . . . I do not believe these people can ever establish a government among themselves that will stand. Carranza has no more control over local commanders or of states or municipalities than if he lived in London."[17]

To another friend he complained: "Conditions here are really hopeless. . . . The country is given over to banditry, the main purpose of the bandits being to live without work and have first call on all the young girls as they arrive at the age of puberty or even before."[18]

But Pershing was not ready to give up. On April 16 he cabled Funston a report on chaotic conditions in Mexico and asked permission to establish a military government in Chihuahua.[19] Two days later he went even further. Forgotten was any petty goal like capturing Villa. What Pershing had in mind was Napoleonic—nothing less than conquering the whole Mexican republic from sea to sea! The plan: first seize Chihuahua City with its railroads, isolating northern Mexican garrisons and forcing them to surrender. Next, move "without delay" on Torreón, Monterrey and the East, whose capture "would easily result." The expedition's cavalry was "sufficient to disperse or drive all Mexican troops . . . [in Chihuahua] an unlimited distance south." Mexican troops were in an "unorganized condition and could make little resistance. . . . The tremendous advantage we now have in penetration into Mexico for 500 miles parallel to the main line of railway south should not be lost. With this advantage a swift stroke now would paralyze Mexican opposition throughout northern tier of states and make complete occupation of entire Republic [a] comparatively easy problem."[20]

Here surely was a case of going overboard, of enlarging the expedition's purpose infinitely beyond its original scope. One wonders how much thought Pershing gave to this proposal which would have had the extremest consequences on Mexican-American relations, on United States participation in World War I, and on world history. He must have been vexed beyond belief to suggest it. It is a proposal born of frustration. In later years he seemed to realize as much, for after treating it in his unpublished "Autobiography," he explained, rather lamely, that his plan was based solely on military considerations, not diplomatic.[21] Even militarily, the United States was in no position in 1916 to undertake readily an operation of such vast proportions.

Nothing came of this grandiose plan because Pershing's superiors said no. President Wilson had the deep-seated conviction, as he explained it to Ray Stannard Baker, that (1) all people, Mexicans included, have the right "to do what they damned pleased with their own affairs," and (2) the first Mexican War (1846–48) was a blot on American honor and should not be repeated. Also, a practical consideration: the U. S. should not be involved in Mexico if war came with Germany.[22] Hence the War Department had vetoed Funston's proposal to lead a second expedition into Mexico, as it had also turned down his request to open a new line of communications with Pershing from Fabens, Texas. As Funston told Pershing: "Diplomatic instead of military considerations seem to govern, as relations between governments [are] apparently strained."[23]

They certainly were. The administration rushed Maj. Gen. Hugh L. Scott, Army Chief of Staff, to the border to confer with Carranza officials. In the meantime it advised Pershing to await the outcome of negotiations.[24]

He did. The four cavalry columns, united under Colonel Brown at Santa Cruz de Villegas ceased to hunt Villa and retired slowly north. San Antonio, which had been an intermediate base, became an advanced one as the expedition drew back. The last airplanes were flown out, condemned as unsafe, and destroyed.[25]

On April 22 General Scott reported on the Mexican situation. Three courses were open. One was that suggested by Pershing: regroup and drive south over Carranzista opposition, seizing key towns and railroads to supply the large number of troops which would be needed. Whether this would capture Villa was doubtful. That elusive fellow could lead them a merry chase all the way down to Yucatan.

The second possibility was simply to forget about it, call off the expedition, and chalk it up to experience—a sort of adventure in frustration. That undoubtedly was what the Mexicans hoped would happen.

The third course was a compromise: withdraw north but do not leave Mexican territory. At Colonia Dublán, the northernmost depot, considerable supplies were on hand. Here the expedition could concentrate and remain indefinitely as an incentive to the Carranza government to kill or capture Villa.

Scott and Funston recommended the third course. They pointed out, however, that the approaching rainy season would make the road from Columbus to Colonia Dublán impassable; troops would therefore have to be supplied via the railroad from Juarez to Casas Grandes.[26]

Anticipating that the War Department would elect the third alternative, Funston cabled Pershing to expect an order to withdraw to Colonia Dublán. Pershing cabled back from Namiquipa asking that the order be delayed.[27] The Santa Maria Valley, where American troops were then located, contained probably 100 participants in the Columbus raid, he said. Many were Villa officers, including Cervantes, his second in command. Several had been arrested and, under questioning, had given information about the others. "By using local Villista prisoners," suggested Pershing, "there is strong probability of capturing most others including Villa himself."

Furthermore, to withdraw now, after the Parral attack, would be considered an act of weakness "and will cause greatest loss [of] American prestige throughout Mexico. . . ." Instead of withdrawing, Pershing recommended that they wait and see if Carranza really intended to capture Villa. "Withdrawal should be conceded only upon condition of actual accomplishment . . . rather than upon promises of future effort." He asked to retire no farther than San Antonio and to resume active pursuit of Villistas.[28]

Funston approved. On April 29, Pershing organized the occupied territory into five districts, each patrolled by a regiment of cavalry. Their areas were apparent from the district names: Namiquipa, Bustillos, Statevó, San Borja, and Guerrero.[29]

Meanwhile Scott and Funston met at Juarez, just across from El Paso, to confer with General Obregón. The conference opened on April 30 under a dark cloud of rumor: Mexico was prepared to go to war unless the Punitive Expedition withdrew immediately.[30] Scott and Funston pressed for Mexican cooperation against Villistas and for the use of Mexican railroads to supply Pershing. Obregón would not hear of it. He spoke of nothing but immediate withdrawal, insisting that Villa was dead, his forces scattered, and the border safe.

To prevent a deadlock, Scott and Funston said they would telegraph Obregón's position to Washington and await an answer. In this they were following War Department instructions that when a deadlock seemed imminent, they should adjourn to gain time to warn Pershing.[31] Washington's reply was temporizing. The United States was willing to retire farther north and to leave entirely *provided* that the border was secure.[32]

This was not good enough. Word went out to a Carranza general on May 1:

"Dispose your troops that they shall be in a position [to] cut off American expeditionary forces now in Chihuahua. The action must be sudden and will take place after the Scott-Obregón conference. It will make no difference what else may be decided upon in conference; unless there is absolute withdrawal of American troops the above plans will be carried out."[33]

Having intercepted this message, Funston immediately informed Pershing of his danger. "Situation very tense, regarded as dangerous. . . . Take all possible precaution against troops from Sonora and against the movement we are informed is in progress from the South. No hope of our being allowed to strike first blow. Suggest desirability of shortening your lines."[34]

In Washington the War Department waited uneasily the word that would plunge the United States into its first war in the twentieth century. "In case matters come to open break," it informed Scott on May 1, "telegraph the following in plain English: *'Send them at once.'*"[35]

The telegram never came. On May 2, Scott mustered all his determination and, with an interpreter and stenographer, closeted himself with Obregón, determined to work out an agreement that would avoid war. Scott told the Mexican "that if he wanted to lose his country, the surest way for him to do it would be to attack Pershing."

The American Chief of Staff had been an old Indian negotiator; it prepared him well for the wily Obregón. Said Scott of the encounter: ". . . an agreement was formulated for discussion, paragraph by paragraph. I thought that as each was decided upon it would be put aside as settled and the next one taken up, but we would agree amicably on two or three paragraphs, which I considered as put out of the discussion, only to find to my surprise that their points were brought into the discussion of the next, as if no previous decisions had been arrived at at all. I was reminded of the web of Penelope, which was knitted in the day only to be undone at night."

The next day, bleary-eyed and exhausted after an all-night session, Scott emerged and sent a wire to Washington:

"An agreement was reached this morning after a continuous struggle of twelve hours duration which was not equalled by any similar struggle with the wildest and most exasperated Indian heretofore encountered."[36]

It had been agreed that the Punitive Expedition would withdraw *immediately* (that satisfied Obregón), but the withdrawal would be *gradual* (that satisfied the United States).[37] Yet within a week it was all nullified. Carranza refused to ratify "on the ground that no date was set for complete withdrawal and the agreement was therefore too indefinite and a danger to Mexico."[38]

Privately, Scott and Funston felt that this was subterfuge. They were convinced that Carranza knew he could not carry out the part of the agreement whereby he guaranteed the United States against border raids. Even during the Scott-Obregón conferences Mexicans had raided two Texas towns, killing four and kidnapping two. Carranza was therefore stalling until his troops were in position to drive Pershing out by force.

To Scott and Funston the American position was grave. "Our line is thin and weak everywhere and inadequate to protect border anywhere if attacked in force," they told Washington. "There are no adequate reserves. There are now many calls for help on border which cannot be given, and we think the border should at once be supported by at least 150,000 additional troops."[39]

On May 9, President Wilson called out the National Guard of Texas, New Mexico, and Arizona. The call-out was pitiful, totaling a little more than 5,000, most of which was infantry, with only one squadron of cavalry and two batteries of field artillery.[40] That same day Funston sent Pershing an alarmist telegram:

"A war with de facto government almost inevitable. You are liable to be attacked any time by large force reaching Chihuahua by train from central Mexico as well as by Sonora troops. Your line is too long and troops scattered too much. For a time we cannot support you. Fall back along your line of communication with view to general concentration of entire force at Colonia Dublán. Such action is imperative. No question of prestige can be entertained as military considerations must govern. If attacked do not allow any preliminary success to induce you to advance too far as danger meeting overwhelming force and having your line of communications cut is too great. Acknowledge and report daily."[41]

As Herbert Mason, Jr., has remarked, Funston was obviously alarmed at the specter of five possible Little Big Horns at Namiquipa,

Bustillos, Satevó, San Borja, and Guerrero, where Pershing's command, spread out and scattered, was liable to be overwhelmed in bits and pieces.[42] Pershing, however, felt that Funston was needlessly panicking.

"[I] do not anticipate molestation unless they have overwhelming numbers coupled with every other possible advantage," he cabled Funston on May 11. "Any assemblage of Mexicans . . . would be without intelligent leadership or organization, and their easy defeat by this command would be certain. Any army they can muster would be nothing but a mob without training or discipline and wth little courage and not to be feared in the slightest."[43]

Pershing may have been a little overconfident, but his words were effective. Funston countermanded his order and told Pershing he could stop his withdrawal at Namiquipa, the northernmost of the five districts.[44]

This he did, but he was beginning to chafe at the futility of it all. No sooner did he organize five districts to renew the pursuit when orders came to withdraw. And now the newspapers, Mexican and American, were speaking of his "retreat," as if he were being forced back by superior arms, or being outgeneraled or outguessed.[45]

"You can state for me," he angrily told Frank Elser of *The New York Times,* "that there never was a command which left the borders of the United States by sea or land that more nearly represented the flower of the American Army or was better qualified to take care of itself in any emergency."

His eyes snapped as he spoke and his teeth fairly spat out the words.

"They can't make this expedition budge one inch unless so ordered. It stands ready to hold its ground, to meet all emergencies, face all contingencies; and I wish you would emphasize that reports of nervousness and feverish preparation are the sheerest nonsense and wildest exaggeration."[46]

True enough, but it was an indication of how the expedition had changed. They had gone in to catch somebody. Now they were concentrated in order to protect themselves.

After mid-May the political situation eased a bit. The troopers, unaware of how tense things were at the diplomatic level, were glad that supplies were at last catching up with them, especially with the flying columns which for weeks had been outrunning everyone except Villa. Now they were heading north and for the first time had enough of what they needed, including "luxuries" like candy, preserves, and tobacco.

No Villistas were hunted and, except for a lucky break, none were captured. As for Carranzistas, Pershing's opinion was that, as long as the expedition stayed put and did not send out roving columns, there was little likelihood of another Parral. Carranza must surely realize the "suicidal outcome of precipitating war with us," he surmised.[47]

Yet if Carranza realized it, he wasn't showing it. Funston kept getting reports of heavy Mexican troop movements north—ostensibly to suppress banditry, but suspiciously large and out of all proportion for such work. Virtually every piece of Mexican field equipment was heading north. Already over 20,000 Mexican troops were stationed in and around Chihuahua City, just south of the expedition, and more were en route. Reports reached Pershing that General Luis Herrera had declared he would attack any American troops still in Mexico after June 1.[48]

Already outnumbered at least two to one, Pershing minimized the danger and disdained Carranza's army. On May 25, he advised against further retreat, saying that his present position threatened Chihuahua City and the railroad. "To withdraw now under the circumstances seems to me yielding ground in face of threats by forces unable to back them up."[49]

As of the above date his main southernmost camp was Namiquipa, although reconnaisance cavalry ranged as far south as Providencia and San Geronimo. Troops north of Namiquipa were mostly occupied in running down rumors regarding Carranza troops on the flanks. Occasionally, however, they came across small bands of Villistas. On May 25, an infantry scouting party killed Candelario Cervantes, Villa's chief lieutenant in the Columbus raid.[50] Earlier that month George S. Patton, Jr., an aide whom Pershing dubbed "The Bandit," dropped Col. Julio Cárdenas, sometime leader of Villa's Dorados, with a pistol shot when he stumbled upon him at a ranch. Patton brought the corpse back to camp draped over an automobile fender like a dead deer and wrote his wife, Bea: "You are probably wondering if my conscience hurts me for killing a man. It does not. I feel about it just as I did when I got my sword fish: surprised at my luck."[51]

During the withdrawal north, Carranza's troops became more aggressive. When Pershing learned that Mexicans at Bachiniva were moving toward Namiquipa, he fired off a warning that "any further advance . . . will be regarded as hostile and will be resisted." He told Funston: "There is an evident movement to scare us back."[52]

Funston prudently counseled less belligerency. "You are instructed to act conservatively," he said. "If a breach does occur the responsibility must be beyond question on Carranza troops."[53]

Reporting the situation to General Scott in Washington, Funston wrote on May 30:

"One thing is sure, and that is if a fight takes place between any of Pershing's force and Carranza troops the fat is in the fire for good. There will be no more hope of localizing the difficulty than of localizing a typhoon. Regardless of the result of such a conflict it will be heralded all over Mexico as a victory, and the whole country will be aflame with the tabasco sauce brand of patriotism prevalent there."[54]

The next day it seemed certain that Carranza had cast the die for war. On May 31 the War Department directed that a telegram be sent to Funston RUSH:

"The following is for you alone and in closest confidence.

"The terms of the Mexican note just received in State Department indicate possibility of very grave situation. Secretary of War directs you instruct General Pershing get his troops promptly in hand. . . ."[55]

Days went by, and the attack did not come. Had it, Pershing would have geen considerably outmanned and outgunned. His force on June 7 numbered 10,542 men, with 20 field artillery pieces and 20 machine guns. Carranzistas at Chihuahua City numbered at least 22,000 and their number was growing. They had about 80 artillery pieces and 100 machine guns. This was to say nothing of the force moving east from Sonora on Pershing's western flank.[56]

In case of attack, Pershing's orders were to flash immediately the news to Funston without waiting to give details, and then try to destroy the attacking force, avoiding extended pursuit or spreading himself too thin. He was to send cavalry east and west to cut the railroads and secure his flanks. Meanwhile Gen. George Bell, Jr., would cross from El Paso and drive fast for Gallego, located half-way between El Paso and Chihuahua City on the railway line, where, as soon as practicable, Pershing was to unite with him. If possible, he was also to take Chihuahua City, the railway junction.[57]

From that town on June 16 came a warning telegram written by Gen. J. B. Treviño, the commander:

"I have orders from my government to prevent, by the use of arms, new invasions of my country by American forces and also to prevent the American forces that are in this state from moving to the south, east or west of the places they now occupy. I communicate this to you for your knowledge for the reason that your forces will be attacked by the Mexican forces if these indications are not heeded."[58]

Pershing's reply, dated the same day, was terse and implacable.

"You are informed that my government has placed no such restriction upon the movement of American forces. I shall therefore use my own judgment as to when and in what direction I shall move my forces in pursuit of bandits or in seeking information regarding bandits. If under these circumstances the Mexican forces attack any of my columns the responsibility for the consequences will lie with the Mexican government."[59]

All of which was summed up in a Pershing remark widely quoted in the American press: "I do not take orders except from my own government."[60]

June wore on in an atmosphere of uneasy tension. James Hopper, who asked Pershing for an interview, learned just how touch-and-go the situation was.

"They are all about us," said Pershing. "Our patrols are in constant contact; we cannot go anywhere without running into Mexican troops; the pursuit is brought to an absolute stand-still. And from all sides we are hearing threats."

"If that's true," said Hopper, "isn't it possible that a clash may occur at any time—since the two armies are so close to each other? And couldn't that start a general conflagration?"

Pershing sat silent a moment, looking down. Hopper felt he was debating whether to answer. Finally he raised his head.

"It's almost impossible that there shouldn't be a clash," he said.[61]

It was not long in coming. On June 18 Pershing, who had moved his headquarters to Colonia Dublán, decided to send a cavalry patrol east to investigate rumors that eight to ten thousand troops were assembling at Ahumada. With the airplanes gone, no other way to gain information was available.[62] To command, Pershing selected Capt. Charles T. Boyd, who had served as his adjutant at Fort William McKinley in the Philippines. Boyd was a West Pointer ('96), a distinguished graduate of the School of the Line ('12) and of the Army Staff College ('16). A good fighting soldier, he also had a sound head on his shoulders. He could be trusted to use discretion.

And discretion was needed, Pershing reminded him. The situation was tense, Treviño was breathing threats, and a clash might bring on a war. He suggested that probably Boyd could find out what he wanted by going no farther east than Santo Domingo Ranch, about eighteen miles short of Ahumada.[63] "This is a reconnaissance only, and you will not be expected to fight. In fact, I want you to avoid a fight if possible. Do not allow yourself to be surprised by superior numbers."[64] On the evening of June 20, Boyd reached Santo Domingo Ranch with C Troop, 10th Cavalry, a Negro regiment with a splendid record. There he met Capt. Lewis S. Morey, commanding K Troop, who had come east from Ojo Federico on the same mission: to investigate the reports of a troop build-up at Ahumada.

At Santo Domingo Ranch, an American foreman who had visited Ahumada recently gave them much valuable information, including the fact that there were several hundred Carranza troops at Carrizal, west of Ahumada. Lt. Henry Adair of C Troop, who had a low opinion of Mexican courage, predicted that if there was any trouble, all the Americans had to do was charge and the Mexicans would run. Lem Spilsbury, a Mormon scout who had lived at Colonia Dublán and whom Pershing had assigned to Boyd's troop, disagreed. "Well, you're just mistaken about that," he interjected. "I know Mexicans that are just as brave as any Americans I have ever heard about, and they are not afraid to die."

As subsequent actions revealed, Boyd believed Adair more than Spilsbury and decided to push on to Carrizal and then to Ahumada to investigate personally.

Leaving the ranch at 4:00 A.M. on June 21, Boyd, the senior in command, marched both troops east and arrived within one mile of Carrizal at 7:30 A.M. He sent ahead Spilsbury, who spoke Spanish, to ask permission of the Mexican commander to pass through the town. "If he asks you what you want to go through for, you tell him that we want to see about a Negro deserter who is reported to be over there."

Spilsbury first encountered Maj. Genevo Rivas who was decidedly unfriendly. "There are no Villistas in this part of the country, and if there are any enemies of yours over here, we're them!"

Rivas sent for Gen. Felix Gómez, the Mexican commander, who came out and conferred with Boyd sitting by the side of the road. He was courteous, but firm in opposing Boyd's advance.

"I have orders to stop any movement of American troops through this town and am therefore duty bound to oppose you. Whether you were one or a thousand, we should try to stop you. However, if you would like to wait here, I will go back to Villa Ahumada and wire General Treviño, our commanding general. If he gives you permission to come through, you will be welcome to do so. But if he does not, we shall have to stop you."[65]

During the conference, Mexican soldiers began to move out and take positions opposite the Americans. Although the position and attitude of Gómez's force indicated that they meant business, Boyd, perhaps recalling Adair's prediction about Mexican cowardice, suddenly broke off the talk. "Tell the son-of-a-bitch that I'm going through!" he exclaimed to Spilsbury. Rising to his feet, he shook his fist at Gómez and said: "God damn you! I've never disobeyed an order yet, and I'm not going to now. I'm going through your goddamned town!"

Gómez, who probably understood enough English to know what had been said, replied with dignity: "You might pass through the town, but you'll have to walk over my dead body." He then returned to his men and Boyd did the same. As the latter mounted up, he said to his horseholder: "Sergeant, we're going to have a fight."[66]

Boyd then addressed Troops C and K.

"My orders are to go east to Villa Ahumada on the other side of this town, and I'm going through and take all of you men with me."[67]

The soldiers cheered. Boyd continued:

"I value each of you as ten Mexicans. Do not let it be said that the American troops fired the first shot. If they fire on us, we will answer them, shot for shot. The only thing I will not forgive is showing your back to the enemy."

Boyd then gave the drill-book command: "Fight on foot, action right."[68]

The troopers dismounted and moved forward on foot. One out of four was occupied in taking the horses to the rear and holding them. Since Troops C and K were skeleton organizations to begin with, together totalling only about eighty fighting men, the removal of the horseholders reduced Boyd's strength by 25 percent right off. He advanced his troopers across an open plain in full view of the Mexicans who were already in position, perhaps some three hundred strong. When Boyd was within about 250 yards, the Mexicans opened fire.

The first shots, especially from the one Mexican machine gun, were high; they went over the Americans' heads but fell squarely among the horseholders to the rear, who had not moved far enough out of range. The horses panicked, stampeded, and fled.

The Americans fired back, at first with deadly effect. General Gómez died instantly, a bullet through his brain. But a short time later so did Boyd, after being twice wounded, and Henry Adair, the other officer of Troop C. Morey, the only officer with Troop K, was wounded early and put out of the fight. Because of faulty cavalry organization at the time, there were no permanent platoons or squads, so that, with officers killed or disabled, the soldiers did not know where to turn for leadership. The two troops began to disintegrate as fighting units. Although there were instances of gallantry, the Americans were driven back and scattered.

American casualties were nine killed and twelve wounded; twenty-four were captured. Mexican casualties, although disputed, were considerably higher.[69]

Word of the clash flashed over the wires. On June 22, Funston dashed off an excited note to Pershing: "Why in the name of God do I hear nothing from you? The whole country has known for ten hours through Mexican sources that a considerable force from your command was apparently defeated yesterday with heavy loss at Carrizal. Under existing orders to you why were they there so far from your line being at such distance that I assume that now nearly twenty-four hours after affair news has not reached you? Who was responsible for what on its face seems to have been a terrible blunder?"[70]

Actually Pershing had heard of the incident on June 21 from General Bell in El Paso, who relayed news which the Mexican consul had heard from Mexico City. Pershing handed the dispatch to his Chief of Staff, De Rosey C. Cabell, without a word and when Cabell finished reading, Pershing said: "That was a deliberate attack."[71]

That afternoon he sent Major Howze with a squadron of cavalry to learn details and to pick up survivors. On the way Howze encountered Captain Morey, four soldiers, and the American foreman of the Santo Domingo ranch. Morey was reticent and didn't want to talk about Carrizal very much. When an officer said it looked like Boyd had bungled badly, he just nodded his head.[72]

After questioning some of the survivors, Pershing asked Funston for authorization to strike back. He had intercepted a Carranza message calling on Villistas to unite with government troops in driving out the Americans.[73] Said Pershing: "Full consideration should be given to fact that Mexican troops fired first. . . . All . . . preparations under way."[74] Funston knew what "all preparations" meant. The Second Mexican War was about to become history. Newsmen were betting on it three-to-one.[75]

On June 25, the War Department vetoed Pershing's request to retaliate. Mexican forces had been building up continually and could be easily reinforced from the South; Pershing's command was small; reinforcing it was difficult and time-consuming. He did not have a single airplane for communication and observation.[76]

Obviously the War Department wanted no conflict until Pershing's forces could be bolstered. Telegrams went out to the commanding generals of the Eastern, Western, and Central Departments, all with the same opening sentence: "Grave necessity for additional troops on border."[77]

While this build-up went on, Funston cautioned Pershing against any more Carrizals. "It is so difficult to understand why 75 men were sent 80 to 90 miles from your lines in the face of unknown large organized force." In the future, "undertake no move that is not thoroughly safe. One more such incident as that of June 21 will raise the morale of the others to such an extent that it will be costly to reduce it again."[78]

Pershing felt this criticism unjustified. "There is absolutely no source [of] information here that is reliable," he explained. "It has been [the] policy [of] this expedition not to be disturbed by alarming unverified reports received from border or elsewhere. Yet such reports must always be investigated. Any other course would be in disregard of safety of command. Many reports of large movement reach here that require sending cavalry patrols 70 to 90 miles to ascertain facts. My opinion [is that] this has been necessary and will be necessary in future."[79]

Confidentially Pershing told Funston that Boyd had failed in prudence at Carrizal. Morey entirely disagreed with him and had argued against advance, but Boyd was adamant and "thought he could bluff it through."[80] As for the future, Pershing finally came round to Funston's viewpoint and recommended that, unless war was contemplated, the expedition should be further concentrated and pulled back. "Our presence here almost certain to bring on clash," he said. "Consider it miraculous we have not already had several clashes in view of necessity of protective patrolling."[81]

Thus matters stood at the end of June, one hundred days after the attack at Columbus.

17

The Last Campaign

From July on, the "quiet period" of the expedition set in. President Wilson had called out the whole National Guard, which numbered over 110,000 men, in mid-June and its presence on the border, coupled with the fact that Carranza had other problems—like fighting 20,000 die-hard guerrillas under Zapata south of Mexico City—gave him second thoughts about attacking anyone.[1]

No National Guard units crossed the border into Mexico; their value was mostly for effect on impressionable Mexicans. Regular Army officers, who saw the guardsmen up close, were not particularly impressed with their training or capabilities.

"It is a pity the militia could not have been called out two months ago," Pershing commented acidly, "so that its hopeless deficiencies might have been shown up to Congress in their true light. To attempt to put dependence upon the militia is absolutely absurd and rediculous [*sic*]. . . ."[2]

Many of the Guard units found life on the border difficult. "This is the most forsaken country the Lord ever made," wrote one New York recruit. "We ought to clean Mexico up, and for punishment make them take back this part of Texas."[3]

Activities during the "quiet period" were mostly reconnaissance and training. "Don't let them stagnate!" said Pershing of troops. "If they get out of the habit of working they won't be in condition when they are needed. Idleness has ruined more armies than battles have. . . . The men are more contented when they have something to do."[4]

Accordingly, he instituted a training course from company right up to the brigade, with particular attention to machine guns and musketry. An inspector called the course "the best I have ever seen."[5] General Funston, who reviewed the troops and inspected all the camps near the end of 1916, told the War Department, "It is a really wonderful command, men and horses absolutely in the pink of condition. They have been kept pretty hard at work at drills and field exercises and in a climate cool enough so that the men could work without wearing themselves out. I think Pershing deserves a tremendous amount of credit for the way he has handled things. . . ."[6]

How the troops regarded Pershing is clear. They respected him. Not a few feared him. There was nothing wishy-washy about him, even though at times he was rather petty—like making a man open his shirt on a hot day to see if he wore the prescribed undershirt.[7] The men thought he was strict, but fair. Nor did they doubt his competence as commander. One veteran who called him an "S.O.B." and said he "hated his guts," added: "But as a soldier, the ones then and the ones now couldn't polish his boots."

Few liked him, in the sense that he inspired warm, personal enthusiasm. "He was very cold and impersonal," one subordinate stated, echoing earlier judgments. "He was a martinet of the first water—a very tough gentleman to deal with. Absolutely ruthless. He was a man that you could never get on friendly terms with; I think that was a studied maneuver on his part."[9] Others qualified this. His fierce mien, said one, which tended to freeze up everyone, considerably softened when he opened his mouth and began to speak. And he could tolerate human foibles. When he encountered a group of soldiers squatting behind an overturned wagon which served both as a windbreaker and concealment, he said not a word about their playing craps, which was against regulations, but told them to move away from the trail "or some lieutenant might see you."[10]

"The inner man was fairminded, generous and sensitive," said S.L.A. Marshall. But "either he was emotionally totally incapable of revealing this to his troops or he mistakenly believed that when a man becomes a professional soldier he cannot act like a warm human being without damaging his command power."[11]

Then, too, Pershing was still recovering from the Presidio tragedy. In Mexico he was a very lonely man.[12] And lonely men do not always put their best foot forward.

One who felt close to Pershing was his aide, George S. Patton, Jr. On one occasion they rode horseback forty miles, hunted antelope, and started back to camp by automobile. Eight miles from camp the car broke down.

Pershing "set the pace," related Patton, "and walked five miles in fifty minutes. The scout and I were nearly killed by the pace and he had to slow down for the remainder of the way on our account." When one remembers that Patton was a famous athlete in his own right (in the 1912 Olympic Games at Stockholm he won fifth place in the pentathalon), his statement is tribute indeed.[13]

On another occasion Pershing sent Patton with a message which had to be carried by plane. When Patton ordered the pilot to take off, the latter objected that the weather was too bad. Patton insisted. Under protest, the pilot took off, muttering something about going to his death. When Patton reported what had happened, Pershing said, "It was not really that important, but if the man is killed, I signed that order." Fortunately, the man was not.[14]

In World War II, when Patton was about to leave for North Africa, he went out to Walter Reed Hospital in Washington, D. C., to say goodbye to Pershing, then in his eighties. Kneeling down in front of the old man, Patton asked for his blessing. Pershing put his hand on his head and said, "May God be with you, Georgie. Would that I could be with you also, but my spirit will march along beside yours." The incident meant much to Patton for he had boundless admiration for his old commander. Patton's daughter said once, "My father thought he was the greatest American soldier and the greatest man that he ever knew. He idolized him."[15]

The biggest problem after July, apart from the perennially disagreeable weather, was morale. No USO existed then for the troops; no recreational facilities were provided by the YMCA, the K of C, the Salvation Army, or Jewish Welfare, as were later provided in World War I.

The soldiers had to make their own recreation: baseball games, boxing matches, card games, "galloping dominoes," and the like. One sergeant later took out of Mexico some twenty thousand dollars he had amassed by gambling.[16] There were occasional hunting parties, but only with an escort large enough to discourage molestation by hostile Mexicans. Those hunters who took along some Apache Scouts (a number of these were with the expedition) were fortunate indeed, for the Apaches were hawk-eyes when it came to trailing animals. One officer went out with the Apaches and brought back seven deer; later he went out without them and did not even *see* one. Commented the Apache Scout commander, Lt. James Shannon: "The amusing thing was that he did not seem to realize that the presence of the Indians had anything to do with finding the deer."[17]

While the Apaches (dubbed "Pershing's Pets") were phenomenally good at following trails, they did have a problem distinguishing friend from foe, Carranzistas from Villistas. To them they were all Mexicans. When Sergeant Chicken encountered a Carranzista detachment, he exclaimed to his white commander: "Heap Mexican. Shoot 'em all!"[18]

One other feature of camp life should be mentioned—and usually is not: the prostitutes. Once active operations ceased, Mexican whores flocked into Colonia Dublán, Nueva Casas Grandes, and other barrios. Troopers met them out in the bush or in the town, and the VD rate skyrocketed. Forbidding the liaisons by regulations or orders was next to impossible.

Later, when the Mormon bishop at Colonia Dublán complained, Pershing authorized the commanding officer of the camp to confer with him to see what might be done. The bishop proposed a restricted district and offered to find a Mexican to manage it. With the army's approval he selected an inconspicuous location well removed beyond the camp limits; the Army guarded the enclosure (known popularly as the "Remount Station") and examined the women regularly for traces of disease.

"Soon," reported Pershing, "we had the traffic under perfect control with a resulting low rate of venereal disease. Everybody was satisfied, as the towns have been kept absolutely clear of that sort of thing. . . . The establishment was necessary and has proved the best way to handle a difficult problem."[19]

In the fall of 1916, Pershing applied for a vacancy in the grade of major general. "Have had more foreign service than any other general officer," he said. "Request full consideration of my record of accomplishment. Also of my present rank as senior Brigadier General of the Army."[20]

Secretary of War Newton D. Baker went over all the Pershing dispatches during the expedition and gave his opinion to President Wilson.

"I am impressed with his general steadiness and good service," he said. It was true that he had shown some "impatience and failure to comprehend the delicate duty intrusted to him," but not more "than would be the case of any soldier who looked at the situation purely from a military point of view."

Baker added one other observation which must have impressed the President. Although Pershing was the son-in-law of Senator Warren, "I have not . . . been able to discover the slightest evidence of political activity on his part."[21]

On September 25 Pershing received a recess appointment as major general.[22] The honor was welcome, but Frances was no longer alive to share his joy. When a friend congratulated him, Pershing replied, "All the promotion in the world would make no difference now."[23]

In September the question of withdrawing the expedition came up.

From a military viewpoint Pershing saw no particular reason against it, since the pursuit of Villa had ceased. From a diplomatic viewpoint, however, he suggested that staying put might be "something of a club that the administration can use over the Mexican government."[24]

Capturing Villa, he told General Scott, "would accomplish little or nothing so far as Mexico is concerned." Someone else would quickly rise up to replace him. "The successful outlaw has always appealed to the mind of the Mexican and probably always will."[25]

On October 9, Scott informed Pershing that there was no prospect of immediate withdrawal. "If you were withdrawn and anything should happen below and you had to go back again where you are, it would be in the nature of a row with the Carranza government, rather than with Villa; so he [President Wilson] prefers to keep you where you are for the time being. How long this is going to continue, none of us know."[26]

Actually, the Wilson Administration was no longer particularly interested in capturing Villa. "People used to tease me about not catching Villa," said Secretary of War Baker later, "but I never dared tell them the truth. I was in hopes they would not catch him. I would not know what to do with him if they did, and Villa captured was much less use to us than Villa at large. As long as he was still at large and running from one hiding place to another, there was an excuse for having Pershing's expedition hang like a pendulum down in Mexico and as long as his army hung down there, no [major] attacks on the border were to be feared because if an attack had come from the east or west of Pershing's line, he could have thrown his army around behind the attacking force and made a curtain between that point and the border and chased any marauders up to the border and captured them there. Every Mexican commander realized it was unhealthy to attack the border as long as Pershing's army was hanging down there like a pendulum. If we had captured Villa, we would have had to retire and then would have the problem of what to do with him, which nobody was particularly clever in suggesting solutions for."[27]

But Pershing still dreamed of capturing Villa. No matter what he said about it meaning "little or nothing," Pancho's escape rankled him.

Pershing (at center) inspecting a mountain battery at Laredo,
Texas, February, 1917
Photograph courtesy Robert A. Vitt, Florissant, Missouri

Pershing's professional pride and his awareness that many considered the expedition a failure spurred him to ask to resume the pursuit.

The answer was the same. No.[28]

At the end of October a deadlock occurred in a commission which had been meeting since September 6 in New London, Connecticut, to negotiate withdrawal. The United States refused to withdraw until the Mexican government did something to make the border safe. Mexico insisted that it *was* safe. Yet all American sources of information contradicted this.[29] Just the previous month, for example, Villa had swept into Chihuahua City at night, opening the penitentiary and freeing the prisoners. When the Carranzista General Treviño attempted to drive him out, his own personal bodyguard deserted and joined Villa, as did most of the Carranzista artillery.[30]

In October a resurgent Villa issued a manifesto against "the abhorred Yankee" and "the unjustified invasion of our eternal enemies, the barbarians of the North. . . ."[31] By November 18 he was in the vicinity of Parral. Later that month, crying "Viva Villa and death to the Gringos," his forces again captured Chihuahua City. A newspaper quoted him as saying, "I will drive them out or make them fight, and after they are gone I will make a gap between the two countries so wide and deep that no American will ever be able to steal Mexican land, gold or oil."[32]

Again Pershing asked to resume operations against Villa. Again the answer was no.[33]

In early January, 1917, it became apparent that the expedition would remain in Mexico little longer. Paradoxically, although Carranza had always insisted on withdrawal, Pershing was convinced that he now was secretly against it. With Villa on the resurgence, Carranza could not hope to stand up to him; only the Americans kept Villa from moving north of Chihuahua City.[34]

On January 28, 1917, the Punitive Expedition began to withdraw. Pershing scheduled a leisurely march, allowing plenty of time to use up the forage on hand and haul out government property. It took a week to cover the 95 miles from Colonia Dublán to Columbus.[35]

There on February 5, Pershing stood on a grandstand and watched his men—the largest force to enter Mexico since the War of 1846–48 —march past. He wore a campaign hat, shirt, boots, and a pistol at his side. "There was no cleaning up for that review," said a trooper. "We looked just natural, so did he."[36]

Thus ended the Punitive Expedition. How does one evaluate it, success or failure? And what were its effects?

Pershing did not catch Villa. If that was the purpose of the expedition, it failed. Nor did he secure the border. During the expedition Villistas crossed it and plundered several Texas towns.[37]

Why did Villa escape? Pershing laid it to two causes: false information from the people and lack of cooperation from the Carranza government. Practically all news that the expedition received of Villa's whereabouts was either entirely misleading or stale.[38] "We do not like the Americans in here," the people said, "because we believe they are in our country to take it. They are pursuing our brother; we do not want him caught."[39] More than one Mexican said he would consider it "a national disgrace" if the Americans captured Villa.[40]

"From the very first," said Pershing, "from the time we crossed the line, we were met by nothing but misinformation and subtle maneuvers to lead us off on wrong trails. And throughout the pursuit we *never* received a bit of correct information till it was too late."[41]

During the campaign many of Villa's followers deserted him and returned to their homes. They must have known his whereabouts and the direction of his march; Carranza commanders must have known too. But, complained Pershing, "they furnished us less cooperation and more deliberately false information than came from any other source."[42]

General Cavazos, for instance, had blocked Tompkins at San Borja when he was in close pursuit of Villa. When finally ordered not to interfere, he said: "I am obeying the orders of my government. But if I had my way, I would not allow you to go one step farther south. I would fight you if I had one man or a thousand men."[43]

However much the Carranzistas and Villistas hated each other, they hated Americans more. "It was like interfering in a family quarrel," said Pershing. "They would fight each other when we were not about, but when we appeared frustration of our plans was the common objective."[44]

This put Pershing in a tremendously embarrassing position. As Col. William A. Ganoe has said: "He had to advance with little transportation through the most trying part of a tensely hostile country. He was allowed to attack one party but not the other, while both were equally antagonistic. He was in the position of the man who had to walk into a hungry leopard's cage with orders to beat Mr. Leopard, but under no conditions resist Mrs. Leopard with her cubs."[45]

But all this is on the assumption that the purpose of the expedition was to capture Villa. Was it?

The purpose was partially contained in the White House announcement which appeared in the press on March 11, 1916. "An adequate force will be sent at once in pursuit of Villa with the single object of capturing him and putting a stop to his forays. This can and will be done in entirely friendly aid of the constituted authorities in Mexico and with scrupulous respect for the sovereignty of that Republic."[46]

The statement could mean two things: (1) the sole object was the capture of Villa, or (2) the object *concerned* Villa and was not a cloak for imperialism. Undoubtedly the second was what the White House wanted to emphasize in view of the remark about Mexican sovereignty. But the American press, in an understandable (but regrettable) desire for a catchy phrase, often printed the statement under a boldface headline like "FUNSTON TOLD TO GET VILLA DEAD OR ALIVE."[47] Thus in the popular mind capturing Villa became the object of the expedition. Actually, Funston never received any such order.

The order which Funston actually received was dated March 10, 1916; it read as follows:

"You will promptly organize an adequate military force of troops under the command of Brigadier General Pershing and will direct him to proceed promptly across the border in pursuit of the Mexican band which attacked the town of Columbus and the troops there on the morning of the ninth instant. These troops will be withdrawn to American territory as soon as the de facto government of Mexico is able to relieve them of this work. *In any event the work of these troops will be regarded as finished as soon as Villa band or bands are known to be broken up."* (Author's italics)[48]

Thus the purpose of the expedition was not to capture Villa, but rather to break up his bands and thus insure the protection of the American border. Catching Villa was incidental to that. Any statement about the "single object" of capturing Villa must be understood in terms of the White House's desire to alleviate Mexican fears of American imperialism.

Further support for this argument appears in the conversation the Chief of Staff, General Scott, had with Secretary of War Baker.

"I want you to start an expedition into Mexico to catch Villa," said Baker.

"Mr. Secretary," Scott replied, "do you want the United States to make war on one man? Suppose he should get on the train and go to Guatemala, Yucatan, or South America; are you going to go after him?"

"Well, no, I am not."

"That is not what you wanted then. You want his *band* captured or destroyed."

"Yes, that is what I really want."

Thereupon the March 10 telegram, quoted above, was sent to Funston. It made no mention of capturing Villa.[49]

Confirmation appears also in the instructions Pershing received on March 14, the day before he entered Mexico: "The President desires that your attention be especially and earnestly called to his determination that the expedition into Mexico is limited to the purposes originally stated, namely *the pursuit and dispersion of the band or bands that attacked Columbus, N. M.,* and it is of the utmost importance that no color of any other possibility or intention be given and, therefore, while the President desires the force to be adequate to disperse the bands in question and to protect communications, neither in size nor otherwise should the expedition afford the slightest ground of suspicion of any other or larger object." (Author's italics)[50]

Undoubtedly Pershing wanted to capture Villa and failure to do so piqued him. As late as December 8, 1916, he was still requesting permission to resume active operations against the bandit.[51]

But this failure was not a failure of the *expedition.* In his unpublished "Autobiography" Pershing wrote: "We had not captured Villa, to be sure, as we had hoped to do, but when active pursuit stopped *we had broken up and scattered his band, which was our original mission."* (Author's italics)[52]

Villa's band which raided Columbus had numbered 485 members. By June 30, 1916, 19 of these had been captured and 273 killed, including famous Villista generals like Julio Cárdenas and Candelario Cervantes, the last named being Villa's ablest lieutenant and the man who had led the actual assault on Columbus. Of those who remained, 108 had been wounded and 60 amnestied by the Carranza government. That left exactly 25 of the original raiders who had not been punished or amnestied and who were still at large.[53]

Even though Villa remained free, his prestige was considerably damaged. Half of his force deserted him on the way to Chihuahua City in November, 1916, and most who stayed did so because of coercion. "I do not think he can ever regain the position he once had," said Pershing as the expedition withdrew.[54]

Many who wrote about the expedition later did not do it justice. Dubbed the "Perishing Expedition," it was depicted as slow, heavy-footed, weighed down by its impedimenta so much that Villa and the Mexicans rode circles around it. According to one writer it was "Villa with his seasoned rebels and his intimacy with the hills, against Pershing with several thousand lumbering, cannon-hampered, rule-encumbered recruits, playing Mexican mountain cat to American domestic rat. The battles were farce. Villa would squat in high caves and review the Pershing army regularly."[55]

This is overdrawn. Clarence Clendenen, a cavalryman himself and a student of the campaign, has remarked: "The actual situation was the direct opposite. It was a game of hare and hounds, with Villa and his bands in the uncomfortable position of the hare."[56] Said Clendenen, in his summary of the expedition: "Actually, the major Villista bands were smashed in every encounter. As for the supposed superiority of the Villistas in guerrilla warfare, it need only be pointed out that *they were surprised in every encounter* and not once were they victorious. And as for the single American defeat, at Carrizal, it is enough to say that two understrength troops of the 10th Cavalry, with their officers killed or wounded, inflicted casualties almost equal to their own total strength, and that the Carranza government changed its tone immediately after the fight. It should be noted also, that when Villa reappeared on the scene, he never came within reach of the expedition, nor did he, as far as available records show, offer violence to Americans, in spite of his bloodcurdling threats. The expedition was far from a failure, even though it did not capture or kill Villa."[57]

Apart from Villa, the expedition had important side effects. It gave military experience to a core of 11,000 men in Mexico, plus thousands of National Guardsmen on the border. The roster of men involved is studded with the names of future military leaders—George S. Patton, Jr., Brehon B. Somervell, John L. Hines, Lesley J. McNair, Benjamin Foulois, U.S. Grant III, Carl Spaatz, Courtney Hodges.

To Pershing, this military experience alone would have justified the expedition. A lifelong advocate of military preparedness, he perennially called for universal military training, stating that it should be a prerequisite for the right to vote.[58]

"No nation can long endure that does not foster a military spirit among its young men . . . ," he said.[59] "Were I in a position to do so I would devote my entire time in attempting to convince our people of the necessity of preparedness."[60] The expedition, to some extent, served this purpose.

It also exposed the inadequacies of a number of "weak sister" colonels. These were weeded out, thus saving time and lives in doing so when World War I came. Pershing said of one of them: "He takes no interest in anything, lacks initiative, and is, upon the whole, hopeless as a regimental commander. The sooner the Army gets rid of men like these . . . the better it will be off."[61]

Not the least of the expedition's advantages was to reveal the pitiful inadequacy of the United States to fight a major war. Practically every military resource which America had was either in Mexico or on the border, yet the whole of it would not have made a respectable advance guard for any of the great European armies. In early 1916 the total amount of U.S. artillery ammunition was estimated to be enough for just three minutes of shooting. No wonder James L. Collins said: "Germany pays no more attention to our notes than does our government to Carranza's and for the very same reason—there is no force to back up our demands."[62]

The expedition showed the need of conscription if war came. Although men were badly needed, General Scott reported that many militia organizations "had great difficulty in getting the requisite number of men to fill their quotas, and some never got them. . . ."[63] Furthermore, the fact that American railroads had difficulty efficiently transporting and supplying 150,000 men on the border suggested that increased federal supervision would be necessary in a future major war.[64]

The expedition was also a testing ground for equipment. It demonstrated that the regulation shoe was too light for a hard campaign; a better shoe was developed and used in World War I. In September, 1916, "rolling kitchens" were tested; they were introduced into the Army the next year. Thirteen types of motor trucks, representing eight manufactures, were sent to the border in 1916 and tested under field conditions. The result was a standardized model in production by 1917.[65] Examples like this could be multiplied. One military historian called the Villa raid on Columbus a "blessing in disguise."[66]

Finally, the expedition contributed to the training of Pershing himself. Its 11,000 troops were the largest contingent he had ever commanded and gave him some preparation, albeit inadequate, for handling the 2,000,000 men he would eventually be commanding in France.

The expedition revealed a number of things about Pershing. One was mentioned by Secretary Baker in recommending him for promotion: "general steadiness and good service."[67] Mexico was a difficult assignment for a soldier. In dealing with Carranzistas he had to walk the tightrope between conciliation and firmness. Too much conciliation would have meant failure to apprehend as many Villistas as he did. Too much firmness could have brought on war with Mexico. In the Philippines, Pershing had built a reputation for knowing how to handle delicate situations. It served him well in Mexico.

Some lapses did occur. Pershing's over-reaction after Parral was one. His seeking permission then to begin a full-scale war with Mexico was, according to Secretary Baker, a "failure to comprehend the delicate duty intrusted to him."[68] Another was Pershing's choice of Captain Boyd for the Carrizal reconnaissance. He either totally misjudged his man or failed to make his conciliatory instructions sufficiently clear, but in any event it resulted in needless loss of life and a serious crisis between the two nations. Perhaps Pershing communicated to Boyd his own contempt for Carranza troops, a contempt not without some Anglo-Saxon prejudice and not altogether justified by the facts. To Pershing, Carranzistas were "a mob without training or discipline and with little courage and not to be feared in the slightest."[69] Boyd learned otherwise at Carrizal. It was not the Mexicans who retreated or were captured.

Pershing had his prejudices. He had the professional soldier's disdain for the non-professional. For all his talk about universal military training, the end product would be to his mind no better than a second-rate soldier compared with the Regular Army. The adjective "goddamn" seemed to find its way in front of the word "National Guard" or "militiaman," when Pershing was holding forth.[70] "I question whether the militia [will] be very strong for the Regular Army when they get back," he wrote disparagingly.[71] "After a few months' service on the border you will hear a great howl go up from them all regarding the hardships they endure and they will be crying to be mustered out."[72] "The brigadier-generals and the major-generals in the National Guard down here, so far as

I have been able to learn, have been abject failures and their men say so. . . ."[73]

By the end of the expedition, Pershing's reputation as a disciplinarian, not to say a martinet, was established. It accompanied him the rest of his life. In France, after the armistice, he would arouse resentment by keeping troops at their training when it seemed to the average doughboy that there was no longer need for it. But Pershing was following the dictum he had used in Mexico: "Men are more contented when they have something to do."[74] Even if the something doesn't make much sense.

He never completely succeeded in separating discipline from pettiness, nor did he in Mexico. Checking for undershirts beneath blouses on a hot day, as we have already noted, was an example.[75] The troops gave him what he deserved: respect. But they would not give him their affection. Save for men on his staff like George Patton, Jr. and James L. Collins, who were permitted to see a side of him that others never did—his sensitivity, his warmth, his humor—Pershing in Mexico and thereafter was what Laurence Stallings was later to name him: The Iron Commander.

He was tough and he expected others to be tough. He roughed it in Mexico and claimed it added ten years to his life.[76] "All the way through he has shown himself to be a man of iron," said Patton.[77]

Man of Iron! Because he wanted to be, or because he had to be? The Punitive Expedition was therapeutic for him, distracting him from thoughts of his dead wife and children. Work was an antidote for sorrow. Pershing was fighting more than Villistas. He was fighting mental depression. "One must get over sorrow or it will break you," he said once to a member of his staff who had a death in the family. "All one can do is to go on with life."[78]

He did go on, despite difficulties which were formidable—unmapped terrain, foul weather, inadequate supplies, misleading information, Carranzista obstruction and attack. The restrictions under which he operated (not being able to use the railroads, nor to enter the towns, nor to retaliate when attacked) were repugnant, as they must be to any soldier. Another general said later, "In war there is no substitute for victory."[79] In the Punitive Expedition there had been no victory, in a soldier's sense of the word.

A contemporary poem by an unknown author summed up what could have been Pershing's sentiments after Parral and Carrizal.

Fifty miles to Carrizal, sage brush, sand and flies,
If a fellow falls behind, well a fellow dies.

Nothing much in front of us but the baking sun;
Less 'n nothing back of us—I mean Washington.
Out in front—Carranza's men, no one safe at night;
Right behind us government, still too proud to fight.

Yesterday our allies stood grinning to the last
While the village cutups stoned us as we passed.
Day before a scout was lost, and found without his toes.
Tomorrow? about tomorrow, the good Lord only knows.

Had a dream the other night and it was a peach—
All the sand was presidents, and every grain a speech;
Every grain was graceful words and every word hot stuff
But a wind across the sage brush called the scintillating bluff.

That is all about myself, except I'm seeing red
Watchful waiting, for a shot to get me in the head;
Guns are not for use, I know, that's the higher law
Down here saying thank you when they punch you in the jaw.

But today we got some news, got it by the grace
Of a Mexican Lieutenant (Jena scars [up] on his face),
Got the news from Carrizal and, we thank God tonight
For Boyd, Adair, and fifty coons, not too proud to fight.

Take their murdered bodies up, calk them from the sun.
We let them die, but now, oh my plot in Arlington!
Dead march, cart 'em across the bridge, a flag atop of each
And ship one to the White House, so a man may make a speech.

Will he see it when it goes past him in its pall,
Will he have the nerve to say anything at all?
Bet your life the brook of words bubbles day and night—
Here's your dead, Your Excellency, still too proud to fight?

Fifty miles to Carrizal, half past time to die;
We don't mind the dying, but we'd like to know the why.
If we weren't sent here to shoot, and we weren't, it is clear,
Tell us, Mr. President, why the h . . . we're here.

What's the use of bluffing, when the Greasers got us right.
He's no kind of talker, but he's not too proud to fight.[80]

After Parral and Carrizal it must have seemed to Pershing as if the Mexican "greasers" did indeed have him in an impossible situation. In such circumstances the natural tendency is towards self pity and in extreme cases, as with MacArthur in Korea, an attempt to undercut government policy. Such conduct was utterly foreign to Pershing. As he told George S. Patton, Jr.:

"When we enter the army we do so with full knowledge that our first duty is toward the government, entirely regardless of our own views under any given circumstances. We are at liberty to express our personal views only when called upon to do so or else confidentially to our friends, but always confidentially and with the complete understanding that they are in no sense to govern our actions."[81]

Confidentially, Pershing made clear his opinion that the United States should intervene in Mexico. "If I expressed myself as vigorously as I feel," he wrote a friend, "it would burn a hole in the note paper."[82] He personally felt that the Punitive Expedition constituted one of the dark pages of American history. "Having dashed into Mexico with the intention of eating the Mexicans raw, we turn back at the very first repulse and are now sneaking home under cover like a whipped cur with his tail between his legs."[83] But all this was expressed privately, or, as Pershing said to Patton, "confidentially." Publicly he kept quiet.

Years later, Gen. George C. Marshall, testifying before a Senate Committee, contrasted the conduct of Pershing in Mexico with MacArthur in Korea when both were hemmed in by political restrictions. Describing Pershing's reaction to the order to cease efforts and retire north, Marshall said,

"He told me he didn't mention that to any of his staff, and that he walked around his tent, and around the bivouac there most of the night, and gave the order the next morning for the beginning of the withdrawal without any explanation whatever to anybody concerned. . . . I think it was a very good model to follow in the Army."[84]

It was. But it hurt terribly at the time. When the order came to call off the Villa hunt, Pershing did something few people thought him capable of. Tough old soldier that he was, in the privacy of his tent, *he wept!*[85]

Despite his obedience, rumors began circulating in Washington in the early months of 1917 that Pershing had criticized Wilson's Mexican policy. Hearing this, Pershing wrote to General Scott, the Chief of Staff. "I . . . assure you that these reports are entirely without foundation. . . . I have been just as guarded in my remarks as I could be. . . . I have realized from the start that the President has been confronted with very serious conditions as to our foreign relations. . . . I have not only not criticized him, but I have stated the above views time and again to others."[86]

Scott gave Pershing's letter to Secretary of War Baker who, in turn, saw that it came before the eyes of the President. But for this, Scott felt, Pershing would never have received the appointment as commander of the A.E.F.[87]

After World War I, George Hinman asked Pershing how it happened that he, a good Republican, received the Number One appointment from a Democratic president. "After all," said Hinman, "you had always been associated with Republican leaders—Charles G. Dawes, Francis E. Warren, etc."

Pershing responded that he had once asked the same question of President Wilson.

"General," was the answer, "when you were down in Mexico you showed you could obey orders."[88]

That this quality counted much with Wilson was revealed by Col.

Edward House, who was asked why Pershing had been selected over Leonard Wood. House replied:

"Well, they're both fine men. But . . . the experience we have had with the two men is that, while I admire Wood very much, as does the President, we felt Wood will do what he's told, but he may do some things he's not told. . . . Pershing will just do what he's told."[89]

On February 19, 1917, Maj. Gen. Frederick Funston dropped dead of a heart attack and Pershing moved up to command the Southern Department in his stead. Douglas MacArthur, a major on the General Staff, remembered the reaction of President Wilson and Secretary of War Baker when he brought them news of Funston's death. "Had the Voice of Doom spoken the result could not have been different. The silence seemed almost like that of death."

The President asked Baker who would take Funston's place if the United States should be involved in the European war. Baker turned to MacArthur.

"Whom do you think the Army would choose, Major?"

"I cannot, of course, speak for the Army," answered MacArthur, "but my own choice would be without question General Pershing."

Wilson looked at MacArthur long and hard. Then he said quietly: "It would be a good choice."[90]

So ended Pershing's career as a frontier cavalryman and guerrilla warrior. He had spent most of his professional life in this work, from the sun-scorched frontier posts in New Mexico as a young officer to the rock-strewn canyons of Chihuahua as a general.

He had begun as a cavalryman in the southwestern United States in 1886, at a time when Geronimo was still living and not just a name in the history books or a cry on some paratrooper's lips. He had seen service in South Dakota in putting down the last major Indian uprising in America. He had trained cadets at Nebraska and West Point, and then served in Cuba, an extension of America's frontier as she moved out to make the Caribbean an American lake. Afterwards came the Philippines and names that he could recall in his sleep, filled with

Promoted to two stars after the Mexican Expedition, Pershing poses stiffly for the photographer at his desk. This kind of public image persuaded most people to think of him as hard and rigid, rather than sensitive and warm as he was in his private relations.

Photograph courtesy of Mr. F. Warren Pershing

memories good and bad: Iligan, Vicars, Maciu, Bacolod, Lake Lanao, the Moros, Fort William McKinley, Zamboanga, Sulu, Bud Dajo, Bud Bagsak. The Philippines was *really* the frontier, America's farthest-flung possession, containing strange people with strange customs. Combat there was, but not the "civilized" kind, not the kind that was going on in Europe in 1917. It was guerrilla war, small unit actions calling for counter-insurgency work. The Chihuahua expedition was more of the same—seeking out an elusive foe, breaking up bandit bands, engaging a foe who lived off the country.

And now, if the United Sates were to engage in the war which was raging on the other side of the Atlantic, it would be for him a new frontier, unlike the old ones he had encountered during his first fifty-seven years. War was different in Europe. He would face a vastly different type of foe and would have to meet and solve problems infinitely more complex and varied. Whether he knew it or not that day as he rode from Palomas, Chihuahua, across the border to Columbus, New Mexico, his days as a frontier cavalryman were over. He had fought his last guerrilla war.

Appendix

Pershing's Falsified Birthday

The accepted date for General Pershing's birthday—the date which he himself gave—is September 13, 1860. But the following conflict with it.

(1) Mrs. Louisa D. Warren, who was present at the birth, told a reporter later that she thought Pershing's birthday was not September 13, but January 13, 1860. It was cold that night, she remembered, and the snow was falling.[1]

(2) The same Mrs. Warren was married in March, 1860. Present at the wedding was Mrs. Pershing and her baby, John, whom she remarked was six weeks old.[2]

(3) Everett T. Tomlinson, a biographer, questioned Pershing's sister, May, in 1918 concerning his birthday. Tomlinson said that one of Pershing's boyhood friends "now living in Waco, Texas, writes that he is positive the General was born in January on the same date of his own birthday and is positive of this because he says as boys they used to celebrate their birthdays on the same date."[3]

(4) In all probability, the person mentioned by Tomlinson was Lee W. Love. A reporter who interviewed Pershing acquaintances in 1918 said in passing: "Mr. Love was born on the same day as Pershing, in the same town, and therefore is, in a way, a twin brother."[4] Love was born January 13, 1860.[5] The city directory and phonebooks of Waco, Texas, do not list any Lee W. Love in 1918, but they do list a Will Love, who may well have been the same person, since the latter on occasion signed himself as W. L. Love.[6]

(5) Pershing attended college at the First District Normal School, Kirksville, Missouri. The records there list his age as twenty when he registered in the spring of 1880. If September 13, 1860, were his birthday, he should have been listed as nineteen.[7]

(6) The United States census for 1870 listed Pershing's age as ten. It was taken August 17, 1870. Again, if September 13, 1860, were Pershing's birthday, he should have been listed as nine.[8]

(7) The United States census for 1860 did not list a *Pershing* for either of the two towns in Missouri where John J. Pershing might have been born: Laclede or Meadville. It did, however, list under Meadville a *Pousing* and the following information:

John F. Pousing, age 26, birthplace Pennsylvania.
Elizabeth Pousing, age 25, birthplace Tennessee.
John Pousing, age six months, birthplace Missouri.[9]

This information is extremely close to what is known of the Pershing family. A census report on them in 1860 would have been almost exactly the same:

John F. Pershing, age 26, birthplace Pennsylvania.
Ann Elizabeth Pershing, age 25, birthplace Tennessee.
John Pershing, . . . , birthplace Missouri.[10]

It seems likely that *Pousing* in the 1860 census was a misspelling or garbling of *Pershing,* and that the families are one and the same. (The census records in the National Archives are in extremely large, bulky books, impossible to carry from door to door in making census. Hence the original census taker's return had to be transcribed later to these large books, presumably by some functionary reading unfamiliar handwriting, a situation which could easily make for errors in transmission, especially in spelling.) The child of this family, named John, was six months old at the time of the census, which was taken July 12, 1860. This would absolutely exclude September 13, 1860, as the date of Pershing's birth.[11]

If September 13, 1860, was not Pershing's birthday, why did he list it as such when he went to West Point as a cadet in 1882? (The West Point records are the earliest extant where Pershing himself noted his birthday). The answer is that Pershing was probably overage when he went to the Military Academy. Twenty-two was the cut-off date.[12] Using September 13, 1860, as his birthday enabled him to qualify by a little under three months, whereas his true birthday would have deprived him of the appointment.

Notes

(Each chapter is footnoted independently.)

The following abbreviations are used in the notes:

"Joseph Lach/Edward Gambish" stands for "Letter from Joseph Lach to Edward Gambish." After the first reference (which will include date and depository), subsequent references will be condensed to: "Lach/Gambish."

Acct	–account
ACP	–Appointment, Commission, Promotion file, Record Group 94, at National Archives, Washington, D. C.
Act	–Acting
AG	–Adjutant General
AGO	–Adjutant General's Office
Asst Adj Gen	–Assistant Adjutant General
Asst SW	–Assistant Secretary of War
CG	–Commanding General
CO	–Commanding Officer
CHB	–Charles H. Brent Papers, Library of Congress, Washington, D. C.
cir	–Circular
CofS	–Chief of Staff
CS	–confidential source. Certain recollections furnished the author by two persons who wished to be unnamed. Cited as CS#1 and CS#2.

DCF —Dorothy Canfield Fisher Papers, in possession of Henry Castor, New York City.

Dept —Department

Dist —District

Div —Division

DS —John J. Pershing Papers in possession of the author, Donald Smythe.

Effcy Rept —efficiency report

Encl —enclosure

ER —Elihu Root Papers, Library of Congress

FEW —Francis E. Warren Papers, Western History Research Center, University of Wyoming, Laramie, Wyo.

FF —Frederick Funston Papers, Kansas State Historical Society, Topeka Kansas

FL —Frank Lanckton Papers, in possession of Mrs. Richard Montgomery, Reston, Va.

FO —Field Orders

FWP —John J. Pershing Papers, in possession of F. Warren Pershing, Southampton, L.I., N.Y.

GCM —George C. Marshall Papers, Marshall Library, Lexington, Va.

GCS —George C. Shaw Papers, in possession of Mrs. Edmund K. Daley, Arlington, Va.

GDM —George D. Meiklejohn Papers, Nebraska State Historical Society, Lincoln, Neb.

GO —General Orders

HFW —Helen Frances Warren (Pershing)

Hq —Headquarters

HTA —Henry T. Allen Papers, Library of Congress

IG —Inspector General

Intvw —interview

JGH —James G. Harbord Papers, Library of Congress

JGH-NYHS —James G. Harbord Papers, New York Historical Society, New York City

JJP —John J. Pershing

JLC —James L. Collins Papers, in possession of Gen. James L. Collins, Jr., Washington, D.C.

LC —Library of Congress, Washington D.C.

LW —Leonard Wood Papers, Library of Congress

MS	–Manuscript
NA	–National Archives, Washington, D.C.
NPRC	–National Personnel Records Center, St. Louis, Mo.
OCT	–Orlando C. Troxel Papers, in possession of Mrs. Richard H. Hawkins, Rye Beach, N.H.
OHRO	–Oral History Research Office, Columbia University, N.Y.
PA	–(John J.) Pershing Autobiography (manuscript written in 1930's)
PP	–(John J.) Pershing Papers, Library of Congress. The accompanying numeral indicates the box number.
rept	–report
RG	–Record Group
SA	–(George C.) Shaw Autobiography (manuscript written in 1930's)
Sec	–Secretary
SO	–Special Orders
SW	–Secretary of War
TAG	–The Adjutant General
TAGO	–The Adjutant General's Office
Tg	–telegram
THB	–Tasker H. Bliss Papers, Library of Congress. The accompanying numeral indicates the box number.
TR	–Theodore Roosevelt
USMA	–United States Military Academy, West Point, N.Y.
WC	–William Cowin Papers, in possession of Mrs. Katherine Phister Cowin, Newton Centre, Mass.
WCB	–William Cary Brown Papers, Western Historical Collections, University of Colorado, Boulder, Colo. The accompanying numeral indicates the box number.
WCF	–William Cameron Forbes Papers, Library of Congress
WCF-H	–William Cameron Forbes Papers, Houghton Library, Harvard University
WD	–War Department
WHT	–William Howard Taft Papers, Library of Congress. The accompanying numeral indicates the volume number.
WSHS	–John J. Pershing Papers, Washington State Historical Society, Takoma, Washington

CHAPTER I: FRONTIER CAVALRYMAN

1. *History of Linn County, Missouri* (Kansas City, Mo., 1882), (Cited herein-after as *History of Linn County*) 593; *St. Louis Times*, Sep. 10, 1919, quoted in K. K. Goodwin, "The Early Life of General John Joseph Pershing, 1860–1881" (unpublished MA thesis, Northeast Missouri State Teachers College, 1954), 23–25; PA, ch I, 7–8, PP 380. (Unless other-wise noted, all reference to PA in this chapter are from PP 380.)

2. PA, I, 1–2. For a history of the Pershing family in America from the coming of Frederick in 1749 down to 1924, see Edgar J. Pershing, *The Pershing Family in America* (Philadelphia, 1924). There is also considerable material on the family in PP 157.

3. PA, I, 3–4; E. J. Pershing, 211; Goodwin, *op. cit.*, 16; George MacAdam, "The Life of General Pershing," *The World's Work*, Vol. 37 (Nov., 1918), 46.

4. PA, I, 3, PP 377; MacAdam, *op. cit.*, 46. See Appendix.

5. "Cypress Lodge Information Form on Mr. Pershing," dated 1897, PP 369; PA, II, 15; E. J. Pershing, *op. cit.*, 404–05; MacAdam, *op. cit.*, 46, 51, 53, 56.

6. PA, I, 7, 10, and II, 4–6; PP 380; PA, I 10, PP 374; MacAdam, *op. cit.*, 51–52; Cypress Lodge Form, PP 369; J. A. Eliott/JJP, Sep. 22, 1919, PP 369; U.S. Census 1860, for Linn Co., Missouri, 37.

   In 1952 the Missouri State Park Board acquired the Pershing house and in 1960 opened it to the public as a permanent shrine and as part of the state park system. For details on the house and how it has been restored to its 1860 appearance, see *The National Tribune–The Stars and Stripes* (Washington, D.C.), Sept. 1, 1960; *The Kansas City Star* (Mo.), Sept. 11, 1960; and *The Review* (Laclede, Mo.), Sept. 13, 1960.

7. MacAdam, *op. cit.*, 53; Everett T. Tomlinson, *The Story of General Pershing* (New York, 1919), 11, 14; *History of Linn County*, 585; Goodwin, *op. cit.*, 26; PA, I, 8, 10–11; Mrs. Alice (Reynolds) Chappell/JJP, Aug. 29, 1915, PP 313; loose sheet on JJP early life, PP 360.

8. Goodwin, *op. cit.*, 27; PA, I, 10–11, and II, 2–3, 5.

9. PA, I, 12, and II, 3, 11.

10. Mrs. J. C. Manning/JJP, Sep. 13, 1924, PP 122; Rev. Arthur E. Winkler, pastor of Laclede Methodist Church/author, Feb. 19, 1960.

11. *Public Ledger* (Philadelphia, Pa.), Sep. 9, 1917; *Indianapolis Star*, Sep. 11, 1960; *The St. Louis Star*, Aug. 30, 1919; *St. Louis Globe-Democrat*, Sep. 28, 1918; *Quincy Daily Herald* (Ill.), May 18, 1918; Arthur A. Jeffrey, "John Pershing—Missourian," *Missouri Ruralist*, XVII (July 5, 1918), 3 and 5; MacAdam, *op. cit.*, 54; clipping, May or June, 1917, Scrapbook VI, 7, PP 386.

12. *Brookfield Argus* (Mo.), July 16, 1948; Samuel E. Carothers/JJP, Dec. 19, 1919, PP 40; MacAdam, *op. cit.*, 53–54; PA, I, 11, and II, 8.

13. PA, I, 13–14.

14. Dorothy Canfield Fisher/Henry Castor, July 30, 1953, DCF.
15. Tomlinson, *op. cit.,* 12; MacAdam, *op. cit.,* 54–55; E. B. Allen/G. E. Adamson, Jan. 29, 1934, PP 369; PA, II, 9–10.
16. Thomas M. Johnson, "Boys, We Had Him Wrong," *American Magazine*, Vol. 105 (May, 1928), 78; Jeffrey, "Pershing—Missourian," 3; JJP, "The Things We Need Today," *American Magazine*, Vol. 114 (Dec., 1932), 19; PA, II, 10.
17. JJP, "We Are At War," *American Magazine*, Vol. 113 (June, 1932), 16–17.
18. Nurse Margaret Cummings intvw, Dec. 30, 1962.
19. *Kansas City Star* (Mo.), July 9, 1918; PA, II, 11, 12, 14; *Brookfield Daily Argus* (Mo.), June 18, 1918, quoted in Goodwin, *op. cit.,* 32; Johnson, *op. cit.,* 80; Allen/Adamson; Goodwin, *op. cit.,* 40, 55. One of Pershing's students, the father of Sen. J. W. Fulbright of Arkansas, remembered him as "a very impressive figure." Sen. Fulbright/author, June 21, 1960.
20. Clipping, Scrapbook VI, 7; *Honolulu Star Bulletin*, Mar. 4, 1931.
21. For example, JJP/R. B. Louden, June 29 and July 3, 1880, PP 120.
22. See Appendix, "Pershing's Falsified Birthday."
23. *Official Register of the Officers and Cadets of the U.S. Military Academy* (West Point, N.Y., 1886), 29.
24. "Descriptive Book of Candidates from 1869 to 1888," USMA Archives; 3310 ACP 86, encl 3, NA; MacAdam, *op. cit.,* 164. Pershing was still riding at 75. F. Warren Pershing intvw, May 26, 1960.
25. Carlisle V. Allen intvw, July 11, 1960.
26. *The Centennial of the United States Military Academy at West Point, New York, 1802–1902* (Washington, D.C., 1904) (Hereinafter cited as *Centennial*), I, 231, 253–58; *1886–1911, In Commemoration of the Twenty-fifth Anniversary of Graduation of the Class of '86, U.S.M.A.* (West Point, N.Y., 1911), (Hereinafter cited as *1886–1911*) 14–15.
27. *Centennial*, I, 136; PA, II, 17; PA, III, 11, PP 377; Avery D. Andrews, *My Friend and Classmate, John J. Pershing* (Harrisburg, Pa., 1939), 28; Ralph Curtin intvw, July 17, 1963; Grades, PP 315; MacAdam, *op. cit.,* 164.
28. *Andrews, op. cit.,* 26.
29. *Ibid.,* 25.
30. Robert L. Bullard, *Personalities and Reminiscences of the War* (New York, 1925), 42–43.
31. *1886–1911,* 6; MacAdam, *op. cit.,* 161; Andrews, *op. cit.,* 24; PA, III, 6.
32. PA, III, 13.
33. General Douglas MacArthur, "Reminiscences," *Life* (Jan. 24, 1964), 71.
34. James G. Harbord, *Serving with Pershing: An Address Delivered before the University Club of Port Chester, Port Chester, N.Y., May 26, 1944* (n.p., n.d.), 16–17; JJP, *My Experiences in the World War* (New York, 1931), I, 88; *Lincoln Morning Journal* (Neb.), June 7, 1936; Andrews, *op. cit.,* 35.
35. PA, III, 10; PP 380.
36. Charles D. Rhodes, "Diary Notes of a Soldier" (typed book-script at LC), 2.

37. James H. Frier, Jr. intvw, Jan. 20, 1970.
38. Andrews, *op. cit.*, 27; *1886–1911 (op. cit.)*, 8; PA, III, 10; Ralph Curtin intvw, July 19, 1960.
39. James H. Frier, Jr. intvw, Jan. 28, 1970; PA, III, 15–16; *1886–1911 (op. cit.)*, 27. For a penetrating analysis of the intellectual atmosphere of West Point in Pershing's time and the shortcomings of the academic system, see T. Bentley Mott, *Twenty Years as Military Attaché* (New York, 1937), 28–45.
40. Frier intvw, Jan. 20, 1970.
41. JJP, *Experiences*, I, 181.
42. S. L. A. Marshall, *Men Against Fire* (New York, 1966), 60–61.
43. James G. Harbord memo of conversation with Avery D. Andrews, June 13, 1934, JGH-NYHS.
44. Ernest D. Scott/author, Aug. 12, 1960.
45. Rhodes, *op. cit.*, 1.
46. GO 7, Jan. 30, 1919, Assoc. of Graduates Files, USMA.
47. *Public Ledger* (Philadelphia), Sep. 9, 1917; Andrews, *op. cit.*, 34, 47; PA, III, 12; MacAdam, *op. cit.*, 166.
48. PA, IV, 3–5.
49. George MacAdam, "The Life of General Pershing," *The World's Work*, Vol. 37 (Jan., 1919), 290.
50. Sophie A. Poe, *Buckboard Days* (Caldwell, Idaho, 1936), 279.
51. Mrs. Seth Cook (Cavanaugh's daughter) intvw, Mar. 16, 1961.
52. MacAdam, *loc. cit.*, 290.
53. Mary Ann Rose Harbottle intvw, Sep. 28, 1961; Bullard, *op. cit.*, 42.
54. MacAdam, *loc. cit.*, 290.
55. PA, IV, 6.
56. *Ibid.*, 7–8; JJP/Julius Penn, Oct. 16, 1887, PP 282.
57. Nelson A. Miles, *Personal Recollections* (Chicago, 1896), 537–40, 543; MacAdam, *loc. cit.*, 291–92; *Annual Report of the Secretary of War for the Year 1888* (Washington, D.C., 1888), I, 125–27.
58. GO 39, Dept. of Arizona, Dec. 24, 1887, PP 315; PA, IV, 10.
59. PA, IV, 10; Tomlinson, *op. cit.*, 48.
60. JJP/Julius Penn, Sep. 30, 1890, PP 282.
61. SO 2, Dist. of N. Mex., Jan. 12, 1889, PP 315; Order 85, Ft Wingate, N. Mex., May 9, 1889, PP 315.
62. MacAdam, *loc. cit.*, 293; PA, IV, 12.
63. D. J. Dolson/JJP, Oct. 22, 1906, PP 281.
64. Col. Carr effcy rept on JJP, May 1, 1890, 3849 ACP 86, NA; PA, IV, 12.
65. Howard Bryan, "A Close Call," *The Albuquerque Tribune*, Nov. 15, 1969, 1, quoting recollections of Russell C. Charlton, who got this from Pershing.
66. PA, IV, 15.
67. Carr effcy rept, May 1, 1890.
68. JJP, "Competitions for 1889," *Journal of the U.S. Cavalry Association*, II

(Dec., 1889), 420; Eugene A. Carr/TAG, Feb. 17, 1889, 1015 ACP 89, NA; JJP effcy rept, May 1, 1890, 3849 ACP 86, NA; JJP/Penn, Nov. 10, 1890, PP 282.
69. PA, IV, 12; marksman certificates, PP 315.
70. Martin F. Schmitt and Dee Brown, *Fighting Indians of the West* (New York, 1948), 332.
71. *Ibid.*, 333–34.
72. William H. Carter, *From Yorktown to Santiago with the Sixth U.S. Cavalry* (Baltimore, 1900), 256–57; PA, V, 1–5.
73. PA, V, 5–6; MacAdam, *loc. cit.*, 293.
74. George MacAdam, "The Life of General Pershing," *The World's Work*, Vol. 37 (Feb., 1919), 451, 458.
75. Virginia Conner, *What Father Forbad* (Philadelphia, 1951), 92.
76. PA, V, 8.
77. *Ibid.*, 6; JJP/Julius Penn, Feb. 14, 1891, PP 282.
78. PA, V, 7.
79. JJP/Penn, *loc. cit.*
80. JJP/TAGO, June 1, 1891, 3871 ACP 91, NA; PA, V, 9–10; MacAdam, *loc. cit.*, 460.
81. PA, V, 11; MacAdam, *loc. cit.*, 460.
82. PA, V, 10–11.
83. *Ibid.*, 11–12.
84. William A. Kobbé/JJP, Nov. 4, 1906, PP 281.
85. Frier intvw, Jan. 20, 1970.
86. PA, IV, 11.
87. *Ibid.*, 7–8; Julius Penn/mother and sister, Sep. 5, 1887, PP 282.
88. Poe, *op. cit.*, 230–31, 280–81.
89. JJP/Asst. Adj. Gen., Dept. of Arizona, Aug. 20, 1890, endorsed by Carr, Aug. 22, 1890, PP 315.

CHAPTER II: COMMANDING CADETS

1. George MacAdam, "The Life of General Pershing," *The World's Work*, Vol. 37 (Feb., 1919), 461.
2. *Semi-Centennial Anniversary Book, The University of Nebraska, 1896–1919* (Lincoln, 1919), 53.
3. James J. Canfield/Hon. Frank L. Stetson, Jan. 25, 1895, 13987/C AGO 1895, NA.
4. *The Sombrero* for 1893–94 (Univ. of Neb. Yearbook), 45; *Boston Sunday Globe*, Aug. 5, 1917; Harry R. Follmer, *Footprints on the Sands of Time* (9

Vols. in 12; n.p., 1950?–1953), Vol. VII, Part II, beginning (pages are unnumbered).
5. Follmer, *op. cit.*, IX, 137, 139; Erwin R. Davenport/author, June 14, 1960. Maj. Gen. Charles D. Herron, CofS, 78th Div, AEF, told me that the first thing Pershing did when a man reported to him was to look him up and down from head to toe regarding neatness and appearance—and this no matter how hot the battle or how the war was going. Herron intvw, June 25, 1960.
6. *Boston Sunday Globe*, Aug. 5, 1917.
7. George MacAdam, "The Life of General Pershing," *The World's Work*, Vol. 37 (Mar., 1919), 542.
8. Davenport/author, *op. cit.*
9. *Ibid.*
10. *Boston Sunday Globe*, Aug. 5, 1917.
11. Davenport/author, *op. cit.*
12. Dorothy Canfield, "A General in the Making," *The Red Cross Magazine*, XIV (Sep., 1919), 20.
13. Charles A. Eliot, "The Early Days of the Pershing Rifles," *The Pershing Rifleman*, IV (May, 1935), 6.
14. John R. Johnson, *Representative Nebraskans* (Lincoln, 1954), 148.
15. *Joplin Globe* (Mo.), Feb. 24, 1918.
16. *History of the Military Department, University of Nebraska, 1876–1941* (Lincoln, 1942), 19; JJP rept to Bd. of Regents, June 12, 1895, 2, Board of Regents Papers, University of Nebraska Archives, RG 1/1/1.
17. E. G. Fechet rept to IG, May 23, 1895, 3–7, PP 315; JJP rept, 1–2.
18. Dorothy Canfield Fisher/Henry Castor, July 30, 1953, DCF.
19. Alvin Johnson, *Pioneer's Progress: An Autobiography* (New York, 1952), 78.
20. Fechet rept, *op. cit.*, 1.
21. Rept on Annual Competitive Drill, Univ. of Neb, by E. G. Fechet, June 3, 1895, 3, PP 315.
22. Follmer, *op. cit.*, I, near end (pages unnumbered); PA, VI, 1, PP 380. (All references to PA in this chapter are from PP 380.)
23. *The Omaha Daily Bee*, June 13, 1892.
24. *History of the Military Department, University of Nebraska, op. cit.*, 17.
25. Follmer, *op. cit.*, I, near end.
26. *Ibid.*, IX, 141; *Sombrero, op. cit.*, 45; *History, op. cit.*, 17–18; *The Omaha Daily Bee*, June 19, 1892; PA, VI, 3.
27. PA, VI, 4; L. H. Robbins [?] /JJP, May 29, 1895, PP 160.
28. James H. Canfield/SW, Dec. 5, 1903, 464287/P AGO 1902, NA.
29. Fisher/Castor, July 30, 1953. Ernest D. Scott, a student in Pershing's 8:00 A.M. mathematics class, remembered his "dissipated" look after "a bad night." Scott/author, Aug. 12, 1960. By 1917, however, Pershing had the reputation of being quite sober. Micheline Resco intvw, Aug. 6, 1965.
30. MacAdam, *op. cit.*, 543.

31. Follmer, *op. cit.,* IX, 146. See also W. Henry Smith/SW, Aug. 6, 1895, PP 281.
32. MacAdam, *op. cit.,* 543.
33. Diploma, PP 419.
34. PA, VI, 5; Bascom N. Timmons, *Portrait of an American: Charles G. Dawes* (New York, 1953), 28.
35. JJP/Ward Pershing, May 3, 1898, FWP.
36. Thomas M. Johnson, "Boys, We Had Him Wrong," *The American Magazine,* Vol. 105 (May, 1928), 84.
37. JJP/wife, Oct. 23, 1907, FWP.
38. JJP/Bd of Regents, Oct. 2, 1891, Board of Regents Papers, University of Nebraska Archives, RG 1/1/1; undated account by Adelloyd Whiting Williams, a student in Pershing's class, sent to author by her grandson, James W. Wheaton, Jan. 3, 1970.
39. Fisher/Castor, July 30, 1953.
40. Alvin Johnson, *op. cit.,* 77–78.
41. *Ibid.,* 78.
42. *Ibid.,* 79–80.
43. Davenport/author, *op. cit.* Pershing claimed he got his "glorious memory" from his mother. PA, VI, 8.
44. PA, VI, 6; Timmons, *op. cit.,* 22–23.
45. Charles G. Dawes, *A Journal of the Great War* (Boston, 1921), I, 61–62.
46. *Ibid.,* I, 23.
47. Canfield/Stetson, *op. cit.*
48. PA, VI, 7–8.
49. JJP rept, 4–5.
50. Dorothy Canfield Fisher/Henry Castor, July 27, 1953, DCF.
51. *Boston Sunday Globe,* Aug. 5, 1917.
52. Army Records Center/author, May 9, 1960.
53. PA, VI, 8–9.
54. George MacAdam, *op. cit.,* 544; J.M.J. Sanno/JJP, June 13, 1896, PP 369.
55. JJP rept to J.M.J. Sanno, Aug. 15, 1896, 1, PP 369; PA, VI, 10–11.
56. Army Records/author.
57. PA, VI, 13–14.
58. Avery D. Andrews, *My Friend and Classmate, John J. Pershing* (Harrisburg, Pa., 1939), 54.
59. PA, VI, 17.
60. Charles D. Herron/author, Aug. 1, 1960.
61. A. H. Sunderland/author, Aug. 3, 1960.
62. William Larkin/author, Aug. 23, 1960.
63. Herron/author, *op. cit.*; Charles D. Herron intvw, June 25, 1960. Confirmation that Pershing inspected at unusual hours appeared in letters to the author in 1960 from the following former cadets: Ernest D. Scott, Aug. 12; C. L. Maguire, Aug. 9; William Ennis, Aug. 2; Robert R. Wood, Aug.

12; Curtis W. Otwell, Aug. 4; Edward Shinkle, Aug. 3; Evan H. Humphrey, Aug. 4.

On the other hand, Gilbert A. Youngberg did not recall any inspections at unusual hours. Youngberg/author, Aug. 5, 1960. And Amos A. Fries, another cadet, told me in an interview on May 14, 1960, that Pershing was liked, that he was "square," that he "set no traps and did not go out of his way to catch anyone."

64. Malin Craig/James G. Harbord, Aug. 1, 1934, JGH–NYHS.
65. Scott/author, Aug. 12 and Nov. 7, 1960.
66. Guy V. Henry/author, Aug. 31, 1960.
67. Herron/author, *op. cit.*
68. Craig/Harbord, *op. cit.* The punishment was actually for thirty days, not ninety. SO 24, Feb. 14, 1898, USMA Archives.

The incident of the water bucket was related in the letters previously cited from Larkin, Henry, Humphrey, Shinkle, Wood, Ennis, Maguire, and Youngberg, as well as in the Aug. 12, 1960 Scott letter and in former cadets John A. Long/author, Aug. 27,1960, and Harvey W. Miller/author, Aug. 9, 1960. Said one former cadet: "Of all the various schemes contrived to get the best of him, I do not recall any that succeeded." William R. Bettison/author, Aug. 4, 1960.

69. Scott/author, Aug. 12, 1960.
70. *Ibid.* A slightly different version is related in Miller/author: "The production, carefully censored, of course, was progressing smoothly when, to the utter consternation of every officer and cadet present, a classmate of mine —a *very minor* character in the performance—stepped to the center of the stage and, like a bolt from the clear, and out of context, announced: 'an eye for an eye, a tooth for a tooth and thirty days for a water bucket.' "
71. Herron intvw. Letters to the author from the following also confirm and/or elaborate on the silence: Bettison, Larkin, Scott, Aug. 12, Long, Maguire, Ennis, Wood, Shinkle, Humphrey.
72. C. L. Maguire/author, *op. cit.*
73. Gilbert A. Youngberg/author, *op. cit.*
74. Herron intvw.
75. Wallace D. Dickinson/JJP, May 19, 1898, PP 316.
76. Letters to author from Youngberg, Maguire, Larkin, Humphrey, Henry, Sunderland, Shinkle, Otwell, Ennis, Long, Scott, Aug. 12. Eugene R. West/author, Aug. 30, 1960.

While four of the above specifically said the term was "Nigger Jack," Gilbert Youngberg cautioned against using an opprobrious term to estimate dislike for Pershing: "The 'tacs,' being so largely responsible for the discipline of the cadets, were regarded by the latter as their 'natural enemies' and were given uncomplimentary monikers quite frequently." Youngberg/author.

The letters to the author from Wood and Bettison denied they ever heard Pershing called "Black Jack" at the Academy. So did Fries and Herron in interviews of May 14 and June 25, 1960. Herron said the only name he ever heard was "John J."

77. Ralph Curtin intvw, July 19, 1960. Another explanation of the name was offered by Lee W. Love, a boyhood companion of Pershing. "He taught an unexpired term of the colored school at Laclede where he obtained the name of Black Jack given by his companions." Love/G. E. Burns, Jan. 2, 1937, loaned author by Lafayette Moore, Laclede, Mo. I have found no other confirmation of this explanation. Pershing, as the text indicates, put the origin of the name at West Point.

78. George V. H. Moseley/author, Sep. 22, 1960; Moseley intvw, Sep. 13, 1960.

79. JJP/TAG, Apr. 16, 1898, 74943 AGO 98, NA.

80. JJP/George D. Meiklejohn, Apr. 17, 1898, 82076 AGO 98, NA.

81. SO 100, Hq of Army, Apr. 29, 1898, USMA Archives.

CHAPTER III: "THE SPLENDID LITTLE WAR"

1. See, for example, Wallace D. Dickinson/JJP, May 7 and 19, 1898; George D. Meiklejohn/JJP, May 24, 1898; J. H. Harley/JJP, June 3, 1898; Charles G. Dawes/JJP, June 2, 1898; Nelson A. Miles/JJP, June 4, 1898 —all in PP 316.

2. Lee Mantle/W. D. Dickinson, May 16, 1898; Meiklejohn/JJP, May 24, 1898; Dawes/JJP, June 2, 1898; H. S. Harwood/JJP, May 25 and June 3, 1898—all in PP 316.

3. PA, VII, 7–8, PP 380. (Unless otherwise noted, all references to PA in this chapter are from PP 380.)

4. *Ibid.*, 8–9. Leonard Wood summed up Tampa in three words: "Confusion. Confusion. Confusion." Hermann Hagedorn, *Leonard Wood* (New York, 1931), I, 155.

5. For details on the embarkation and the trip see Herschel V. Cashin *et al.*, *Under Fire with the Tenth U.S. Cavalry* (New York, 1899), 67–79, and Herbert H. Sargent, *The Campaign of Santiago de Cuba* (Chicago, 1907), II, 1–24. J. F. C. Fuller has a clear, concise account of the whole Santiago campaign in his *Decisive Battles of the U.S.A.* (New York, 1953), 333–62. A longer, more recent account is Frank Freidel's *The Splendid Little War* (Boston, 1958).

6. Richard Harding Davis, *The Cuban and Porto Rican Campaigns* (New York, 1898), 86.

7. PA, VII, 6, 10.

8. JJP diary, June 18, 1898, PP 316.

9. T. G. Steward, *The Colored Regulars in the United States Army* (Philadelphia, 1904), 157; PA, VII, 11.

10. JJP diary, June 19, 1898.

11. PA, VII, 12; JJP, Address on the Campaign of Santiago, Nov. 20, 1898, 6–7, PP 369.

12. PA, VII, 12–13; Davis, *op. cit.*, 116.

13. JJP Address *(op. cit.)*, 7–8; Davis, *op. cit.*, 102, 124.

14. PA, VII, 12–13. For another description of the landing, see Walter Millis, *The Martial Spirit* (Boston, 1931), 263–68.

15. PA, VII, 13; JJP diary, June 24, 1898; JJP Address *(op. cit.)*, 11.

16. Davis, *op. cit.*, 174–75.

17. JJP diary, July 4, 1898.

18. James G. Harbord, *The American Army in France, 1917–1919* (Boston, 1936), 43–44. Harbord states here that he got the incident from Maj. Gen. F.R. McCoy in 1934.

19. Davis, *op. cit.*, 180.

20. PA, VIII, 1. For other accounts of the battle of San Juan Hill, July 1, 1898, which begins here, see Millis, *op. cit.*, 269–92 (emphasizing American blundering); Sargent, *op. cit.*, II, 108–32; Cashin, *op. cit.*, 84–98; Matthew F. Steele, *American Campaigns* (Washington, 1909), I, 605–608; Private St. Louis (Alfred C. Petty), *Forty Years After* (Boston, 1939), 34–67; Thomas J. Vivian, *The Fall of Santiago* (New York, 1898), 155–82; E. L. N. Glass (comp. and ed.), *The History of the Tenth Cavalry, 1866–1921* (n.p., 1921), 33–34; William A. Ganoe, *The History of the United States Army* (2d ed. rev.; New York, 1942), 380–85; Theodore Roosevelt, *The Rough Riders* (Statesman Ed.; New York, 1904), 112–56; Charles J. Post, *The Little War of Private Post* (Boston, 1960), 161 ff. A good map of the battlefield is in Sargent, *op. cit.*, II, 94.

21. Steele, *op. cit.*, I, 605; JJP Address *(op. cit.)*, 13; PA, VIII, 1.

22. Davis, *op. cit.*, 178, 203; PA, VIII, 1.

23. Steele, *op. cit.*, I, 605–06; Davis, *op. cit.*, 219; PA, 155, PP 374; PA, VIII, 2, PP 380. Leonard Wood called this incident "one of the most ill-judged and idiotic acts I ever witnessed." Hagedorn, *op. cit.*, I, 174.

24. Davis, 204, 208, 212; JJP Address *(op. cit.)*, 15–16; PA, 156, PP 374; PA, VIII, 3, PP 380; Steele, *op. cit.*, I, 606.

25. Post, *op. cit.*, 178.

26. George MacAdam, "The Life of General Pershing," *The World's Work*, Vol. 37 (Apr., 1919), 691.

27. Baldwin/JJP, Nov. 30, 1898, PP 316; JJP 201 file, NPRC, citing 303229 AGO 1898, NA.

28. Davis, *op. cit.*, 218.

29. JJP/Edward Rosewater, July 19, 1898, PP 369. (I have reparagraphed Pershing's account.)

30. Richard O'Connor, " 'Black Jack' of the 10th," *American Heritage*, Vol. 28 (Feb., 1967), 106.
31. PA, VIII, 4; JJP Address *(op. cit.)*, 18.
32. JJP Address *(op. cit.)*, 19–20. For the precarious American situation after the battle, see Davis, *op. cit.*, 224, 235, 244, 247, 262. For the discussion the evening of July 1 as to whether to withdraw from San Juan Hill to a stronger position, see Hagedorn, *op. cit.*, I, 179, and PA, VIII, 5.
33. PA, VIII, 8.
34. JJP diary, Aug. 5, 1898.
35. JJP Address *(op. cit.)*, 21–22.
36. PA, VIII, 6; JJP effcy. rept., 1897–1899, 3849 ACP 86, NA; JJP/TAG, Mar. 31, 1900, PP 281.
37. *The Centennial of the United States Military Academy at West Point, New York, 1802–1902* (Washington, 1904), (Hereinafter cited as *Centennial*) I, 762; Davis, *op. cit.*, 125–32, 247–48; PA, VIII, 6–7.
38. For an excellent description of daily life in the trenches during this truce and after the surrender, see Charles D. Rhodes, "Diary Notes of a Soldier" (typed bookscript at LC), 27–48.
39. PA, VIII, 9–10.
40. JJP Address *(op. cit.)*, 22–23.
41. *Ibid.*, 24½; Hagedorn, *op. cit.*, I, 180; Davis, *op. cit.*, 281–82; Society of Santiago de Cuba, *The Santiago Campaign* (Richmond, Va., 1927), 202–04; JJP/George D. Meiklejohn, Aug. 2, 1898, GDM.
42. Davis, *op. cit.*, 278–79.
43. PA, VIII, 7.
44. *Ibid.; Boston Sunday Post*, Dec. 22, 1918.
45. Baldwin/JJP, Nov. 30, 1898, PP 316.
46. Beck/JJP, Feb. 20, 1899, PP 316.
47. Rhodes, *op. cit.*, 38–39; JJP Address *(op. cit.)*, 25–26.
48. PA, VIII, 10–11; *Centennial, op. cit.*, I, 764; JJP/George D. Meiklejohn, Aug. 2, 1898, GDM.
49. William Cowin/wife, Aug., 1898, in Katherine Phister Cowin, "Army Kaleidoscope," 70 (unpublished autobiography).
50. Steele, *op. cit.*, I, 610; PA, VIII, 12.
51. PA, IX, 1, PP 380.
52. PA, IX, 1, PP 378.
53. PA, IX, 1, PP 380.
54. Wheeler/TAG, July 16, 1898, 281430 AGO 99, NA.
55. Everett T. Tomlinson, *The Story of General Pershing* (New York, 1919), 84. Pershing was eventually awarded the Silver Star "for gallantry in action against Spanish Forces at Santiago, Cuba, July 1, 1898." GO 3, WD, Feb. 28, 1925, JJP 201 file, NPRC.
56. Wood/TAG, July 30, 1898, 134350 ACP 86, NA; commission diploma, PP 419.

57. Quoted in Richard Hofstadter, *The American Political Tradition and the Men Who Made It* (New York, 1967), 97. See also letters between JJP and Assistant Secretary of War George D. Meiklejohn, 1897–1901, concerning promotion, GDM.

58. Harbord, *op. cit.*, 43.

59. JJP Address, *(op. cit.)* 18.

60. Charles R. Codman, *Drive* (Boston, 1957), 159.

61. JJP Address *(op. cit.)*, 23.

62. George D. Meiklejohn/JJP, Dec. 20, 1898, 185234 AGO 99, NA.

63. James G. Harbord, *Serving with Pershing: An Address Delivered before the University Club of Port Chester, N. Y., May 26, 1944* (n.p., n.d.), 3–4.

64. *Annual Report of the Chief of the Division of Insular Affairs to the Secretary of War for the Year 1901* (Washington, 1901), 34. Pershing served from Mar. 10 to Aug. 24, 1899.

65. PA, VIII, 1, PP 376.

66. PA, IX, 3–4; PA, X, 1.

67. July 13, 1899, PP 64.

68. George MacAdam, "The Life of General Pershing," *The World's Work*, Vol. 38 (May, 1919), 86.

69. SO 192, Hq of Army, Aug. 17, 1899, PP 317; PA, IX, 3.

70. SO 208, Hq of Army, Sep. 6, 1899, 274747 AGO 99, NA; W. H. Carlson/JJP (tg), Aug. 30, 1899, PP 281; JJP/wife, Dec. 31, 1911, PP 3; PA, X, 3.

71. PA, X, 2, 7, PP 380; PA, 193, PP 374.

72. PA, X, 5, PP 378.

73. JJP/George D. Meiklejohn, Apr. 5, 1900, PP 317.

74. PA, X, 5–6, PP 375.

75. JJP/Meiklejohn, Apr. 5, 1900, PP 317; PA, X, 11.

76. JJP/Meiklejohn, Apr. 5, 1900, PP 317.

77. JJP/D. M. Butler, Sep. 12, 1900, PP 317.

78. JJP/Meiklejohn, *loc. cit.*

79. PA, X, 8.

80. *Ibid.;* PA, X, 17, PP 378.

81. 1276789 AGO 07, NA.

82. SO 48, Hq of Army, Feb. 27, 1901, PP 317.

83. PA, X, 11.

84. SO 194, Hq of Army, Aug. 20, 1901, 389894 AGO 01, NA.

85. PA, X, 11–12.

86. JJP 1902 effcy rept, 3849 ACP 86, NA; PA, X, 13; Army Records Center/author, May 9, 1960.

87. PA, X, 12.

88. *Ibid.*, 12–13; William C. Forbes/Lindley M. Garrison, Apr. 11, 1913, WCF-H.

89. PA, X, 12–13.

CHAPTER IV: ILIGAN: MAKING FRIENDS WITH THE MOROS

1. Rutherford H. Platt, "There Was a Captain by the Name of Pershing," *The World's Work*, Vol. 67 (Dec., 1923), 182.
2. GO 8, 10 and 4, Iligan, Nov. 3, 14, 1901, Jan. 29, 1902, PP 317.
3. Platt, *op. cit.*, 182.
4. Moro was Spanish for Moor, a follower of Mohammed.
5. Frederick Palmer, *John J. Pershing, General of the Armies* (Harrisburg, Pa., 1948), 61.
6. PA, X, 13–14, PP 380. (Unless otherwise noted, all references to PA in this chapter are from PP 380.)
7. A sultan was the highest Moro religious and political authority; a datto, the principal adviser or tribal leader, and also a war chief; a pandita, a head priest.
8. R. S. Stevens rept. to AG, Dept of Mindanao-Jolo, Jan. 31, 1901, PP 370; JJP rept to same AG, Feb. 20, 1902, PP 370.
9. PA, 214, PP 374.
10. George MacAdam, "The Life of General Pershing," *The World's Work*, Vol. 38 (May, 1919), 92; Frederick Palmer, *Bliss, Peacemaker* (New York, 1934), 89; Platt, *op. cit.*, 183; PA, X, 14; Amos Fries intvw, May 14, 1960; W. Cameron Forbes Journal, 1st Series, IV, 65, LC.
11. PA, X, 15.
12. JJP paper on Moros, n.d., PP 370.
13. PA, X, 15.
14. *Ibid.*, 8, 15; JJP MS, "Conquest of the Moros," PP 278.
15. PA, X, 18.
16. JJP, "Conquest of Moros" *(op. cit.)*; Stevens rept; William T. Sexton, *Soldiers in the Sun* (Harrisburg, Pa., 1939), 278.
17. Stevens rept.
18. PA, X, 15.
19. Platt, *op. cit.*, 185.
20. George T. Bowman/William C. Sanger, May 15, 1903, PP 370. The citation refers to the Moro practice of killing people with the diagonal down-thrust.
21. PA, X, 15–16.
22. *Ibid.;* JJP rept, Feb. 20, 1902.
23. PA, X, 16.
24. *Ibid.*, 17–18; JJP rept, Feb. 20, 1902.
25. PA, 217, PP 374.
26. George W. Davis/William H. Taft, Mar. 10, 1906, PP 281.
27. JJP rept, Feb. 20, 1902.
28. Ben Lear/author, Feb. 18, 1960; George A. Hunt, *The History of the Twenty-seventh Infantry* (Honolulu, 1931), 22–23. MacAdam, *op. cit.*, 87–88.

29. JJP rept to AG, Div of Philippines, May 10, 1902, PP 370.
30. JJP/George W. Davis, Apr. 12, 1902, PP 279.
31. *Proclamation*, PP 370.
32. JJP rept, May 10, 1902; JJP/various sultans, Apr. 18, 1902, PP 370.
33. J.P. Sanger/JJP, Apr. 16, 1902, PP 370.
34. PP 370.
35. JJP/Charles Magoon, Jan. 28, 1903, PP 370; JJP rept, May 10, 1902.
36. JJP/George W. Davis (tg), April [May?] 1, 1902, PP 317; JJP/Magoon.
37. PA, XI, 3.
38. *Ibid.*
39. JJP rept, May 10, 1902.
40. *Ibid.;* PA, XI, 3.
41. Hunt, *op. cit.,* 23–24; Clarence Deems rept, May 18, 1902, 6–7, 9, PP 370; PA, XI, 3, 5.
42. Davis/Taft, *op. cit.*
43. *Ibid.;* May 13, 1902 tg, PP 317; PA, XI, 4.
44. J.P. Sanger/George W. Davis, May 13, 1902, PP 370.
45. JJP/Magoon; PA, 221–22, PP 374.

CHAPTER V: CAMP VICARS

1. PA, XI, 4, PP 380.
2. *Ibid.*
3. PA, 223, PP 374.
4. A cotta was a Moro fort.
5. PA, XI, 5, XII, 1, PP 380.
6. JJP /George W. Davis (n.d.), PP 1.
7. Baldwin/George W. Davis, June 17, 1902, PP 370. (I have rearranged the sentence order.)
8. JJP diary, June 30, 1902, PP 370.
9. George W. Davis/SW, Mar. 10, 1906, PP 281.
10. JJP rept to TAG, Dept. of Mindanao-Jolo, May 15, 1902, PP 370.
11. Another name for the Dept. of Mindanao-Jolo.
12. Davis/TAG, Feb. 19, 1903, PP 281.
13. JJP paper on Moros (n.d.), PP 370.
14. PA, XI, 8, PP 380.
15. JJP/George W. Davis, Mar. 14, 1903, PP 370.
16. PA, XI, 8, PP 380.
17. JJP/Charles Magoon, Jan. 28, 1903, PP 370; PA, 229, PP 374.
18. PA, XI, 9, PP 380; PA, 225, PP 374.
19. Robert Patterson/Asst SW, Dec. 22, 1903, PP 281.

20. PA, XI, 10, PP 380.
21. *Ibid.,* 10–11.
22. JJP paper on Moros; JJP/Magoon, *op. cit.*
23. PA, XI, 10, PP 380; Charles Cameron/David P. Barrows, Sep. 24, 1909, PP 320; JJP/Magoon, *op. cit.*
24. PA, XI, 10, PP 380.
25. Patterson/Asst SW, *op. cit.*
26. George MacAdam, "The Life of General Pershing," *The World's Work,* Vol.38 (May, 1919), 96–97.
27. JJP diary, May 26, 1902.
28. PA, XI, 6–7, 14, PP 380; PA, 225, PP 374.
29. JJP diary, June 22, 1902.
30. PA, XI, 13, PP 380.
31. JJP/Magoon, *op. cit.*
32. JJP diary, July 19, 1902.
33. *Ibid.,* July 20–21, 1902; JJP/Magoon, *op. cit.*
34. PA, XI, 14, PP 380.
35. *Ibid.*
36. Amos A. Fries intvw, May 14, 1960.
37. PA, XI, 15, PP 380.
38. *Army and Navy Journal,* Apr. 2, 1910.
39. JJP diary, Aug. 12–13, 16, 1902; JJP/George W. Davis, Aug. 28, 1902, PP 317; *The Evening Star* (Washington, D. C.), Oct. 23, 1902.
40. GO 5, Vicars, Aug. 17, 1902, PP 317.
41. Ben Lear/author, Feb. 18, 1960; PA, XI, 15, PP 380.
42. *Annual Reports of the War Department for the Fiscal Year Ended June 30, 1903* (Washington, D.C., 1903), III, 6.
43. JJP/Davis, Aug. 28, 1902.
44. Adna R. Chaffee/Samuel S. Sumner (tg), Sep. 5, 1902, PP 370.
45. PA, 247, PP 374.
46. *Ibid.*
47. SA, III, 274, GCS.
48. FO 9, Vicars, Sep. 17, 1902, PP 370; JJP 1st rept on Maciu expedition, Oct. 15, 1902, 1, PP 317; PA, 247, PP 374.
49. JJP diary, June 11, 1902.
50. FO 9, *op. cit.*
51. PA, XII, 2, PP 380.
52. *Ibid.,* 1.
53. JJP 1st rept, 2–3; PA, XII, 2–3, PP 380; PA, 248–49, PP 374.
54. PA, XII, 2–3, PP 380.
55. JJP 1st rept, 4–5; PA, XII, 3, PP 380; PA, 249, PP 374.
56. PA, 251, PP 374.
57. *Ibid.*
58. *Ibid.,* 250–51.
59. PA, XII, 4–5, PP 380; PA, 252–53, PP 374.

60. FO 17, Vicars, Sep. 25, 1902, PP 317; PA, XII, 5, PP 380; PA, 254, PP 374.
61. PA, XII, 6, PP 380.
62. *Ibid.;* JJP 2d rept on Maciu expedition, Oct. 15, 1902, 5, PP 317.
63. JJP 2d rept, 5–6.
64. *The Manila Times,* Oct. 22, 1902; Rowland Thomas, "Pershing—United States Soldier," *The World's Work,* Vol. 13 (Nov., 1906), 8181.
65. Kelton L. Pepper intvw, Nov. 13, 1960; PA, XII, 7, PP 380; JJP 2d rept, 6.
66. JJP acct of service, 1902–1903, PP 317; JJP 2d rept, 7–8; PA, XII, 7–8, PP 380.
67. PA, XII, 8, PP 380.
68. JJP/Charles Magoon, Jan. 28, 1903, PP 370.
69. PA, 270, PP 374; PA, XII, 8, PP 380.
70. PA, XIII, 1, PP 380.
71. JJP diary, June 23, 1902.
72. PA, 245, PP 374.
73. JJP/Samuel S. Sumner, Dec. 18, 1902, PP 370; PA, XIII, 1–2, PP 380.
74. Acct of visit, Feb. 11, 1903, PP 281; PA, XIII, 2, PP 380.
75. MacAdam, *op. cit.,* 97.
76. JJP/George W. Davis, Mar. 14, 1903, PP 370; PA, XIII, 2, PP 380.
77. PA, XIII, 2–3, PP 380.
78. PA, XIII, 3, PP 380; PA, 246, PP 374.
79. PA, XIII, 1, PP 380.
80. PA, 246, PP 374.
81. Bacolod/Vicars, Oct. 9, 1902, PP 319.
82. George C. Shaw, "Around Lake Lanao" (1905 MS), 12, located in SA, III, GCS; *Annual Reports of the War Department for the Fiscal Year Ended June 30, 1903* (Washington, D.C., 1903), III, 300; JJP rept on period June 30, 1902-May 15, 1903, PP 317.
83. JJP/Sumner *(op. cit.)*; JJP/Davis, Jan. 23 and Mar. 14, 1903, PP 370.
84. JJP/Samuel S. Sumner (tg), Mar. 21, 1903, PP 370
85. Samuel S. Sumner/JJP, Apr. 2, 1903, PP 279.
86. George W. Davis/Samuel S. Sumner, Mar. 30, 1903, PP 317.

CHAPTER VI: THE MARCH AROUND LAKE LANAO

1. PA, XIII, 4, PP 380. (Unless otherwise noted, all references to PA in this chapter are from PP 380.)
2. JJP rept on Bacolod expedition, May 15, 1903, I, PP 317; George C.

Shaw/wife, Apr. 17, 1903, GCS; George C. Shaw, "Around Lake Lanao," (1905 MS), 12, located in SA, III, GCS.
3. Shaw, *op. cit.* 12–13; SA, III, 328–29, GCS.
4. JJP/Samuel S. Sumner, Apr. 16, 1903, PP 370; CS #1 intvw, Mar. 13, 1961.
5. Shaw, *op. cit.,* 13–14.
6. *Ibid.,* 14; JJP rept, *op. cit.,* 1–2.
7. Shaw, *op. cit.,* 14–15.
8. *Ibid.,* 15.
9. JJP/Samuel S. Sumner (tg), Apr. 7, 1903, PP 370; Shaw, *op. cit.*, 15–17; JJP rept, *op. cit.,* 1–2, 5–6; PA, XIII, 4–5; George A. Hunt (comp.), *The History of the Twenty-seventh Infantry* (Honolulu, 1931), 99.
10. JJP/[George Meiklejohn], Apr. 27, 1903, quoted in clipping, PP 373.
11. A panandungan was a retired sultan who served as counsellor, often with more influence than the reigning sultan.
12. A. Henry Savage Landor, *Gems of the East* (New York, 1904), 293.
13. Ben Lear/author, Feb. 18, 1960.
14. Shaw, *op. cit.,* 19.
15. *Ibid.,* 20; JJP/[Meiklejohn] *op. cit.;* Chaplain George D. Rice, Field sermon, Apr. 12, 1903, PP 317.
16. JJP/[Meiklejohn], *op. cit.*
17. Shaw, *op. cit.,* 21.
18. *Ibid.,* 22–23; JJP/[Meiklejohn], *op. cit.*
19. JJP/George T. Bowman, Apr. 23, 1903, PP 370.
20. Robert V. Patterson/Asst SW, Dec. 22, 1903, PP 281.
21. JJP/[Meiklejohn], *op. cit.*
22. PA, XIII, 6.
23. Shaw, *op. cit.,* 28.
24. JJP/Samuel S. Sumner (tg), Apr. 16, 1903, PP 370.
25. Shaw, *op. cit.,* 30.
26. *Ibid.,* 30–31.
27. JJP/[Meiklejohn], *op. cit.*
28. Samuel S. Sumner/JJP, Apr. 21, 1903, PP 317.
29. JJP/Samuel S. Sumner, Apr. 24, 1903, PP 370.
30. Samuel S. Sumner/JJP (tg), May 1, 1903, PP 317.
31. Hunt, *op. cit.,* 102; JJP/someone at Pantar, May 6, 1903, PP 3.
32. Shaw, *op. cit.,* 32–36.
33. George T. Bowman/Asst SW, May 15, 1903, PP 370; PA, XIII, 1, 8.
34. Shaw, *op. cit.,* 36–37.
35. *Ibid.;* Landor, *op. cit.,* 299; PA, XIII, 8–10; JJP summary of Taraca expedition, May 12, 1903, PP 370.
36. Frank P. Helio, Jr., "A Trip around Lake Lanao" (1903 MS), 7, PP 370.
37. Shaw, *op. cit.*, 47–48.
38. PA, XIII, 10.

39. JJP recapitulation for period June 30, 1902-May 15, 1903, 15, PP 317; JJP/TAG at Zamboanga (tg), May 12, 1903, PP 370.
40. Helio, *op. cit.*, 13; Shaw, *op. cit.*, 48; PA, XIII, 10–11.
41. Cholera.
42. Samuel S. Sumner/JJP, May 10, 1903, PP 317.
43. GO 39, Div of Philippines, May 13, 1903, PP 317.
44. PA, XIII, 11.
45. Quoted, Davis/SW, Mar. 10, 1906, PP 281.
46. Preston/(man named Wardman), July 15, 1903, PP 281.
47. Avery D. Andrews, *My Friend and Classmate, John J. Pershing* (Harrisburg, Pa., 1939), 61.
48. W. F. Lewis/TAG at Zamboanga, May 15, 1903, PP 281; PA, XIII, 11–12.
49. Lt. George C. Shaw, however, said that after the Bacolod fight "Capt. Pershing came and put his hand on my shoulder and said, 'Good work, you are the fine soldier I thought you were.' " SA, III, 310.
50. Lear/author, Feb. 18, 1960.
51. JJP/[Meiklejohn], *op. cit.*
52. Andrews, *op. cit.*, 61.
53. Robert L. Bullard, *Personalities and Reminiscences of the War* (Garden City, N. Y., 1925), 44.
54. *Ibid.*, 45.
55. JJP/George W. Davis, Mar. 14, 1903, PP 370.
56. Moros living around Lake Lanao.
57. Bowman/Asst SW, *op. cit.*
58. JJP MS, "Conquest of the Moros" (dated sometime before 1908), PP 278.
59. JJP/Charles Magoon, Jan. 28, 1903, PP 370.
60. A. H. Sunderland/author, Aug. 3, 1960.
61. Kelton L. Pepper/author, Oct. 27, 1960; Pepper intvw, Nov. 13, 1960.
62. C. C. Booth/author, July 20, 1960
63. Lear/author, Feb. 10, 1960.
64. Bowman/Asst SW, *op. cit.*

CHAPTER VII: LOVE AND MARRIAGE

1. JJP/G. A. and W. B. King, June 27, 1942, PP 324.
2. PA, XIV, 7–8, PP 380.
3. JJP acct of service, June 1903-June 1904, 3849 ACP 86, NA.
4. GO 155, WD, Sep. 17, 1904, PP 373; *Fort Lesley J. McNair* (Washington, D.C. [1950]), 9; George S. Pappas, *Prudens Futuri: The U.S. Army War College, 1901–1967* (Carlisle Barracks, Pa., 1967), 40, 46–47.

5. Avery D. Andrews/JJP, Nov. 16, 1903, PP 281.
6. Theodore Roosevelt/Andrews, Nov. 17, 1903, PP 281.
7. TR Message, Dec. 7, 1903, PP 371.
8. George W. Davis/JJP, June 16, 1903, PP 281.
9. PA, XIV, 11.
10. Charlotte H. Conant/JJP, Sep. 28, 1915, PP 313.
11. *Boston Sunday Post*, Jan. 19, 1919. (Recollection of the event, based on an interview with Sen. F. E. Warren.)
12. Harold F. Wheeler, "The Romance of General Pershing," *The Ladies' Home Journal*, XXXVI (July, 1919), 8.
13. FWP diary, Dec. 9, 1903, PP 1.
14. Wheeler, *op. cit.*, 7.
15. PP 1.
16. Wheeler, *op. cit.*, 7; *Boston Sunday Post*, Jan. 19, 1919.
17. GO 65, WD, Dec. 22, 1903, PP 373; FWP diary, Dec. 23 and 29, 1903.
18. HFW diary, Dec. 29, 1903.
19. JJP/HFW, Mar. 1 and 14, 1903, FWP; HFW/JJP, Mar. 3, and Apr. 27, 1904, FWP.
20. JJP/HFW, Feb. 14, 1904, FWP.
21. HFW/JJP, Feb. 22, 1904, FWP.
22. JJP/HFW, Mar. 1, 1904, FWP.
23. JJP/HFW, Apr. 3, 20, 1904; HFW/JJP, Feb. 4, Apr. 29, 1904, FWP.
24. JJP/HFW, Aug. 22, 1904, FWP.
25. Mark Sullivan, *Our Times* (New York, 1927), II, 547.
26. HFW/JJP, Oct. 1, 1904, FWP.
27. JJP/HFW, Dec. 20, 1904, FWP.
28. JJP/HFW, Feb. 14 and 29, 1904, FWP.
29. HFW/JJP, Oct. 2, 1904, FWP.
30. HFW/JJP, Oct. 4, 1904, FWP.
31. HFW/JJP, Oct. 12, 1904, FWP.
32. HFW/JJP, Oct. 2, 1904, FWP.
33. JJP diary, Dec. 25, 1905, DS; PA, XIV, 11; Wheeler, *op. cit.*, 8.
34. Asst AG/JJP, Dec. 27, 1904, PP 158.
35. George MacAdam, "The Life of General Pershing," *The World's Work*, Vol. 38 (May, 1919), 99; *Boston Sunday Post*, Jan. 19, 1919.
36. JJP diary, Dec. 28, 1904, DS; Wheeler, 8; PA, XIV, 11; MacAdam, *op. cit.*, 99.
37. JJP diary, DS.
38. JJP/Thomas Swobe, Jan. 17, 1905, PP 281.
39. JJP/Hamilton Bowie, Jan. 11, 1905, PP 281.
40. PA, XIV, 12.
41. *Lake City Herald* (Utah), Jan. 27, 1905; *Army and Navy Register*, Jan 28, 1905.
42. Katherine Beach/JJP, Sep. 18, 1906, PP 281; *Boston Sunday Post*, Jan. 19, 1919.
43. JJP diary, Jan. 26, 1905, DS.

44. *Ibid.*, Jan. 30–31, 1905.
45. *Ibid.*, Feb. 7, 1905.
46. Marcella Tallant, "The Rescuer I'll Never Forget," *This Week Magazine*, Sep. 20, 1959, 30–31, 33.
47. JJP diary, Feb. 17, 20, 1905, DS.
48. *Ibid.*, Feb. 23, 1905.
49. *Ibid.*, Feb. 24, 1905. (Paragraphing and punctuation added.)

CHAPTER VIII: PROMOTION AND SCANDAL

1. JJP diary, Feb. 14, March 5, 9, 1905, DS.
2. *Ibid.*, March 11, 1905; PA, XV, 6–7, PP 380.
3. PA, XV, 9.
4. Frederick Palmer, *With My Own Eyes* (Indianapolis, 1933), 248.
5. PA, XV, 12.
6. *Ibid.*, 13; JJP rept on Manchuria, 10, 21, PP 371.
7. Frederick Palmer, *John J. Pershing, General of the Armies* (Harrisburg, Pa., 1948), (Hereinafter cited as *Pershing*) 61.
8. JJP notebook, (n.d. but probably 1905), PP 2.
9. JJP diary (n.d.), PP 2.
10. *Kansas City Star* (Mo.), Jan. 11, 1931.
11. JJP pencil draft on Manchuria, 5, PP 323.
12. JJP, *My Experiences in the World War* (New York, 1931), I, 106.
13. JJP rept, 63, PP 371; JJP statement on machine guns (n.d.), PP 324.
14. JJP criticism of Russian preparedness (n.d.), PP 323.
15. *The Detroit News*, July 19, 1948.
16. Palmer, *Pershing (op. cit.)*, 59.
17. JJP/wife, June 16, 1905, FWP.
18. Palmer, *Pershing (op. cit.)*, 60.
19. JJP diary, Mar. 9, 1905, DS.
20. *Ibid.*, Mar. 19, 1905.
21. *Ibid.*, Mar 29 and April 12–13, 1905.
22. *Ibid.*, Apr. 20, 1905.
23. *Ibid.*, Mar. 30–31, 1905.
24. Edgar J. Pershing, *The Pershing Family in America* (Philadelphia, 1924), 404. Mrs. Pershing's name was Helen Frances, although she commonly dropped the first name.
25. Diploma, PP 419.
26. *New York Sun*, Sep. 17, 1906.
27. *St. Louis Post-Dispatch* (Mo.), Editorial, Oct. 3, 1906.
28. Carter W. Clarke intvw, Feb. 8, 1960.
29. TR/F.E. Warren, Nov. 18, 1910, PP 371. See also John J. Leary, Jr., *Talks*

with T.R. (Boston, 1920), 296–98. T.R. was wrong in thinking that Senator Warren had never spoken to him concerning Pershing's promotion before it was announced. See Senator Warren/JJP, Mar. 11, 12, 1906, FEW.

30. *The Baltimore Sun*, Dec. 11, 1906; *Washington Herald*, Dec. 21, 1906. Actually, there was objection in committee which Senator Warren, by adroit maneuver, managed to silence, so that the Committee reported out unanimously in favor of the promotion. The Senator also managed to avoid a discussion of the question on the Senate floor. See Senator Warren/JJP, Dec. 11, 1906, FEW.

31. See George W. Davis/SW, Mar. 10, 1906, PP 281; Guy H. Preston/(man named Wardman), July 15, 1903, PP 281; Avery D. Andrews, *My Friend and Classmate, John J. Pershing* (Harrisburg, Pa., 1939), 61. One cannot but be impressed with the consistently laudatory statements about Pershing, both before and after his promotion, in his 201 file, NPRC.

32. ER, Vol. 176, pt. 3.

33. James G. Harbord, *The American Army in France, 1917–1919* (Boston, 1936), 46. JJP's 201 file lists the following Adjutant General's Office documents regarding promotion to brigadier general: 464287; 464287/D,H,I,J,L,M,N,P,R,Y; 503860; NPRC.

34. JJP/Elmer J. Burkett, Nov. 21, 1903, PP 281.

35. Palmer, *Pershing (op. cit.)*, 65.

36. *Kansas City Star* (Mo.), Jan. 11, 1931; F.E. Warren/JJP, Mar. 29, 1905, FEW; F.E. Warren/Mrs. JJP, Apr. 15, 1905, FEW.

37. JJP/F.E. Warren, Oct. 2, 1916, FWP.

38. JJP/F.E. Warren, Oct. 24, 1916, FWP.

39. Nurse Margaret Cummings intvw, Dec. 30, 1962. For Senator Warren's influence in furthering the movement for Pershing's promotion, see his letters to Pershing of Mar. 11, 12, 16, 19, Apr. 20, May 10, Aug. 31, Sep. 25, Oct. 24, 30, Nov. 3, 7, 24, Dec. 11, 1906, and his letters to Mrs. Pershing of Feb. 4 and Dec. 11, 1906—all in FEW.

40. Quoted, *The Chicago Daily Tribune*, Dec. 19, 1906.

41. *The Washington Post*, Dec. 21, 1906.

42. George W. Davis/JJP, Sep. 16, 1906, PP 281. Later General Davis told Senator Warren: "The story about Pershing is absolutely true as to every particular—the building, the children, the woman, and all—only it was not Pershing; it was another officer who is not now in the army." F. E. Warren/JJP, Jan. 21, 1907, FEW.

43. O.G. Villard/W.H. Taft, Nov. 16, 1906, WHT 128.

44. Dec. 20, 1906, WHT 4.

45. *The Washington Herald*, Dec. 21, 1906.

46. Wife/JJP, Oct. 17, 1906, FWP.

47. *The Washington Herald*, Dec. 21, 22, 1906.

48. Thomas Swobe/F.E. Warren, Nov. 19, 1906, PP 281.

49. *The Omaha Herald* (Neb.), Dec. 21, 1906.

50. Guy H. Preston/JJP, Nov. 27, 1906, PP 281.
51. 1222216 MSO 07, NA.
52. *Ibid.* In an affidavit dated Jan. 19, 1907 Joaquina stated that she had been repeatedly approached by "various Americans" who offered her money to falsely state that Pershing had lived with her and supported her.
53. *Ibid.* Senator Warren told Pershing that the Secretary of War "seemed to me to be entirely satisfied. . . ." F. E. Warren/JJP, July 29, 1907, FEW.
54. *The Washington Post*, June 7, 1913.
55. *Ibid.*
56. W. G. [Hoare?] /JJP, Jan. 31, 1907, PP 281.

CHAPTER IX: FORT WILLIAM McKINLEY

1. Army Records Center/author, May 9, 1960; PA, XVI, 2–3, PP 378. (Unless otherwise noted, all references to PA in this chapter are from PP 378.)
2. PA, XVI, 3.
3. Avery D. Andrews, *My Friend and Classmate, John J. Pershing* (Harrisburg, Pa., 1939), 68.
4. PA, XVI, 4–5.
5. "Military Posts in the Philippines—Fort William McKinley," 2, n.d., unsigned acct by staff officer, c. 1907 or 1908, PP 371. (Cited hereinafter as "McKinley.")
6. Andrews, *op. cit.*, 68.
7. McKinley, *op. cit.*, 5.
8. Andrews, *op. cit.*, 68.
9. William P. Duvall/Act SW, Dec. 4, 1907, PP 371.
10. *Ibid.*
11. Mrs. John Wainwright intvw, May 12, 1961; "McKinley," *op. cit.*, 3.
12. George MacAdam, "The Life of General Pershing," *The World's Work*, Vol. 38 (May, 1919), 101.
13. Mrs. Richard Hawkins intvw, Jan. 26, 1963.
14. *Star-Bulletin*, Honolulu, Jan. 30, 1931.
15. PA, XVI, 8.
16. *Ibid.*
17. Andrews, *op. cit.*, 67.
18. Army Records Center/author; PA, XVI, 10.
19. JJP rept on maneuvers, Feb. 15, 1908, 19–21, PP 371.
20. *Ibid.*, 26.
21. Cris Emmett, *In the Path of Events with Colonel Martin Labor Crimmins, Soldier, Naturalist, Historian* (Waco, Texas, 1959), 204.

22. Trip itinerary, PP 279; PA, XVII, 1–2, PP 379; Mrs. JJP diary, Aug. 24, 1908, PP 2.
23. Mrs. JJP diary, Sep. 16, 1908.
24. *Ibid.*
25. PA, XVII, 9.
26. *Ibid.*
27. *Ibid.*, 10; WD/JJP, Oct. 28, 1908, 1444729 AGO 08, NA.
28. PA, XVII, 11–12.
29. *Ibid.*, 13; Army Records Center/author; TAG/JJP, Jan. 20, 1909, PP 279; JJP/James F. Smith, Nov. 16, 1908, WSHS.
30. JJP/TAG, Mar. 3, 1909, 1496419 AGO 09, NA; TAG/JJP, May 24, 1909, 1526212 AGO 09, NA; JJP/TAG, Sep. 24, 1909 (tg), PP 278: Medical record, Army and Navy General Hospital, Hot Springs, Ark., Admission date: May 26, 1909, JJP 201 file, NPRC.
31. Ralph Curtin intvw, July 17, 1963.
32. PA, XVI, 11; XVII, 15.
33. HFW/JJP, Dec. 1, 1910, FWP.
34. Guy H. Preston/JJP, Nov. 27, 1906, PP 281.
35. Adjectives used in condolence letters after Frances' death in 1915, PP 313, 314 *passim.*
36. Dorothy Canfield Fisher/Henry Castor, July 27, 1953, DCF.
37. JJP diary, Feb. 24, 1905, DS.
38. Alice Roosevelt Longworth intvw, Mar. 15, 1961; Mrs. Hanson Ely intvw, Apr. 11, 1961.
39. JJP/wife, Oct. 23, 1907, FWP.
40. JJP/wife, Oct. 28, 1907, FWP.
41. Wainwright intvw.
42. *Ibid.*
43. Edward Bowditch intvw, Dec. 29, 1960.
44. Wainwright intvw.
45. JJP/Cecil A. Lyon, Jan. 15, 1905, PP 281.
46. *New York Evening Post*, Dec. 20, 1906; B. E. Brewer/author, July 12, 1960.
47. Letcher Hardeman/JJP, Sep. 17, 1906, PP 281.
48. JJP/Leonard Wood, Mar. 9, 1914, LW.

CHAPTER X: GOVERNOR OF THE MORO PROVINCE

1. The Moro Province was organized in Sep., 1903. The first governor was Maj. Gen. Leonard Wood (1903–1906) and the second, Brig. Gen. Tasker H. Bliss (1906–1909).

2. Population estimate of May 19, 1913, PP 279; PA, XVIII, 7, PP 379.
3. JJP/William Cameron Forbes, Dec. 24, 1909, PP 76.
4. JJP/J. Franklin Bell, Apr. 2, 1911, PP 371.
5. Bell/Wood, Apr. 3, 1911, PP 371.
6. JJP/Forbes, *op. cit.*
7. PA, XVIII, 8–9; JJP/Tasker H. Bliss, Dec. 3, 1909, PP 371.
8. JJP/Forbes, *op. cit.*
9. Robert Ginsburgh, "Pershing as His Orderlies Know Him," *The American Legion Monthly*, V (Oct., 1928), 11.
10. PA, XVIII, 9.
11. Summary of Marahui meeting, PP 371.
12. Ginsburgh, *op. cit.*, 10.
13. *Ibid.*, 11.
14. JJP/Forbes, Aug. 2, 1911, PP 76.
15. *Ibid.*; JJP, *Annual Report of the Governor of the Moro Province, for the Fiscal Year Ended June 30, 1913* (Zamboanga, 1913), (Hereinafter cited as *Report . . . for 1913*) 87–88; unsigned article in PP 371.
16. JJP, *Report . . . for 1913 (op. cit.)*, 57.
17. The Government of the Moro Province, *Annual Report of Brig. Gen. John J. Pershing, U.S. Army, Governor of the Moro Province, for the Year Ending June 30, 1911* (Zamboanga, 1911), 6–7; Program, The Moro Province Fair at Zamboanga, Feb. 7–14, 1911, PP 371; W. Cameron Forbes, *The Philippine Islands* (Boston, 1928), I, 511.
18. JJP, *Report . . . for 1913 (op. cit.)*, 12.
19. *Ibid.*, 26–27; quote is from PA, XX, 8–9, PP 379.
20. PA, XX, 8–9.
21. *Ibid.*, 6; JJP, *Report . . . for 1913 (op. cit.)*, 30.
22. PA, XX, 6; JJP, *Report . . . for 1913 (op. cit.)*, 29.
23. PA, XX, 8; William Cameron Forbes, "Journal," 1st Series, V, 217, WCF.
24. JJP, *Report . . . for 1913 (op. cit.)*, 12.
25. *Ibid.*, 10.
26. JJP, "A Few Words of Advice," *The Sulu News*, June 30, 1911.
27. Arthur S. Pier, *American Apostles to the Philippines* (Boston, 1950), 121; JJP, *Report . . . for 1913 (op. cit.)*, 3; PA, XX, 3.
28. Leonard Wood/J. Franklin Bell, Nov. 30, 1910, PP 371.
29. "Zamboanga"/*Army and Navy Journal*, Apr. 20, 1912, PP 382.
30. PA, XX, 5–6.
31. *Ibid.*, 5.
32. JJP/Clarence Edwards, Feb. 9, 1910, PP 69.
33. JJP/Martin Egan, May 2, 1910, PP 69.
34. JJP/Editor, *Army and Navy Register*, Apr. 8, 1911, PP 371; PA, XVIII, 3, 11; Bell/Wood, *op. cit.*
35. Bell/Wood, *op. cit.*
36. Fair Program *(op. cit.)*, PP 371.

37. PA, XX, 11.
38. Fair Program *(op. cit.)*, PP 371.
39. Bell/Wood, *op. cit.*; Ginsburgh *(op. cit.)*, 11; *The Evening Missourian* (Columbia, Mo.), Aug. 2, 1919.
40. JJP, *Report . . . for 1913 (op. cit.)*, 64–65.
41. James G. Harbord/Leonard Wood, Oct. 7, 1910, Private Letters, III, JGH.
42. *Ibid.*; PA, XVIII, 7; JJP, "Observations on Philippine Independence," May 10, 1913, PP 371. (Hereinafter cited as "Observations.")
43. JJP/Leonard Wood, Nov. 20, 1913, PP 371; JJP, *Report . . . for 1913 (op. cit.)*, 64.
44. JJP, "Observations" *(op. cit.)*.
45. JJP/Forbes.
46. JJP/Leonard Wood, Feb. 11, 1910, PP 371; JJP/James G. Harbord, Nov. 3, 1913, PP 278.
47. JJP, "Observations" *(op. cit.)*; Allen S. Fletcher/JJP, Oct. 18, 1914, PP 371.
48. JJP/TAGO, June 10, 1910, PP 371.
49. JJP/TAGO, Aug. 21, 1914, PP 280.
50. Private Letters, III, JGH.
51. JJP/James G. Harbord; JJP, *Report . . . for 1913 (op. cit.)*, 66–67; Forbes/Frank Carpenter, Aug. 25, 1917, WCF-H.
52. Wood/Forbes, Dec. 2, 1909, WCF-H.
53. Charles Brent/Forbes, Feb. 26, 1914, WCF-H.
54. Harbord/Wood, *op. cit.*
55. *Ibid.* Harbord got this first-hand from an influential Zamboanga lawyer who was supported in his story by two others.
56. Harbord/Wood, Mar. 13, 1911, JGH.
57. Harbord/Wood, Oct. 29, 1911, JGH.
58. Harbord/H. H. Bandholtz, JGH.
59. PP 278.
60. Corinna Lindon Smith/author, June 25, 1963.
61. Encl, JJP/TAGO, Oct. 15, 1913, 2016194, RG 94, NA.
62. "Journal," Nov. 4, 1909, WCF.
63. *Ibid.*, Mar. 10, 1910, WCF.
64. George MacAdam, "The Life of General Pershing," *The World's Work*, Vol. 38 (May, 1919), 101–02.
65. Forbes/William H. Taft, Dec. 27, 1911, WHT.
66. Forbes/SW, June 21, 1913, PP 278.

CHAPTER XI: DISARMING THE MOROS

1. *The World* (New York), Sep. 21, 1913.
2. JJP/William Cameron Forbes, Dec. 24, 1909, PP 76.
3. Hugh L. Scott, *Some Memories of a Soldier* (New York, 1928), 314.
4. For details on the juramentado, see Scott, *op. cit.,* 315; PA, X, 10, PP 380; clippings and articles in PP 326 and 371; *Annual Reports of the War Department for the Fiscal Year Ended June 30, 1903* (Washington, D.C., 1903), III, 304–05; Rutherford H. Platt, "There Was a Captain by the Name of Pershing," *The World's Work*, Vol. 67 (Dec., 1923), 183; *Mindanao Daily Herald*, Feb. 14, 1911.
5. *The World* (New York), Sep. 21, 1913.
6. J. Franklin Bell/JJP, May 23, 1911, PP 371; C. C. Booth/author, Mar. 20, 1960; Platt, 183–84.
7. Scott, *op. cit.*, 372.
8. *Ibid.*, 364.
9. JJP, "Annual Report as Governor of the Moro Province," Aug. 15, 1912, (Hereinafter cited as "Report as Governor . . .") 11, PP 371; JJP/Francis E. Warren, Feb. 9, 1912, PP 371; PA, XVIII, 10–11, PP 379.
10. John P. Finley rept to JJP, Jan. 1, 1910, PP 320; JJP rept to TAG, June 30, 1910, PP 371; JJP/J. Franklin Bell, Apr. 2, 1911, PP 371.
11. JJP/J. Franklin Bell, Aug. 23, 1912, PP 371.
12. JJP/J. Franklin Bell, Apr. 22, 1911, PP 371.
13. Wood/James G. Harbord, Dec. 4, 1911, Private Letter File, IV, JGH.
14. *Ibid.*
15. JJP/Bell, Apr. 22, 1911.
16. PA, XVIII, 11.
17. JJP/Forbes, July 28, 1911, PP 76.
18. Forbes/JJP, Aug. 17, 1911, PP 76.
19. W. Cameron Forbes, *The Philippine Islands* (Boston, 1928), II, 24–25.
20. JJP, "Report as Governor . . ." *(op. cit.)*, 11–12; PA, XVIII, 12.
21. *The Sulu News*, Oct. 31, 1911.
22. JJP/J. Franklin Bell, Oct. 23, 1911, PP 371 (author's italics).
23. *Ibid.*
24. *Ibid.*
25. PA, XVIII, 12–13.
26. JJP/diary, Dec. 1, 1911, PP 3.
27. At Camp Vicars, 1902–1903.
28. JJP/wife, Dec. 2, 1911, PP 3.
29. *Ibid.*; PA, XVIII, 13.
30. Hugh L. Scott, former governor of Sulu.
31. JJP/wife, Dec. 8, 1911, PP 3.
32. PA, XVIII, 13.
33. Dec. 6, 1911, PP 371.
34. JJP/wife, Dec. 21, 1911, PP 3.

35. JJP/wife, Nov. 29, and Dec. 3, 1911, PP 3.
36. *Ibid.*, Dec. 5, 1911, PP 3.
37. JJP, "Report on Bud Dajo Operations," May 31, 1912, (Hereinafter cited as ". . . Bud Dajo . . .") 1, PP 371; PA, XVIII, 13.
38. JJP/wife, Dec. 14, 1911, PP 3.
39. JJP, "Bud Dajo . . ." *(op. cit.)*, 1.
40. Scott, *op. cit.*, 379–80.
41. JJP/wife, Dec. 16, 1911, PP 3; JJP, ". . . Bud Dajo . . ." *(op. cit.)*, 1.
42. JJP/Bell, Dec. 16, 1911, PP 371. (Paragraphs inverted.)
43. JJP, ". . . Bud Dajo . . ." *(op. cit.)*, 1–2.
44. JJP/wife, Dec. 17, 1911, PP 3.
45. JJP, ". . . Bud Dajo . . ." *op. cit.*, 2.
46. *Ibid.*; W.O. Boswell diary, Dec. 21, 1911, PP 371. (W.O. Boswell was an officer with Pershing during this campaign. His wife had been maid of honor at JJP's wedding.)
47. JJP/wife, Dec. 21, 1911, PP 3.
48. JJP/wife, Dec. 22, 1911, PP 3; JJP, ". . . Bud Dajo . . ." *(op. cit)*, 2–3; Boswell diary, Dec. 20, 1911.
49. Boswell diary, Dec. 22, 1911.
50. Robert L. Bullard, *Personalities and Reminiscences of the War* (Garden City, N.Y., 1925), 91–92. (Bullard later changed his opinion.)
51. JJP, ". . . Bud Dajo . . ." *(op. cit.)*, 2.
52. *Ibid.*, 3.
53. *Ibid.*; Boswell diary, Dec. 23–24, 1911.
54. JJP/wife, Dec. 24, 25, 1911, PP 3.
55. JJP, ". . . Bud Dajo . . ." *(op. cit.)*, 3.
56. A datto was a tribal adviser or chief, and also a war leader.
57. JJP/Joseph T. Dickman, Jan. 5, 1912, PP 64; JJP, ". . . Bud Dajo . . ." *(op. cit.)*, 3–4; Boswell diary, Dec. 25–26, 1911; JJP, "Report as Governor . . ." *(op. cit.)*, 12.
58. Forbes/SW, WHT 425; Boswell diary, Dec. 27, 1911.
59. Scott, *op. cit.*, 380.
60. JJP/Warren, *op. cit.*; JJP, ". . . Bud Dajo . . ." *(op. cit.)*, 4.
61. Wood/Harbord, *op. cit.*
62. Scott, *op. cit.*, 379–80.

CHAPTER XII: "THE GOOD OLD DAYS AT ZAMBOANGA"

1. JJP/Charles Cameron, Aug. 10, 1917, PP 38.
2. Thomas M. Johnson, "Boys, We Had Him Wrong!" *American Magazine,*

CV (May, 1928), 84; Christian A. Bach and Henry Noble Hall, *The Fourth Division* (n.p., 1920), 239; James G. Harbord, *Leaves From a War Diary* (New York, 1925), 130.

3. See JJP/wife, Dec., 1911 letters, PP 3.
4. JJP/wife, Dec. 4, 5, 28, 1911, PP 3.
5. JJP/wife, Dec. 4, 5, 18, and Nov. 28, 1911, PP 3.
6. James L. Collins intvw, Dec. 29, 1962.
7. JJP/wife, Dec. 31, 1911, FWP. (Some verses omitted.)
8. Photos, PP 280; PA, XVIII, 3–4, 6, PP 379.
9. PA, XVIII, 5.
10. *Ibid.*
11. Robert Ginsburgh, "Pershing as His Orderlies Know Him," *American Legion Monthly*, V (Oct., 1928), 64.
12. Richard O'Connor, *Black Jack Pershing* (New York, 1961), 98.
13. Ginsburgh, *op. cit.*, 64.
14. George MacAdam, "The Life of General Pershing," *The World's Work*, Vol. 38 (May, 1919), 102.
15. *Ibid.*; Bishop Charles Brent diary, Jan. 23, 1910, CHB.
16. William Cameron Forbes, *The Philippine Islands* (Boston, 1928), II, 451; Forbes, "Journal," 1st series, IV, 260, WCF.
17. Forbes, "Journal," *op. cit.*, 442–43.
18. Henry J. Reilly intvw, May 26, 1960.
19. Henry T. Allen/JJP, Feb. 14, 1912, PP 280; JJP/Allen, May 15, 1912, PP 280.
20. *The Denver News*, June 1, 1912.
21. JJP/Francis E. Warren, Feb. 9, 1912, PP 371.
22. JJP/Francis E. Warren, Nov. 6, 1912, FWP.
23. James Ross/JJP, Oct. 22, 1913, FWP; *New York Evening World*, May 27, 1912 and June 6, 1913. Extended correspondence regarding the suit is in "Miscellaneous Items . . . Pershing Materials," FEW.
24. JJP/J. Franklin Bell, July 13, 1911, PP 371. On taking over a command Pershing gave the impression of being unnecessarily strict and harsh. Later, however, as a unit shaped up, people came to appreciate the merit of Pershing's sternness. James L. Collins, "Impressions of General Pershing," n.d., JLC.
25. William H. Oury/author, Apr. 13, 1961.
26. *Oklahoma City Times*, Sep. 2, 1960.
27. Ginsburgh, *op. cit.*, 66.
28. *Ibid.*, 11.
29. B. E. Brewer/author, July 12, 1960.
30. *Ibid.*
31. *Ibid.*
32. Allen J. Greer/author, Sep. 19, 1960.
33. Brewer/author, *op. cit.*
34. Frederick Palmer, "John J. Pershing—Plower," *Collier's*, May 3, 1919, 6.

35. JJP/TAG, June 30, 1910, PP 371.
36. *Ibid.*
37. *Ibid.*
38. G.F. Edwards/Frank Lanckton, Oct. 27, 1928, FL.
39. *Life*, Oct. 18, 1913, PP 347.
40. JJP/J. Franklin Bell, Feb. 23, 1912, PP 371; JJP/J. Franklin Bell, Apr. 29, 1913, PP 279; JJP/Leonard Wood, July 9 and Nov. 20, 1913, PP 371.
41. JJP/TAG, June 30, 1910, PP 371.
42. Intvw, radio station WRC, Washington, D.C., Sep. 12, 1960. See also James L. Collins, "Impressions of General Pershing," n.d., JLC.
43. JJP/TAG, June 30, 1910, PP 371.
44. *Ibid.*
45. *Ibid.*; U.S. War Department, *Annual Report of the Secretary of War, 1916* (Washington, D.C., 1916), 24.
46. Russell F. Weigley, *The History of the United States Army* (New York, 1967), 400–01.
47. Ginsburgh, *op. cit.*, 64.
48. MacAdam, *op. cit.*, 102.
49. Oury/author, *op. cit.*
50. Bell/JJP, June 30, 1911, PP 371.
51. Brewer/author, *op. cit.*
52. Palmer, *op. cit.*, 6.

CHAPTER XIII: THE BUD BAGSAK CAMPAIGN

1. PP 371.
2. William W. Gordon/JJP, Jan. 14, 1913, PP 278.
3. Gordon/JJP, Feb. 25, 1913, PP 278; J. Franklin Bell/TAG, July 3, 1913, PP 278.
4. JJP/J. Franklin Bell, Mar. 11, 1913, PP 371; JJP/William Cameron Forbes, Feb. 7, 1913, PP 76.
5. James G. Harbord/Leonard Wood, Apr. 18, 1913, Private Letters, V, JGH.
6. PA, XIX, 8, PP 379.
7. *Ibid.*, 8–9.
8. JJP/J. Franklin Bell, Mar. 12, 1913, PP 278.
9. Gordon/JJP, Feb. 24, 25, 1913, PP 278.
10. Gordon/JJP, Mar. 8, 1913, PP 278; JJP/Bell, Mar. 12, 1913.
11. JJP, "Report of Bud Bagsak Operations," Oct. 15, 1913, (Hereinafter cited as "... Bud Bagsak ...") 2–3, PP 371; K. L. Sherman, "Pershing and a World Peace," *Survey Graphic*, XXIX (Nov., 1940), 551.

12. PA, XIX, 9.
13. James L. Collins, "The Battle of Bud Bagsak and the Part Played by the Mountain Guns Therein," *The Field Artillery Journal*, XV (Nov.-Dec., 1925), (Hereinafter cited as "The Battle of Bud Bagsak") 560. James L. Collins, author of the article, was JJP's right-hand man during the whole operation.
14. Although most Philippine Scouts were Filipinos, some were Moros. The 51st and 52nd Companies, which led the final attack on Bagsak, were Moro troops.
15. Collins, *op. cit.*, 560; JJP, ". . . Bud Bagsak . . ." *(op. cit.)*, 3; James L. Collins diary, June 10, 1913, JLC.
16. Collins, *op. cit.*, 560; Collins diary, June 10, 1913, JLC.
17. George C. Shaw/Mr. and Mrs. William R. Davis, Aug. 30, 1913, GCS; SA, V, 483; GCS.
18. Shaw/Davises, *op. cit.*
19. Collins, *op. cit.*, 562; JJP, ". . . Bud Bagsak . . ." *(op. cit.)*, 3–4; Collins diary, June 10, 1913, JLC.
20. JJP, ". . . Bud Bagsak . . ." *(op. cit.)*, 5–6; Collins, *op. cit.*, 563.
21. JJP, ". . . Bud Bagsak . . ." *(op. cit.)*, 6; George C. Shaw, "Mixing with the Moros," *Arms and the Man*, LIV (Aug. 28, 1913), 433.
22. SA, V, 486; JJP, ". . . Bud Bagsak . . ." *(op. cit.)*, 7; Collins diary, June 11, 1913, JLC.
23. George C. Shaw, "Report of Operations against Mt. Bagsak," June 18, 1913 (Hereinafter cited as "Report . . . Mt. Bagsak"), 1–2, 4, GCS; SA, V, 486–87; Collins diary, June 11, 1913, JLC.
24. Shaw, "Report . . . Mt. Bagsak" *(op. cit.)*, 1.
25. JJP, ". . . Bud Bagsak . . ." *(op. cit.)*, 7–8; Collins diary, June 11, 1913, JLC.
26. Shaw/Davises, *op. cit.*; JJP, ". . . Bud Bagsak . . ." *(op. cit.)*, 7–8.
27. Shaw, "Report . . . Mt. Bagsak" *(op. cit.)*, 2.
28. JJP/Shaw, June 11, 1923, GCS.
29. Collins, "The Battle of Bud Bagsak . . ." *(op. cit.)*, 564; SA, V, 488.
30. Shaw, "Report . . . Mt. Bagsak" *(op. cit.)*, 2; Collins diary, June 11, 1913, JLC.
31. SA, V, 489.
32. Shaw, "Mixing with the Moros" *(op. cit.)*, 433, 436; Collins diary, June 12, 1913, JLC.
33. Shaw/Davises, *op. cit.*; SA, V, 489–90; Collins diary, June 12, 1913 JLC.
34. SA, V, 489–90; Shaw, "Mixing with the Moros" *(op. cit.)*; Collins diary, June 12, 1913, JLC.
35. JJP, ". . . Bud Bagsak . . ." *(op. cit.)*, 9; Shaw, "Mixing with the Moros," *(op. cit.)*, 436.
36. Collins, "The Battle of Bud Bagsak . . ." *(op. cit.)*, 566; Collins diary, June 12, 1913, JLC.
37. *Ibid.; Ibid.*

38. JJP, ". . . Bud Bagsak . . ." *(op. cit.)*, 9–10; Shaw, "Mixing with the Moros," *(op. cit.)*, 436; Collins diary, June 14, 1913, JLC.
39. Collins, "The Battle of Bud Bagsak . . ." *(op. cit.)*, 566; JJP, ". . . Bud Bagsak . . ." *(op. cit.)*, 10.
40. JJP, ". . . Bud Bagsak . . ." *(op. cit.)*, 10.
41. JJP/wife, June 19, 1913, PP 371.
42. JJP, *The Annual Report of the Governor of the Moro Province, for the Fiscal Year Ended June 30, 1913* (Zamboanga, 1913), 65. The Moros' bravery excited Pershing's admiration. In a memo to his troops after the battle, he said, "In this hour of exultation let us not forget the vanquished foe . . . [who] fought with an unswerving courage and a superb gallantry that was the admiration of all. Let our assurances of good will be extended to him in his defeat, and let no opportunity be allowed to pass by to do a kindly act, or to extend a word of encouragement to this brave people." Memo, JJP/James L. Collins, June 19, 1913, JLC.
43. JJP/wife, June 19, 1913, PP 371; Shaw, "Report . . . Mt. Bagsak" *(op. cit.)*, 3, SA, V, 494; Collins, *loc. cit.*, 568; Ralph G. Craven, "Report on the Bagsak Operations," June 20, 1913, encl 21 of 2114117 AGO 1914, NA; Collins diary, June 15, 1913, JLC.
44. George C. Charlton/TAG, Sep. 7, 1913, PP 279; Collins, "The Battle of Bud Bagsak . . ." *(op. cit.)*, 568.
45. George P. Stallman/TAG, Sep. 14, 1913, PP 279.
46. JJP/wife; PA, XVIII, 19; Collins diary, June 15, 1913, JLC.
47. Collins, "The Battle of Bud Bagsak . . ." *(op. cit.)*, 569; Collins diary, June 15, 1913, JLC.
48. James L. Collins intvw, July 31, 1962; George C. Charlton, "Report on Bagsak Operations," June 30, 1913, encl 58 of 2114117 AGO 1914, NA; JJP, ". . . Bud Bagsak . . ." *(op. cit.)*, 10–11; Shaw/Davises *op. cit.*
49. JJP/Bell Mar. 11, 1913, PP 371.
50. JJP, ". . . Bud Bagsak . . ." *(op. cit.)*, 3; Sherman, *op. cit.*, 551.
51. JJP/Gordon, Apr. 10, 1913, PP 278.
52. PA, XIX, 8–9.
53. JJP/Forbes. See also: JJP/William W. Gordon, Jan. 20, 1913, PP 83.
54. Collins, "The Battle of Bud Bagsak . . ." *(op. cit.)*, 560; Collins diary, June 11, 1913, JLC.
55. *The Washington Herald*, July 31, 1913; *Army and Navy Journal of the Philippines*, Aug. 9, 1913, PP 278.
56. JJP/CG, Philippines Dept, Sep. 28, 1913, 2016194 AGO 1913, NA.
57. *Army and Navy Journal of the Philippines*, Aug. 9, 1913, PP 278.
58. An action in 1906 under Gen. Leonard Wood in which women and children were killed.
59. CS No. 1 intvw, Mar. 13, 1961. (Author was shown the letter.)
60. Bell/WD, July 3, 1913, PP 278. See also: James L. Collins, "Impressions of General Pershing," n.d., JLC.

61. Forbes/SW, June 21, 1913 (tg), PP 278; Forbes/Wood, July 7, 1913, WCF-H.
62. Endorsement, Nov. 24, 1913, PP 371.
63. JJP/Leonard Wood, July 9, 1913, PP 371.
64. Edward Bowditch/JJP, June 2, 1913, PP 279.
65. George C. Charlton/TAG, *op. cit.*
66. JJP/TAG, Sep. 30, 1913, PP 279.
67. Endorsement of Oct. 8, 1913, on JJP/TAG, Sep. 30, 1913, 2098044 AGO 1913, NA.
68. Sherman, *op. cit.*, 552n; WD Press Release, "General Pershing Declines Award of Distinguished Service Cross," Jan. 23, 1922, JJP 201 file, NPRC; George C. Marshall/James F. McKinley, Dec. 5, 1934, JJP 201 file, NPRC.
69. JJP/May Pershing, Sep. 23, 1940, FWP; "Memo for the Press," Sep. 12, 1940, GCM; WD Press Release, "The President Presents Distinguished Service Cross to General Pershing," Sep. 13, 1940, JJP 201 file, NPRC; Sherman, *op. cit.*, 552n.

CHAPTER XIV: TRAGEDY AT THE PRESIDIO

1. Robert Ginsburgh, "Pershing as His Orderlies Know Him," *The American Legion Monthly*, V (Oct., 1928), 10.
2. JJP/TAG, Aug. 21, 1914, PP 280; Health memo, Aug. 30, 1914, PP 279; JJP/J. Franklin Bell, Oct. 18, 1913, PP 371.
3. JJP/George Deshon, June 2, 1914, PP 64; *The San Francisco Examiner*, Apr. 24, 1914.
4. JJP/Deshon, *op. cit.*; JJP/Deshon, Mar. 6, 1915, PP 64.
5. JJP/Deshon, June 2, 1914; *The San Francisco Examiner*, Apr. 24, 1914.
6. G0 13, WD, Apr. 26, 1914, quoted in tg, Tasker H. Bliss/JJP, Apr. 26, 1914, THB 141.
7. *The Press* (Philadelphia), Aug. 27, 1914; Timothy G. Turner, *Bullets, Bottles, and Gardenias* (Dallas, 1935), 203.
8. Turner, *op. cit.*, 203; PA, XXII, 9–10, PP 379.
9. JJP/Hugh L. Scott, Oct. 18, 1914, PP 372.
10. PA, XXII, 6.
11. Carlos E. Husk/JJP, Sep. 4, 1914, PP 372; JJP/Husk, Sep. 14, 1914, PP 372.
12. JJP/William W. Wotherspoon, Aug. 10, 1914, PP 217.
13. JJP/wife, May 11, 1915, FWP.
14. *New York Times*, May 11, 1915; JJP/wife, May 14, 1915, FWP.

15. George MacAdam, "The Life of General Pershing," *The World's Work*, Vol. 38 (June, 1919), 148.
16. JJP/wife, Apr. 25, 1915, FWP.
17. FWP/JJP, Feb. 2, 20, 1915, FWP.
18. FWP/JJP, Aug. 15, 1915, FWP.
19. FWP/JJP, Mar. 18, 1915, FWP.
20. Harold F. Wheeler, "The Romance of General Pershing," *The Ladies Home Journal*, XXXVI (July, 1919), 44; William O. Boswell/author, May 18, 1963; *The San Francisco Examiner*, Aug. 28, 29, 1915; CS #2/author, May 1, 1961. An extensive file of newspaper clippings concerning the fire and funeral is in Scrapbook #32, FEW.
21. *The San Francisco Examiner*, Aug. 28, 1915; CS #2/author.
22. CS #2/author, May 1, 1961, Feb. 8, 1963, and Mar. 4, 1963.
23. *El Paso Herald*, Sep. 8, 1915.
24. CS #2/author, May 1, 1961.
25. Wheeler, *op. cit.*, 44.
26. *El Paso Herald*, Sep. 8, 1915.
27. CS #2/author, May 1, 1961.
28. S. L. A. Marshall in *The Detroit News*, Jan. 8, 1931 and July 15, 1948; Marshall intvw, June 13, 1961. Marshall was in the office with Walker.
29. Collins intvw, Dec. 29, 1962; Collins/"Sweetheart," Aug. [27], 1915, JLC.
30. *San Francisco Chronicle*, Aug. 30, 1915; Frank A. Helm/George Adamson, Oct. 7, 1948, PP 92. For Pershing's distress during the train trip to San Francisco, tramping up and down the passenger coach nearly all night, see James L. Collins/"Sweetheart," [Aug. 28, 1915], JLC.
31. Henry H. Whitney/JJP, Oct. 9, 1915, PP 211.
32. Helm/Adamson, *op. cit.*; Collins intvw; James L. Collins/author, Jan. 16, 1963; Proceedings, Presidio Investigation Board, Aug. 27, 1915, FWP.
33. *The San Francisco Examiner*, Aug. 30, 1915; Helm/Adamson, *op. cit.*
34. Helm/Adamson, *op. cit.*
35. H. Congar Pratt intvw, May 1, 1960; Nellie Tayloe Ross intvw, May 8, 1961; *San Francisco Chronicle*, Aug. 30, 1915. "To see four hearses following each other and to realize that only a few days before that these four were healthy happy carefree members of a single family was a sight to unnerve the strongest." James L. Collins/"Sweetheart," Aug. 31, 1915, JLC.
36. Wheeler, *op. cit.*, 44; *San Francisco Chronicle*, Aug. 29, 1915.
37. George Eller intvw, Dec. 28, 1960.
38. Villa letter, PP 314. Unwittingly Warren Pershing lightened his father's sorrow. Besides being the last living link with Frances, he distracted Pershing by constantly asking questions about everything and by keeping Pershing busy looking after him. James L. Collins/"Sweetheart" [Aug. 30, 1915], JLC.
39. JJP/Mrs. Robert H. Winn(?), n.d., PP 208.

40. JJP/Charles H. Brent, Dec. 5, 1916, PP 34.
41. JJP/George Deshon, Apr. 29, 1917, PP 64.
42. JJP/wife, May 4, 1915, FWP.
43. John C. Hughes intvw, Oct. 30, 1964. See also JJP/George C. Marshall, Oct. 6, 1927, PP 124.
44. James H. Frier, Jr. intvw, Jan. 20, 1970.
45. Mrs. John D. Wainwright intvw, May 12, 1961; F. Warren Pershing intvw, May 26, 1960.
46. PA, XXI, 6, PP 379.
47. Mrs. J. Borden Harriman intvw, Apr. 18, 1961.
48. Charles G. Dawes, *A Journal of the Great War* (Boston, 1921), I, 22–23.
49. Henry J. Reilly intvw, May 26, 1960.
50. Wainwright intvw, *op. cit.*
51. Dorothy Canfield Fisher/Henry Castor, July 30, 1953, DCF.
52. Collins intvw. As Collins lived closer to Pershing than any others whom I have quoted (Collins was his aide in the Philippines, in Mexico, and in France), his remarks probably come closest to the truth. He insisted that any attempt to paint Pershing as taking the news like an unfeeling robot or reacting to it in such a way that his whole character changed from hot to cold is pure fiction.

CHAPTER XV: CHASING VILLA

1. Haldeen Braddy, "Pancho Villa at Columbus," *Southwestern Studies*, III (Spring, 1965), 15; quote from Richard O'Connor, *Black Jack Pershing* (New York, 1961), 138.
2. Braddy, *op. cit.*, 29, 33.
3. Herbert M. Mason, Jr., *The Great Pursuit* (New York, 1970), 26–64.
4. Braddy, *op. cit.*, 36.
5. Samuel F. Bemis, *A Diplomatic History of the United States* (5th ed.; New York, 1965), 550–51.
6. James A. Sandos, "German Involvement in Northern Mexico, 1915–1916: A New Look at the Columbus Raid," *The Hispanic American Historical Review*, L (Feb., 1970), 70–88.
7. Undated statement of Charles W. Hoffmann, sergeant of the guard at the execution. (Lent to author by Col. Clarence C. Clendenen.)
8. Thomas A. Bailey, *A Diplomatic History of the American People* (6th ed.; New York, 1958), 561.
9. "Mexican Situation, 1916," WCD 6474–381, 1, PP 372.
10. Frederick Funston/TAG, PP 372.
11. "Mexican Situation, 1916," *op. cit.*, 3.

12. Newton D. Baker, "The Secretary of War During the War," Army War College lecture, May 11, 1929, 5, PP 354.

13. JJP, "Report of the Punitive Expedition," Oct. 10, 1916, (Hereinafter cited as "Report") 1, PP 372; PA, XXII, 11, PP 379.

14. Funston/TAG, Apr. 10, 1916, PP 372; TAG/Funston, Apr. 11, 1916, PP 372; George Marvin, "Invasion or Intervention?" *The World's Work*, Vol. 32 (May, 1916), 40.

15. SW/Funston, Oct. 30, 1915, THB 194.

16. Baker, *op. cit.*, 5.

17. U.S. Department of State, *Papers Relating to the Foreign Relations of the United States, 1916* (Washington, D.C., 1925), (Hereinafter cited as *Foreign Relations, 1916*) 509–12; Hugh L. Scott/Frederick Funston, Mar. 27, 1916, FF.

18. Hugh L. Scott, *Some Memories of a Soldier* (New York, 1928), 530–31; Hugh L. Scott/Frederick Funston, Mar. 24, 27, 1916, FF.

19. JJP, "Report" *(op. cit.)*, 57–58.

20. O'Connor, *op. cit.*, 126.

21. Glendon Swarthout, *They Came to Cordura* (New York, 1959), 9.

22. James L. Collins/wife, Mar. 23, 1916, JLC. Besides dust, troopers were vexed by scorpions which crawled into their boots at night when they took them off. Mason, *op. cit.*, 85–86.

23. Swarthout, *op. cit.,* 7.

24. Frederick Funston, Memo, Mar. 12, 1916, RG 120, NA.

25. Frank Tompkins, *Chasing Villa* (Harrisburg, Pa., 1934), 72–73.

26. JJP, "Report" *(op. cit.)*, 7, 48.

27. *Ibid.,* 6–7; WD/JJP, Mar. 15, 1916 (tg), PP 372.

28. JJP, "Report" *op. cit.,* 7; James Hopper/JJP, July 1, 1916, PP 372.

29. Tompkins, *op. cit.,* 76–77; JJP, "Report," *(op. cit.),* 7.

30. PA, XXIII, 3, PP 379; JJP, "Report" *op. cit.,* 7–8.

31. JJP, "Report" *(op. cit.),* 5–6, 8.

32. *Foreign Relations, 1916,* 485, 488, 515–17, 588; Baker, *op. cit.,* 4.

33. JJP, "Report" *(op. cit.),* 10.

34. *Foreign Relations, 1916, op. cit.,* 559.

35. JJP, "Report" *(op. cit.),* 10.

36. E. L. N. Glass (ed.), *The History of the Tenth Cavalry, 1866–1921* (n.p., 1921), 70; PA, XXIII, 3–4; Tompkins, *op. cit.,* 89; Clarence C. Clendenen, *Blood on the Border* (New York, 1969), 241–43; William C. Brown, "Address to the Lions Club," n.d., 7, and "Report on Operations of the 10th Cavalry," May 7, 1916—both in WCB 7; William C. Brown diary, Mar. 19, 1916, WCB 38.

37. JJP, "Report" *(op. cit.),* 8.

38. *The New York Times*, Apr. 4, 1916; Frank B. Elser, "General Pershing's Mexican Campaign," *The Century*, IC (Feb., 1920), (Hereinafter cited as "Campaign") 437.

39. Elser, *op. cit.,* 438.

40. Mason, *op. cit.,* 94–95.

41. JJP, "Report" (op. cit.), 11–12.
42. Tompkins, op. cit., 121–22, 188.
43. James L. Collins/George E. Adamson, June 29, 1934, PP 372; Brown, "Address" op. cit., 7.
44. New York American, Apr. 5, 1916.
45. Ibid.
46. Samuel F. Dallam, "The Punitive Expedition of 1916," Cavalry Journal, XXXVI (July, 1927), 386.
47. Ibid.
48. Henry T. Allen/wife, Apr. 2, 5, 1916, HTA.
49. Dallam, op. cit., 389, 398.
50. Clarence C. Clendenen, The United States and Pancho Villa (Ithaca, 1961), 264n.
51. JJP/Hugh L. Scott, Sep. 23, 1916, PP 372.
52. Mason, op. cit., 83. See also: James L. Collins/mother, May 23, 1916, JLC.
53. JJP/Funston, Mar. 25, 1916, PP 372; Clendenen, Blood on the Border (op. cit.), 244.
54. Frank B. Elser, "Pershing's Lost Cause," American Legion Monthly (July, 1932), (Hereinafter cited as "Cause") 44; Elser, "Campaign" (op. cit.), 438–39; New York Tribune, Apr. 21, 1916.
55. Elser, "Campaign" (op. cit.), 440.
56. USAF Historical Division, The United States Army Air Arm, April 1861 to April 1917, USAF Historical Studies: No. 98 ([San Antonio], 1958), 173.
57. Undated statement of Charles L. Bolté, who got this from John L. Hines, (author's file).
58. William B. Cowin/wife, Mar. 27, 1916, WC.
59. Ibid.
60. Cowin/wife, Apr. 7, 1916, WC.
61. PA, XXIII, 7; JJP, "Report" op. cit., 14–15; Clendenen, Blood on the Border (op. cit.), 233–40; Mason, op. cit., 95–99.
62. New York American, Mar. 28, 1916.
63. Elser, "Campaign" (op. cit.), 441.
64. Tompkins, op. cit., 117–18.
65. Ibid., 162–63.
66. Edgar S. Gorrell, "Why Riding Boots Sometimes Irritate an Aviator's Feet," U.S. Air Service, XVII (Oct., 1932), 24–25; JJP, "Report" op. cit., 86; PA, XXIII, 6.
67. Benjamin D. Foulois, "Reminiscences," 27, OHRO.
68. JJP preliminary rept, Mar. 27, 1916, AGO 2387731, RG 120, NA.
69. Gorrell, op. cit., 24.
70. New York World, Apr. 3, 1916.
71. Mason, op. cit., 116; Calvin W. Hines, "First Aero Squadron in Mexico," American Aviation Historical Society Journal, X (Fall, 1965), 195.
72. The New York Times, Apr, 8, 1916.

73. Elser, "Campaign" (*op. cit.*), 442; Hines, *op. cit.*, 195; [Benjamin Foulois], "Report of the First Aero Squadron, Signal Corps, with Punitive Expedition, U.S.A., for Period March 15 to Aug. 16, 1916," WCB 7.
74. JJP, "Report" (*op. cit.*), 18.
75. Tompkins, *op. cit.*, 131.
76. *Ibid.*, 131-34, 160-61.
77. Robert Dunn, "With Pershing's Cavalry," *Collier's*, Sep. 23, 1916, 8.
78. JJP/Funston, Apr. 14, 1916, PP 372; *The New York Times*, Apr. 13, 1916; Elser, "Cause" (*op. cit.*), 45.
79. Funston/Scott, Apr. 5, 1916, FF.
80. O'Connor, *op. cit.*, 133-34.
81. JJP/Francis E. Warren, Apr. 19, 1916, FWP.
82. PA, XXIII, 10.
83. JJP, "Report" (*op. cit.*), 19; Tompkins, *op. cit.*, 159-60; James L. Collins/ "Families," Apr. 24, 1916, JLC; Report, CO 11th Cavalry to CG, Punitive Expedition, June 8, 1916, 9-10, WCB 7.
84. JJP, "Report" (*op. cit.*), 59.
85. John A. Porter, "The Punitive Expedition," *Quartermaster Review*, XII (Jan.-Feb., 1933), 26, 28; Frederick Funston/Hugh L. Scott, Apr. 5, 1916, FF.
86. Katherine Phister Cowin, "Army Kaleidoscope," 32, WC.
87. Cowin/wife, Apr. 7, 1916, WC.
88. Vernon G. Olsmith, *Recollections of an Old Soldier* (San Antonio, 1943), 16.
89. JJP, "Report" (*op. cit.*), 40; Elser, "Campaign" (*op. cit.*), 434.
90. JJP, *My Experiences in the World War* (New York, 1931), I, 240; JJP, "What the Punitive Expedition Has Accomplished," PP 347; JJP, "Report" (*op. cit.*), 41.
91. Funston/TAG, Apr. 10, 1916, PP 372.
92. Elser, "Campaign" (*op. cit.*), 444.
93. *The New York Times*, Apr. 14, 19, 1916; Elser, "Campaign" (*op. cit.*), 444.
94. Elser, "Campaign" (*op. cit.*), 446; Elser," Cause" (*op. cit.*), 46.
95. JJP/Funston, Apr. 14, 1916, PP 372.
96. *Ibid.*
97. JJP/Funston, PP 372.
98. JJP, "Report" (*op. cit.*), 109–10; Raymond Reed, "The Mormons in Chihuahua" (unpublished MA thesis, University of New Mexico, 1938), 52–54, 57–59; Tompkins, *op. cit.*, 160–61.
99. George MacAdam, "The Life of General Pershing," *The World's Work*, Vol. 38 (June, 1919), 151.
100. *Ibid.*; JJP, "Report" (*op. cit.*) 60.
101. JJP, "Report" (*op. cit.*), 51–52.
102. *New York Tribune*, Apr. 21, 1916; Elser, "Campaign" (*op. cit.*), 445.

CHAPTER XVI: PARRAL AND CARRIZAL

1. Frank Tompkins, *Chasing Villa* (Harrisburg, Pa., 1934), 135.
2. *Ibid.*, 135–37; Haldeen Braddy, *Pershing's Mission in Mexico* (El Paso, 1966), 27–31; JJP, "Report of the Punitive Expedition," Oct. 10, 1916, (Hereinafter cited as "Report.") 21–22, PP 372.
3. Tompkins, *op. cit.*, 137.
4. *Ibid.*, 137–38.
5. *Ibid.*, 138; Braddy, *op. cit.*, 31–32.
6. Tompkins, *op. cit.*, 138–42.
7. *Ibid.*, 142; JJP, "Report" (*op. cit.*), 94.
8. Frank B. Elser, "General Pershing's Mexican Campaign," *The Century*, IC (Feb.., 1920), (Hereinafter cited as "Campaign") 446; JJP/Frederick Funston, Apr. 14, 1916, PP 372.
9. Tompkins, *op. cit.*, 136, 156–57.
10. George B. Rodney, *As a Cavalryman Remembers* (Caldwell, Idaho, 1944), 262–63; William C. Brown, "Address to the Lions Club," n.d., 12–13, and "Report on Operations of the 10th Cavalry," May 7, 1916—both in WCB 7.
11. Tompkins, *op. cit.*, 136, 156–57; JJP/Funston, *op. cit.*
12. JJP/Funston, *op. cit.*
13. Elser, "Campaign" (*op. cit.*), 446; Elser, "Pershing's Lost Cause," *American Legion Monthly* (July 1932), (Hereinafter cited as "Cause"), 47.
14. JJP/Hugh L. Scott, Sep. 23, 1916, PP 372.
15. James Hopper intvw, PP 372.
16. Robert Dunn, *World Alive* (New York, 1956), 238.
17. JJP/Enoch H. Crowder, June 15, 1916, PP 56.
18. JJP/Joe Breckons, May 23, 1916, PP 34.
19. PP 372.
20. JJP/Funston, Apr. 18, 1916, PP 372.
21. PA, XXIII, 12, PP 379.
22. Ray Stannard Baker, *American Chronicle* (New York, 1945), 286; Newton D. Baker, "The Secretary of War During the War," Army War College lecture, May 11, 1929, 4–5, PP 354; Joseph P. Tumulty, *Woodrow Wilson as I Know Him* (Garden City. N. Y., 1921) 157–60.
23. Funston/JJP, April 18, 1916, PP 372.
24. Funston/JJP, Apr. 19, 1916, PP 372.
25. JJP, "Report" (*op. cit.*), 23, 44, 51, 90.
26. Scott/SW, Apr. 22, 1916, THB 200.
27. Funston/JJP, Apr. 23, 1916, PP 372; JJP/Funston, Apr. 24, 1916, PP 372.
28. JJP/Funston, Apr. 24, 1916.
29. Funston/JJP, Apr. 24, 1916, PP 372; JJP, "Report" (*op. cit.*), 24–26, 50.
30. Funston/WD, Apr. 29, 1916, PP 372; U.S. Department of State, *Papers*

Relating to the Foreign Relations of the United States, 1916 (Washington, D.C., 1925) (Hereinafter cited as *Foreign Relations, 1916*), 533.
31. Scott/SW, Apr. 30, 1916, PP 372; WD/Funston, Apr. 30, 1916, PP 372.
32. Henry P. McCain/Scott, Apr. 30, 1916, PP 372.
33. Venustiano Carranza/Gen. Anulfo Gomez, quoted in W. S. Scott/Funston, May 1, 1916, PP 372.
34. Funston/JJP, May 1, 1916, PP 372.
35. TAG/Hugh L. Scott, May 1, 1916, THB 200.
36. Hugh L. Scott, *Some Memories of a Soldier* (New York, 1928), 525–28; *Foreign Relations, 1916, (op. cit.)*, 537–38.
37. Scott and Funston/SW, May 3, 1916, in *Foreign Relations, 1916 (op. cit.)*, 537–39.
38. Scott and Funston/SW, May 9, 1916, THB 200.
39. *Ibid.*
40. Herbert M. Mason, Jr., *The Great Pursuit* (New York, 1970), 174.
41. PP 372.
42. Mason, *op. cit.,* 183.
43. PP 372.
44. Funston/JJP, May 11, 1916, PP 372.
45. *Ibid.*; PA, XXIII, 15–16, PP 379.
46. Elser, "Campaign" (*op. cit.*), 447.
47. JJP/Funston, May 14, 1916, PP 372.
48. Funston/SW, May 23, 28, 1916, PP 372; Funston/JJP, May 19, 1916, PP 372.
49. JJP/Funston, PP 372.
50. Tompkins, *op. cit.,* 219; JJP "Report" (*op. cit.*), 26.
51. Martin Blumenson (ed.), *The Patton Papers* (Boston, 1972), I, 336; Patton/JJP, Sep. 24, 1920, PP 155.
52. Funston/WD, May 29, 1916, PP 372. This communication quoted verbatim JJP's message to Funston.
53. Funston/JJP, May 29, 1916, PP 372.
54. Frederick Funston/Hugh L. Scott, May 30, 1916, FF.
55. Tasker H. Bliss/TAG, May 31, 1916, THB 202.
56. "Mexican Situation, 1916," WCD 6474–381, 15, PP 372; Funston/SW, May 23, 28, 1916, PP 372.
57. Funston/JJP, June 12, 17, 1916, PP 372.
58. JJP, "Report" (*op. cit.*), 30.
59. *Ibid.*
60. *Ibid.*
61. JJP/James Hopper, July 11, 1916, PP 372.
62. JJP "Memo on Carrizal Fight," n.d., PP 372.
63. *Ibid.*; S. L. A. Marshall intvw, June 13, 1961; PA, XXIII, 18.
64. JJP memo for Inspector General of Punitive Expedition, June 30, 1916, Punitive Expedition Records, Box 70, NA.
65. H. B. Wharfield, "The Affair at Carrizal," *Montana,* XVIII (Autumn,

1968), 36; Karl Young, "A Fight That Could Have Meant War," *The American West*, III (Spring,1966), 20–21.

66. Clarence C. Clendenen, *Blood on the Border* (New York, 1969), 307; Young, *op. cit.*, 21.

67. Wharfield, *op. cit.*, 36.

68. Clendenen, *op. cit.*, 307.

69. *Ibid.*, 305–11; JJP/Funston, June 22, 1916, PP 372; *Foreign Relations, 1916, op. cit.*, 593–94, 596; JJP, "Memo" (*op. cit.*); JJP, "Report" (*op. cit.*), 30-31, 94; Raymond Reed, "The Mormons in Chihuahua" (unpublished MA thesis, University of New Mexico, 1938), 68–71; Mason, *op. cit.*, 210–11; James L. Collins diary, June 22–26, 1916, JLC.

70. Funston/JJP, June 22, 1916, PP 372.

71. JJP/Funston, June 21, 1916, PP 372; PA, XXIII, 19; Collins diary, June 21, 1916, JLC.

73. JJP/Funston, June 21, 23, 1916, PP 372.

74. JJP/Funston, June 22, 1916, PP 372.

72. JJP/Funston, June 21, 1916, PP 372; PA, XXIII, 19; Mason, *op. cit.*, 212.

75. Elser, "Campaign" (*op. cit.*), 447.

76. Memo, Tasker H. Bliss/TAG, June 25, 1916, THB 203.

77. *Ibid.*

78. Funston/JJP, June 25, 1916, PP 372.

79. JJP/Funston, June 26, 1916, PP 372.

80. *Ibid.* Pershing said later that he "especially cautioned him [Boyd] against exactly what happened." JJP/Henry T. Allen, June 23, 1916, PP 9. On the other hand, Boyd's widow showed me carbons (but not the originals) of letters to her from Orlando C. Troxel, a friend of Boyd, stating that his orders were to go all the way to Ahumada. Troxel/ Mrs. Charles Boyd, June 27, 1916, Dec. 11, 1916, and Apr. 17, 1917, OCT.

81. JJP/Funston, June 26, 1916, PP 372.

CHAPTER XVII: THE LAST CAMPAIGN

1. Frederick Funston/JJP, June 27, 1916, PP 372; Tasker H. Bliss/CofS, June 28, 1916, THB 203; Herbert M. Mason, Jr., *The Great Pursuit* (New York, 1970), 216–222.

2. JJP/Joe Breckons, May 23, 1916, PP 34.

3. "From a National Guardsman," *Outlook*, CXIII (Aug. 2, 1916), 773.

4. *The Globe* (New York), c. Aug. 1, 1916, PP 384.

5. G.O. Cress/CG, Southern Dept, May 3, 1917, PP 372; PA, XXIII, 21,

PP 370. Copies of the instruction program are in the John L. Hines Papers, Box 12, LC.

6. Frederick Funston/Hugh L. Scott, Feb. 7, 1917, FF.
7. E. A. Roberts/author, July 16, 1961; Robert H. Fletcher/author, May 23, 1961.
8. H. N. Eidson/author, Dec. 15, 1961.
9. Carter Weldon Clarke intvw, Feb. 10, 1960.
10. *Star-Bulletin* (Honolulu), Mar. 4, 1931; J. Stewart Richardson, "Pershing, in Spirit, Is Again Over There," *The New York Times Magazine*, Aug. 13, 1944, 45.
11. *The Detroit News,* Sep. 11, 1960.
12. JJP/George Deshon, Apr. 29, 1917, PP 64.
13. *The Los Angeles Examiner,* Oct. 13, 1916; Editors of the Army Times, *Warrior: The Story of General George S. Patton* (New York, 1967), 37.
14. Ruth Patton Totten/author, Nov. 5, 1966.
15. *Ibid;* Charles R. Codman, *Drive* (Boston, 1957), 146.
16. Clarence C. Clendenen, *Blood on the Border* (New York, 1969), 330, 339.
17. James A. Shannon, "With the Apache Scouts in Mexico," *Journal of the U. S. Cavalry Association,* XXVII (Apr., 1917), 544.
18. *Ibid.,* 546; *Star-Bulletin* (Honolulu), Mar. 4, 1931; Clendenen, *op. cit.,* 330.
19. Hugh L. Scott/JJP, Jan. 8, 1917, PP 372; JJP/Hugh L. Scott, Jan. 21, 1917, PP 372; Leonard Wood diary, Jan. 4, 1918, LW.
20. JJP/Charles S. Farnsworth, Sep. 22, 1916, PP 158.
21. Newton D. Baker/Woodrow Wilson, Sep. 23, 1916, 3849 ACP 86, NA.
22. Hugh L. Scott/JJP, Sep. 25, 1916, PP 181. Pershing jokingly inquired whether his new rank would give him more latitude in searching out Villa. "If a Brigadier General can be permitted to go 500 miles, possibly a Major General should be given a radius of 1000 miles." JJP/Virginia Collins, Oct. 17, 1916, JLC.
23. JJP/T. Bentley Mott, Oct. 2, 1916, PP 141.
24. JJP/Hugh L. Scott, Sep. 23, 1916, PP 372.
25. *Ibid.*
26. Scott/JJP, Oct. 9, 1916, PP 372.
27. Newton D. Baker, "The Secretary of War During the War," Army War College lecture, May 11, 1929, 5, PP 354.
28. JJP/Hugh L. Scott, Oct. 21, 1916, PP 372.
29. Hugh L. Scott/JJP, Oct. 30, 1916, PP 372; Hugh L. Scott/Frederick Funston, Oct. 27, 1916, FF.
30. U.S. Department of State, *Papers Relating to the Foreign Relations of the United States, 1916* (Washington, D. C., 1925) (Hereinafter cited as *Foreign Relations, 1916*), 609–10.
31. *Ibid.,* 617, 620, 480; JJP/Hugh Scott, Nov. 18, 1916, PP 372.

32. Quoted in Richard O'Connor, *Black Jack Pershing* (New York, 1961), 138.
33. M. H. Barnum/JJP, Dec. 8, 1916, PP 21.
34. JJP/Tasker H. Bliss, Jan. 7, 1917, PP 372.
35. JJP/Hugh L. Scott, Jan. 21, 1917, PP 372.
36. *Star-Bulletin* (Honolulu), Mar. 10, 1931. (This was one of a series of veterans' recollections run by the newspaper on the occasion of the publication of his book.)
37. U. S. War Department, *Annual Report, 1916* (Washington, D. C., 1916), I, 118.
38. JJP, "Report of the Punitive Expedition," Oct. 10, 1916, 11, PP 372.
39. JJP/James Hopper, July 11, 1916, PP 372.
40. JJP, "Report" (*op. cit.*), 11.
41. JJP/Hopper, *op. cit.*
42. PA, XXIII, 5; In contrast, Pershing cooperated with Carranza forces to the extent of authorizing the loan of American motor trucks to a garrison at Ascención for chasing bandits. JJP/Charles S. Farnsworth, Sep. 13, 1916, Farnsworth Papers, Museum of New Mexico.
43. JJP/Hopper, *op. cit.*
44. PA, XXIII, 4.
45. William A. Ganoe, *History of the U. S. Army* (New York, 1942), 460.
46. *Foreign Relations, 1916* (*op. cit.*), 484.
47. *New York American,* Mar. 11, 1916.
48. WD/Funston, PP 372.
49. Hugh L. Scott, *Some Memories of a Soldier* (New York, 1928) (Hereinafter cited as *Some Memories*), 519-20.
50. Omar Bundy/JJP, Mar. 14, 1916, PP 372.
51. M. H. Barnum/JJP, Dec. 8, 1916, PP 21.
52. PA, XXIII, 22.
53. JJP, "Report" (*op. cit*), 94, 97.
54. JJP/Hugh L. Scott, Jan. 4, 1917, PP 372.
55. Anita Brenner, *Idols Behind Altars* (New York, 1929), 211-12.
56. Clendenen, *op. cit.,* 232.
57. *Ibid.,* 340.
58. *Wyoming Tribune* (Cheyenne), Feb. 21, 1917.
59. JJP, Dec. 5, 1916 statement, PP 374.
60. *The Times* (El Paso), Aug. 10, 1916.
61. Mason, *op. cit.,* 220; Frederick Funston/Hugh L. Scott, Feb. 7, 1916, FF; James L. Collins diary, Apr. 28, 1916, JLC.
62. James L. Collins/mother, June 9, 1916, JLC; Mason, *op. cit.,* 84; U.S. War Department, *Annual Report of the Secretary of War, 1916* (Washington, D. C., 1916), 24.
63. Scott, *Some Memories (op.cit.)*, 523.
64. Russell F. Weigley, *The History of the United States Army* (New York, 1967), 351.

65. Robert K. Sawyer, "Viva Villa! " *Military Review,* XLI (Aug., 1961), 61, 67, 70.
66. Ganoe, *op. cit.,* 463.
67. Baker/Wilson, *op. cit.*
68. *Ibid.*
69. JJP/Frederick Funston, May 11, 1916, PP 372.
70. Clarke intvw.
71. JJP/William R. Sample, Oct. 31, 1916, PP 179.
72. JJP/Guy Preston, May 22, 1916, PP 164.
73. JJP/Francis E. Warren, Jan. 20, 1917, FWP.
74. *The Globe* (New York), c. Aug. 1, 1916.
75. Roberts/author, *op. cit.*; Fletcher/author, *op.cit.*
76. *The Globe, op.cit.*
77. *Los Angeles Examiner,* Oct. 13, 1916.
78. John C. Hughes intvw, Oct. 30, 1964.
79. Douglas MacArthur, Address to Congress, Apr. 19, 1951, in *The New York Times,* Apr. 20, 1951.
80. According to Col. Charles W. Hoffmann, who sent me a copy, the poem was originally published in *Collier's,* but I was unable to find it there. It was reprinted in the *Mexican Border Veterans Bulletin* in April, 1957. Hoffmann said the poem was "indicative of the total disgust that pervaded the Punitive Expedition for the 'too proud to fight' theory of President Wilson. Every officer and man in the Expedition carried a copy of this poem in his pocket until it wore out. My enlistment was to terminate in April, 1917, and I had my mind made up that if we were to continue on this policy I would go to Canada and enlist, I was so utterly disgusted." Hoffmann/author, Oct. 30, 1969.
81. JJP/George S. Patton, Jr., Oct. 16, 1916, PP 155.
82. JJP/U. S. Stewart, July 6, 1916, PP 190.
83. JJP/Francis E. Warren, Jan. 20, 1917, FWP.
84. U. S. Congress, Senate, *Military Situation in the Far East, Hearings before the Committee on Armed Services and the Committe on Foreign Relations,* 82d Cong., 1st Sess., 1951, I, 381.
85. Micheline Resco intvw, May 21, 1965.
86. JJP/Hugh L. Scott, March 3, 1917, PP 372.
87. Scott, *Some Memories* (*op. cit.*), 532.
88. George Hinman intvw, Mar. 26, 1961; see also Newton D. Baker War College lecture, *op. cit.,* 5, and Charles G. Dawes, *A Journal of the Great War* (Boston, 1921), I, 45.
89. James T. Williams, "Reminiscences, " OHRO.
90. *The National Tribune-The Stars and Stripes* (Washington, D. C.), Sep. 1, 1960.

APPENDIX: PERSHING'S FALSIFIED BIRTHDAY

1. *St. Louis Times,* Sep. 8, 1919, quoted in Katherine Kleiss Goodwin, "The Early Life of General John Joseph Pershing, 1860–1881" (unpublished MA thesis, Northeast Missouri State Teachers College, 1954), 20.
2. *Ibid.*
3. Everett T. Tomlinson/May Pershing, Aug. 1, 1918, PP 369.
4. Burris A. Jenkins, "Seven Places of Birth," *Kansas City Star* (Missouri), July 9, 1918, 5.
5. Lee W. Love affidavit, Mar. 12, 1938, before May B. Brown, Notary Public, Los Angeles County. (Copy furnished author by Lafayette Moore of Laclede, Mo.)
6. Waco, Texas, City Directory, 1917–18; W. L. Love/G. E. Bruns, Jan. 2, 1937. (Copy furnished author by Lafayette Moore.) The address for both W. L. Love and Lee W. Love in this and the previous footnote is the same: 1424 Cloverdale Ave., Los Angeles, Calif.
7. Orville E. Bowers, college registrar/author, Feb. 11, 1960. Significantly, while the family Bible of Pershing's sister, Mary Elizabeth (Mrs. Daniel M. Butler), lists September 13, 1860, as the date of his birth, the word *September* is in different ink than the rest of the entry, showing evidence of erasure and correction. John J. Pershing Papers, Nebraska State Historical Society.
8. U. S. , Bureau of the Census, "Linn County, Missouri: 1870, Population," 37, NA.
9. U.S. Bureau of the Census,"Linn County, Missouri: 1860, Population," 121, NA.
10. JJP Vital Statistics Questionnaire, n.d., Assoc. of Graduates Files, USMA.
11. 1860 census as cited in footnote 9.
12. SW/JJP, Nov. 10, 1881, PP 315.

Bibliography

Manuscripts in Public Depositories

Agora Society, Wellesley College, Wellesley, Mass.:
  John J. Pershing Papers.
Association of Graduates Offices, USMA, West Point, N. Y:
  John J. Pershing File.
Butler Library, Columbia University, N.Y.C.:
  James H. Canfield Papers.
Eisenhower Library, Abilene, Kansas:
  Courtney H. Hodges Papers.
Georgetown University, Washington, D. C.:
  Mrs. Henry C. Corbin Papers.
Houghton Library, Harvard University, Cambridge, Mass. :
  Theodore Roosevelt Papers.
  William Cameron Forbes Papers.
Huntington Library, San Marino, Cal. :
  Frank D. Baldwin Papers.
Kansas State Historical Society, Topeka, Kansas:
  Frederick Funston Papers.
Library of Congress, Washington, D. C. :
  Henry T. Allen Papers.
  Newton D. Baker Papers.
  Ray Stannard Baker Papers.
  Tasker H. Bliss Papers.
  Charles H. Brent Papers.
  William Jennings Bryan Papers.
  Robert L. Bullard Papers.
  Frank W. Carpenter Papers.
  Henry C. Corbin Papers.
  Charles G. Dawes Papers.

William Cameron Forbes Papers.
Lloyd C. Griscom Papers.
James G. Harbord Papers.
John L. Hines Papers.
Robert Lansing Papers.
Frank McCoy Papers.
John J. Pershing Papers.
Theodore Roosevelt Papers.
Elihu Root Papers.
Hugh L. Scott Papers.
Charles P. Summerall Papers.
William Howard Taft Papers.
Woodrow Wilson Papers.
Leonard Wood Papers.
Marshall Library, Lexington, Va.:
George C. Marshall Papers.
Museum of New Mexico, Santa Fe, N.M.:
Charles S. Farnsworth Papers.:
National Archives, Washington, D.C.:
John J. Pershing Papers.
Census Bureau Papers.
War Department Papers.
National Personnel Records Center, St. Louis, Mo.:
John J. Pershing 201 File.
Nebraska State Historical Society, Lincoln, Neb.:
Samuel R. McKelvie Papers.
George D. Meiklejohn Papers.
John J. Pershing Papers.
New York Historical Society, N.Y.C.:
James G. Harbord Papers.
John J. Pershing Papers.
Theodore Roosevelt Papers.
New York Public Library, N.Y.C.:
James H. Canfield Papers.
John J. Pershing Papers.
Hugh L. Scott Papers.
Francis E. Warren Papers.
Office of the Chief of Military History, Washington, D. C.:
John J. Pershing File.
Oral History Research Office, Columbia University, N. Y.C.:
Horace M. Albright Reminiscences.
Boris Alexander Bakhmeteff Reminiscences.
Henry Breckinridge Reminiscences.
Henry Bruere Reminiscences.
Holger Cahill Reminiscences.

Reed M. Chambers Reminiscences.
William Lockhart Clayton Reminiscences.
William Wilson Cumberland Reminiscences.
Haven Emerson Reminiscences.
Benjamin D. Foulois Reminiscences.
John P. Frey Reminiscences.
Perrin Galpin Reminiscences.
Lloyd C. Griscom Reminiscences.
William E. Harkness Reminiscences.
Leslie Irvin Reminiscences.
Clarence B. Kelland Reminiscences.
Langdon P. Marvin Reminiscences.
Eugene Meyer Reminiscences.
Carl E. Milliken Reminiscences.
John F. O'Ryan Reminiscences.
Arthur W. Page Reminiscences.
DeWitt Clinton Poole Reminiscences.
George Rublee Reminiscences.
Francis R. Stoddard Reminiscences.
James W. Wadsworth Reminiscences.
Clyde D. Wagoner Reminiscences.
James T. Williams, Jr. Reminiscences.
Pershing Boyhood Home Memorial Shrine, Laclede, Mo.:
    Pershing Family Papers.
Sterling Memorial Library, Yale University, New Haven, Conn.:
    Gordon Auchincloss Papers.
    Edward M. House Papers.
    Vance C. McCormick Papers.
    Frank L. Polk Papers.
United State Military Academy Library and Archives, West Point, N.Y.:
    Guy V. Henry, Jr. Papers
    John J. Pershing File.
    Eben Swift, Jr. Papers.
University of Nebraska Archives, Lincoln, Neb.:
    Board of Regents Papers.
    Chancellor's Papers.
    Military Department Papers.
University of Vermont, Burlington, Vt.:
    Dorothy Canfield Fisher Papers.
Washington State Historical Society, Takoma, Wash.:
    John J. Pershing Papers.
Wellesley College Library, Wellesley, Mass.:
    John J. Pershing Papers.
Western Historical Collections, University of Colorado, Boulder, Colo.:
    William Cary Brown Papers.

Western History Research Center, University of Wyoming, Laramie, Wyo.:
Francis E. Warren Papers.

Manuscripts in Private Collections

Henry Castor, c/o Franklin Watts, Inc., 575 Lexington Ave., New York City:
Dorothy Canfield Fisher Papers.
James L. Collins, Jr., 3625 Ordway, N.W., Washington, D.C.:
James L. Collins Papers.
Mrs. Katherine Phister Cowin, Lakeview Rest Home, Newton Centre, Mass.:
William B. Cowin Papers.
Mrs. Edmund K. Daley, 976 N. Quantico, Arlington, Va.:
George C. Shaw Papers.
Lt. Col. Elliott L. Johnson, Department of History, USAF Academy, Colo.:
Hugh A. Drum Papers.
Mrs. Judith Ely Glocker, 949 Elder Lane, Jacksonville, Fla.:
Hanson E. Ely Papers.
Mrs. Richard H. Hawkins, Rye Beach, N.H.:
Orlando C. Troxel Papers.
Mrs. Richard Montgomery, 11597 N. Shore Dr., Reston, Va.:
Frank Lanckton Papers.
F. Warren Pershing, Halsey Neck Lane, Southampton, N.Y.:
Helen Frances Warren (Pershing) Papers.
John J. Pershing Papers.
Miss Micheline Resco, 5 rue des Renaudes, Paris 17, France:
F. Warren Pershing Papers.
John J. Pershing Papers.
Mrs. Crawford Shaeffer, 218 N. Riverside Drive, Edgewater, Fla.:
Crawford Shaeffer Papers.
Donald Smythe, S.J. John Carroll University, Cleveland, Ohio:
John J. Pershing Papers.

Interviews

Allen, Carlisle V. Washington, D.C., July 11, 1960.
Andel, John. Washington, D.C., May 10, 1960.
Baukhage, Mrs. H. R. Washington, D.C., July 26, 1966.

Bliss, Edward Goring. Washington, D.C., July 27, 1966.
Boone, Joel T. Washington, D.C., Apr. 28, 1961.
Bowditch, Edward. New York, Dec. 29, 1960.
Brause, Jacob. Washington, D.C., Sep. 28, 1960.
Cabell, Edith M. Washington, D.C., June 25 and July 22, 1960.
Clarke, Carter Weldon. Washington, D.C., Feb. 10, 1960.
Cochrun, Mrs. James L. Akron, O., Sep. 23, 1970.
Collins, James L. Alexandria, Va., July 31 and Dec. 29, 1962.
Confidential Source No. 1. Washington, D.C., Mar. 13, 1961.
Cook, Mrs. Seth. Washington, D.C., Mar. 16, 1961.
Cowin, Mrs. Katherine Phister. West Newton, Mass., July 11, 1970.
Criswell, Robert L. Washington, D.C., Feb. 10, 1961.
Crystal, Thomas L. New York, May 26, 1960.
Cummings, Margaret. Washington, D.C., Dec. 30, 1962.
Curtin, Ralph A. Washington, D.C., July 19, 1960; July 15, 17, 22, 1963; Aug.
    1, 1963.
Daley, Mrs. Edward. Arlington, Va., July 2, 1960.
Davies, John M. Washington, D.C., May 3, 1961.
Ebner, Roy. Wheaton, Md., Apr. 5, 1961.
Egan, Mrs. Martin. New York, Apr. 24, 1961.
Eller George P. New York, Dec. 28, 1960.
Elliott, Dabney O. Washington, D.C., Apr. 13, 1961.
Ely, Mrs. Hanson. Washington, D.C., Apr. 11, 1961; Blue Ridge Summit, Pa.,
    July 4, 1961; Woodstock, Md., Aug. 15, 1963.
Epstein, Harold. New York, Dec. 29, 1960; Oct. 29, 1964.
Frank, Walter H. Washington, D.C., July 14, 1960.
Frier, James H., Jr. Cleveland, Jan 20, 28, 1970.
Fries, Amos A. Washington, D.C., May 14, 1960.
Ginnetti, Ernest. Washington, D.C., May 3, 1961.
Hains, John P. Washington, D.C., Apr. 17, 1961.
Harbottle, Mary Ann Rose. San Diego, Cal., Sep. 28, 1961 (interviewed by
    Marion F. Humphrey, Jr.).
Harriman, Mrs. J. Borden. Washington, D.C., Apr. 18, 1961.
Hart, Franklin A. Washington, D.C., Mar. 21, 1961.
Hawkins, Mrs. Richard. Baltimore, Jan. 26 and Feb. 2, 1963.
Hayes, Mrs. Edward A. Chicago, Apr. 29, 1967.
Heiberg, Louise Cromwell Brooks MacArthur Atwill. Washington, D.C., Mar.
    9, Apr. 5, 10, 1961.
Heister, John J. Washington, D.C., Apr. 11, 1961.
Herron, Charles D. Bethesda, Md., June 26, 1960.
Hershey, Burnet. New York, Dec. 29, 1966.
Hinman, George W. Washington, D.C., July 22, 1960; Mar. 26, 1961.
Hinman, Mrs. George W. Washington, D.C., Apr. 7, 1961; Mar. 27, 1966.
Holcomb, Thomas. Washington, D.C., Mar. 21, 1961.
Holle, Charles G. Washington, D.C., July 20, 1960.

Horgan, John L. Washington, D.C., May 5, 1961.
Hughes, John C. New York, Oct. 30, 1964.
Jones, Richard S. Washington, D.C., July 28, 1966.
Kass, Garfield I. Washington, D.C., Apr. 7, 1961.
Kauffman, Benjamin F. Washington, D.C., Mar. 24, 1960.
Keatley, G. Harold. Washington, D.C., Apr. 5, 1961.
Kelly, Charles C. Washington, D.C., Mar. 4, 1961.
Kelly, Thomas J. Miami, Fla., Nov. 14, 1962.
Kenedy, Eugene T., S.J. Washington, D.C., Jan. 15, 1961.
Kienle, Alfred, S.J. Washington, D.C., Mar. 6, 1961.
Kines, Louis B., S.J. New York, Dec. 29, 1960.
King, John T. Baltimore, May 15, 1961.
Lanckton, Mrs. Frank. Washington, D.C., May 2, 1961.
Leidesdorf, Samuel D. New York, Dec. 27, 1960.
Longworth, Mrs. Nicholas (Alice Roosevelt). Washington, D.C., Mar. 7, 15, 1961.
Mangum, James E. Washington, D.C., July 10, 30, 1963.
Mangum, Mrs. James E. Washington, D.C., July 10, 1963.
March, Mrs. Peyton C. Washington, D.C., Dec. 11, 1960; Mar. 11, 16, 1961; Apr. 14, 1961.
Marietta, S. U. Washington, D.C., July 2, 1960.
Marshall, S. L. A. Arlington, Va., June 13, 1961.
McCoy, Mrs. Frank R. Washington D.C., Apr. 5, 1961.
McNeil, Edwin C. Washington, D.C., Mar. 17, 1961.
Miller, Paul C. Washington, D.C., June 15, 1961.
Moginier, Madam Celia. Paris, France, Aug. 26, 1965.
Moseley, George Van Horn. Washington, D.C., Sep. 12–13, 1960.
Mueller, Charles R. Washington, D.C., Apr. 9, 1961.
Mueller, Paul J. Washington, D.C., July 31, 1963.
North, Thomas. Washington, D.C., Mar. 14, 1961.
Pepper, Kelton Lyon. Washington, D.C., Nov. 13, 1960.
Pershing, Eli R. Washington, D.C., May 8, 1961.
Pershing, F. Warren. New York, May 26, 1960; Southampton, N.Y., Aug. 14, 1966.
Pratt, H. Conger. Washington, D.C., May 1, 1960.
Purdon, Mrs. Eric. Washington, D.C., June 25, 1960.
Reilly, Henry J. New York, May 26, 1960.
Resco, Mlle. Micheline. Paris, France, May 21, Aug. 3, 6, 8–14, 16, 24–30, 1965; April 12–May 1, 1966.
Reynolds, Russel B. Washington, D.C., June 28, 1960; Apr. 28, 1961.
Robinett, Paul McD. Washington, D.C., Apr. 13, 1961.
Ross, Mrs. Nellie Tayloe. Washington, D.C., May 8, 1961.
Runk, William. Washington, D.C., May 7, 1960.
Schneider, J. Thomas. Washington, D.C., Mar. 17, 1961.
Schuyler, Edwin C. Washington, D.C., Apr. 6, 1961.

Shaeffer, Crawford. Washington, D.C., Feb. 16, 1964.
Shaw, Charles B. Washington, D.C., July 25, 1963.
Siefert, George J., Jr. Washington, D.C., Apr. 6, 1961.
Skilton, John. New York, Apr. 24, 1961.
Smith, Mrs. Corinna Lindon. New York, June 27, 1963.
Sorley, Lewis. Washington, D.C., Apr. 17, 1961.
Stathis, Mrs. Getty. Alexandria, Va., May 6, 1961.
Totten, James. Washington, D.C., July 29–30, 1966.
Twitchell, Heath. Camp Springs, Md., Aug. 7, 1970.
Villaret, Gustave. Chevy Chase, Md., July 6, 8, 1960.
Virden, John M. Chevy Chase, Md., Mar. 6, 8, 22, 1961; July 31, 1962.
Wainwright, John D. Washington, D.C., May 12, 1961.
Wainwright, Mrs. John D. Washington, D.C., May 12, 1961.
Whiting, Lawrence H. Chicago, Apr. 28, 1967.
Whitley, George R. Arlington, Va., July 30, 1966.
Wood, Mrs. John S. Washington, D.C., Apr. 7, 1961.

Correspondence

Agar, Herbert. Petworth, Sussex, England, Nov., 19, 1963.
Allen, Hugh. New York, Sep. 28 and Oct. 11, 1960.
Andrews, Hugh P. Portland, Ore., Apr. 9, 1961.
Army Records Center, St. Louis, Mo., May 9, 1960.
Bechely, Francis C. Los Angeles, Mar. 22, 1961
Bettison, William T. Wynnewood, Pa., Aug. 4, 1960.
Bliss, Edward Goring. Washington, D.C., July 27, 1966.
Boatner, Mark, Jr. Jackson, La., May 23, 1961.
Boehs, Charles J. San Antonio, Tex., May 31, 1961.
Booth, C. C. Dallas, Mar. 20 and July 20, 1960.
Boswell, James O. San Francisco, Feb. 28, 1963.
Boswell, John P. San Francisco, Sep. 12, 1963.
Boswell, William O. Cairo, United Arab Republic, May 18, 1963.
Bowers, Orville, Registrar, Northeast Missouri State Teachers College, Kirks-
    ville, Mo., Feb. 11, 1960.
Boykin, Neal L. Apr. 2, 1961.
Brabson, F. W. Staunton, Va., Sep. 25, 1960.
Brewer, B. E. Lexington Park, Ky., July 12, 1960.
Brimberry, John H. San Jose, Cal., Mar. 19, 1960.
Butz, Bright B. St. Petersburg, Fla., June 30, 1961.
Cabell, Edith M. Washington, D. C., July 5, 20, 25, 1960.
Chudly, Mrs. Edward. Lincoln, Neb., Apr. 2, 1960.

Clark, Charles B. St. Petersburg, Fla., Aug. 1, 1960.
Clayton, W. L. Houston, Sep. 4, 1963.
Clinton, Edward. Baltimore, Feb. 7, 1960.
Cochran, Paul. Mann's Choice, Pa., Feb. 10, 1960.
Coleman, Miles, Outwood, Ky., Mar. 14, 1960.
Collins, James L. Alexandria, Va., Dec. 29, 1962; Jan. 16 and Mar. 28, 1963.
Confidential Source No. 2. Apr. 1 and May 1, 1961; Feb. 8 and Mar. 14, 1963.
Conklin, H. W. El Paso, Nov. 21, 1962.
Coop, Basil C. Belmont, Cal., Mar. 19, 1960.
Craven, Thomas, Jr. Scranton, Pa., Mar. 29, 1961.
Crivello, William A. Alton, Ill., Mar. 14, 1960.
Cronin, Gerald. St. Petersburg, Fla., Nov. 3, 1961.
Curtin, Ralph A. Washington D.C., Aug. 16, 1963; Jan. 9, 1964.
Davenport, Erwin R. Miami Beach, June 14, 1960.
Davison, Roland. Paget West, Bermuda, Jan. 28 and Feb. 19, 1963.
Dawes, Beman Gates, Jr. Cincinnati, Jan. 16 and Apr. 6, 1961.
Dawes, C. Burr. Columbus, O., May 30 and June 6, 1961.
Dawes, Henry. Hartford, Conn., May 8, 1961.
Demarest, Mrs. Glenn. Brookfield, Mo., July 15, 1960.
Dodds, Harold W. Princeton, N.J., Aug. 2, 1960.
Doherty, James F. Mill Valley, Cal., Mar. 21, July 30 and Oct. 10, 1960.
Downs, Mrs. Norton. Bryn Mawr, Pa., Mar. 8, 1960.
Dunn, Mrs. Cary. Miami, Fla., Nov. 8, 1961.
Dupuy, R. Ernest. Arlington, Va., Apr. 10, 1961.
Eidson, H. H. Tulsa, Okla., Dec. 15, 1961.
Ennis, William P. Vineyard Haven, Mass., Aug. 2, 1960.
Farnsworth, Robert J. Los Angeles, Nov. 20, 1962.
Fletcher, Robert H. Leesburg, Va., May 23, 1961.
Fulbright, Sen. J. W. Washington, D. C., June 21, 1960.
Furnos, Sally L. Oakland, Cal., June 10 and July 24, 1961.
Gates, John M. Wooster, O., Jan. 7, 1971.
Gerhart, Charles I. Lawrenceville, Ill., Mar. 26, 1960.
Goldsmith, Myron B. San Francisco, Aug. 17, 1961.
Good, Arthur. Kansas City, Kans., Mar. 19, 1960.
Green, Mrs. Roy M. Lincoln, Neb., Nov. 19, 1962.
Greene, Paul. State Dept. of Education, Jefferson City, Mo., Feb. 18, 1960.
Greer, Allen J. San Clemente, Cal., Sep. 19, 1960.
Grendon, Arthur de. St. Louis, Mo. Mar. 12, 1960.
Gutleben, Dan. Walnut Creek, Cal., Oct. 14, 1960.
Hanes, Murray S. Springfield, Ill., Oct. 5, 1960.
Harts, William W. Madison, Conn., July 20, 1960.
Hartshonn, Elizabeth P. New Hope, Pa., Apr. 17, 1961.
Hawkins, Mrs. Richard H. Rye Beach, N. H., June 8, 1961.
Henry, Guy V. Chevy Chase, Md., Aug. 31, 1960.
Herring, Grover, Sep. 25 and Dec. 6, 1970.

Herron, Charles D. Bethesda, Md., Aug. 1, 1960; Nov. 13, 1962.
Hoffmann, Charles W. Santa Barbara, Cal., Oct. 27, 30, 1969.
Holiday, John. Los Angeles, Cal., Jan. 28, 1971.
Humphrey, Evan H. San Antonio, Aug. 4, 1960.
Immaculée, Sister. St. Mary of the Woods, Ind., Jan. 18, 1963.
Jones, Everett N. Kansas City, Mo., Mar. 19, 1960.
Jorgensen, O. M. Manhattan, Kan., Mar. 17, 1960.
Kass, Garfield I. Washington, D. C., Apr. 21, 1961.
Kassel, Mrs. Murray M. Middletown, N. Y., Feb. 8, 1960.
Kelly, Mrs. D. T. New York, Feb. 22, 1960.
Kenedy, Eugene L., S. J. New York, Jan. 28 and Feb. 8, 1961.
Ketterman, C. W. Bloomington, Ind., May 1, 1967.
Kilcullen, Gerald. Jamaica, N. Y., Nov. 13, 1960.
Lambert, John H. Washington, D. C., Sep. 26, 1960.
Lamme, Mrs. T. T. Laclede, Mo., Mar. 17, 1960.
Larkin, William. Los Angeles, Cal., Aug. 23, 1960.
Lear, Ben. Memphis, Feb. 10, 18, 1960.
Lee, Walter R., Sr. Jackson, Miss., Sep. 26, 1960.
Lipkin, Florence. New York, Apr. 29, 1960.
Lippmann, Walter. Washington, D.C., Sep. 14, 1964.
Long, John D. Baltimore, Md., Aug. 27, 1960.
Lynn, Miles R., Jr. Emlenton, Pa., Nov. 20, 1961.
MacAdam, Mrs. George. Scarsdale, N. Y., May 12, 1960.
MacArthur, Douglas. New York, Sep. 17 and Oct. 13, 1960.
McClary, G. R. N. Miami, Fla., July 25, 1961.
McFarland, E. L. Rock Island, Ill., Mar. 25, 1960.
McKay, James V. Washington, D. C., May 24, 1961.
McKinstry, C. H. Santa Barbara, Cal., Sep. 17, 1960.
Magruder, L. B. Rumson, N. J., July 11, 17, 1961.
Maguire, C. L. Wickenburg, Ariz., Aug. 9, 1960.
Mahoney, Tom. New York City, Feb. 14, 1960.
Mangum, James E. Washington, D.C., Aug. 17 and Dec. 14, 1963.
Marietta, Shelley U. Washington, D.C., Sep. 25, 1960.
Marsh, Ralph E. Kansas City, Mo., Mar. 16, 1960.
Marshall, Katherine Tupper. Southern Pines, N. C., Apr. 26, 1961.
Marshall, S. L. A. Birmingham, Mich., Jan. 19, 1963.
Mathews, William R. Tucson, Ariz., Feb. 12, 1960.
Mauer, Charles A. Blythe, Cal., Aug. 15, 1961.
Merrill, Adelbert. Portland, Me., Feb. 7 and 21, 1960.
Miller, Harvey W. Syracuse, N. Y., Aug. 9, 1960.
Moginier, Celia S. Paris, France, Sep. 15, 1965.
Molski, John A. Chicago, Ill., May 1, 1960.
Montfort, Harold de. N. Orleans, La., Nov. 24, 1961.
Moore, Lafayette. Laclede, Mo., June 2, Sep. 22, and Oct. 20, 1960.
Morgan, Harold A. Merrill, Wisc., Mar. 29, 1961.

339

Moseley, George Van Horn. Atlanta, Ga., July 19, Aug. 10, Sep. 22, and Nov. 7, 1960.
Mulloney, D. H. Columbus, O., Apr. 30, 1961.
Munday, Charles V. San Antonio, Tex., Aug. 26, 1961.
O'Connell, Mrs. Frank B. Lincoln, Neb., Aug. 2, 1960.
O'Donnell, Joseph M. Archivist, USMA, West Point, N. Y., Mar. 10 and Aug. 18, 1960; Feb. 24, 1967.
Otwell, Curtis W. Palo Alto, Cal., Aug. 4, 1960.
Oury, William H. Apr. 13, 1961.
Parker, F. LeJ. Charlestown, S.C., Sep. 24 and Oct. 9, 1960.
Parr, Perry. Colorado Springs, Colo., Sep. 5, 1961.
Patton, George S. Washington, D. C., Nov. 25, 1966.
Pegler, Westbrook. New York, Dec. 16, 1960.
Petter, K. L. Port Richey, Fla., Oct. 27 and Dec. 10, 1960.
Perkins, George T. Morgan Hill, Cal., Mar. 27, 1963.
Reid, L. Leon. Pittsburgh, Pa., Sep. 16, 1960.
Reilly, Henry T. New York, June 19, July 7, and Sep. 13, 1960; May 3, 1961.
Resco, Mlle. Micheline. Paris, France, Aug. 18 and Oct. 21, 1964; Sep. 15, 1965.
Rickenbacker, Eddie. New York, July 20, 1960.
Rinard, Claude. Milwaukee, Wisc., Oct. 17, 1960.
Roberts, Charles D. Chevy Chase, Md., Oct. 1, 1960.
Roberts, E. A. Carlsbad, N. M., July 16, Sep. 25, Nov. 3, and Dec. 3, 1961.
Rosario, Luis del, S.J. Archbishop of Zamboanga, Philippines, July 19, 1960.
Ryle, Walter. Kirksville, Mo., Jan. 20, 1960.
Scott, Ernest D. Miami, Fla., Aug. 12 and Nov. 7, 1960.
Schmidt, C. J. Blair, Neb., Oct. 4, 1960.
Schneider, J. Thomas. Washington, D. C., May 28, 1963.
Shapland, Lester B. Hettinger, N.D., May 11, 22, 1963.
Shepherd, Lemuel C., Jr. Warrenton, Va., Mar. 18, 1961.
Shinkle, Edward. San Francisco, Cal., Aug. 3, 1960.
Siefert, George J., Jr. Washington, D. C., June 18, 1961.
Simons, Marji. Pres., Agora Society, Wellesley College, Feb. 8 and Mar. 5, 1963.
Singleton, Ann. Orlando, Fla., Mar. 15, 1960; July 19, 1961.
Smith, Corinna Lindon. Norman, Okla., Jan. 23, 1961; Dublin, N. H., June 25–26, 29, and Aug. 28, 1963.
Stacy, Barney H. Weatherford, Tex., Oct. 19, 1960.
Stephens, Mrs. Flecta M. State Historical Society, Columbia, Mo., June 29, 1960.
Straw, Harry J. Muncie, Ind., Oct. 21, 1960.
Sunderland, A. H. Hampton, Va., Aug. 3, 1960.
Surgner, Stanley G. Philadelphia, Pa., July 26, 1960.
Sweeney, Walter C. San Francisco, Cal., Oct. 10, 1960.
Taylor, John M. Arlington, Va., June 17, 1961.
Thomas, Floyd E. Tucson, Ariz., June 20 and July 7, 1960.

Totten, Ruth Patton. Washington, D. C., Nov. 5, 1966.

The Tribune-Herald. Waco, Tex., July 25, 1960.

Turner, Marion. DeSoto, Mo., Mar. 14, 1960.

Vance, John R. Corte Madera, Cal., Sep. 13, 1960.

Virden, John M. Chevy Chase, Md., Mar. 24, June 12, and July 17, 1961.

Wade, T. R. Sec., Cypress Lodge No. 227, A.F. and A.M., Brookfield, Mo.,
May 16, 1960.

Watson, Mark S. Baltimore, Md., May 5, 1961.

Weeks, Sinclair. Lancaster, N. H., July 30, 1960.

Wenger, Samuel S. Lancaster, Pa., Jan. 23, 1961.

West, Eugene R. Washington, D. C., Aug. 30, 1960.

Whipp, Mrs. Elmer. Frederick, Md., Apr. 5, 1962.

Wilkinson, J. P. Asst. Director for Libraries, Univ. of Nebraska, Lincoln. Neb.,
July 8, 1960.

Williams, Irvin. Sumner, Mo., Mar. 27, 1960.

Willis, George G. Greenville, S. C., Mar. 23, 1965.

Winkler, Arthur E. Pastor, Methodist Church, Laclede, Mo., Feb. 19, 1960.

Winslow, Mabel E. Washington, D. C., May 11, 1961.

Withers, W. R. Greensboro, Ala., Sep. 27, 1960.

Wood, Robert E. Chicago, Ill., Aug. 12, 1960.

Woodruff, J. A. Coronado, Cal., Aug. 18, 1960.

Yates, Halsey E. San Francisco, Cal., May 24, 1962.

Youngberg, Gilbert A. Jacksonville, Fla., Aug. 5, 1960.

Autobiographies and Memoirs

Andrews, Avery D. *My Friend and Classmate, John J. Pershing.* Harrisburg, Pa.,
1939.

Baker, Ray Stannard. *American Chronicle.* New York, 1945.

Bigelow, John, Jr. *Reminiscences of the Santiago Campaign.* New York, 1899.

Bonsal, Stephen. *The Fight for Santiago.* New York, 1899.

Brown, William C. *The Punitive Expedition.* Tucson, 1921.

Bullard, Robert L. *Personalities and Reminiscences of the War.* New York, 1925.

Cloman, Sidney A. *Myself and a Few Moros.* New York, 1923.

Codman, Charles R. *Drive.* Boston, 1957.

Conner, Virginia. *What Father Forbad.* Philadelphia, 1951.

Daniels, Josephus. *The Cabinet Diaries of Josephus Daniels, 1913–1921.* ed. E.
David Cronin. Lincoln, 1963.

————. *The Life of Woodrow Wilson, 1856–1924.* Philadelphia, [1924].

————. *The Wilson Era: Years of Peace, 1910–1917.* Chapel Hill, N.C., 1944.

Davis, Richard Harding. *The Cuban and Porto Rican Campaigns.* New York,
1898.

Dawes, Charles G. *A Journal of the Great War.* 2 vols. Boston, 1921.

_____. *A Journal of the McKinley Years.* Chicago, 1950.

Dierks, Jack Cameron. *A Leap to Arms: The Cuban Campaign of 1898.* Philadelphia, 1970.

Dunn, Robert. *World Alive: A Personal Story.* New York, 1956.

Evans, Robley D. *An Admiral's Log: Being Continued Recollections of Naval Life.* New York, 1910.

Funston, Frederick. *Memories of Two Wars.* New York, 1911.

Griscom, Lloyd C. *Diplomatically Speaking.* Boston, 1940.

Harbord, James G. *The American Army in France, 1917–1919.* Boston, 1936.

_____. *Serving with Pershing: An Address Delivered before the University Club of Port Chester, Port Chester, N. Y., May 26, 1944.* n.p.,n.d.

Hobbes, Horace P. *Kris and Krag: Adventures Among the Moros of the Southern Philippine Islands.* n.p., 1962.

Hoffmann, Max von. *The War of Lost Opportunities.* London, 1924.

Houston, David F. *Eight Years with Wilson's Cabinet.* Garden City, N.Y., 1926.

Howard, O. O. *My Life and Experience Among Our Hostile Indians.* Hartford, Conn., 1907.

Janis, Elsie. *So Far, So Good.* New York, 1932.

Johnson, Alvin. *Pioneer's Progress: An Autobiography.* New York, 1952.

Landor, A. Henry Savage. *Everywhere: The Memoirs of an Explorer.* Vol. II. New York, 1924.

_____. *The Gems of the East.* New York, 1904.

Lane, Franklin K. *The Letters of Franklin K. Lane, Personal and Political.* ed Anne Wintermute Lane and Louise Herrick Wall. Boston, 1922.

Leary, John J., Jr. *Talks with T. R.* Boston, 1920.

March, Peyton C. *The Nation at War.* Garden City, N. Y., 1932.

Marcosson, Isaac F. *Before I Forget: A Pilgrimage to the Past.* New York, 1950.

MacArthur, Douglas. *Reminiscences.* New York, 1964.

Miles, Nelson A. *Personal Recollections.* Chicago, 1896.

_____. *Serving the Republic.* New York, 1911.

Miley, John D. *In Cuba with Shafter.* New York, 1899.

Mott, T. Bentley. *Twenty Years as Military Attaché.* New York, 1937.

Olsmith, Vernon G. *Recollections of an Old Soldier.* San Antonio, 1963.

Palmer, Frederick. *With Kuroki in Manchuria.* New York, 1904.

_____. *With My Own Eyes: A Personal Story of Battle Years.* Indianapolis, 1933.

Parker, James. *The Old Army: Memories, 1872–1918.* Philadelphia, 1929.

Parker, John H. *History of the Gatling Gun Detachment, Fifth Army Corps, at Santiago.* Kansas City, Mo., 1898.

Pershing, John J. *My Experiences in the World War.* 2 vols. New York, 1931.

Poe, Sophie A. *Buckboard Days.* Caldwell, Idaho, 1936.

Post, Charles J. *The Little War of Private Post.* Boston, 1960.

Roosevelt, Theodore. *An Autobiography.* New York, 1920.

_____. *The Rough Riders.* New York, 1902.

Rouse, Henry Clark. *Travelling around the World with General Nelson A. Miles: Extracts from Home Letters, October 1, 1902 to February 15, 1903.* New York, 1904.

Scott, Hugh L. *Some Memories of a Soldier.* New York, 1928.

Slayden, Ellen Maury. *Washington Wife.* New York, 1963.

Smith, Corinna Lindon. *Interesting People: Eighty Years with the Great and Near Great.* Norman, Okla., 1962.

Standing Bear, Luther. *My People the Sioux.* Boston, 1928.

St. Louis, Private [Alfred C. Petty]. *Forty Years After.* Boston, 1939.

Sullivan, Mark. *The Education of an American.* New York, 1928.

Tumulty, Joseph P. *Woodrow Wilson as I Know Him.* Garden City, N.Y., 1921.

Wheeler, Joseph. *The Santiago Campaign, 1898.* Boston, 1898.

White, John R. *Bullets and Bolos: Fifteen Years in the Philippine Islands.* New York, 1928.

Published Primary Sources

Annual Reports of the Boards of Visitors to the U. S. Military Academy: 1882–86, 1897–98.

Annual Report of the Chief of the Division of Insular Affairs: 1901.

Annual Report of the Chief of Staff: 1916.

Annual Reports of the Commanding General of the Army: 1898, 1901–02.

Annual Reports of the Commanding General, Department of Mindanao: 1910–11.

Annual Reports of the Governor of the Moro Province: 1910–13.

Annual Reports of the Public Schools of the State of Missouri: 1879–82.

Annual Reports of the Secretary of War: 1882–86, 1888, 1891, 1898–1903, 1914, 1916–17.

Annual Reports of the Superintendent of the U.S. Military Academy: 1882–86, 1897–98.

Annual Reports of the War Department: 1897–99, 1901–04, 1911–13, 1916.

Blumenson, Martin, ed. *The Patton Papers, 1885–1940.* Boston, 1972.

Congressional Directory, 59th Cong., 2d Sess., 1906.

1886–1911, In Commemoration of the 25th Anniversary of Graduation of the Class of '86, U.S.M.A. West Point, N. Y., 1911.

First Class Annual of the Class of '86, United States Military Academy, N. Y., for the Year 1887. Poughkeepsie, N. Y., 1887.

Fourteenth Annual Catalogue of the Missouri State Normal School, First Normal District, for the School Year 1880–81, with Announcements for School Year 1881–82. Hannibal, Mo., 1881.

Harper's Pictorial History of the War with Spain. 2 vols. New York, 1899.

The Hesperian [University of Nebraska biweekly], 1891–95.

The Howitzer, 1898 [U. S. Military Academy Yearbook].

The Hundredth Night Entertainment Given by the U. S. Corps Cadets, February 20, 1886. Poughkeepsie, N. Y., 1886.

McClure, Nathaniel F., ed. *Class of 1887, United States Military Academy: A Bibliographical Volume to Commemorate the 50th Anniversary of Graduation at West Point, N. Y., June, 1937.* Washington, D.C., 1938.

Mexican Foreign Office. *Diplomatic Dealings of the Constitutionalist Revolution in Mexico.* Mexico City, n.d.

The Mindanao Herald, Historical and Industrial Number Commemorating a Decennium of American Occupation of the Land of the Farthest East and Nearest West. Zamboanga, Philippines, 1909.

Official Register of the Officers and Cadets of the U. S. Military Academy: 1882–86, 1897–98.

Regulations of the U. S. Military Academy at West Point, New York. Washington, D.C., 1883.

Reunion of the Class of '86, United States Military Academy, in Honor of the 55th Anniversary of its Graduation on June 12, 1886. West Point, N. Y., 1941.

Rice, George D. *Photographs of the Battle of Bacolod.* n.p., [1903].

Reports of Military Observers Attached to the Armies in Manchuria during the Russo-Japanese War. 5 parts. Washington, D. C., 1906–07.

The Sombrero [University of Nebraska Yearbook]: 1892, 1894.

U. S. Congress. Senate. Committee on Armed Services and the Committee on Foreign Relations. *Hearings on the Military Situation in the Far East.* 82d Cong., 1st Sess., 1951.

U. S. Congress. Senate. Committee on Foreign Affairs. *Investigation of Mexican Affairs.* 66th Cong., 2d Sess., 1920.

U. S. Department of State. *Papers Relating to the Foreign Relations of the United States: 1916–17.*

————. *Papers Relating to the Foreign Relations of the United States: The Lansing Papers, 1914–1920.* 2 vols. Washington, D. C., 1939–40.

The University of Nebraska. *Catalogue, 1892.* Lincoln, 1892.

————. *The Colleges, Courses of Study, Departments of Instruction, 1894–95.* Lincoln, 1894.

————. *Twelfth Biennial Report, Board of Regents.* Lincoln, 1894.

Published Primary Articles

Brent, Charles H. "Tutoring the Philippines," *Yale Review*, VI (July, 1917), 715–26.

Bullard, R. L. "Road Building Among the Moros," *The Atlantic Monthly*, XCII (Dec., 1903), 818–26.

Canfield, Dorothy. "A General in the Making," *The Red Cross Magazine*, XIV (Sep., 1919), 19–23, 66–68.

Collins, James L. "The Battle of Bud Bagsak and the Part Played by the Mountain Guns Therein," *Field Artillery Journal*, XV (Nov.-Dec., 1925), 559–70.

Cramer, Stuart W., Jr. "The Punitive Expedition from Boquillas," *Journal of the U. S. Cavalry Association*, XXVII (Nov., 1916), 200–27.

Dallam, Samuel F. "The Punitive Expedition of 1916: Some Problems and Experiences of a Troop Commander," *The Cavalry Journal*, XXXVI (July, 1927), 382–98.

Dunn, Robert. "With Pershing's Cavalry," *Collier's*, Sep. 23, 1916, 8–9, 25–26, 28.

Elser, Frank B. "General Pershing's Mexican Campaign," *The Century*, IC (Feb., 1920), 433–47.

————. "Pershing's Lost Cause," *The American Legion Monthly*, XIV (July, 1932), 14–15, 44–47.

"Field Notes from Mexico and Border," *Journal of the U. S. Cavalry Association*, XXVII (Nov., 1916), 171–82.

Gorrell, Edgar S. "Why Riding Boots Sometimes Irritate an Aviator's Feet," *U. S. Air Services*, XVII (Oct., 1932), 24–30.

Hayward, William. "Cut Up Pershing's Breeches," *Boston Sunday Globe*, Aug. 5, 1917.

Howe, Jerome W. "Campaigning in Mexico, 1916," *Journal of Arizona History*, VII (Autumn, 1966), 123–37.

————. "Chasing Villa," *Journal of the Worcester Polytechnic Institute*, XIX (July, 1916), 380–87.

Landor, A. Henry Savage. "Experience in the Philippines," *Harper's Weekly*, May 14, 1904, 760–62.

MacArthur, Douglas. "Reminiscences," *Life*, Jan. 17, 1964, 54–59; Jan. 24, 1964, 66–74.

Morey, Lewis, S. "The Cavalry Fight at Carrizal," *Journal of the U. S. Cavalry Association*, XXVII (Jan., 1917), 449–56.

Patton, George S., Jr. "Cavalry Work of the Punitive Expedition," *Journal of the U. S. Cavalry Association*, XXVII (Jan., 1917), 426–33.

Pershing, John J. "Competitions for 1889," *Journal of the U. S. Cavalry Association*, II (Dec., 1889), 420.

————. "Practical Patriotism," *Quartermaster Review*, II (July-Aug., 1923), 3–4.

————. "Stand by the Soldier," *The National Geographic Magazine*, XXXI (May, 1917), 457–59.

————. "The Things We Need Today," *The American Magazine*, CXIV (Dec., 1932), 18–19, 82, 84.

————. "To the Ages," *The American Legion Monthly*, XVI (June, 1934), 7–11, 40.

———. "We Are at War," *The American Magazine*, CXIII (June, 1932), 15–17, 72, 74.

"Philippine Islands. Jolo. Extract from a Letter of Father William McDonough, March 19, 1911," *Woodstock Letters*, XL, No. 3 (1911), 398–99.

Schneider, J. Thomas. "General Pershing and I," *The Saturday Evening Post*, Apr. 27, 1963, 70, 72, 74.

Shannon, James A. "With the Apache Scouts in Mexico," *Journal of the U.S. Cavalry Association*, XXVII (Apr., 1917), 539–57.

[Shaw, George C.] "Mixing with the Moros," *Arms and the Man*, Aug. 28, 1913, 433, 436.

Swift, Eben, Jr. "Experience in Mexico," *Journal of the U. S. Cavalry Association*, XXVII (Nov., 1916), 232–35.

"The Attack on Our Cavalry at Parral," *Journal of the U. S. Cavalry Association*, XXVII (Nov., 1916), 249–53.

Troxel, O. C. "The Tenth Cavalry in Mexico," *Journal of the U. S. Cavalry Association*, XXVIII (Oct., 1917), 199–208.

Williams, S. M. "The Cavalry Fight at Ojo Azules," *Journal of the U. S. Cavalry Association*, XXVII (Jan., 1917), 405–408.

Worcester, Dean C. "The Non-Christian People of the Philippine Islands," *The National Geographic Magazine*, XXIV (Nov., 1913), 1158–1256.

Published Secondary Works

Addresses at the Unveiling of the Portrait of General John J. Pershing Upon the Occasion of the Opening of the Army War College. Washington, D. C., 1924.

Allen, Douglas. *Frederic Remington and the Spanish-American War*. New York, 1971.

Andrews, Peter. *In Honored Glory: The Story of Arlington*. New York, 1966.

The Army War College: A Brief Narrative, 1901–1952. Carlisle Barracks, Pa., 1952.

Azoy, A. C. M. *Charge!: The Story of the Battle of San Juan Hill*. New York, 1961.

Baclagon, Uldarico S. *Philippine Campaigns*. Manila, 1952.

Baker, Ray Stannard. *Woodrow Wilson: Life and Letters*. Vol. VI, Garden City, N. Y., 1937.

Baldwin, Alice. *Memoirs of the Late Frank D. Baldwin*. Los Angeles, 1929.

Beaver, Daniel R. *Newton D. Baker and the American War Effort, 1917–1919*. Lincoln, Neb., 1966.

Bemis, Samuel F. *A Diplomatic History of the United States*. 5th ed. New York, 1965.

Bernardo, C. Joseph, and Bacon, Eugene H. *American Military Policy: Its Development Since 1775*. Harrisburg, Pa., 1957.

Blount, James H. *The American Occupation of the Philippines, 1898–1912.* New York, 1913.

Braddy, Haldeen. *Cock of the Walk: The Legend of Pancho Villa.* Albuquerque, N. M., 1955.

———. *Pershing's Mission in Mexico.* El Paso, Tex., 1966.

Brenner, Anita. *Idols Behind Altars.* New York, 1929.

Brimlow, George F. *Cavalryman Out of the West: Life of General William Carey Brown.* Caldwell, Idaho, 1944.

Brininstool, Earl A. *Fighting Indian Warriors.* Harrisburg, Pa., 1953.

Brown, Dee. *Bury My Heart at Wounded Knee.* New York, 1971.

Calero, Manuel. *The Mexican Policy of President Woodrow Wilson as It Appears to a Mexican.* New York, 1916.

Carter, William H. *Creation of the American General Staff.* Washington, D. C., 1924.

———. *From Yorktown to Santiago with the Sixth U. S. Cavalry.* Baltimore, 1900.

———. *The Life of Lieutenant General Chaffee.* Chicago, 1917.

Cashin, Herschel V. *et. al. Under Fire with the Tenth U. S. Cavalry.* New York, 1899.

The Centennial of the United States Military Academy at West Point, New York, 1802–1902. 2 vols. Washington, D. C., 1904.

Chadwick, French Ensor. *The Relations of the United States and Spain: The Spanish-American War.* 2 vols. New York, 1911.

Chandler, Melbourne C. *Of Garry Owen in Glory: The History of the Seventh United States Cavalry Regiment.* [Annadale?], Va., 1960.

Clendenen, Clarence C. *The United States and Pancho Villa: A Study in Unconventional Diplomacy.* Ithaca, N. Y., 1961.

———. *Blood on the Border.* New York, 1969.

Cloman, Sydney A. *Myself and a Few Moros.* New York, 1923.

Cline, Howard F. *The United States and Mexico.* Rev. ed. New York, 1963.

Coffman, Edward M. *The Hilt of the Sword: The Career of Peyton C. March.* Madison, Wisc., 1966.

———. *The War To End All Wars: The American Military Experience in World War I.* New York, 1968.

Colby, Elbridge. *American Militarism.* Washington, D. C., 1934.

Compendium of History and Biography of Linn County, Missouri. Chicago, 1912.

Cosmas, Graham A. *An Army for Empire.* Columbia, Mo., 1971.

Cramer, Clarence H. *Newton D. Baker: A Biography.* Cleveland, 1961.

Cullum, George W. *Biographical Register of the Officers and Graduates of the U. S. Military Academy at West Point, N. Y.* 3d ed. Vol. III and IV. Boston, 1891.

Deutrich, Mabel E. *Struggle for Supremacy: The Career of General Fred C. Ainsworth.* Washington, D. C., 1962.

Downey, Fairfax. *Indian-Fighting Army.* New York, 1941.

Drury, John. *Historic Midwest Houses.* Minneapolis, 1947.

Dupuy, R. Ernest. *The Compact History of the United States Army.* New York, 1956.

————. *Men of West Point: The First 150 Years of the United States Military Academy.* New York, 1951.

————. *Where They Have Trod: The West Point Tradition in American Life.* New York, 1940.

Dupuy, R. Ernest, and Dupuy, Trevor N. *Brave Men and Great Captains.* New York, 1959.

Editors of the Army Times. *The Yanks Are Coming: The Story of General John J. Pershing.* New York, 1960.

————. *Warrior: The Story of General George S. Patton.* New York, 1967.

Elliott, Charles B. *The Philippines to the End of the Commission Government: A Study in Tropical Democracy.* Indianapolis, 1917.

Ellis, Edward S. *The Indian Wars of the United States.* Grand Rapids, Mich., 1892.

Emmett, Cris. *In the Path of Events with Colonel Martin Labor Crimmins, Soldier, Naturalist, Historian.* Waco, Texas, 1959.

Esposito, Vincent J. (ed.) *The West Point Atlas of American Wars.* 2 vols. New York, 1959.

Farago, Ladislas. *Patton: Ordeal and Triumph.* New York, 1964.

Finegan, Philip M., S. J. *Fr. William M. McDonough, S. J.: A Sketch.* n.p., *ca.* 1926.

Fitzgibbons, Russell H. *Cuba and the United States, 1900–1935.* Menasha, Wisc., 1935.

Fleming, Thomas J. *West Point: The Men and Times of the United States Military Academy.* New York, 1969.

Follmer, Harry R. *Footprints on the Sands of Times; Memoirs.* 9 vols. in 12. n.p., [1950?] –53.

Forbes, William Cameron. *The Philippine Islands.* 2 vols. Boston, 1928.

Forman, Sidney. *West Point: A History of the United States Military Academy.* New York, 1950.

Fort Lesley J. McNair, Washington, D. C.: A Brief History of the Post. Washington, D. C., [1950].

Freidel, Frank. *The Splendid Little War.* Boston, 1958.

Frye, William. *Marshall, Citizen Soldier.* Indianapolis, 1947.

Fuller, J. F. C. *Decisive Battles of the U. S. A.* New York, 1953.

Ganoe, William Addleman. *The History of the United States Army.* Rev. ed. New York, 1942.

————. *Soldier Unmasked.* Harrisburg, Pa., 1939.

Gibbons, Edward. *Floyd Gibbons, Your Headline Hunter.* New York, 1953.

Glass, E. L. N. (comp. and ed.) *The History of the Tenth Cavalry, 1866–1921.* n.p., 1921.

Godson, William F. H., Jr. *The History of West Point, 1852–1905.* Philadelphia, 1934.

Grunder, Garel A., and Livezey, William E. *The Philippines and the United States.* Norman, Okla., 1951.

Guzmán, Martín L. *Memoirs of Pancho Villa.* Austin, Tex., 1965.

Hagedorn, Hermann. *Leonard Wood: A Biography.* 2 vols. New York, 1931.

Hans, Frederic M. *The Great Sioux Nation.* Minneapolis, 1964.

Harris, Larry A. *Pancho Villa and the Columbus Raid.* El Paso, Texas, 1949.

Hatch, Alden. *George Patton: General in Spurs.* New York, 1950.

Herr, John K., and Wallace, Edward S. *The Story of the U. S. Cavalry, 1775–1942.* Boston, 1953.

Hill, Jim Dan. *The Minute Man in Peace and War: A History of the National Guard.* Harrisburg, Pa., 1964.

Hines, Calvin W. *The Mexican Punitive Expedition of 1916.* San Antonio, Texas, 1962.

The History of Linn County, Missouri. Kansas City, Mo., 1882.

History of the Military Department, University of Nebraska, 1876–1941. Lincoln, Neb., 1942.

Hobbs, William H. *Leonard Wood: Administrator, Soldier, and Citizen.* New York, 1920.

Hoyer, Eva Hood. *Sixteen Exceptional Americans: Biographical Sketches.* New York, 1959.

Hunt, Frazier. *The Untold Story of Douglas MacArthur.* New York, 1954.

Hunt, George A. *The History of the Twenty-Seventh Infantry.* Honolulu, 1931.

James, D. Clayton. *The Years of MacArthur:* Volume I, 1880–1941. Boston, 1970.

Johnson, Edward A. *History of Negro Soldiers in the Spanish-American War.* Raleigh, N. C., 1899.

Johnson, John Reuben. *Representative Nebraskans.* Lincoln, Neb., 1954.

Johnson, Virginia W. *Unregimented General: A Biography of Nelson A. Miles.* Boston, 1962.

Johnson, Willis Fletcher. *Life of Sitting Bull and History of the Indian War of 1890–'91.* n.p., 1891.

Keenan, George. *Campaigning in Cuba.* New York, 1899.

King, James T. *War Eagle: A Life of General Eugene A. Carr.* Lincoln, Neb., 1963.

Krieger, Herbert W. *The Collection of Primitive Weapons and Armor of the Philippine Islands in the United States National Museum.* Washington, D. C., 1926.

Law, Frederick Houk. *Modern Great Americans.* New York, 1926.

Leech, Margaret. *In the Days of McKinley.* New York, 1959.

Leach, Paul R. *That Man Dawes.* Chicago, 1930.

Leopold, Richard W. *Elihu Root and the Conservative Tradition.* Boston, 1954.

LeRoy, James A. *The Americans in the Philippines: A History of the Conquest and the First Years of Occupation with an Introductory Account of the Spanish Rule.* 2 vols. Boston, 1914.

Liddell Hart, B. H. *Reputations Ten Years After.* Boston, 1928.

Link, Arthur S. *Woodrow Wilson and the Progressive Era, 1910–1917.* New York, 1954.

———. *Wilson*. Vol. III: *The Struggle for Neutrality, 1914–15*. Princeton, 1960. Vol. IV: *Confusions and Crises, 1915–16*. Princeton, 1964. Vol. V: *Campaign for Progressivism and Peace*, Princeton, 1965.

Lockmiller, Davis A. *Enoch H. Crowder: Soldier, Lawyer and Statesman*. Columbia, Mo., 1955.

Lodge, Henry Cabot. *The War with Spain*. New York, 1899.

Löhndorff, Ernst F. *Bestie Ich in Mexiko. Wahre Erlebnisse*. Bremen, 1927.

Lynk, Miles V. *The Black Troopers, or the Darking Heroism of the Negro Soldiers in the Spanish-American War*. Jackson, Tenn., 1899.

McCracken, Harold. *Pershing: The Story of a Great Soldier*. New York. 1931.

The Man Who Dared To Be Different. Laclede, Mo., 1958.

Manley, Robert N. *Centennial History of the University of Nebraska*. Lincoln, 1969.

Margo, Dr. A. *Who, Where, and Why Is Villa?* New York, n.d.

Marshall, S. L. A. *Men Against Fire*. New York, 1966.

Mason, Herbert M., Jr. *The Great Pursuit*. New York, 1970.

Matthews, William, and Wector, Dixon. *Our Soldiers Speak, 1775–1918*. Boston, 1943.

Mellor, William Bancroft. *Patton: Fighting Man*. New York, 1946.

Merrill, James M. *Spurs to Glory*. Chicago, 1966.

Millis, Walter. *Arms and Men, A Study in American Military History*. New York, 1956.

———. *The Martial Spirit: A Study of Our War With Spain*. Boston, 1931.

Miller, David Humphreys. *Ghost Dance*. New York, 1959.

Nelson, William H., and Vandiver, Frank E. *Fields of Glory: An Illustrated Narrative of American Land Warfare*. New York, 1970.

O'Connor, Richard. *Black Jack Pershing*. Garden City, N. Y., 1961.

O'Laughlin, John Callan. *Pershing*. New York, 1928.

Olson, James C. *J. Sterling Morton*. Lincoln, Neb., 1942.

Palmer, Frederick. *Bliss, Peacemaker*. New York, 1934.

———. *John J. Pershing, General of the Armies: A Biography*. Harrisburg, Pa., 1948.

———. *Newton D. Baker: America at War*. 2 vols. New York, 1931.

Palmer, John McAuley. *America in Arms: The Experience of the United States with Military Organization*. New Haven, 1941.

———. *Washington, Lincoln, Wilson: Three War Statesmen*. New York, 1930.

Pappas, George S. *Prudens Futuri: The U. S. Army War College, 1901–1967*. Carlisle Barracks, Pa., 1967.

Perry, Milton F., and Parke, Barbara W. *Patton and His Pistols*. Harrisburg, 1957.

Pershing, Edgar Jamison. *The Pershing Family in America: A Collection of Historical and Genealogical Data, Family Portraits, Traditions, Legends and Military Records*. Philadelphia, 1924.

Pier, Arthur S. *American Apostles to the Philippines*. Boston, 1950.

Pinchon, Edgcumb. *Viva Villa! A Recovery of the Real Pancho Villa*. New York, 1933.

Pogue, Forest C. *George C. Marshall: Education of a General, 1880–1939.* New York, 1963.

Portrait and Biographical Record of Clay, Ray, Carroll, Chariton and Linn Counties, Missouri. Chicago, 1893.

Reeder, Red. *Heroes and Leaders of West Point.* New York, 1970.

Reeves, Ira L. *Military Education in the United States.* Burlington, [Vt.?], 1914.

Reinhardt, George C., and Kintner, William R. *The Haphazard Years: How America Has Gone to War.* Garden City, N. Y., 1960.

Richardson, Robert Charlwood, Jr. *West Point: An Intimate Picture of the National Military Academy and of the Life of the Cadet.* New York, 1917.

Rodney, George Brydges. *As a Cavalryman Remembers.* Caldwell, Idaho, 1944.

Romney, Thomas C. *The Mormon Colonies in Mexico.* Salt Lake City, 1938.

Saleeby, Najeeb M. *The Moro Problem: An Academic Discussion of the History and Solution of the Problem of the Government of the Moros of the Philippine Islands.* Manila, 1913.

Sargent, Herbert H. *The Campaign of Santiago de Cuba.* 3 vols. Chicago, 1907.

Schmitt, Martin F., and Dee Brown. *Fighting Indians of the West.* New York, 1948.

Schuster, Ernest Otto. *Pancho Villa's Shadow.* New York, 1947.

Sears, Joseph H. *The Career of Leonard Wood.* New York, 1919.

Semi-Centennial Anniversary Book, The University of Nebraska, 1869–1919. Lincoln, Neb., 1919.

Semmes, Harry H. *Portrait of Patton.* New York, 1955.

Sexton, William Thaddeus. *Soldiers in the Sun: An Adventure in Imperialism.* Harrisburg, Pa., 1939.

Shively, James R. (ed.). *Writings from Willa Cather's Campus Years.* Lincoln, Neb., 1950.

Shoemaker, Robert H., and Paris, Leonard A. *Famous American Generals.* New York, 1946.

Simmons, Lucy. *History of Northeast Missouri State Teachers College.* Kirksville, Mo., 1927.

Sixty-seventh Annual Report of the Association of Graduates of the United States Military Academy at West Point, New York, June 11, 1936. Newburgh, N. Y., [1936].

Smith, Dale O. *U. S. Military Doctrine: A Study and Appraisal.* New York, 1955.

Smith, Daniel M. *Robert Lansing and American Neutrality, 1914–1917.* Berkeley, 1958.

Society of Santiago de Cuba. *The Santiago Campaign.* Richmond, Va., 1927.

Spaulding, Oliver Lyman. *The United States Army in War and Peace.* New York, 1937.

Steele, Matthew Forney. *American Campaigns.* 2 vols. Washington, D. C., 1909.

Stevens, Louis, *Here Comes Pancho Villa: The Anecdotal History of a Genial Killer.* New York, 1930.

Steward, T. G. *The Colored Regulars in the United States Army.* Philadelphia, 1904.

Sullivan, Mark. *Our Times: The United States, 1900–1925.* Vol. II: *America Finding Herself.* New York, 1927.

Swarthout, Glendon. *They Came to Cordura.* New York, 1959.

Teitelbaum, Louis M. *Woodrow Wilson and the Mexican Revolution, 1913–1916.* New York, 1967.

Thomas, Robert S. and Allen, Inez V. *The Mexican Punitive Expedition.* Washington, D. C., 1954.

Thompson, Jay A. *The Columbus, N. M. Raid on the 13th U. S. Cavalry on Thursday, March 9, 1916, by Poncho* [*sic.*] *Villa and His Mexican Bandits.* n.p., n.d.

Thweatt, Hiram H. (comp.). *What the Newspapers Say of the Negro Soldier in the Spanish-American War and the Return of the 10th Cavalry.* 2d ed., n.p., n.d.

Timmons, Bascom N. *Portrait of an American: Charles G. Dawes.* New York, 1953.

Todd, Frederick P. *Cadet Gray: A Pictorial History of Life at West Point as Seen through Its Uniforms.* New York, 1955.

Tomlinson, Everett T. *Story of General Pershing.* New York, 1919.

Tompkins, Frank. *Chasing Villa: The Story Behind the Story of Pershing's Expedition into Mexico.* Harrisburg, Pa., 1934.

Toulmin, Harry Aubrey, Jr. *With Pershing in Mexico.* Harrisburg, Pa., 1935.

Turner, Timothy G. *Bullets, Bottles and Gardinias.* Dallas, 1935.

Utley, Robert M. *The Last Days of the Sioux Nation.* New Haven, Conn., 1963.

USAF Historical Division. *The United States Army Air Arm, April 1861 to April 1917.* USAF Historical Studies: No. 98. [San Antonio], 1958.

Vandiver, Frank E. *John J. Pershing.* Morristown, N.J., 1967.

————*John J. Pershing and the Anatomy of Leadership.* U. S. Air Force Academy, Colorado, 1963.

Vestal, Stanley. *New Sources of Indian History, 1850–1891.* Norman, Okla., 1934.

Violette, E. M. *History of the First District State Normal School, Kirksville, Missouri.* Kirksville, 1905.

Vivian, Thomas J. *The Fall of Santiago.* New York, 1898.

Wagner, Arthur L. *Report of the Santiago Campaign, 1898.* Kansas City, Mo., 1908.

Waugh, Elizabeth Day. *West Point.* New York, 1944.

Wellard, James. *General George S. Patton, Jr.: Man Under Mars.* New York, 1946.

Wellman, Paul I. *Death on the Prairie: The Thirty Years' Struggle for the Western Plains.* New York, 1934.

Register of Graduates and Former Cadets, United States Military Academy. New York, 1953.

Weigley, Russell F. *The History of the United States Army.* New York, 1967.

West Point Sesquicentennial, 1802–1952. Buffalo, 1952.

Wharfield, H. B. *Tenth Cavalry and Border Fights.* El Cajon, Cal., 1965.

White, John R. *Bullets and Bolos: Fifteen Years in the Philippine Islands.* New York, 1928.

Whitman, S. E. *The Troopers: An Informal History of the Plains Cavalry, 1865–1890.* New York, 1962.

Williams, T. Harry. *Americans at War: The Development of the American Military System.* n.p., 1960.

Wiltsey, Norman B. *Brave Warriors.* Caldwell, Id., 1963.

Wolff, Leon. *Little Brown Brothers.* New York, 1961.

Worcester, Dean C. *The Philippines Past and Present.* New York, 1930.

Wormser, Richard. *The Yellowlegs: The Story of the United States Cavalry.* Garden City, N. Y., 1966.

Zabriskie, Alexander C. *Bishop Brent: Crusader for Christian Unity.* Philadelphia, 1948.

Zaide, Gregorio F. *Philippine History and Civilization.* Manila, *ca.* 1939.

———. *Political and Social History of the Philippines.* 2 vols. Manila, 193[5?].

Published Secondary Articles

"A Continuing Mexican Trouble," *World's Work,* Vol. 37 (June, 1916), 137–138.

"A Pacifist Secretary of War," *Literary Digest,* LII (Mar. 18, 1916), 701.

Adams, Cyrus C. "Northern Mexico, the Scene of Our Amy's Hunt for Villa," *Review of Reviews,* LIII (Apr., 1916), 421–23.

Andrews, Marshall. "Our 1st Aerial Combat Force," *Washington* [D. C.] *Sunday Post,* May 26, 1929, 6–7.

Archer, Jules. "Woodrow Wilson's Dirty Little War," *Mankind,* I (Feb., 1968), 44–55.

Bellah, James Warner. "Gen. Pershing Stood Alone," *Army-Navy-Air Force Register,* Sep. 17, 1960, 24–25.

———. "A Tribute to John J. Pershing," *The American Legion Magazine,* LXIX (Aug., 1960), 10–11, 49–51.

" 'Black Jack' Pershing Knew What He Wanted," *The Literary Digest,* Apr. 21, 1928, 34, 36.

Braddy, Haldeen. "Myths of Pershing's Mexican Campaign," *Southern Folklore Quarterly,* XXVII (Sep., 1963), 181–85.

———. "Pancho Villa at Columbus: The Raid of 1916 Restudied," *Southwestern Studies,* III (Spring, 1965), 1–43.

———. "Pancho Villa's Capitulation: An Inside Look," *Password,* I (Spring, 1969), 9–12.

———. "Revolution: Agony South of the Border," *Montana,* XIX (Oct., 1969), 32–45.

Briscoe, Edward E. "Pershing's Chinese Refugees in Texas," *Southwestern Historical Quarterly,* LXII (Apr., 1959), 467–88.

Britton, Rollin J. "Joseph H. Burrows," *The Missouri Historical Review*, XXII (Oct., 1927), 3–12.

Bryan, Howard. "A Close Call," *The Albuquerque Tribune*, Nov. 15, 1969, 1.

Burdick, Eugene. "Journey across the Pacific," *Holiday*, XXVIII (Oct., 1960), 52–60, 70–74, 82–86, 94–98, 105–108, 110–13, 115–17, 119, 132–33, 135, 137–39, 142–43, 145–57.

Bye, George T. "John Joseph Pershing, Typical American," *The Landmark*, I (June, 1919), 348–50.

"C. in C. to the C.-in-C." *The American Legion Magazine*, XXVI (Feb., 1939), 32–34, 57–59.

"Captain Pershing." *Munsey's Magazine*, XXX (Oct. 1903), 43–46.

Carll, George S., Jr. "Americans Remember 'Black Jack' Pershing," *Army-Navy-Air Force Register*, Sep. 17, 1960, 23.

"Carranza Mentions the Door," *Literary Digest*, LII (June 10, 1916), 1689–1690.

Clendenen, Clarence C. "The Punitive Expedition of 1916: A Re-evaluation," *Arizona and the West*, III (Winter, 1961), 311–20.

Coffman, Edward. "Army Life on the Frontier, 1865–98," *Military Affairs*, XX (Winter, 1956), 193–201.

Connolly, C. P. "Senator Warren of Wyoming," *Collier's*, Aug. 31, 1912, 10–11, 30.

Cosmas, Graham. "Military Reform After the Spanish-American War: The Army Reorganization Fight of 1898–1899," *Military Affairs*, XXXV (Feb., 1971), 12–18.

De Weerd, H. A. "Pershing and the Anvil Chorus," *Infantry Journal*, XLIII (Mar.–Apr., 1936), 99–103.

"Drifting Toward Intervention in Mexico," *Literary Digest*, LII (May 27, 1916), 1515–1517.

Eliot, Charles A. "The Early Days of the Pershing Rifles," *The Pershing Rifleman*, IV (May, 1935), 6–7.

"End of the Chase after Villa," *Current Opinion*, LX (May, 1916), 304–05.

Epperson, Ivan H. "Missourians Abroad. No. 1. Major General John J. Pershing," *The Missouri Historical Review*, XI (April-July, 1917), 313–23.

Ferrard, Eugene A., Jr. "Early Educational Experiences of General Pershing," *USAF Instruction Journal*, III (July, 1965), 21.

[Finegan, Philip M., S. J.] "Father McDonough in the Philippines," *Woodstock Letters*, LVI (Oct., 1927), *11–*32.

Fleming, Thomas J. "Pershing's Island War," *American Heritage* (August, 1968), 32–35, 101–04.

"Flying into Mexico," *Literary Digest*, LII (April 15, 1916), 1103.

Forman, Sidney. "Lessons in Leadership: John J. Pershing," *The Military Engineer*, XLIX (March–April, 1957), 105.

"Funston and Pershing, the Generals in Charge of the Chase after Villa." *Current Opinion*, LX (May, 1916), 318–20.

"General Pershing and the Red Cross," *The Red Cross Magazine*, XII (May, 1917), 173.

"General Pershing at 81 Reminds Americans that Their Army Can Be Great," *Life*, Sep. 29, 1941, 62.

"Gen. Pershing Fulfilled His Ancestor's Hope," *The Missouri Historical Review*, XIII (July, 1919), 356.

Ginsburgh, Robert. "Pershing as His Orderlies Know Him," *The American Legion Monthly*, V (Oct., 1928), 9–11, 64–68; (Nov., 1928), 12–15, 52–57.

Greenway, John. "The Ghost Dance," *American West*, VI (July, 1969), 42–47.

Hervier Paul–Louis. "American Silhouettes," *The Living Age* (Sep. 21, 1918), 744–47.

Hines, Calvin W. "First Aero Squadron in Mexico," *American Aviation Historical Society Journal*, X (Fall, 1965), 190–97.

Hoffmann, Charles W. "The Final Saga of Our Horse Cavalry," *The Westerners Brand Book*, VIII (1959), 15–22.

Hopper, James. "What Happened at Columbus," *Collier's* (Apr. 15, 1916), 11–12, 32, 34, 36–37.

———. "A Little Mexican Expedition," *Collier's*, LVII (July 15, 1916), 1–2, 22–24.

———. "Browsing on the Border," *Collier's*, LVII (May 27, 1916), 1–2, 27, 30–32.

———. "Pancho Villa," *Collier's*, LVII (April 29, 1916), 8–10, 43–46.

———. "Twin Towns on the Border," *Collier's*, LVII (Aug. 19, 1916), 1–3, 27–38.

———. "Wilson and the Border," *Collier's*, LVII (July 8, 1916), 7–8, 23–25.

Hughes, Rupert. "The Big Hike," *Collier's*, LVIII (Nov. 11, 1916), 5–6, 24–26, 28.

———. "The Case of the National Guard," *Collier's*, LVII (May 20, 1916), 7–8, 31–32.

James, Marquis. "Pershing," *The American Legion Magazine*, XLV (Sep., 1948), 30, 33.

Jeffrey, Arthur A. "He Understands Pershing," *Everybody's Magazine*, XL (May, 1919), 80.

Jenkins, Burris A. "Seven Places of Birth," *Kansas City Star* (Missouri), July 9, 1918.

Johnson, J. R. "Colonel John Miller Stotsenburg: A Man of Valor," *Nebraska History*, L (Winter, 1969), 339–57

Johnson, Thomas M. "Boys, We Had Him Wrong!" *The American Magazine*, CV (May, 1928), 11–13, 78, 80, 82, 84, 86, 88.

Liddell Hart, B. H. "Pershing," *The Atlantic Monthly*, CXL (Aug., 1927), 166–77.

"Life of the Border–A Guardsman's Letter," *Outlook*, CXIII (Aug. 23, 1916), 946–947.

Loth, David. "The Charge Up San Juan Hill," *The American Legion Magazine* (Feb., 1970), 28–32, 46, 48–49.

MacAdam, George. "The Life of General Pershing," *The World's Work,* Vol. 37 (Nov., 1918–Apr., 1919), 42–56, 161–72, 281–93, 449–61, 539–36, 681–97; Vol. 38 (May, June, and Sep., 1919), 86–103, 148–58, 537–52.

McClernand, E. J. "The Santiago Campaign," *Infantry Journal,* XXI (Sep., 1922), 280–302.

Mahoney, Tom. "The Columbus Raid," *Southwest Review,* XVII (Jan., 1932), 161–71.

———. "When Villa Raided New Mexico," *The American Legion Monthly,* LXXVII (Sep., 1964), 10–11, 40, 42–44.

"Making Over the Army of the United States," *Current Opinion,* LX (May, 1916), 308–11.

Markey, D. John. "That Was Pershing," *American Legion Magazine,* XLVI (Jan., 1949), 28–29, 34–36, 38–39.

Marshall, George C. "John Joseph Pershing," *Assembly,* VIII (Apr., 1940), 6–8.

Marshall, S. L. A. "Pershing Fought Grief Under the Desert Stars," *The Detroit News,* Jan. 8, 1931, 1–2.

Marvin, George. "Bandits and the Borderland," *World's Work,* Vol. 32 (Oct., 1916), 656–663.

———. "Invasion or Intervention?" *World's Work,* Vol. 32 (May, 1916), 40–62.

———. "The First Line of Defense in Mexico," *World's Work,* Vol. 32 (Aug., 1916), 416–424.

———. "The Quick and the Dead on the Border," *World's Work,* Vol. 32 (Jan., 1917), 295–311.

Mason, Gregory. "Mexico—From the Inside Looking Out," *Outlook,* CXIII (May 10, 1916), 92–96.

———. "Our Citizens in Arms," *Outlook,* CXIII (July 5, 1916), 546–549.

"Messages from Mexico," *World's Work,* Vol. 32 (Aug., 1916), 430–436.

"Mexico and the Militia," *Outlook,* CXIII (May 31, 1916), 233–234.

Mills, Elizabeth H. "The Mormon Colonies in Chihuahua after the 1912 Exodus," *New Mexico Historical Review,* XXIX (July and Oct., 1954) 165–182, 290–310.

Minnigerode, Fitzhugh Lee. "General John J. Pershing," *Current History,* XXXIV (May, 1931), 175–78.

———. "General Pershing Still on Duty for the Nation," *The New York Times Magazine,* Apr. 4, 1937, 4, 26, 28.

Mooney, James. "The Ghost-Dance Religion and the Sioux Outbreak of 1890," *Fourteenth Annual Report of the Bureau of Ethnology to the Secretary of the Smithsonian Institution, 1892–93.* Part 2. Washington, D. C., 1896, 641–1136.

Munch, Francis J. "Villa's Columbus Raid: Practical Politics or German Design?" *New Mexico Historical Review,* XLIV (July, 1969), 189–214.

"Notes on Campaigning in Mexico," *Journal of the U. S. Cavalry Association,* XXVII (July, 1916), 63–66.

O'Connor, Richard. " 'Black Jack' of the 10th," *American Heritage,* XVIII (Feb., 1967), 14–17, 102–107.

"Old Soldier," *Time,* Nov. 15, 1943, 55–56, 58, 60.

"Our Unprepared Militia," *Literary Digest,* LII (June 3, 1916), 1617.

"Our Unpreparedness Revealed by Villa," *Literary Digest,* LII (Apr. 1, 1916), 883–886.

Palmer, Frederick. "John J. Pershing—Plower," *Collier's,* May 3, 1919, 5–6, 30, 32, 34, 36–37.

———. "Pershing at 75: The Story of a Soldier," *The New York Times Magazine,* Sep. 8, 1935, 4–5, 13.

Perrenot, Earle E. "The National Guard Fiasco," *Out West,* XLIV (Aug., 1916), 79–81.

"Pershing, a Great Soldier of the Republic," *The Literary Digest,* Sep. 27, 1919, 39–42, 46.

"Pershing Collection of Philippines and South American Curios Given to Smithsonian," *Hobbies,* LV (January, 1951), 145.

"Pershing's 'Jinx' Birthday, and Something about His Boyhood," *The Literary Digest,* Sep. 7, 1918, 58–59, 61–62, 64.

Platt, Rutherford H. "There Was a Captain by the Name of Pershing," *The World's Work,* Vol. 67 (Dec., 1923), 181–85.

Porter, John A. "The Punitive Expedition," *The Quartermaster Review,* XII (Jan.–Feb., 1933), 19–30.

Ranson, Edward. "Nelson A. Miles as Commanding General, 1895–1903," *Military Affairs,* XXIX (Winter, 1965–66), 179–200.

Reilly, Henry J. "Cavalry in Modern War," *Journal of the U. S. Cavalry Association,* XXVII (Nov., 1916), 294–97.

Richardson, J. Stewart. "Pershing, in Spirit, Is Again Over There," *The New York Times Magazine,* Aug. 13, 1944, 44–46.

Richardson, W. P. "Some Observations Upon the Sioux Campaign of 1890–91," *Journal of the Military Service Institution,* XVIII (May, 1896), 512–31.

Rippy, J. Fred. "Some Precedents of the Pershing Expedition into Mexico," *Southwestern Historical Quarterly,* XXIV (Apr., 1921), 292–316.

Sandos, James A. "German Involvement in Northern Mexico, 1915–1916: A New Look at the Columbus Raid," *The Hispanic American Historical Review,* L (Feb., 1970), 70–88.

Savage, Laird. "Fort Wingate," *New Mexico,* XXXVIII (Aug., 1960), 32–33, 37–39.

Sawyer, Robert K. "Viva Villa," *Military Review,* XLI (Aug., 1961), 60–75.

Scrimsher, Lila G. "General Pershing's Love Story," *Sunday World–Herald Magazine* (Omaha), (July 29, 1962), 8, 10.

Shane, Ted. "These Are the Generals—Patton," *The Saturday Evening Post,* Feb. 6, 1943, 19, 81–82.

Shaw, W. B. "Pershing on the Trail," *Review of Reviews,* LIII (April, 1916), 419–21.

Sherman, K. L. "Pershing and a World Peace," *Survey Graphic,* XXIX (Nov., 1940), 551–54.

Simmons, Lucy and Selby, P. O. "The Northeast Missouri State Teachers College and Its Founder, Joseph Baldwin," *The Missouri Historical Review,* XXII (Jan., 1928), 157–170.

Smith, Richard W. "Philippine Constabulary," *Military Review,* XLVIII (May, 1968), 73–80.

Smythe, Donald, S. J. "Lt. John J. Pershing at the Grand Canyon," *Montana,* XIII (Apr., 1963), 11–23.

"Soldiering with Pershing in the Philippines," *The Literary Digest* (Nov. 17, 1928), 52–54.

Spring, Agnes W. "When the Last Trumpet Sounds," *True West,* XVII (May–June, 1970), 32–34, 56–59.

Stanley, Peter W. "William Cameron Forbes: Proconsul in the Philippines," *Pacific Historical Review,* XXXV (Aug., 1966), 285–301.

Stewart, William G. "Why Does This Area Grow Great Generals?" *Army,* XXI (June, 1971), 44–45.

Stivison, Roy E. and Della Mavity McDonnell. "When Villa Raided Columbus," *New Mexico Magazine,* XXVIII (Dec., 1950), 17–19, 37, 39, 41, 43, 45.

"The Columbus Raid," *Journal of the U. S. Cavalry Association,* XXVII (Apr., 1917), 490–96.

"The Motor Truck in Mexico," *Literary Digest,* LII (May 27, 1916), 1599.

"The National Guard Demonstrates Some Facts," *The World's Work,* Vol. 32 (Sep., 1916), 485–486.

"The Spirit of the Guardsman," *Outlook,* CXIII (Aug. 9, 1916), 815.

"The Story of the Week," *Independent* (July 3, 1916), 8.

"The Swearing in the Militia," *Literary Digest,* XLII (June 24, 1916), 1866–67.

Thomas, Rowland. "Pershing—United States Soldier," *The World's Work,* Vol. 13 (Nov., 1906), 8179–82.

Ueland, Alexander. "John J. Pershing, Crusader and Mason," *The New Age,* LXVIII (Dec., 1960), 19–23.

U.S. Congressional Record, 66th Cong., 1st Sess., 1919, LVIII, Part 5, 4463–68.

————. 91st Cong., 2d Sess. (Dec. 15, 1970), CXVI, No. 201, S 20151–52.

"Villa's American Allies," *Literary Digest,* LII (April 8, 1916), 951–954.

"Villa's Lesson," *World's Work,* Vol. 32 (May, 1916), 18.

Virden, John M. " 'Black Jack' Was All Soldier Every Day," *Army–Navy–Air Force Register and Defense Times,* Sep. 17, 1960, 28.

Wallace, Andrew. "The Sabre Retires: Pershing's Cavalry Campaign in Mexico, 1916," *The Smoke Signal,* No. 9 (Spring, 1966), 1–24.

Wallis, George A. "Pancho's Raid Not Forgotten," *Infantry,* LIII (July–Aug., 1963), 9–12.

"What To Do With Mexico," *Literary Digest,* LII (May 20, 1916), 1438–1440.

"What War with Mexico Means," *World's Work,* Vol. 32 (Aug., 1916), 425–430.

Wharfield, H. B. "The Affair at Carrizal," *Montana*, XVIII (Autumn, 1968), 24–39.

Wheeler, Harold F. "Pershing's Beautiful Marriage Romance," *Boston Sunday Post* (Jan. 19, 1919), 39–40.

———. "The Romance of General Pershing," *The Ladies Home Journal*, XXXVI (July, 1919), 7–8, 44.

"When Pershing Put Discipline into the 'Varsity Rifles.'" *The Literary Digest* (Apr. 5, 1919), 46, 48, 50.

"When 'Johnny Comes Marching Home' to Laclede, Missouri," *The Literary Digest* (Sep. 13, 1919), 70, 72.

"Who's Who—and Why," *The Saturday Evening Post* (Dec. 2, 1911), 27.

Wolff, Leon. "Black Jack's Mexican Goose Chase," *American Heritage*, XIII (June, 1962), 22–27, 100–106.

Young, Karl. "A Fight That Could Have Meant War," *The American West*, III (Spring, 1966), 16–23, 90.

Newspapers

General Pershing subscribed to a clipping service, with the result that the Pershing Papers in the Library of Congress contain more than a score of scrapbooks, each 200 pages, bulging with press clippings. Many of these are repetitive, covering the same event in different newspapers. Because of this, and because a list would be impossibly long, no formal listing of newspapers based on the Pershing Papers appears here.

Besides the above named collection, the following newspapers furnished material for this book:

The Army and Navy Journal, Apr. 2, 1910; Apr. 20, 1912; June 13, 1936; July 17, 24, 31 and Aug. 7, 1948.

The Army and Navy Journal of the Philippines (Manila), Aug. 9, 1913.

Army and Navy Register (Washington, D.C.), Jan. 28, 1905; Apr. 8, 1911.

The Baltimore News Post, Sep. 26, 1960.

The Baltimore Sun, Dec. 11, 1906; Jan. 27, 1929; Aug. 29, 1960.

Boston American, June 27, 1916.

Boston Sunday Globe, Aug. 5, 1917.

Boston Sunday Post, Nov., 1918–Feb., 1919.

Brookfield Argus (Mo.), July 16, 1948.

The Brookfield Gazette (Mo.), Sep. 29, 1917.

The Chicago Daily Tribune, Dec. 19, 1906; Nov. 28, 1916.

Cheyenne State Leader, Aug. 28–Sep. 1, 1915.

The Commercial Appeal (Memphis), Sep. 13, 1960.

The Daily News Bulletin (Brookfield, Mo.), Sep. 15, 1960.
The Denver News, June 1, 1912.
The Detroit News, Jan. 1–15, 1931; July 15–23, 1948; Sep. 11, 1960.
El Paso Herald, Sep. 8, 1915.
El Paso Herald Post, Mar. 14, 1961.
The Evening Missourian (Columbia, Mo.), Aug. 2, 1919.
Evening Post (New York), Dec. 20, 1906.
The Evening Star (Washington, D. C.), Aug. 26, 1899; Oct. 23, 1902; Sep. 12–13, 1960.
First Illinois Cavalryman (Brownsville, Tex.), July 22–Oct. 15, 1916.
Fond Du Lac Commonwealth Reporter (Wisc.), July 13, 1939.
Honolulu Star Bulletin, Jan. 30, Mar. 4, 10, 1931.
Indianapolis Star, July 4, 1927; Sep. 11, 1960.
Joplin Globe (Mo.), Feb. 24, 1918.
The Kansas City Star (Mo.), July 9, 1918; June 1, 1930; Jan. 11, 1931; July 18, 1948; Sep. 11, 1960.
Kansas City Times (Mo.), Sep. 9, 1930.
Laclede News (Mo.), Dec. 29, 1881.
Lake City Herald (Utah), Jan. 27, 1905.
Lincoln Morning Journal (Neb.), June 7, 1936.
Linneus Bulletin (Mo.), Oct. 27, 1881.
Los Angeles Examiner, May 4 and Oct. 13, 1916.
The Manila Times (Philippines), Oct. 22, 1902.
Milwaukee Sentinel, July 4, 1937.
Mindanao Daily Herald (Zamboanga, Philippines), Feb. 14, 1911 and June 21, 1913.
Missouri Ruralist (Fayette, Mo.), July 5, 1918.
The National Tribune–The Stars and Stripes (Washington, D.C.), Sep. 1, 8, 15, 1960.
New Orleans Times–Picayune, Aug. 28, 1915.
New York American, Mar. 11–April 30 and June 20–30, 1916.
New York Evening World, May 27, 1912.
New York Herald, Apr. 16, 1916.
New York Sun, Sep. 17, 1906; Aug. 2, 1914.
The New York Times, Aug. 30, 1882; July–Sep., 1883; June 3–13, 1886; Apr. 4–19 and May 5, 1916; Nov. 13, 1921; June 15, 1924; Mar. 6, 1936; Apr. 20, 1951; Sep. 12–13, 1960.
New York Tribune, Apr. 21, 1916.
Oklahoma City Times, Sep. 2, 1960.
The Omaha Daily Bee, June 13–21, 1892.
The Omaha Herald, Dec. 21, 1906.
Ottumwa Courier (Iowa), Jan. 24, 1931.
The Pittsburgh Post, Apr. 29, 1914.
Pointer View (West Point, N.Y.), Sep. 9, 16, 1960.
The Press (Philadelphia), Aug. 27, 1914.

Public Ledger (Philadelphia), Sep. 9, 1917.
Quincy Daily Herald (Ill.), May 18, 1918.
The Review (Laclede, Mo.), Sep. 13, 1960.
Richmond News Leader (Va.), Dec. 11, 1937.
Richmond Times–Dispatch (Va.), Dec. 18, 20, 1937.
San Francisco Chronicle, Aug. 28–Sep. 10, 1915.
The San Francisco Examiner, Apr. 24, 1914; Aug. 28–31, 1915.
Sioux City Journal (Iowa), Jan. 7, 1907.
Spectator (Palmyra, Mo.), Oct. 3, 1917.
St. Louis Globe Democrat, Sep. 28, 1918, Jan. 27, 1928.
St. Louis Post–Dispatch, June 10, 1917.
The St. Louis Star, Aug. 29–30, 1919.
St. Louis Times, Sep. 8, 1919.
The Sulu News (Zamboanga, Mindanao, Philippines), June 30–Dec. 31, 1911.
Sunday News (New York), May 26, 1940.
The Sunday Star (Washington, D.C.), Dec. 29, 1935; Nov. 1, 1959.
Sunday Times Magazine (Manila, Philippines), Sep. 2, 1962.
The Times (El Paso), Aug. 28, 1915 and Aug. 10, 1916.
Trenton Weekly Republican and Tribune (Mo.), June 14, 1917.
Tulsa Daily World, Okla., Sep. 13, 1960.
Voice of the First U. S. Army (Governors Island, N. Y.), Sep. 1, 1960.
The Washington Herald, Dec. 10, 21, 22, 1906; July 31, 1913.
The Washington Post, Sep. 19 and Dec. 21, 1906; June 7, 1913; May 26, 1929;
    Mar. 6, 1938; Sep. 12–13, 1960.
Washington Times (D.C.), Dec. 21, 1906.
The World (New York), Dec. 9, 1906; Sep. 21, 1913; Apr. 3, 1916.
Wyoming Tribune (Cheyenne), Feb. 21, 1917.

Miscellaneous Sources

Armstrong, Henry E. "The Pursuit of Villa." Review of *Chasing Villa,* by Frank
    Tompkins. *The New York Times Book Review* (Sep. 8, 1935).
Cole, George D. "Brush Fire War, 1916 Style." (Unpublished MA thesis,
    McNeese State University, 1962.)
Curtin, Ralph A. Address to the Chevy Chase (Md.) Citizens Association in
    1948 or 1949, reviewing Frederick Palmer's book, *John J. Pershing, General
    of the Armies.* (Loaned to the author by Mr. Curtin.)
Fain, Samuel S. "The Pershing Punitive Expedition and Its Diplomatic Back-
    ground." (Unpublished MA thesis, University of Arizona, 1951.)
Flowers, Paul. "Pershing and Lear," in *Greenhouse.* Memphis, Tenn. 1964,
    26–27.

Guerrilla Warrior

Gonzáles, Daniel. "The Fight at Carrizal." Translation of Mexican account of the Carrizal incident by a participant. (Loaned to the author by Col. Clarence C. Clendenen.)

Goodwin, Katherine K. "The Early Life of General John Joseph Pershing, 1860–1881." (Unpublished MA thesis, Northeast Missouri State Teachers College, 1954.)

Johnson, Robert Bruce. "The Punitive Expedition: A Military, Diplomatic, and Political History of Pershing's Chase after Pancho Villa, 1916–1917." (Unpublished Ph.D. dissertation, University of Southern California, 1964.)

King, Jeff. An interview by the Press of an old Navajo Indian scout who rode with Pershing at Ft. Wingate, N. M. (Rexographed.) (Loaned to the author by Wallace Terry of *The Washington* (D.C.) *Post.*)

Love, Lee W. Statement before May B. Brown, Notary Public, Los Angeles, Mar. 12, 1938.

McDonough, Joseph C. "The Political and Military Background of the Mexican Punitive Expedition." (Unpublished MA thesis, Georgetown University, 1957.)

Marshall, S. L. A. Review of *Black Jack Pershing,* by Richard O'Connor, *The New York Times Book Review* (Sep. 3, 1961), 6, 12.

Pixton, John E., Jr. "The Early Career of Charles G. Dawes." (Unpublished Ph.D. dissertation, University of Chicago, 1952.)

Reed, Raymond. "The Mormons in Chihuahua: Their Relations with Villa and the Pershing Punitive Expedition, 1910–17." (Unpublished MA thesis, University of New Mexico, 1938.)

Rhodes, Charles D. "Diary Notes of a Soldier." (Typed bookscript, five copies in existence. Author consulted the copy at the Library of Congress, where it is classified and filed as a book, rather than a manuscript.)

Shadley, Frank William. "The American Punitive Expedition into Mexico, 1916–1917." (Unpublished MA thesis, College of the Pacific, 1952.)

U.S. Department of the Army, Office of the Chief of Information. *General of the Armies John J. Pershing Centennial, 1860–1960.* n.p., 1960. (Compilation of press clippings throughout the United States and elsewhere on the occasion of the celebration of the Pershing centennial. Loaned to the author by Lt. Col. Lee J. Fishkin.)

U. S. Department of the Army, Office of the Chief of Information, Military District of Washington. "Tribute to General John J. Pershing." A Washington, D. C. radio broadcast over Station WRC on Sep. 12, 1960, featuring interviews with Ralph A. Curtin, J. Thomas Schneider, and James L. Collins.

U. S. Department of Defense, Office of Armed Forces Information and Education. "The Pershing Story." (1960 film.)

Index

Adair, Henry: 256, 258
Adam, Emil: 23
Aero Squadron, 1st: 232
Aguadores River: 51
Ahumada: 256–257
Aircraft, Army: 140, 232–233, 248
Allen, Henry T.: 226–227, 234, 244
Amil (chief): 186, 188, 193, 197, 200
Andrews, Avery D.: 11, 13, 40, 108,
   111–112
Apache: 16, 20
Apache Scouts: 264
Aremain: 77
Arizona National Guard: 251
Aserraderos: 48
Ashurst, Henry F.: 218
Associated Press: 238
Ayres, Charles G.: 52

Bachiniva: 229–230, 234, 254
Bacolod: 79–80, 86–87, 91, 93,
   95–103, 106–107
Bader, C. F.: 131
Badlands region: 21–22
Baker, Newton D.: 220, 233, 254, 271,
   274–275, 279–280
Baker, Ray Stannard: 247, 265
Baldwin, Frank D.: 78–80, 107

Baldwin, Theodore A.: 52, 56
Ball, George: 255
Balloons, Army: 51
Barnum, Malvern-Hill: 54, 57
Barry, Thomas H.: 126
Baruch, Bernard M.: 36
Basilan: 153, 189
Basilan Strait: 176
Bates, John C.: 53
Bayabao: 89
Bayan: 77, 86, 91–92, 97
Beck, William H.: 56
Bell, J. Franklin: 126–127, 145, 153,
   157, 159, 162, 164, 166, 169,
   178–180, 184, 186, 200, 203, 259
Best, Jack: 29
Bethel, Walter A.: 11
Big Foot: 22–23
Binidayan: 84–85
Birnie, Upton, Jr.: 40
Black Mts.: 16
Blakeslee, H. W.: 238
Bliss, Tasker H.: 220
Boca Grande: 220
Booth, C. C.: 110
Boswell, Anne Orr: 208–209, 213
Bowditch, Edward: 203
Bowman, George T.: 109–110

Index

Boyd, Charles T.: 256–260, 275
Brent, Charles H.: 157, 178, 214
Brigade, 8th: 205, 222
Brown, William C.: 225–226, 238, 244, 248
Bryan, William Jennings: 39, 220
Bud Bagsak: 157, 160, 186–204
Bud Dajo: 157, 160, 168–175, 186, 188, 203
Buffalo Bill: 25
Bukidnon Strip: 163
Bullard, Robert L.: 8–11, 101–102, 104, 109, 171, 174
Bun Bun: 190–193
Bunga: 193–198, 200
Burtt, Wilson B.: 40
Bustillos: 249, 252
Butt, Archibald W.: 118

Cabell, De Rosey C.: 240, 259
Calarian Prison: 172
Cameron, Don: 37
Camp Keithley: 182–183
Camp Overton: 182, 189
Camp Vicars: 78–94, 102, 104, 106, 108–109
Canfield, James H.: 27, 33, 37
Capistrano: 62
Cárdenas, Julio: 253, 272
Carpenter, Frank: 157
Carr, Eugene A.: 19–21
Carranza, Venustiano: 206, 218–221, 227, 232–236, 238–241, 246, 248–251, 253–260, 266–269, 271, 274
Carrizal: 256–260, 273, 275, 278
Casas Grandes: 237, 248
Cavalry Journal: 20
Cavalry Regiments
    6th: 14, 21–22
    7th: 224, 226, 229
    8th: 190
    10th: 6, 39, 45–59, 222, 225–226, 238, 244, 256–259, 273
    11th: 226, 238
    13th: 226, 230, 238, 241
    15th: 64
Cavazos, José: 234, 236, 269
Caviglia, Enrico: 123–124
Cervantes, Candelario: 248, 272
Chaffee, Adna R.: 75, 77–78, 86, 93

Charlton, George C.: 189, 198–200, 204
Cheyenne Reservation: 22
Chicago Tribune: 238
Chickamauga Park: 46, 58
Chicken, Sgt. (Apache): 264
Chihuahua: 218, 221–222, 225, 227, 244, 246–247, 249, 251
Chihuahua City: 233, 240, 247, 253–255, 268, 271
Cienéguita: 231, 234
Civil War period: 1–2
Clark, C. H.: 128–129
Clendenen, Clarence C.: 272
Cloman, Sidney: 128, 130
Cody, William F.: 25
Collins, James L.: 183, 189, 197, 199–200, 211, 216, 221, 274, 276
Colonia Dublán: 224–227, 232, 237, 240, 248, 251, 256, 264, 268
Columbus, N.M.: 206, 217–221, 232, 237, 248, 253, 268, 272, 274
Communications problems: 239–240
Confederate raiders: 1–2
Conner, Fox: 40
Conscription, need for: 274
Corregidor: 179
Corsivart, Charles: 123–124
Corwine, Richard M.: 131
Cotabato: 154, 167
Coutts Station: 39
Cowin, William B.: 229, 237
Craig, Malin: 41–42
Craven, Ralph G.: 199
Cree: 39
Crimmins, Martin L.: 138
Crowder, Enoch H.: 246
Crozier, William: 118

Daiquirí: 48
Dairen: 121
Dani, Bela de: 123–124
Dargue, Herbert A.: 233
Davao: 144, 154
Davenport, Erwin R.: 36
Davis, George W.: 65, 75, 80, 93, 105–106, 109, 112, 126, 128
Davis, Richard Harding: 52, 55
Davis, Robert C.: 40
Dawes, Charles G.: 34, 36–37, 39, 119, 216, 279

DeShon, George: 60
Díaz, Porfirio: 217
Dilamo: 102
Dickinson, Jacob M.: 155, 157
Diki Diki: 154
Division, 1st: 222
Dodd, George A.: 229–230
Drinking, soldiers: 14–15
Duncan, George B.: 11
Dunn, Robert: 238, 246
Duvall, William P.: 178

Edwards, Clarence R.: 152
Edwards, G.F.: 182
Egan, Martin: 153
El Caney: 53
El Paso: 221, 225, 237, 240, 255
El Paso Herald: 210
El Pozo: 50–51
Elser, Frank: 228, 230, 233–235,
    237–239, 245, 252
Engineer operations: 150, 237
Engle, Emil: 237
Equipment, testing: 274
Erwin, James B.: 224–226, 229
Etzel, Maj. von: 123–124
Evans, Ellwood W.: 225
Evans, Robley D.: 85

Fabens, Tex.: 247
Fechet, Edmond G.: 30
Field Artillery, 6th: 222
Fierro, Rodolfo: 206
Fisher, Dorothy Canfield: 5, 33, 35, 38,
    141, 216
Fling, Fred Morrow: 29
Forbes, William Cameron: 145–146,
    151, 159–161, 163–164, 173,
    178–179, 187, 200
Forsyth, William D.: 75
Fort Assiniboine: 40
Fort Bayard: 14–15
Fort Bliss: 206
Fort Leavenworth: 20
Fort Riley: 179
Fort Stanton: 16, 20
Fort William McKinley: 133, 138, 159
Fort Wingate: 19
Foulois, Benjamin D.: 232, 240, 273
Frendendall, Ira L.: 131
Frier, James H., Jr.: 214

Funston, Frederick: 220, 222, 233, 235,
    237, 240, 245–255, 259–260, 262,
    270, 280

Gallagher, Matt: 218
Gallego: 255
Ganassi: 76–77
Ganoe, William A.: 270
García, Calixto: 48
Garley, Thomas: 131
Gata: 91, 103, 107
Geary, SS: 190
Genassi, Sultan of: 84
Geronimo: 14, 280
Ghost Dance: 21–23
Gibbons, Floyd: 238
Glover's turkeys: 5
Goethals, George W.: 142
Gómez, Felix: 256–257
Gordon, William W.: 186, 188
Gorrell, Edgar S.: 232
Grande, Datto: 86
Grant, Ulysses S., III: 273
Greer, Allen J.: 181
Griensen, Elisa: 242
Grimes, George S.: 50
Griscom, Lloyd: 117, 121
Guanduali: 89
Guaun: 88–89
Guaymas: 220
Guerrero: 224, 229–230, 249, 252

Hachita: 220, 224
Hafer, Sgt.: 100
Hanna, Mark A.: 39
Hannibal-St. Joseph R.R.: 3, 6
Harbord, James G.: 60, 156–159, 175,
    187
Harriman, J. Borden: 216
Hayama, Japan: 125
Heffner, Bill: 66–67
Heintzelman, Stuart: 40
Helm, Frank P.: 131, 211–213
Helmick, Eli A.: 87
Herndon, William H.: 58
Herrera, Luis: 235, 238, 253
Hersey, Mark L.: 11
Hines, John L.: 228, 273
Hinman, George: 279
Hodges, Courtney H.: 273
Hoffman, Max von: 123–124, 142

Index

Holtzclaw, Clifton: 2
Hopper, James: 245, 255–256
House, Edward M.: 280
Howze, Robert L.: 226, 236, 238–239, 244, 259
Huerta, Victoriano: 217
Hunsaker, Irvin L.: 232
Hunter, Hubert S.: 210
Huntsville, Ala.: 60

Iligan: 64–78, 101, 106, 108
Infanta, José: 77
Infantry Regiments
 1st: 48
 6th: 222
 7th: 222
 8th: 193
 10th: 222
 11th: 222
 13th: 222
 16th: 222
 71st N.Y.: 51
Isabela: 189

Japanese Army: 121–122
Jewell, SS: 190
Johnson, Alvin: 35–36
Jolo: 144, 146, 153, 162, 165–166, 169, 173, 186–204
Journal of the U.S. Cavalry Association: 20
Juarez: 248–249
Juramentado, tradition of: 161–163

Kawodi, Japan: 179
Kent, Jacob F.: 50–52
Kettle Hill: 51–53
Kingsbury, Henry P.: 135–136
Kirksville, Mo.: 6
Knox, [William] Frank[lin]: 53
Kobbé, William A.: 24, 64
Kromer, Leon B.: 40, 216
Kuroki, Tamemoto: 122

Laclede, Mo.: 1–4
Lake Butig: 85
Lake Lanao: 64, 68–81, 89–110, 163, 200
Lanao: 144, 146, 154, 159, 165
Lanckton, Frank: 146–148, 178, 205, 211
Landing operations: 48

Languasan Hill: 193–196, 202
Las Guásimas: 50
Lassiter, William: 118
Lati Ward: 186–188
Lawton, Henry W.: 53
Lear, Ben: 86, 100, 107, 110
Leona, SS: 47–48
Levi (cook): 66–67, 106
Life: 182
Lincoln, Abraham: 58
Lindsey, Elmer: 226
Linek: 77
Linok: 95, 107
Lippincott, Aubrey: 243
Lomax, Henry: 1, 4
Loring, Sylvester C.: 90
Love, Capt.: 5
Lozano, Ismael: 241–243
Lumbayanague: 89
Lusitania, SS: 206–207
Lynnburg, Tenn.: 230

MacArthur, Arthur: 111, 142
MacArthur, Douglas: 8, 111, 278, 280
Maciu: 80, 86–91, 102, 106, 110
Macon, Mo.: 3
Madaya, Sultan of: 74
Madero, Francisco: 217
Madumba: 95
Magoon, Charles E.: 34, 109, 113, 118
Maguire, C. L.: 43
Maine, USS: 45
Malabang: 75, 81, 84, 87
Malanos. *See* Lake Lanao
Malaria, outbreak of: 56–57
Mandi (Datto): 188
Mangas Colorado: 14–15
Manibilang, Ahmai: 68–77
Manila: 61
Manila American: 127, 130–131, 179
Manila Times: 90, 153
Maps, deficient: 237
Marahui: 70–71, 76, 93, 101–104, 147–148
March, Peyton C.: 11
Marias River: 39
Markham, Edwin M.: 43
Marshall, George C.: 278
Marshall, S. L. A.: 263
Mason, Herbert, Jr.: 227, 251
Mataling Falls: 86–87

Matunkup: 193–197
McAndrew, James W.: 11
McCarthy Light Guards: 30
McIntyre, Frank: 11
McKinley, William: 55, 58–59
McKinney, Carl F.: 193–195
McLean, John: 202
McNair, Lesley J.: 273
McNair, William S.: 87–89
Meadville, Mo.: 3
Meiklejohn, George: 60, 97
Menoher, Charles T.: 11
Merritt, Wesley: 13
Mexican National R.R.: 224
Mexico
  agreement with U.S.: 224–225,
    249–251
  communications problems: 239–240
  conquest, Pershing's plan: 246–247
  engineer operations: 237
  evaluation of: 269–274
  force strength: 273
  as training ground: 273–274
  mission in: 220, 270–271
  morale of troops: 264–265
  political turmoil: 217–218
  Scott-Obregón conference: 249–251
  sentiment against: 218–220
  supply problems in: 253
  terrain features: 221–222, 227, 230
  transportation system: 221
  weather: 225, 228
  withdrawal from: 252–261, 265–269,
    278–279
Miles, Nelson A.: 16–19, 39–40, 47, 55
Military Academy: 6–7, 12–13
Military Engineer: 203
Mills, Albert L.: 112, 126, 129
Mills, Ogden: 37, 176
Mindanao: 64–65, 144, 153, 159, 172
Mindanao Herald: 152
Mogollon Mts.: 14
Moji, Japan: 121
Montauk Point, N.Y.: 57
Monterrey: 247
Morey, Lewis S.: 256, 259–260
Moros
  economy, improvement of: 150–153
  educational system: 150–151, 157
  exploitation of: 145–146, 152
  investments among, U.S.: 152–153

Filipinos, relations with: 150,
    154–155
  lawlessness; 163–164, 173–174
  legal and prison reform: 148, 150
  medical care: 150
  population: 144
  slavery, practice of: 147, 163–164
Morris, Frank: 75
Morrison, Jasper: 128, 130
Moseley, George Van Horn: 40, 44
Mukden: 121–122
Musica: 225

Namiquipa: 225–226, 236, 240, 245,
    248–249, 252–253
National Fencibles: 30
National Guard: 251, 261, 273
Nevares, Modesto: 231
New London conference: 268
New Mexico National Guard: 251
New Orleans, SS: 190
New York Evening Post: 128–129
New York Times: 228, 238, 246, 252
New York Tribune: 238
New York World: 179, 232, 238
Nichols, Taylor A.: 189, 193–194,
    196–197
Nicolas Channel: 47
Nogales, Ariz.: 206
North Lake Moros: 77
Nueva Casas Grandes: 264

Oato: 101
Obregón, Alvaro: 218, 224, 249–251
Ojo Federico: 256
O.K. Trail: 182
Omaha drill competition: 30–33
Orr, Anne Decker: 118
Oury, Harry: 36
Oury, William H.: 180

Page, William T.: 131
Palmer, Frederick: 68, 123–124, 127
Palomas: 224
Pandapatan: 77–78, 81, 91, 93, 97, 107
Pantar: 101
Pantaun: 88–89
Parang: 75
Parral: 231, 238, 240, 244–246, 249,
    268, 275, 278
Patrick, Mason M.: 11

Index

Patterson, Robert U.: 101
Patton, George S., Jr.: 59, 253–254,
  263, 273, 276, 278
Peek, George P.: 100
Pepper, Kelton L.: 110
Pershing, Anne: 140, 212
Pershing, Anne Elizabeth (Thompson):
  3–5
Pershing, Frances (Warren): 112–120,
  142, 207–216
Pershing, Francis Warren: 140,
  176–178, 207, 210, 212–213
Pershing, Grace: 116
Pershing, Helen Elizabeth: 125, 212
Pershing, James: 116, 119
Pershing, John Fletcher: 1–4, 119
Pershing, John Joseph
  ambition: 8–11, 46, 58, 110
  American soldier, opinion of: 122
  ancestry: 1–4
  at Army War College: 111, 116
  Black Jack, origin of: 44
  boyhood: 1–6
  at Bud Bagsak: 186–204
  at Bud Dajo: 168–175, 186, 188, 203
  cadet days: 6–14
  at Camp Vicars: 78–94, 102, 104,
    106, 108–109
  civilian control, attitude toward:
    155–157, 220–221, 279
  command experience: 7–8, 23–24,
    29–30, 39, 107–108, 133, 205, 274
  commendations: 20–21, 52, 58, 80,
    104–105, 159–160, 173
  courtship and family life: 111–119,
    140–142, 175–178, 184, 207–208
  criticized: 157–158, 202–204, 235,
    260, 273
  Cuba service: 47–59
  decorations: 204
  directive to on Villa: 271
  as disciplinarian: 28–29, 40–45,
    66–67, 106–107, 148–150,
    180–181, 184, 262, 275–276
  early service: 14–26
  as educator: 6, 27–38, 40–45,
    150–151
  at El Paso: 205–207, 228
  family, loss of: 207–216
  family, support of: 116
  at Fort Assiniboine: 38
  at Fort Bayard: 14–15
  at Fort Bliss: 206
  at Fort Leavenworth: 20
  at Fort Riley: 179
  at Fort Stanton: 16, 20
  at Fort William McKinley: 133, 138,
    159
  at Fort Wingate: 19
  generals as classmates: 11
  German army, observation of: 139
  Grant, resemblance to: 7
  health: 140, 175, 205
  humor: 180–181, 246
  at Iligan: 64–78, 101, 106, 108
  Indian campaigns: 14–24, 39
  intelligence, failure in: 269
  Japanese army, observation of: 122,
    125, 137–138, 178–179
  at Lake Lanao: 94–110
  law degree: 33–34
  memory: 29, 36
  in Mexico: 220–279
  Military Academy, influence of: 7,
    12–14
  Military Academy, service at: 40–45
  militia, disdain for: 25, 261–275
  misconduct alleged: 127–132, 179,
    202–204
  modesty: 12
  morale, maintaining: 264–265
  Moros, pacification of: 61, 64–110,
    161–174, 186–204
  Moros, service among: 144–160
  national defense, stress on: 182–184,
    206–207, 273
  Negroes, service with. See Cavalry
    Regiments, 10th
  newsmen, relations with: 225–226,
    228–229, 233–235, 245–246
  personal characteristics: 5–8, 12,
    25–26, 107, 141–142, 146, 148,
    159, 173–174, 184–185, 216,
    262–263
  Philippines service: 60–110, 133–138,
    140–205
  poetry by: 176
  at Presidio: 205, 212
  professionalism: 13, 15, 20–21,
    24–26, 58–59, 107–108, 122–123,
    142–143, 159, 180–181
  promotions: 58, 62, 64, 105–106,

111–112, 125, 127, 142, 265, 274, 280
and prostitution: 264–265
and public opinion: 202–203
religion, practice of: 4–5, 147, 178
Russia and Europe, tour of: 138–140
in Russo-Japanese War: 117, 121–125
soldiers, relations with: 136–137, 142, 181–182, 185, 262–263
Southwest service: 114
as speaker: 5, 11
as student: 6, 20
supply problems: 46–47, 50, 54–56, 59–60, 221, 236–237, 248, 253
tact: 67–84, 274–275
training, stress on: 29, 133–135, 142–143, 262
at University of Nebraska: 6, 27–38
venereal disease, control of: 264–265
at Walter Reed Hospital: 6
war, attitude toward: 55, 59, 62
Washington service: 39–40, 60–61, 111, 140
writing facility: 20
Pershing, Mary Margaret: 175, 212
Pershing, May: 116
Pershing Rifles, origin: 33
Pfoershing, Frederick: 2
Philippine Constabulary: 146, 157–158
Philippine Insurrection. *see* Moros
Philippine Scouts: 145, 170–172, 180, 189–200
Pine Ridge Reservation: 21, 23
Placido, Padre Tel: 71
Poore, Benjamin A.: 11
Porcupine Creek: 23
Preston, Guy H.: 105, 130, 141
Providencia: 253
Pujagan: 193–197, 200
Pulpit Pass: 240
Puyacabao: 193–197

Rank, place in Army: 25
Railroads, inadequacy of: 274
Regular Army, state of: 184, 273–274
Reilly, Henry J.: 179, 216
Remein: 104
Richley, Jay: 243
Rivas, Genevo: 257
Rodgers, Henry: 131
Rodney, George B.: 244

Roosevelt, Franklin D.: 53, 204
Roosevelt, Theodore: 40, 56, 58, 111–112, 118, 125–127, 142
Root, Elihu: 105–106, 126
Rosebud River Reservation: 21
Ross, James: 131
Ross, Nellie Tayloe: 213
Rucio: 225
Russell, Phil: 36

St. Louis Post-Dispatch: 125
Sajuduciman (priest); 91–92
Samar, SS: 169, 173
Sample, William R.: 240
Sampson, William T.: 47
San Antonio de los Arenales: 231, 244, 248–249
San Borja: 234, 236, 249, 252, 269
San Francisco de Borja: 231
San Geronimo Ranch: 228, 234, 238, 253
San Juan Hill: 50–53
San Juan River: 52
San Miguel de Babicora: 224–225
San Ramon: 149–150, 159
Sanchez, Juan: 218
Sandford, C. M.: 129
Santa Cruz de Herrera: 231, 234, 239, 245
Santa Cruz de Villegas: 243–244, 248
Santa Isabel: 218
Santa Maria River and Valley: 227, 248
Santo Domingo Ranch: 236
Santiago campaign: 51, 55–58
Satevó: 238, 240, 245, 249, 252
Sauir: 89
Scott, Hugh L.: 162–163, 167, 169, 173–174, 220, 235, 248–251, 254, 266, 271, 274, 279
Sealy Rifles: 30
Seit Lake: 166
Shafter, William T.: 47, 50, 56
Shannon, James: 264
Shaw, George C.: 100, 190–197, 199
Sheldon, George L.: 30
Sherman, William T.: 10
Shinn, Zellar H.: 128, 131
Siasi: 189
Siboney: 50, 54, 56
Sierra Blanca, Tex.: 206
Simonds, George S.: 40

Index

Sioux Indian Scouts: 23–24
Somervell, Brehon B.: 273
Sonora: 224, 240, 250–254
Spaatz, Carl: 273
Spain, war with: 45, 183
Spilsbury, Lem: 256
Stallings, Laurence: 276
Standing Rock Reservation: 22
Stevens, R. S.: 70
Subanos: 163–164
Sugunaimi, Japan: 179
Sulu: 144, 153, 188
Sulu News: 151, 165
Sumner, Samuel S.: 87, 89, 93, 102, 104, 126
Sunderland, Archibald H.: 110
Swobe, Thomas: 128, 130

Taft, William Howard: 117–118, 128–130, 137, 142, 160
Taglibi: 166–167, 174, 188
Tallant, Marcella: 119
Talub: 89, 102
Tampa, Fla.: 46
Tampico: 205
Tangul (Datto): 84
Taraca: 77, 91, 102–104, 106
Tarango, Gen.: 238
Tauagan: 89
Texas, raids on: 251, 269
Texas National Guard: 251
Thayer, Sylvanus: 6
Tompkins, Frank: 226, 230, 233–234, 236–244, 269
Toral, José: 54–55
Torreón: 247
Tracy (cowboy): 226
Treviño, J. B.: 255–256, 268
Trucks, Army use: 221, 237, 274
Turner, Frederick G.: 243

Utrecht, Byron C.: 232, 238

Valle de Zaragoza: 234, 241
Van Natta, Thomas F.: 193, 195, 197–198
Vera Cruz: 205, 220
Vicars. *See* Camp Vicars
Villa, Francisco (Pancho): 205–206, 213, 217–265
Villard, Oswald Garrison: 128–129

Walcutt, Charles: 7
Walker, Norman: 210–211
Warren, Francis E.: 106, 113, 117, 126–127, 142, 179, 279
Warrenton, Mo.: 3
Washington Herald: 129
Water, scarcity of: 14–15
West, Frank: 169
Wheedon, Bert: 36
Wheeler, Joseph: 50–52, 58
Williams, Sumner M.: 236
Wilson, Henry H.: 34
Wilson, Woodrow: 207, 247, 251, 261, 265–266, 279–280
Wint, Theodore J.: 58
Wood, Leonard: 58, 126–127, 129, 131, 135, 142–143, 145, 156–158, 164, 168, 173–174, 187, 280
Wooten, William P.: 41
Wounded Knee Creek: 23–24
Wovoka: 21
Wright, SS: 189–190, 202
Wright, Wilbur: 140, 142

Yaqui: 230
Ygnacio, Joaquina B.: 128–131
Young, Charles: 244
Young, Samuel B. M.: 47, 126
Youngberg, Gilbert A.: 43

Zamboanga: 61, 64, 144, 151–152, 155, 163, 169, 173, 175–185
Zamboanga Fair: 153–154, 157, 159
Zapata, Emiliano: 218, 261
Zuñi: 19